TRAVELER

south africa

south africa

National Geographic
Washington, D.C.

CONTENTS

Pages 2–3: Tembe Elephant Park, home to the province's biggest elephant herd.
Opposite: Coastline of Camps Bay near Cape Town, with Twelve Apostles mountains behind

TRAVELING WITH EYES OPEN

Alert travelers go with a purpose and leave with a benefit. If you travel responsibly, you can help support wildlife conservation, historic preservation, and cultural enrichment in the places you visit. You can enrich your own travel experience as well.

To be a geo-savvy traveler:

- Recognize that your presence has an impact on the places you visit.

- Spend your time and money in ways that sustain local character. (Besides, it's more interesting that way.)

- Value the destination's natural and cultural heritage.

- Respect the local customs and traditions.

- Express appreciation to local people about things you find interesting and unique to the place: its nature and scenery, music and food, historic villages and buildings.

- Vote with your wallet: Support the people who support the place, patronizing businesses that make an effort to celebrate and protect what's special there. Seek out shops, local restaurants, inns, and tour operators who love their home—who love taking care of it and showing it off. Avoid businesses that detract from the character of the place.

- Enrich yourself, taking home memories and stories to tell, knowing that you have contributed to the preservation and enhancement of the destination.

That is the type of travel now called geotourism, is defined as "tourism that sustains or enhances the geographical character of a place—its environment, culture, aesthetics, heritage, and the well-being of its residents." To learn more, visit National Geographic's Center for Sustainable Destinations at *www. nationalgeographic.com/travel/sustainable.*

.

south africa

ABOUT THE CONTRIBUTORS

Roberta Cosi is a writer and editor who was born and raised in Johannesburg. An intrepid traveler, she is passionate about exploring South Africa and all the country has to offer.

Richard Whitaker Born and educated in South Africa, Richard Whitaker studied at the University of the Witwatersrand in Johannesburg, then took further degrees in Classics at the universities of Oxford and St. Andrews. After decades teaching at universities in Durban and Cape Town, he began a second career as a writer. He has traveled widely in Europe and southern Africa.

Samantha Reinders Photographer Samantha Reinders *(www.samreinders.com)* is not one hundred percent certain when her career actually began, but thinks it was a concoction of experiences such as riding shotgun in her father's beloved LandRover on the dust roads of southern Africa, exploring the curious hills of Appalachia, or sandwiched between two other photographers in the press pool in the Oval Office. Either way, her choice of career has, among other things, allowed her to chase penguins, fly on Air Force One, swim with sharks, and meet interesting people—from businessmen to homeless men, and from grannies at a bake-sale to a triple murderer behind bars.

Reinders has a master's in Visual Communication from Ohio University. Her work has appeared in *U.S. News & World Report, Time, The New York Times, L'Express, Der Spiegel, Park Avenue, The Chicago Tribune,* and *The London Financial Times.*

In 2005 she moved back to her native South Africa—and the dust roads that feed her soul. She currently lives in Cape Town, pursuing stories there and abroad.

Charting Your Trip

No two provinces in South Africa are alike—here you will find a whole world in one country. Whether you're looking to lie on the beach or visit world-class museums, trek across a desert or spot some of the world's most magnificent wildlife, sip fine wines or sample Cape Malay cuisine, South Africa has it all.

What to Pack

Dress codes in South Africa stress informality. Shorts, sandals, and a T-shirt are commonly worn in warm weather, and would be perfectly acceptable dress for lunch at many places (though not at expensive restaurants), and even for seaside dining. Skirt, long pants, and open-neck shirt are the norm for dinner or theater. If you're safari bound, take appropriate brown, olive green, or khaki clothing for bush walking, binoculars, hiking boots, backpack, water bottle, sun hat, sunblock, and your prescriptions (including malaria medication for the lowveld and far northeast coast).

With so much on offer, planning an itinerary may seem a daunting task, but it all depends on how much time you have. If you are only visiting for one week, a trip to Cape Town and a safari in a Big-Five area—with elephant, lion, leopard, buffalo, and rhino—such as the Kruger National Park, are an absolute must. You could consider flying directly to Cape Town, spending three nights in this exciting, cosmopolitan city, and then flying on to your safari for three nights. With more time, far-flung attractions await.

Most South African cities are not well served by safe, efficient public transport suitable for tourists. Thus many visitors use rental cars to travel within and between the country's cities. The country has a good, in many parts excellent, network of asphalt and gravel roads. It is perfectly feasible for you to drive your own or rental vehicle on safari, through the country's national and private game reserves. Most of these are accessible by ordinary sedan car, though a few require a 4WD vehicle.

Keep in mind, however, that South Africa is a large country. Travel by air is a good choice if you have a limited amount of time. The national carrier, South African

King of the Big Five

Airways (SAA), flies between all the cities and larger towns in the country, while its Airlink and South African Express services fly in smaller aircraft to many regional destinations.

For something truly extravagant, consider taking the Blue Train or one of the Rovos Rail journeys, which run on a few set routes within southern Africa. Remember, though, that these trips, which run from one or two overnights for the trip between Cape Town and Pretoria, are not about speed but about sightseeing in luxury from the comfort of your armchair.

Cape Town

The "Mother City" can't help but capture your heart. The surrounding mountains and oceans make it scenically captivating, while its 300-year settler history gives it a cultural and historical edge second to none. Beautiful, sophisticated, colorfulful with its multicultural heritage, it's a city you must not miss. First on your list is to climb Table Mountain, whether on foot or by rotating cable car. The dramatic views from the top of this iconic hill are astounding. For the shoppers out there, the Victoria & Alfred Waterfront, perched along a working harbor, is a definite must, and from there you can board a ferry to Robben Island, where Nelson Mandela was infamously imprisoned. A day driving around the Cape Winelands is a real treat, not only for its gustatory delights, but also for the exceptional scenery. And a visit to Kirstenbosch National Botanical Gardens, known as one of the Seven Magnificent Botanical Gardens of the World, should be scheduled. Cape Town has an international airport, and is therefore easily accessible, but if you are flying into Johannesburg it is only a two-hour direct flight to the Mother City.

Surrounding Cape Town: If you have more than just a few days in Cape Town, there are many day trips well worth your while. Why not drive to Cape Point, with its dramatic views of crashing oceans, or over to the east coast of the peninsula, where you can walk among penguins on Boulders Beach or browse antique stores in colorful Kalk Bay. A trip up the West Coast, especially during the Namaqualand flower season, allows for dramatic scenery and easy strolls through arty villages, whereas the wineland towns of Stellenbosch, Paarl, and Franschhoek offer a perfect, lazy afternoon of touring.

If you have an extra week or so, take a trip to the Garden Route, a pleasant, five-hour drive from Cape Town, which is a stretch of exquisite coastline encompassing small coastal towns and beautiful beaches—South Africans flock in droves here in summer.

NOT TO BE MISSED:

A Big Five safari   161, 176–185

The view of Cape Town from the top of Table Mountain   76–77

Wine tasting in the Winelands   102–107

A quick lesson on South Africa's troubled past at Cape Town's Robben Island or Johannesburg's Apartheid Museum   69, 72–73 & 209–210

The Garden Route's small towns and beaches   110–115

The Drakensberg mountains and their San rock art   157–161

A visit to a township such as Soweto in Johannesburg   212–215

An African sunset from one of South Africa's beautiful beaches   122, 129, 135–136, 154–155

A drive through the desolate Kalahari Desert   251–263

Going on Safari

The Kruger National Park, two hours west from Cape Town by air (or an exhausting three-day drive), is the world's oldest game reserve, and it continues to attract more than half a million visitors every year. Besides the Big Five (lion, leopard, elephant, buffalo, and rhino), the park is home to other exciting animals such as giraffes, zebras, cheetahs, hippos, impalas, and hyenas, all of which you can observe at close range in their natural habitat. The park has a network of 1,200 miles (2,000 km) of partially paved roads, which make for easy and comfortable game drives. The more adventurous visitors can find countless sandy side roads to explore on their own.

There are many different types of accommodations to choose from in the park, ranging from private lodges to regular camps. Most camps have their own restaurants and can organize game drives and walks for you. Whatever type of accommodation you choose, it is advisable make reservations in advance.

There are many other game reserves in South Africa, some of the more popular being Addo Elephant Park and the Mountain Zebra National Park in the Eastern Cape, the Golden Gate Highlands National Park in the eastern Free State, and the

Tipping Etiquette

Tipping is customary in South Africa. In a restaurant you should tip 15 to 20 percent of your bill. For larger parties, restaurants sometimes add the tip themselves.

Tour guides and drivers are tipped R15 per person on the tour per day, and this amount will be split between the staff.

Hotel porters are tipped between R2 and R5 per bag. If you have your own car, note that gas station attendants are usually tipped R2–R5. See also p. 278.

Tourist Safety

Crime is unfortunately a reality in South Africa, especially in Johannesburg; being aware can ensure your safety.

STREETWISE:
- Avoid dark, isolated areas at night.
- Travel in groups; stick to well-lit, busy areas.
- Never carry large amounts of cash.
- Avoid wearing loud jewelry or flashing your camera around.
- Use only taxis recommended by your hotel, restaurant, or tourist center.

CARWISE:
- Always plan your route in advance, and keep a map in the car.
- In the cities lock your car doors and keep your windows closed at all times.
- Place valuables in the trunk of the car.
- Avoid parking in dark areas, and park as close to where you are going as possible.
- Never pick up strangers.

HOTELWISE:
- Never leave your luggage unattended in the lobby or any other public areas.
- Lock your valuables in the safe provided in your hotel room or at the front desk.
- If someone knocks unexpectedly, check who it is, before opening the door.
- Always keep your room locked.
- Keep a copy of your documents—credit card information, passport, etc.—in the hotel safe.

Looking out over Verneuk Pan, site of the first land-speed record in 1929

Tankwa Karoo National Park in the Northern Cape. All of them offer superb game viewing and an unforgettable African experience.

If You Have More Time

Gauteng Province: Johannesburg, Gauteng's capital, is an electric city; its currents of ambition and excitement zap through you the minute you step into this busy metropolis. An excursion to the Soweto Township, the active gold mines, the Lesedi Cultural Village, and the Apartheid Museum, not to mention some of the finest shopping malls around, should not be missed. From Johannesburg you can easily access the Cradle of Humankind, home of copious evolutionary relics, and Sun City, the "Las Vegas" of South Africa.

KwaZulu-Natal Province: Durban, with its warm waters, colonial architecture, and diverse cultures, is a friendly city to visit. The coasts to its north and south offer some of the country's finest scuba diving, game-watching, beaches, and coastal towns. With more time, take a drive through the rustic and quaint Midlands Meander, or go horseback riding and hiking over the Drakensberg mountain range.

How to Call Home

To make an overseas phone call, you will first have to dial 00, which is the international access code from South Africa. You will then dial the country and area codes, and the phone number. For the United States you would dial 001 and the number, and for the United Kingdom you would dial 0044 and the number. Various international calling cards are available. The most widely used is Telkom WorldCall Prepaid Calling Card. While these cards may not give the best rates, they are reliable and can be used to make local or international calls from any private or public landline telephone. If you have an international cell phone, bear in mind that roaming costs are high, and that many of the more rural areas and game reserves do not have a signal.

History & Culture

Jacaranda tree in full bloom, Pretoria

South Africa Today

It is difficult to generalize about South Africa, as any visitor will soon find out. How do you sum up a country that speaks 11 official languages, has vibrant cities combining informal Third World settlements with First World hotels and shopping malls, and boasts landscapes ranging from thick bush to lush green mountains, semidesert plateaus, and miles of magnificent sandy beaches?

On safari here you can view the Big Five: elephant, lion, leopard, buffalo, and rhino. If you have a taste for adventure you can go white-water rafting in the Western Cape or Free State, mountain climbing and hiking in the Drakensberg, or scuba diving off Africa's southernmost tropical reefs at Sodwana Bay. But there is also plenty to occupy those with more urban tastes—shopping for local sculpture and beadwork, dining on distinctive South African cuisine and fine local wines, or attending live jazz, quality theater, or dance.

The skylines of South Africa's cities today bristle with cranes, as a massive building boom goes forward. New housing developments—from low-cost dwellings to luxury apartments—are daily reshaping the urban landscape. Huge excitement surrounds the Soccer World Cup, awarded to South Africa for 2010, with stadiums mush-rooming in Cape Town, Durban, and Johannesburg, and new hotels springing up to accommodate the anticipated crowds of tourists and spectators.

Just 3.9 million international tourists visited South Africa in 1994, the year of the first democratic elections, but that number is expected to swell to 10 million by 2010. Apart from the World Cup, what draws all these visitors to the southern tip of Africa and keeps them coming back? More than anything, it is the combina-tion of first-rate facilities, such as the hotels, shops, and restaurants of Cape Town's world-famous Victoria & Alfred Waterfront, with the hundreds of thousands of square miles of unspoiled wilderness in reserves as dif-ferent as the Kruger National Park, Addo Elephant Park, or Hluhluwe Imfolozi Game Reserve. Add to this bounty an advanced, modern banking system, excellent physical infrastructure of harbors, roads, and airports, and you have a winning formula for tourism.

The New South Africa

Since 1994, this country has popularly been known as the "New South Africa." The label is appropriate, as a spirit of renewal has inspired the nation. Millions of people, excluded before, now have access to education, housing, medical clinics, electricity, clean water—and, most important, the right to vote. The healthy economy in the new millennium has enjoyed a period of sustained growth, longer than any experienced before in South Africa's history. Assertive media, free of state interference, keep the populace informed and the government on its toes.

South Africans are justifiably proud of their post-1994 institutions, such as the country's constitution, hammered out in the early 1990s by groups across the political spectrum and widely acknowledged to be one of the most liberal in the world. The constitution above all expresses the people's determination to put behind them the discrimination of the recent past and to secure their right to freedom of association, freedom to participate in government and in the economy, and freedom of expression and of the press. South Africans have made much use, too, of their new Constitutional

Pretoria's Union Buildings, official seat of the South African government

Court, the function of which it is to test parliament's laws and decisions of the lower courts against the agreed constitutional principles.

People & Languages

Due to its history, South Africa possesses a remarkably diverse population. Very small numbers of Bushmen (also known as San), who were the original hunter-gatherer inhabitants of the region, still live in the northwestern parts of the country, though now mainly in settled communities. Along the east coast live people known collectively as the Nguni, their two main groupings being the Zulu of KwaZulu-Natal and the Xhosa of the Eastern Cape. An offshoot of the Nguni, the Ndebele, migrated to the interior in the 17th century and today occupy parts of Limpopo and Mpumalanga Provinces. Sotho-speaking people, related to the inhabitants of neighboring Lesotho, are spread through much of the Free State, Gauteng, Limpopo, and Mpumalanga. Smaller ethnic groups include the Venda in the extreme north, Tsonga in the northeast, and Tswana occupying land to either side of the South Africa–Botswana border. In general, ethnic identities are a good deal stronger in rural areas than in the cities, where economic and class distinctions carry greater weight.

A large segment of the population of the Western Cape consists of so-called Coloured people. ("Coloured" in South Africa means something different than elsewhere in the world.) Chiefly Afrikaans-speaking (Afrikaans being the local version of Dutch), Coloureds are descended from Dutch settlers at the cape, their slaves, who came mainly from Malaysia and Indonesia, and indigenous people of the region.

Alongside these groupings live many immigrants and their descendants, chiefly from England and Holland, but also from several other European countries. In earlier centuries sizable immigrations have come, too, from Malaysia and the Indian subcontinent. A new phenomenon since 1994 has been the influx into South Africa's large cities of many economic migrants from other African countries, especially Mozambique, Angola, Zimbabwe, and the Congos.

The total population of South Africa is estimated to be nearly 49 million, made up as follows: African 79.8 percent, European descent 9 percent, Coloured 8.8 percent, Indian/Asian descent 2.4 percent. No one knows for sure how many illegal immigrants are currently in South Africa; estimates range between two million and five million.

Although linguistic and ethnic allegiances remain strong, citizens of the country are beginning to forge a national identity and to regard themselves as South Africans first, and Xhosa, Sotho, Zulu, or English- or Afrikaans-speaking second.

South African Phrases

South African English has some interesting idiosyncrasies:

Bakkie	pickup truck
Braai	barbecue
Brah	best friend
Bundu	bushveld
Gogga	insect
Howzit	hello
Just now	shortly, not right now
Kloof	ravine
Koppie	rocky hill
Lekka chow	good meal
Lekker	great
Robot	traffic light
SMS	text message
Takkies	running shoes

Inside a Basotho homestead near Matatiele, the Eastern Cape

Given the diversity of the South African population, the architects of the country's new constitution were faced with a problem: Which should be South Africa's official language? They settled on a compromise. All 11 languages spoken in the country became official languages. In theory, every citizen has the right to be educated and to communicate with officialdom in their own mother tongue—though the constitution wisely adds that this right may be exercised only where practicable.

In practice, although in South Africa there are more mother-tongue speakers respectively of Zulu (23.8 percent), Xhosa (17.6 percent), and Afrikaans (13.3 percent) than there are of English (8.2 percent), the latter is by far South Africans' most common second language. Visitors to all the major cities and tourist destinations will find no difficulty communicating in English. In many small towns Afrikaans dominates, though English is still understood. Only in remote rural areas will English-speaking visitors some-times find communication difficult.

Most South Africans warmly welcome visitors to their country. Don't be surprised if the locals want to know who you are, where you come from, whether you are married, or how many children you have. Once you have started talking, it is not unusual for them to invite you into their home or to share a meal.

Cities

Books and photographic essays on Africa sometimes give the impression that the continent is an empty wilderness, populated by more wild animals than people.

Although a nature lover's dream, South Africa also has large, modern, bustling cities, home to many millions of inhabitants. The population of these cities is rapidly increasing as migrants stream in from rural areas in search of jobs and better social services for themselves and their families. Cape Town, with its Cape Dutch and colonial buildings, still has a strongly European feel. Johannesburg's many street traders and teeming inner-city apartment blocks make it very much a city of Africa, whereas the large immigrant Indian population of Durban lends that city its own unique style. Everywhere in the cities you will see minibus taxis that stop any place to pick up or drop off passengers. A remarkable product of the entrepreneurial spirit, these taxis first began to offer their services in the 1980s, taking people

Long Street in Cape Town, a popular entertainment hub

where they wanted and needed to go, to destinations not served by regular buses and trains. Look out for the intriguing nicknames painted on these taxis: names like Pay My Bills, Risky Business, Fatal Attraction, and Lover Boy. But tourists should take care and use only taxis recommended by their hotel or restaurant.

During the past decade, the citizens of Cape Town have been amused to see their city and its surroundings appear as the background to movies, TV features, and commercials supposedly set in other parts of the world. Cars that should be driving on the left appear on screen zooming down the right side of the road. Big-name Hollywood stars are often seen in the city. Movies recently completed here include *Flashbacks of a*

Fool, starring Daniel Craig, and J. M. Coetzee's *Disgrace*, starring John Malkovich. What draws filmmakers to Cape Town, apart from the relatively low costs of filming, are the fine weather, the clarity of the light, and the enormous variety of locations. Within a two-hour radius of the city they can find cityscapes of all sorts, Mediterranean coastline and vineyards, semidesert plains, hills and mountains, forests and lakes.

In 2006 local filmmaking received a huge boost when *Tsotsi*, directed by South African Gavin Hood, received the Academy Award for Best Foreign Language Film.

Sports

South Africa is a sports-crazy nation. So an excellent way to get into conversation with locals is to ask them about their favorite team. By far the largest sport, in terms of spectators and participants, is soccer (or football, as they call it); the top 16 professional teams are organized into the Premier Soccer League. Earn kudos with soccer fans by knowing the nicknames of their favorite teams, such as the Beautiful Birds, the Buccaneers, and the Clever Boys for the Moroka Swallows, Orlando Pirates, and Bidwest Wits (a university team); or, more simply, Chiefs for the enormously popular Kaizer Chiefs. The awarding of the 2010 Soccer World Cup to South Africa has given the sport locally a huge boost, with the national team of the host country qualifying automatically for the finals.

Second in popularity is rugby. This sport, with a large following particularly among Afrikaans speakers, is currently riding the crest of a wave, since the national team, the Springboks, won the 2007 World Cup in France. Major annual competitions pit South African rugby teams against squads from Australia and New Zealand in the Tri-Nations and the Super 14 leagues, while provincial teams compete for the prestigious more-than-100-year-old Currie Cup.

Earn kudos with soccer fans by knowing the nicknames of their favorite teams, such as the Beautiful Birds, the Buccaneers, and the Clever Boys for Moroka Swallows, Orlando Pirates, and Bidwest Wits.

The English first brought cricket to South Africa in the 19th century. The game has taken root here and is gaining support among all sectors of the population. South Africa's national cricket team, the Proteas, has achieved success both in test matches (the longer, five-day form of the game) and one-day internationals, and is ranked consistently among the top three in the world in these forms of cricket.

Other popular sports include road racing and cycling, both of which stage annual events attracting mass participation. The Cape Pic 'n Pay Argus Cycle Tour, a 68-mile (109 km) route through the stunning scenery of the Cape Peninsula, is the largest timed event of its kind in the world. Some 35,000 riders, mostly locals, but also thousands of international entrants, participate in March each year. In road racing, between 10,000 and 14,000 South Africans and overseas visitors compete annually in the 54-mile (87 km) Comrades Marathon. This ultramarathon, run each June from Durban to Pieter-maritzberg (the opposite way in alternate years), has a history going back to 1921, when veterans started the race to commemorate comrades who had died in World War I. The more recent Two-Oceans Marathon, first run in 1970, takes place each Easter weekend. The event actually comprises two races, a 35-mile (56 km) ultramarathon and a 13-mile

(21 km) half marathon, both along the roads of the Cape Peninsula. About 25,000 runners take part annually.

Economy

Until the second half of the 19th century, South Africa's economy was based exclusively on agriculture. Then came the discovery of diamonds at Kimberley in 1867 and of gold on the Witwatersrand in 1886. For nearly a century after, gold and diamond mining and their related industries—explosives, cement, and engineering—formed the backbone of the economy. The extraction of other raw materials, such as coal, iron ore, vanadium, manganese, and platinum, has also grown in importance. But the manufacturing sector, producing clothing, textiles, and vehicles, and paper and wood products, both for the domestic market and for export, has gradually expanded its share of gross domestic product.

Due to South Africa's lack of domestic oil reserves, from 1950 on the government invested heavily in technology to produce oil from the country's abundant coal supplies, and later also from natural gas. The resultant partially state-owned company, Sasol, was for many years a heavy burden on the taxpayer. But with rapidly rising oil prices in the new millennium, its unique technology has become profitable.

Since democratization and the lifting of international sanctions in the early 1990s, the South African economy has transformed itself. One of the success stories has been the wine industry. In 1993 the country exported 6.5 million gallons (24.6 million l) of wine. By 2008 the figure had grown to more than 80 million gallons (300 million l), about 50 percent of that volume going to the United Kingdom. The Netherlands, Germany, Scandinavia, and the United States are also important export markets for South African wines. In the production of beer, too, South Africa has become a world leader. In 2002 South African Breweries bought out the U.S.'s Miller Brewing Company. Since that acquisition, the newly named SABMiller has become the largest brewer in the world, after an expansion in China.

Today South Africa, with its excellent transport, communications, and financial infrastructure, is the economic powerhouse of the African continent. Local mining, construction, financial services, telecommunications, hotel, and retail companies have rapidly expanded northward, establishing a strong presence in the rest of Africa. The South African economy is booming: As of late September 2006, the market capitalization of the Johannesburg Stock Exchange stood at U.S. $579.1 billion, making it the 16th largest stock exchange worldwide. ∎

EXPERIENCE:
Help Build a Home

In a country where unemployment and homelessness are rife, helping to build homes is a fantastic volunteer option. There are several charities that organize such projects, all with the aim of eradicating the crisis of people living in shacks with no amenities. To find out more about donating your time or funds, contact: **Habitat for Humanity** (tel 021/670-2046, www.habitat. org.za); or the **Niall Mellon Townships Initiative** (tel 021/426-2543, www .irishtownship.com). Most charities offer one-day to one-week programs.

Curios and crafts, Blyde River Canyon

History of South Africa

After centuries of conflict, South Africa is coming together as a unified nation. Its history has been marked by clashes between the Khoikhoi, part of a larger group, the Khoisan, the African farmers who came from the north, and the European settlers who arrived by sea beginning in the 17th century.

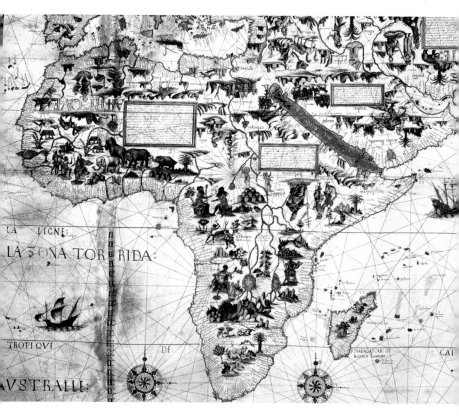

Mid-16th-century map of Africa

Beginnings & Prehistory

If history is the record of human activity, it does not reach much farther back than in South Africa, home to some of the earliest hominids and members of the species *Homo sapiens*. Spectacular discoveries by paleontologists in South Africa have proved that our evolutionary ancestors have lived here continuously for at least 2.5 million years.

Our own species, *Homo sapiens*, originated in Africa some 200,000 years before the present. Very recent investigations of a cave at Pinnacle Point—near Mossel Bay on South Africa's Garden Route—has pushed back the date for cultural activity among modern humans by nearly 100,000 years. As early as 164,000 years ago, cave dwellers here not only crafted small stone blades to be attached to sticks as spear or arrow points, they also used ocher, probably for symbolic cultural purposes.

The first inhabitants of South Africa of whom we have any real knowledge are the Bushmen (San), who today still live in small numbers in the Kalahari Desert. Evidence for their presence in southern Africa goes back at least 20,000 years. For many millennia this Stone Age people pursued a hunter-gatherer way of life that fit perfectly with their environment. The women gathered edible plants while the men hunted. In caves formerly occupied by Bushmen, investigators have dug up the bones of several types of antelope, dassies (the rock hyrax), and tortoises. Remains of rhino, hippo, and elephant show that the Bushmen sometimes hunted these animals, too, probably by the use of pitfalls. Bushmen were not always on the move. Sometimes they lived in caves along the coast, where they ate fish, shellfish, and seals. The remains of rocky walls they built in the sea to form tidal fish traps can still be seen at several places on the southwestern coast. Some of the hunter-gatherer San split off to become herders, known as Khoisan.

Iron Age Farmers

A new chapter in South African prehistory opened around A.D. 200, the beginning of the Early Iron Age, with the arrival of small groups of Bantu-speaking people in the northern part of the country. They interacted and intermarried with the Khoisan, as can be seen from the click-sounds that entered their language. Also like the Khoisan, the darker newcomers herded goats, sheep, and cattle. But their culture was crucially different in that they made pottery, smelted iron to make tools and weapons, and farmed crops: varieties of millet, sorghum, groundnuts, and melons. (Corn, which later became a staple, was obtained from the Portuguese at some time between the 16th and 18th centuries.) Being farmers, they stayed in one place, living in small settled village communities.

With the beginning of the Late Iron Age, from A.D. 1200 on, significant changes occurred, as new waves of Nguni and Sotho-speaking peoples moved into the highveld and down the east coast of South Africa.

Later Iron Age settlements numbered in the thousands. The new arrivals lived in large extended family units, housed in round huts, and built dry stonewalls joining their huts together to form pens for their domestic animals. Sometimes the huts themselves were made of stones piled into a beehive shape.

Hominid Discoveries

In 1924 the anatomist Raymond Dart at the University of the Witwatersrand identified a fossilized skull from Taung, North West Province, as belonging to a species between ape and man. The species, named *Australopithecus africanus* (southern African ape), is believed to have lived 2.5 million years ago and is known as the Taung Child. Paleontologist Robert Broom discovered several more fossilized bones of the species in the caves around Sterkfontein. His most spectacular find, in 1947, was the almost complete skull of an individual, known as Mrs. Ples (from her scientific designation *Plesianthropus transvaalensis*, almost human from the Transvaal). More likely Ples is a he.

In the 1990s Dr. Ron Clarke with Stephen Motsumi and Nkwane Molefe unearthed the nearly complete skeleton of an *Australopithecus* who walked upright, but had forelimbs adapted to climbing. Dubbed Little Foot, he may have walked four million years ago.

These Late Iron Age settlements have left some impressive artistic and material remains. Near the town of Lydenberg the so-called Lydenberg Heads were discovered, several elaborately worked, bell-shaped ceramic artifacts with human features. At Mapungubwe, in the far north of the country, iron, copper, tin, and gold were worked, and the settlement was part of trade networks that extended to the Indian Ocean, Arabia, and the Far East. Tortoiseshell and ivory were traded for textiles, glass beads, and porcelain from China. Hilltop burials containing rich grave goods—among them the famous gold Mapungubwe rhinoceros—provide evidence of a stratified class system, with the ordinary people occupying the area at the foot of the hill.

This Late Iron Age culture, based on farming, herding, and some trading, remained within the arable summer rainfall area of South Africa—on the highveld, the central high plateau, and along the east coast down to the Great Fish River—due to the type of crops being cultivated there. Its village way of life proved remarkably stable, remaining unchanged in essentials until the 19th century. But already from the 18th century on, expansion of European settlement out of the cape and into the interior brought increasing pressures for change.

Early European Contacts

The Portuguese navigator, Bartholomeu Dias (ca 1450–1500), was the first European to round the southern tip of Africa, in 1488. Dias did not see the Cape Peninsula on his outward voyage, as he passed it far to the south, but he put in there on his return and named the place the Cape of Good Hope.

A portrait of Jan van Riebeeck, of the Dutch East India Company

Portuguese efforts to reach India via the southern African sea route continued through the late 15th century. Finally Vasco da Gama (ca 1460–1525) succeeded in 1497, after a voyage during which he put in at St. Helena Bay, Mossel Bay, and, on Christmas Day, at a place on the east coast he named Terra do Natal (the name Natal persists today in the name of the province KwaZulu-Natal). Many convoys of ships from Portugal and other European nations sailed around southern Africa in the 150 years that followed. Ships' logs and accounts by shipwreck survivors tell of contacts with the Khoikhoi at the cape and the Nguni people on the east coast that were sometimes friendly, sometimes hostile.

Dutch Settlement at the Cape

In 1652 Europeans established a more permanent presence at the Cape of Good Hope, only now it was the Dutch rather than the Portuguese who took the lead. The Dutch East India Company (often abbreviated to VOC, from the Dutch Vereenigde Oost-Indische Compagnie) by now dominated European trade with India and the East. But they had a problem: On the long voyage around Africa their crews were suffering and dying from scurvy, due to a vitamin C deficiency. The company's solution was to send out an official, Jan van Riebeeck (1619–1677), with orders to establish a garden at the cape where fresh fruit and vegetables would be grown to supply their passing fleets. The VOC never intended to establish a permanent colony at the cape, but as time passed their officials settled in; many so-called *trekboers* (nomadic farmers) rejected the VOC's authority and began to move into the interior to farm on their own account. In time they established towns such as Stellenbosch, Swellendam, and Tulbagh.

> Protestant refugees from France—the Huguenots—settled in the Franschhoek Valley in 1688. They planted vines and established the wine industry in South Africa.

As the trekboers moved into traditional Khoikhoi pasturelands, the Khoikhoi fought back, but their weapons were no match for the settlers' superior technology, guns, and horses. A smallpox epidemic in 1713, which killed many whites, decimated the Khoikhoi, who had little resistance to the disease.

When the settlers at the cape complained of a shortage of labor, the VOC allowed slaves to be imported. Successive expeditions brought many thousands of slaves from the Far East, especially Malaysia and Indonesia, as well as from elsewhere in Africa. The presence of slaves and slave labor had far-reaching consequences for the social history of the Western Cape. From as early as in 1656 some slaves were freed, or were able to buy their freedom. Some of them married free Dutchmen, others set up as independent tavern owners, artisans, and craftsmen.

A new element was added to the Dutch population in 1688, when a large group of Huguenots, Protestant refugees from France, arrived at the cape. Settling in the Franschhoek Valley, they soon blended in with the Dutch, losing their French language. The Huguenots planted vines and established the wine industry in South Africa.

By the late 18th century, Cape Town was a busy port town, where fresh produce was brought in from the interior and sold to passing ships, while imported goods were sold to the farmers. Dutch settlement now extended well up the west coast as far as Springbok and to the northeast as far as Graaff-Reinet. The Khoisan who had formerly lived in the region retreated to more remote areas, were killed, or reduced to the status of servants. But in the 1770s along the Great Fish River, the trekboers encountered and clashed repeatedly with a much more formidable adversary, the settled Xhosa, with weapons of iron. At the same time, events in faraway Europe were to have a profound effect on the history of the cape and of South Africa as a whole.

British Occupation of the Cape

After the Dutch monarchy had been toppled and replaced by a revolutionary French-dominated republic in 1795, Britain saw her lucrative trade with the East threatened. She immediately sent troops, who occupied the cape in the same year. Forced by diplomatic means to withdraw in 1802, the British returned to the cape in 1805, this time for good. The new administration courted popularity with the Dutch inhabitants by abolishing the hated VOC monopoly on trade, and guaranteeing freedom of religion and language. In 1807 the slave trade was abolished, though slaves could still be owned. As the numbers of British increased, they introduced to the cape distinctively English religious and domestic architecture, commercial and legal practices, and institutions such as the press, debating, horse racing, and cricket. They also built schools and made better provisions for the education of the poor.

In 1820, 4,000 English immigrants—the so-called 1820 settlers—were given a free passage to the cape and gifts of land along its eastern frontier. The intention was to create a buffer zone between the inhabitants of the cape and the Xhosa, who were vigorously resisting incursions into their territory. In a series of brutal conflicts lasting through the early decades of the 19th century up until 1852, the British, using firepower and scorched-earth tactics, weakened and eventually broke Xhosa resistance. Decimated by warfare, starvation, and disease, the Xhosa population was greatly reduced. Large areas of their former territory were now occupied by European settlers.

Expansion Outward from the Cape

It was not only the Xhosa who came into conflict with the British. Many Boers (Dutch farmers) in the eastern cape felt alienated by British ways, and by what they regarded as unwarranted legal interference in their relations with their Khoisan and slave labor. For them the abolition of slavery at the cape in 1834 was the last straw. From that date on, successive bands of Voortrekkers (pioneers) left the cape in ox wagons with their wives, children, and servants and trekked into the interior across the Orange and Vaal Rivers and the Drakensberg. This migration became known as the Great Trek. After many battles with the African groups who already lived in these territories, the Voortrekkers set up a series of republics—free, they hoped, of all British influence. These Boer republics occupied the areas that later came to be known as the Orange Free State, between the Orange and Vaal Rivers; the Transvaal, north of the Vaal; and Natal, between the Drakensberg and the Indian Ocean.

From 1824 onward a band of English-speaking adventurers had already established itself in Natal, in Durban Bay. Although the men represented themselves as pioneers and explorers, it seems to have been mainly greed for ivory and other trade goods that drove them.

They constantly tried to have Britain annex Port Natal. The authorities refused. But when the Voortrekkers declared the Republic of Natalia in 1838, the British did not recognize its independence, but sent soldiers to Port Natal who defeated the Voortrekker forces. In 1843 the British finally annexed Natal, and two years later made it part of the Cape Colony.

Rise & Fall of the Zulu Kingdom

On the east coast of South Africa, both English traders and Voortrekkers encountered a powerful new political force: the Zulu kingdom. Its strong, charismatic leader, Shaka (ca 1787–1828), through a blend of ruthless force and diplomatic persuasion, had welded scattered clans and homesteads together into a nation, with its heartland north of the Tugela River. He organized the young Zulu men into regiments by age group, thus creating a large, disciplined, and highly effective army, which owed allegiance directly to him, as king, and not to any local chief. Shaka

Voortrekkers defend themselves against attacking Zulus in "The Battle of Blauwkrantz."

gave a hospitable reception to the Englishmen who arrived in his territory, allowing them to trade in ivory even though this right was an exclusive royal prerogative.

In 1828 Shaka was assassinated by his half brother, Dingane (ca 1795–1840), who succeeded him as king. Ten years later, Dingane fought a series of bloody battles with the Voortrekkers who had invaded his territory. This lead to a split in the Zulu kingdom, when Mpande (1798–1872), also a half brother of Shaka, sided with the Boers against Dingane, defeated him, and ousted him from the Zulu kingship in 1840. Mpande was to rule for more than 30 years, eventually being succeeded by his son, Cetshwayo (ca 1826–1884), in 1872. Then the British intervened, determined to create a unified South Africa out of the existing patchwork of colonies, Boer republics, and independent territories such as the Zulu kingdom.

In 1879 Britain launched an unprovoked attack on Cetshwayo's land. Three infantry columns marched into Zululand—only to be heavily defeated. At the hill of Isandlwana they were met by a 20,000-strong Zulu army, who wiped out nearly 1,200 British troops. But in the battles that followed, at Rorke's Drift, Khambula, and Gigindlovu, the Zulus were beaten and their power broken. Cetshwayo went into exile, and the British annexed Zululand in 1887.

Indians in Natal

Between 1860 and 1911, a new element entered into the mix of South African peoples, as more than 150,000 indentured Indian laborers were brought to Natal to work in the sugarcane plantations. In terms of their indenture, or contract, laborers were bound to a planter for five years; they could sign on for another five years, after which they would be free workers, or return to India. Despite the harsh conditions, about half chose to remain, farming on their own account, or becoming shopkeepers and traders. Despite social and legal discriminations, many Natal Indians were very successful.

Diamonds & Gold

Between 1866 and 1886, with the discovery of diamonds and gold, the nature of South African society changed forever. The country's economy, until then based on agriculture and trade, was rapidly being transformed into one centered around mining, which required massive amounts of capital and labor, and its associated industries. Modern communications reached into the interior, with the railway arriving in Kimberley in 1885.

In 1866, on a farm near Hopetown on the Orange River, a 15-year-old boy picked up a pretty glittering pebble. He thought of it as just a plaything, but it proved to be a diamond. Then nearby in 1871, at the site of the future Kimberley, diggers unearthed the top of a pipe of igneous rock that contained a king's ransom in diamonds. The diamond rush was in full swing. Within two years the population of the new mining town of Kimberley had grown to 50,000 diggers and laborers, and the site of the diamond-bearing pipe, formerly a small hill, had become the "Big Hole," some 650 feet (200 m) deep. Soon individual claims were bought out by capitalists such as Cecil John Rhodes (1853–1902) and Barney Barnato, who vied for control of the diamond fields. Rhodes, with ready access to foreign capital, won the contest. By 1890 his new De Beers company fully controlled all the diggings and could regulate the volumes of diamonds that came onto the market, as it continued to do for more than one hundred years.

In 1886 a surveyor, George Harrison, discovered the fabulously wealthy gold-bearing reef on the Witwatersrand in the Transvaal. Another rush followed, this time for gold. The city of Johannesburg mushroomed on the veld; by 1905 it had a population of 150,000. But the individual diggers soon found out that the main seam lay deep underground, and to exploit it would require a huge injection of labor and capital. Again Rhodes became involved through his Consolidated Gold Fields company. A Chamber of Mines had formed already in 1887 to represent the interests of the mine owners.

Recruiting agents scoured the South African countryside for labor. The colonial government assisted by imposing taxes on rural Africans that forced them into the cash economy to earn the money to pay their taxes. The thousands of African laborers who ended up working in the gold mines were strictly controlled. Their pay was low, they were forbidden to unionize or to move from one mine to another for higher wages. Many ended up living in townships on the fringes of the mining towns. The fault lines that were to divide South Africans for a century began to open up.

The South African War

Earlier in the 19th century, Britain's imperial ambitions had brought her into conflict with the Boers. In 1852, by the Sand River Convention, she had formally recognized the existence of Boer republics in the Orange Free State and Transvaal. But in 1877, taking advantage of divisions among the Boers and conflict with their African neighbors, Britain invaded and officially annexed the Transvaal. The Boers rose up against their colonial masters. Open conflict broke out in 1880, but ended the following year with the signing of the Pretoria Convention, by which the Transvaal achieved self-government. The president of the new state, the South African Republic (SAR), was a man who would play a key role in the future: Paul Kruger.

After the discovery of gold on the Witwatersrand, new tensions arose between the SAR and the British, represented by their colonial administration at the cape. The so-called *uitlanders* (foreigners) in the SAR, mainly English speakers, were agitating for citizen rights and the vote. Disputes arose between the SAR and the Cape Colony over control of the railways. The British believed that Kruger was obstructive in refusing to allow new deep-mining technology to be used. Then in 1895, a British-backed raid, orchestrated by Rhodes, was launched to overthrow the SAR by military force. The raid failed and the ringleaders were arrested, but thereafter war was inevitable.

In 1899 came the first hostilities of the South African War (also known as the Boer War, or the Anglo-Boer War). The war, pitting loosely organized Boer commandos against a professional British army, was fought on a number of fronts. The Boers tied up large numbers of enemy troops by laying siege to the British-held towns of Kimberley in the south, Ladysmith in northern Natal, and Mafeking in the northwest. After considerable Boer successes at Colenso and Spioenkop in Natal, the fighting came to a stalemate, with the Boers unable to advance, and the British unable to lift the sieges.

Britain then committed large numbers of troops to the war—by the end nearly 450,000, against 90,000 Boers—under the command first of Lord Roberts, then of Lord

> Between 1866 and 1886, with the discovery of diamonds and gold, the nature of South African society changed forever.

Kitchener. The British forces soon lifted the Boer sieges and occupied Bloemfontein, Johannesburg, and Pretoria. Kruger went into exile in 1900, dying in Switzerland in 1904. The regular war was over, but now a guerrilla war began, as Boer commandos under their generals, Christiaan de Wet (1854–1922) and Jan Smuts (1870–1950), harassed the British forces and blew up railway lines. But through a policy of burning farms and confining Boer families and their African workers in concentration camps, where many thousands died, the British eventually broke enemy resistance. In 1902 the war ended. By the Treaty of Vereeniging, the Boer republics surrendered their independence and gave allegiance to the British crown.

Union & After

Just eight years after the end of the South African War, in 1910, the colonies of the cape and Natal and the former Boer republics of the Orange Free State and Transvaal came together to form the Union of South Africa. But this union was a white man's arrangement: Apart from a limited franchise in the cape, blacks were given no voting rights in the newly united country.

During the first half of the 20th century, white politics were dominated by the South African Party of Louis Botha (1862–1919) and Smuts, and J. B. M. Hertzog's (1866–1942) breakaway National Party. The former stood for reconciliation between English and Afrikaans speakers, and represented the interests of English capital; the latter stood for Afrikaner nationalism, while representing interests of the poor white working class. Both were equally determined to exclude blacks from power.

Rise of Nationalisms: Black leaders and intellectuals had petitioned the British government since the beginning of the 20th century to gain voting rights and political representation. But their efforts failed, culminating in their exclusion from the Union of 1910. In response, two years later, black leadership came together to form the body that in 1923 would change its name to the African National Congress (ANC). The ANC, under its new leader, John Dube (1871–1946), immediately had to deal with one of the worst pieces of discriminatory legislation in the country's history. The 1913 Natives Land Act laid down that blacks, although they made up 76 percent of the population, could own only 7.5 percent (later increased to 13 percent) of land in South Africa's territory. The ANC made numerous appeals and fought hard against the act, but without success. In the decades that followed, the ANC launched many peaceful protests and supported workers' strikes, against the social, legal, and political discrimination under which black people suffered.

Gandhi in South Africa

In 1893 a recently qualified young lawyer named Mohandas Gandhi arrived in Durban from India. It was in Natal that Gandhi took his first steps in anticolonial politics, defending the rights of local Indians, putting together petitions, and organizing political meetings. Especially important for the future was the creation of a political organization, the Natal Indian Congress, in 1894. After 1902 Gandhi became active in Transvaal politics as well, and was jailed several times. It was here that he developed his famous policy of passive resistance, Satyagraha. Gandhi finally returned to India in 1914–by then he was a seasoned political organizer.

ANC supporters welcome the return of political exiles to Soweto, 1989.

Afrikaner nationalism, which would in the future be ranged against the ANC, began in the late 19th century as a language movement. Speakers of Afrikaans fought to have their language—developed from Dutch with words introduced by slaves from the East—accorded official status. In time the nationalist cause was embodied in a political body, the National Party (NP), representing above all Afrikaans-speaking, working-class whites. The party drew support from those many Afrikaners who still vividly remembered the abuses of British colonialism and who chafed under the dominion of Britain.

Apartheid Era

When Jan Smuts returned to South Africa after playing a leading role in World War II, it was expected that he and his South African Party would win the elections. But it was the Afrikaner National Party that triumphed in 1948 with its policy of apartheid, absolute separation between the races. The NP remained in power until 1994, and in 1961, South Africa broke all ties with Britain and became a republic.

Racism and racial discrimination were nothing new in South Africa, having been supported for centuries by English and Afrikaner alike. But the NP legislated discrimination on a massive scale. Its successive leaders, especially the ideologue Hendrik Verwoerd (prime minister 1958–1966), made apartheid a reality through laws that prohibited marriage and even sex between black and white (Prohibition of Mixed Marriages and Immorality Acts); kept the races apart in post offices, in parks, on the beaches, and all public places (Separate Amenities Act); legislated different living areas for them (Group Areas Act); and removed blacks from "white" universities (the ironically named Extension of University Education Act). According to the NP's grand scheme, blacks would be permitted to stay only temporarily in "white" South Africa to sell their labor, their movements regulated by the passbooks they were forced to carry at all times. They then had to return to their "own areas," the Bantustans (as they came to be known), where alone they could be citizens and exercise the vote.

The Nationalists passed ever more restrictive laws banning black opposition parties like the Communist Party and, later the ANC and the Pan-Africanist Congress. They also encroached on the rule of law, through house arrests and detention of their opponents without trial. In the 1980s, as the NP regime began to lose its grip on power, it surrendered authority to the military and police. Successive states of emergency were declared, under cover of which the regime's adversaries were tortured and killed with impunity.

Opening Parliament in February 1990, Prime Minister F. W. de Klerk declared that all restrictions on political activity would be lifted. A week later, after nearly 28 years behind bars, Nelson Mandela walked to freedom.

Black Resistance

The newly formed ANC was at first cautious in its dealings with the authorities. The communists and unions successfully represented the interests of the black poor. But with the coming of apartheid in 1948, the ANC and its allies became far more militant, organizing bus boycotts and a general campaign of defiance of unjust laws, which led to the arrest of thousands of its members. In 1955 a widely representative Congress of the People met to adopt the Freedom Charter, a document setting out the principles of a nonracial democratic South Africa.

In 1959 militants led by the charismatic Robert Sobukwe (1924–1978) broke away from the ANC to form the Pan-Africanist Congress (PAC). The PAC organized a campaign against carrying the hated passbook in which tens of thousands took part. On March 21, 1960, at Sharpeville in the southern Transvaal, police opened fire on unarmed PAC marchers, killing 69 and wounding 180, an action that earned worldwide condemnation and is remembered to this day as the Sharpeville Massacre. The government's response was to declare a state of emergency and to ban the ANC and PAC. Left no other option, black organizations launched a campaign of armed resistance. Oliver Tambo (1917–1993) became leader of the ANC in exile, while inside the country Nelson Mandela (b. 1918) and others of Umkhonto we Sizwe (Spear of the Nation, abbreviated MK) organized sabotage of strategic and economic targets, always trying to avoid loss of life. But in 1963, the police rounded up virtually the whole leadership of MK, and they were put on trial. Mandela and eight others were sentenced to life imprisonment and were transferred to Robben Island to begin serving their sentences.

With its leadership jailed and exiled, black resistance was quelled for more than a decade. In 1976, schoolchildren in the black township of Soweto, near Johannesburg, began to protest against the compulsory use of Afrikaans in their schools. When children were killed by police, the protests snowballed into a sustained, countrywide uprising. From this time on, South Africa was in a constant state of low-level civil war during which thousands died. MK guerrillas launched armed incursions into the country from newly decolonized neighbor states, and civilians were targeted in bombing campaigns. Black leaders, such as Archbishop Desmond Tutu (b. 1931), succeeded in having the country made the target of international economic, sporting, and artistic sanctions. As the powerful trade unions organized a series of successful consumer boycotts and strikes, South Africa's economy began to show signs of strain. The National Party regime made halfhearted attempts at reform, but always stopped short of giving the black majority what it actually wanted, universal suffrage in a unified South Africa.

Coming of Democracy

By the late 1980s, the white regime was negotiating secretly with the ANC. Then, opening parliament in February 1990, Prime Minister F. W. de Klerk (b. 1936) dropped a bombshell by announcing that all proscribed parties would be unbanned and all restrictions on political activity lifted. A week later, after nearly 28 years behind bars, Nelson Mandela walked to freedom. After several years' more violence, and complex multiparty negotiations, South Africa's first democratic elections were held peacefully in 1994. With the ANC winning an overwhelming majority, Nelson Mandela became the country's first democratic president, and South Africa's new constitution came into force, guaranteeing basic freedoms and civil rights. Discriminatory legislation has been repealed, and basic services such as medical care, clean water, electricity, and housing, have been extended to millions. For several years in the mid-1990s the Truth and Reconciliation Commission, created by parliament,

Nelson Mandela revisits the cell where he had been incarcerated for almost 30 years.

heard testimony from hundreds of witnesses about human rights abuses that occurred during the apartheid era. The commission's report, presented in 1998, acknowledged abuses both by the apartheid government and the liberation forces.

In 1999 Mandela stepped down, and Thabo Mbeki (b. 1942) became president. Mbeki was reelected in 2004 for a second five-year term. Though the economy boomed during his presidency, his legacy has been marred by a corrupt arms deal, lack of action on HIV/AIDS, and a weak policy on dictatorship in neighboring Zimbabwe. In December 2007 the ANC conference chose as its new leader the controversial Jacob Zuma (b. 1942), who is set to succeed Mbeki after the elections scheduled for 2009. ■

Food & Drink

South Africa's food and drink are as varied as the country's population and different climatic zones. Mediterranean cape, highveld, and subtropical KwaZulu-Natal have contributed their wines, fruit, meat, fish, and vegetables. Africa, Asia, Holland, and Britain have each placed their own distinct stamp on local cuisine.

Indigenous South African cooking is based chiefly on boiled or roasted meat and *pap,* a stiff white porridge made from ground *mielies* (corn), often served with greens, such as the spinach-like *morogo* (as it's known in Sotho) or *imifino* (Zulu). Today, though, the mix is often spiced up with chili, tomato, and onions, and chicken may be used as meat rather than beef or game. For a typical Xhosa dish,

Lambert's Bay, a West Coast seafood hot spot, specializes in fully catered seafood meals on the beach.

try *umngqusho*, consisting of *samp* (crushed corn kernels) and lima beans combined with flavoring ingredients such as herbs, lemon, onions, and chilies. If you are feeling particularly adventurous, you may want to sample so-called mopane worms (actually dried caterpillars of the emperor moth). African restaurants in the larger South African cities nowadays tend to serve dishes from all over the continent, featuring ingredients such as couscous, groundnuts, millet, and sweet potatoes, as well as a great variety of grilled game meats.

Quintessentially South African is the style of cooking known as Cape Malay, which fused the cuisine of the Dutch at the cape with that of the slaves they brought from Indonesia. Well-known Cape Malay dishes are *bobotie*, curried minced meat topped with an egg custard; tasty *bredies*, stews made with lamb, or with tomatoes, but always including *waterblommetjies* (the humbly named but very palatable cape pondweed); and *sosaties*, spiced kebabs of chicken, lamb, pork, or beef. The main dish is often served with rice, colored yellow with *borrie* (turmeric), and *blatjang* (spicy chutney made from a variety of fruits, but usually including apricots).

Afrikaners, descended from the Dutch settlers of the cape, developed characteristic foodstuffs of their own that are still popular today. Among these are *biltong*, air-dried

meat, flavored with salt and coriander and cut into long, thin strips; *boerewors* (farmer's sausage), made from coarsely chopped meat, also spiced with coriander; and *potjiekos*, vegetables and meat—usually lamb, beef, or game—spiced and flavored to the cook's individual taste, and stewed in a three-legged cast iron pot over an open fire. Deep-fried dough is also popular, in the form of either plain rounded *vetkoek*, or fat cake, as an accompaniment to meat dishes; or *koeksusters*, plaited strips of dough soaked in very sweet syrup, as a dessert. A Cape Dutch dessert that you will often find on the menu is malva pudding, a kind of caramelized sponge cake, made with apricot jam, sometimes spiced with ginger, served hot and accompanied by ice cream or custard.

On any visit to South Africa, you are sure to encounter the *braaivleis* (literally, roast meat, usually shortened to *braai*) or barbecue, a type of outdoor cooking done by South Africans of every background. Individual practitioners pride themselves on their secret recipes for marinades and sauces, and their patented methods for getting the fire and coals just right. All kinds of meat—steaks, boerewors, chops, chicken, sosaties—may be *braaied*, as well as fish, and vegetables such as mielies (corn), potatoes, and onions. Green salads and potato salad often accompany the *braai*, as do local red wine and beer to wash down the food.

In restaurants all along the South African coast, you should have no difficulty finding fresh seafood of excellent quality. KwaZulu-Natal specializes in game

Young vendors hawk their wares to passing motorists in the Eastern Cape.

fish, prawns, and shrimps. Knysna, at the heart of the Western Cape's Garden Route, has become famous for its locally produced fresh oysters. In Cape Town try *kingklip* or *kabeljou* (cod), both firm-fleshed white fish. The west coast, from Cape Town to Lambert's Bay, is well known for its spiny lobsters (called crayfish locally) and mussels. The most common freshwater fish on South African menus is trout, introduced into the country's dams and streams by British immigrants.

During the post-1994 tourist boom, South African cooking has come of age. The country's chefs have created a distinct fusion cuisine, combining local and international foods in original ways. Carpaccio made from springbok, ostrich, or even smoked crocodile tail now features on restaurant menus, as does grated biltong, used to flavor deep-fried Camembert or salads. Look out for intriguing dishes such as kudu in black cherry sauce, crayfish risotto, grilled salmon on sweet-potato mash, or ostrich fillet with goat-cheese ravioli.

International cuisine is well represented in South Africa. Indian restaurants have a strong presence in Durban, with its large population from the subcontinent. But in the cities visitors will also be able to find French, German, Greek, Italian, Middle Eastern, Portuguese, Chinese, Thai, and Japanese cooking, as well as traditional British pub food.

Wine lovers are spoiled for choice in South Africa. The Western Cape with its Mediterranean climate has been in the business of making wine since the arrival of the

> **Carpaccio made from springbok, ostrich, or even smoked crocodile tail now features on restaurant menus, as does grated biltong, used to flavor deep-fried Camembert or salads.**

French Huguenots in 1688. Today there are hundreds of different labels on the market—reds, whites, sparkling, and fortified wines—most of good to excellent quality. Due to the hot climate, South African wines are typically powerful and fruity, with a relatively high alcohol content of 11.5 percent to 14.5 percent.

For red wines, Cabernet Sauvignon, Merlot, and Shiraz are the most common cultivars, often combined in good blends. Pinot Noir is rarer, though some of the coastal vineyards have succeeded with this variety. Visitors should sample some Pinotage, a variety created in 1924 right here in South Africa, by crossing the Pinot Noir grape with the Cinsault. Among white wines, the most popular are those created from the Sauvignon Blanc, Chardonnay, Chenin Blanc, and Colombard varieties. While it is invidious to single out specific producers, the Springfield, Hamilton Russell, Vergelegen, and Diemersfontein estates have all been consistent performers in recent years.

If you like a good port, try those produced around the little Western Cape town of Calitzdorp, by the Boplaas or De Krans wineries. From the same region (though expensive and hard to find) comes a superb port made by the tiny Axe Hill estate. South Africa also bottles some excellent sherries, and five- and ten-year-old brandies. With dessert, drink a local sweet wine, produced from Muscadel or Hanepoort grapes. After dinner sip one of the country's popular cream liqueurs: Cape Velvet, or Amarula Cream, made from the fruit of the indigenous marula tree.

Beer drinkers can enjoy a range of locally produced lagers and ales, bottled, canned, or available on draft in pubs. The giant SABMiller brewery dominates the market with its ubiquitous Castle lager. But in the Western Cape, the small independent breweries, Mitchell's in Knysna and Birkenhead near Hermanus, produce high-quality bottled and draught ale. Those who prefer a German-style lager should ask for Windhoek, a beer

EXPERIENCE:
Brewery Tours

In a country mainly known for wine, the brewing business is not to be underestimated. European recipes are combined with African ingredients (for example, sorghum) for a unique drink.

Several breweries around Cape Town offer tours, but the ultimate target lies along the Beer Route in the northwestern KwaZulu-Natal. Starting around Durban, the route snakes through the countryside hitting eight breweries along the way. Highlights include the monolithic **SABMiller Brewery** in Prospecton (9–11 Jeffels Rd., tel 031/910-1111), the tiny **Zululand Brewing Company** in Eshowe (28 miles/45 km NW of Dukuza R66 & N2, tel 035/474-4919, www.zulubeer.com), and the **Shongweni Brewery** in the Shongweni Valley (off B1, tel 031/769-2061, www.shongwenibrewery.com).

Although you can find tours that will take you from place to place, the area is large and spread out, so renting a car is the best bet. For maps, times, and accommodations, visit the official site: http://beer.kzn.org.za.

brewed in accordance with German standards and imported from neighboring Namibia. If you want to go indigenous, try traditional local beer. The production of this drink is the preserve of women, who brew it from corn and sorghum malt, which they combine with yeast and water, then steep, boil, and filter. The resulting drink is opaque and creamy, with a low alcohol content of 3 percent. ■

Land & Landscape

Physically, South Africa consists of a vast, high inland plateau edged by mountain ranges that fall away to a narrow coastal plain. Within this simple structure, the country displays an astonishing variety of striking landscapes: the emerald green mountains of the Drakensberg range, the spectacular Blyde River Canyon, the dune and swamp system of St. Lucia, the starkly beautiful, arid Karoo and Richtersveld, the red sands of the Kalahari, and the weirdly twisted layers of the Cape Fold Mountains.

South Africa is an enormous country of 470,979 square miles (1,219,912 sq km), situated between the warm Indian Ocean in the east and the colder Atlantic in the west, with a coastline that runs northeast and northwest for 1,860 miles (3,000 km). The highest point in the country is the peak of Injisuthi, in the Drakensberg mountains, reaching 11,424 feet (3,408 m).

Rainfall is poor over most of South Africa, apart from the east coast. Just two major rivers flow through the country. The 1,367-mile-long (2,187 km) Gariep River, formerly known as the Orange, rises in the highlands of Lesotho and meets the sea in the extreme northwestern corner of South Africa, at Alexander Bay; while its tributary, the Vaal River, rises in eastern Mpumalanga, then flows for 700 miles (1,120 km) to its confluence with the Gariep River southwest of the town of Kimberley.

Coastline

Palm trees and lush, green, broad-leafed vegetation dominate the landscape along the subtropical east coast of KwaZulu-Natal. Miles and miles of magnificent sandy beaches border the Indian Ocean in this region and down along the sparsely populated, remote Wild Coast (the north coast of the Eastern Cape). The Eastern Cape coastline as a whole is characterized by picturesque river deltas, often with bluffs and lagoons, where short rivers from the interior meet the sea, as at the vacation towns of Gonubie, near East London, and Kenton-on-Sea.

The stretch of coast from Mossel Bay east to beyond Plettenberg Bay is known as the Garden Route. Its lakes, lagoons, green rolling hills, bushy coastal dunes, and fine beaches make the Garden Route one of the most popular tourist areas in

South Africa. The Tsitsikamma National Park here is home to some of the few remaining areas of indigenous temperate forest in South Africa.

As the coast runs southwest to the southernmost point of Africa at Cape Agulhas, and then northwest to Cape Town, it gradually becomes drier, cooler, and rockier. The west coast of South Africa, washed by the Atlantic Ocean and the cold Benguela Current, is very different from the Indian Ocean side. This is a region of freezing blue waters, pounding waves, sea mists, and long white beaches, alternating with seaweed-fringed rocky shore and many miles of dunes.

Mountains

Lying roughly parallel to the coast, inland of the coastal plain, mountain ranges form a barrier to much of the South African interior. In the southwestern corner of the country, the Cederberg range northwest of Cape Town and the Hex River,

Giant's Castle Game Reserve, a World Heritage site in the Drakensberg range

the Riviersonderend and Tsitsikamma ranges, and the Outeniqua Mountains all belong to a single geological system. Known as the Cape Fold Belt, these mountains had their beginnings 400 million years ago, when deep layers of sediment were laid down in the southern ocean. Then, 250 million years ago, a great convulsion of the Earth's crust twisted and folded the resultant quartzitic sandstone into the awe-inspiring formations visible today. Some spectacular passes cut through these Western Cape mountains. If you have your own car, you should take the time to drive over the high Swartberg Pass, between Prince Albert and the Cango Caves, or at least through the more accessible passes at Meiringspoort, on the N12 just north of De Rust, or Seweweekspoort, off the R62 near Ladismith. You will be rewarded with the breathtaking sight of enormous rock bands swirled, twisted, and arched into fantastic shapes, as if formed by a child from modeling clay. Associated with the Cape Fold mountains are many hot springs, most notably at Citrusdal, Caledon, Montagu, and Barrydale.

....

Tourists flock to the dry plains of Namaqua, northwest of Cape Town, in late August and September when countless orange, purple, white, and red spring daisies and flowering succulents come into bloom.

....

Stretching up the eastern side of South Africa through KwaZulu-Natal and Mpumalanga Provinces, the Drakensberg range has a very different, more recent geological history. Around 180 million years ago, huge volumes of basalt welled up and then eroded over millennia to form these mountains, with their precipitous cliffs and soaring peaks. In Mpumalanga the process of erosion has created the magnificent escarpment—where the high interior falls rapidly away to the lowveld—and scenic wonders such as the Blyde River Canyon. In KwaZulu-Natal, the Ukhuhlamba-Drakensberg features natural amphitheaters and bright green grassy slopes intersected by clear mountain streams.

Highveld & Lowveld

Highveld (*veld* is an Afrikaans word meaning "wide open rural spaces") refers to the raised central plateau of South Africa, 4,500 to 6,000 feet (1,370–1,820 m) above sea level. In the past, most of the central and southern part of this area was covered by grassland, though now much of it is inhabited or under cultivation, especially with corn and sunflowers. The northern, somewhat lower, expanses of the highveld, mainly in Limpopo Province, still retain a good deal of their bushveld and woodland vegetation. Look out for trees such as the ubiquitous silver cluster-leaf (*Terminalia serica*), the stately marula (*Sclerocarya birrea*), favored by elephants when in fruit, and the striking knobthorn (*Acacia nigrescens*), with thorns growing directly from the raised knobs that cover its trunk.

Lying at the foot of the eastern escarpment, the lowveld is home to the Kruger National Park and many private game reserves. This hot, humid, malarial region is characterized in the south by dense thorn forest, with graceful green-barked fever trees (*Acacia xanthophloea*), and in the drier north by mopane scrub (*Colophospermum mopane*). Here you can expect to see South Africa's Big Five, the elephant, lion, leopard, buffalo, and rhino, as well as many types of antelope—among them kudu, impala, nyala, and bushbuck—and more than 500 species of birds.

Sunrise over Kgalagadi Transfrontier Park, the Northern Cape

Arid Interior

The Karoo, stretching from east to west inland of the southern coastal mountain ranges, came into being between 240 million and 190 million years ago. Surrounded by high mountains, the region formed the bottom of an inland sea, in which sediments settled over a period of 50 million years. When the sea dried out, the sedimentary layers were exposed to reveal an outstanding fossil record of reptiles, but also of fishes, invertebrates, and plants. Most intriguing are the abundant fossils of the Therapsid family, creatures that combined features of both mammals and reptiles. The modern Karoo is a place of bleak beauty, with low flat-topped hills and wide open plains, where sheep graze on the sparse vegetation, and the only sound is the clank of the windmills bringing water up from underground.

The dry plains of Namaqua, northwest of Cape Town, attract few visitors during most of the year. But tourists flock here in late August and September when countless orange, purple, white, and red spring daisies and flowering succulents come into bloom.

Beyond Namaqua, tucked into the extreme northwestern corner of South Africa, is the moonlike landscape of the Richtersveld. The rugged broken hills are home to tiny succulent plants, tall quiver trees (*Aloe dichotoma*), Hartmann's mountain zebra, and small rock hyraxes. If you think you see a person standing on the skyline in the blazing heat, chances are you are mistaken—it is probably a *halfmens* (Afrikaans for "half person"), the humanlike succulent tree, *Pachypodium namaquanum*. ■

Giraffes amid the treetops at the Sibuya Game Reserve

Animals

The abundant animal life of South Africa attracts droves of local and international tourists each year to the country's wild places. The Big Five are a major drawing card, but so are the many antelope, primates, other mammals, reptiles, and birds. Here are just a few of the specimens you are most likely to see.

Mammals

Dassie: Visitors to the mountains of the Western Cape will almost certainly see these small, agile, brown rock hyraxes basking on the rocks or scuttling under an overhang. Unlikely though it may seem, dassies are anatomically closely related to elephants.

Giraffe: Tallest of all animals, giraffes are wonderfully camouflaged by their dappled brown and white markings. If you spot one browsing the treetops, look hard and you are likely to see others hidden in the bushveld.

Hippopotamus: Despite its jovial appearance, the water-dwelling hippo is a dangerous animal, particularly if you get in its way as it leaves or heads for the water. Look for its ears and its eyes just breaking the surface, and listen for its low grunting sounds.

Porcupine: Porcupines are shy, nocturnal, burrowing animals. While you are unlikely to see them, you may well find their sharp, black-and-white striped quills on the ground.

Warthog: With their protruding tusks, bristly gray bodies, short snouts, and tails held stiffly upright, these small, compact animals have a slightly comical air. In the early summer, watch for parents and their young as they trot single file through the bush.

Zebra: One of the most visible animals on the plains, black-and-white-striped zebras are often found grazing together with wildebeest. When alarmed, they give a high yelping call.

Antelope

Eland: Looking like large cattle, handsome fawn gray eland graze in herds of up to 50 strong. Identify them by their exceptionally thick neck and hanging, bearded dewlap.

Gemsbok: Found in the dry, semidesert of South Africa, gemsboks are distinguished by their very long, dead-straight horns, and black-and-white legs and faces.

Impala: These small, graceful, russet, white-stomached antelope with curving horns are the most common of the bushveld antelope. You will see them in large groups, accompanied in spring by numerous young ones.

Kudu: The males, large, gray-brown, with narrow white vertical stripes on the body, and huge spiraling horns, are the most majestic of the antelope.

Nyala: Nyalas may at first glance be mistaken for kudu, as they have similar striped bodies; but their horns are not as twisted, and they have distinctive yellow legs and a large fringe under the body.

Springbok: Small, cinnamon-colored, with white underparts, a broad chocolate brown stripe on the flanks, and lyre-shaped horns, springbok are found in large numbers in the Karoo and dry, semidesert areas.

Wildebeest: Large, gray antelope with horns that spread outward and up, wildebeest come in two varieties, blue and black. Blue wildebeest are larger, with black tails; black wildebeest are smaller, with white tails.

Primates

Baboons: Widespread in South Africa, baboons, with their long black muzzles, small close-set eyes, and thick gray-brown coats, can be seen in large family groups, with a male acting as lookout. Although in some places baboons are used to humans, you should never feed them, as they can be dangerous.

Vervet monkeys: These light gray, small, agile, long-tailed primates are easily distinguishable by their black faces. They are found mainly in the eastern part of the country, in groups of up to 20.

An impala at the Hluhluwe-iMfolozi Park, the dominant species in many savannas

Vervet monkey, Sodwana Bay

Birds

African penguin: Two colonies of these birds (formerly called jackass penguins for their loud braying call) are found in the Western Cape, at Boulders near Simon's Town, and at Betty's Bay. Standing 27.5 inches (70 cm) tall, they have a black stripe across the chest and are the only species that breed in Africa.

Blue crane: The best place to see the graceful blue crane, South Africa's national bird, is in the fields of the Overberg region of the Western Cape. Slender-necked, 41 inches (105 cm) tall, blue cranes gather in pairs or groups of ten or more. In flight they give a loud, low, belling call.

Helmeted guineafowl: This small bird with red

....

The best place to see the graceful blue crane, South Africa's national bird, is in the fields of the Overberg region of the Western Cape.

....

cap, blue neck, and dark gray, white-flecked body is most often seen in groups, even in cities, feeding on the ground.

Yellow-billed hornbill: Of several varieties of hornbill, the species you are most likely to see in the bushveld is this one. Somewhat comical

in appearance, it has a large yellow bill, angry-looking bare, red skin around the eye, and black-and-white plumage.

Ibises: Two types, both with long curved bills, are commonly found in South Africa. The Hadeda ibis has brown plumage with an iridescent blue-green sheen and utters loud, harsh cries as it flies to and from its feeding grounds. The Sacred ibis, white, with black head, neck, and rump, inhabits dams and swampy areas.

Kori bustard: Seldom seen outside game reserves, the kori bustard, standing 53 inches (135 cm) tall, is the world's heaviest flying bird. It walks slowly on long yellow legs and has a dark crest, brown plumage, black spots on the upper wings, and white underparts.

Lilac-breasted roller: With its blue underparts, brown upper body, and lilac breast and throat, this bird can easily be spotted flying or perching in the bushveld.

Raptors: South Africa has a wealth of raptors, including the lammergeyer, with its large wingspan, up to 110 inches (280 cm); the White-headed fish eagle, notable for its haunting cry; the jackal buzzard, often seen perching on poles at the side of the road; and the light-gray-and-white pale chanting goshawk.

Secretary bird: Standing as tall as 59 inches (150 cm), the majestic secretary bird can easily be recognized by its orange face, loose black feathers behind the head, gray body, and black underparts as it stalks on yellow legs.

Reptiles

Crocodile: The species that occurs locally in the north and east is the olive-colored Nile crocodile, nearly 10 feet long (3 m).

Snakes: South Africa has hundreds of species, some poisonous and a few deadly; most are shy and avoid encounters with humans.

Water monitor: Reaching up to 63 inches (160 cm) in length, this is the largest of the African lizards and may be seen basking alongside rivers and lakes.

Right: Gray-crowned crane, Umbeni River Bird Park

Arts & Literature

From cave paintings of the early San people to vivid contemporary visual arts, from banned writing during apartheid to Nobel Prize novels, the arts of South Africa thrive, an expression of its multicultural ambience.

Literature

South African writing—the novel, drama, poetry—by now has a history stretching back nearly 200 years. This literature speaks in multiple voices, in Xhosa, Zulu, and other African languages, in English, and Afrikaans. It speaks about the experience of Europeans trying to adapt to a land strange to them, and the feelings of dispossession, loss, and rebellion of indigenous peoples. Here we will concentrate on literature in English and Afrikaans.

Black Literature in English: The country's first major black writer in English was newspaper editor and prominent ANC intellectual Sol Plaatje (1876–1932). Apart from numerous political writings, he published the novel *Mhudi* (1930), a romance of love and war, about the Batswana woman, Mhudi. The Zulu author Herbert Dhlomo (1903–1956), in the 1930s and 1940s, produced dramatic works on black leaders such as the Zulu kings Shaka and Cetshwayo.

A performance of *The Lion King,* Johannesburg

After World War II, a number of novels and autobiographical works appeared, recording the realities of life for black people in South Africa. Peter Abrahams (b. 1919) published *Mine Boy* (1946), describing racial discrimination against migrant laborers in mining Johannesburg, and *Tell Freedom* (1954), the story of his upbringing in South Africa. *Down Second Avenue* (1959) by Es'kia Mphahlele (b. 1919) is a moving and engaging account of the author's boyhood in the Transvaal during the 1920s and 1930s. William (Bloke) Modisane's (1923–1986) autobiography *Blame Me on History* (1963) was banned by the apartheid government for its critical stance. Modisane, along with Mphahlele, Can Themba (1924–1969), and Todd

Matshikiza (1921–1968), was a key figure of the so-called *Drum* generation. As writers of short stories and reportage for the black magazine *Drum*, hugely popular during the 1950s, they created a snappy, urban, American-influenced style. The world of their writings was one of *tsotsis* (gangsters) and their molls, beauty queens, jazz, and shebeens (illicit bars).

With the political repression of the 1960s to 1990s, many black writers went into exile; those who remained turned to protest. Poetry enjoyed a renaissance, as poets Mongane Wally Serote (b. 1944), Sipho Sepamla (1932–2007), Oswald Mtshali (b. 1940), Mafika Gwala (b. 1946), and the poet cum orator Mzwakhe Mbuli (b. 1958) read their work to huge audiences at political rallies. The literary magazine *Staffrider* provided a vehicle for many protest poets. The novel *Emergency* (1964) by Richard Rive (1932–1989) dealt with the troubles after Sharpeville, and *Buckingham Palace: District Six* (1987) with the destruction of the mixed-race neighborhood of his youth.

South African Literature Today

Since 1994 there has been a convergence in South African literature, with increasing numbers of authors choosing to make their work available in English. André Brink continues to publish in that language, as do successful novelists like Afrikaner Étienne Van Heerden (b. 1954), *The Long Silence of Mario Salviati*; and Zakes Mda, *The Whale Caller*. The Afrikaans poet Antjie Krog has earned a considerable reputation with her works of reportage in English, among them, *Country of My Skull*, on the Truth and Reconciliation Commission. One of the most exciting new writers of the post-apartheid period is Ivan Vladislavic, whose fictional works *The Folly* (1993), *The Restless Supermarket* (2001), and *Exploded View* (2004) plot the course of South Africa's transition to a new kind of society.

Afrikaans Literature: Afrikaans literature started to emerge with the late 19th-century movement to have the language recognized as an independent entity, but only fully developed with the second language movement of the 1920s.

One of the first notable writers was Totius (real name: Jakob Daniel Du Toit, 1877–1953), translator of the Bible into Afrikaans and prolific lyric poet. The works of Eugene Marais (1871–1936), a number of which have been translated into English, include both poetry and philosophical works on natural history, the best known being *The Soul of the White Ant* (Afrikaans 1925, English 1937). Other important figures were the poet Jan Celliers (1865–1940) and poet, playwright, novelist, and food writer Louis Leipoldt (1880–1947).

A major writer emerged in the 1930s, N. P. van Wyk Louw (1906–1970), both an academic scholar of Afrikaans and a poet and playwright. His best known works are his first volume of poems, *Alleenspraak (Monologue)* of 1935, his poetic epic *Raka* (1941), dealing with problems of violence and culture, and the historical drama, *Germanicus* (1956). D. J. Opperman (1914–1985), a significant poet for several decades, first came to notice with his collection *Heilige beeste (Holy cattle)* of 1945.

Fresh winds blew through Afrikaans literature with the arrival of the controversial Sestigers (writers of the 1960s), novelists Étienne Leroux (1922–1989), André Brink (b. 1935), and poets Ingrid Jonker (1933–1965) and Breyten Breytenbach (b. 1939). Strongly influenced by the French avant-garde, the Sestigers opened up what had been a rurally focused literature to new urban, cosmopolitan trends.

South African English Literature: The first English South African writer to gain an international reputation was the novelist Olive Schreiner (1855–1920). Well ahead of her time, in her novels *Story of an African Farm* (1883) and *Trooper Halkett of Mashonaland* (1897), the free-thinking Schreiner reflected on issues of feminism, agnosticism, race relations, and British imperialism in southern Africa.

Life in South Africa at the turn of the 19th century forms the backdrop to the satirical novels of Douglas Blackburn (1857–1929). His writings—such as *Prinsloo of Prinsloosdorp* (1899) and *A Burgher Quixote* (1903) satirizing the corruption of Paul Kruger's Transvaal—have recently enjoyed something of a revival.

In 1925 a group of rebellious young South African writers, Roy Campbell, Laurens van der Post, and William Plomer, founded the satirical literary magazine *Voorslag (Whiplash).* The magazine was short-lived, but all three went on to have long and successful literary careers, at first in South Africa, later in Europe.

Apart from the *Voorslag* group, the most important writers between World War I and II were the novelists Pauline Smith (1882–1959) and Sarah Gertrude Millin (1889–1968). Smith wrote with empathy of small-town life in the Karoo, while the prolific Millin was limited by her conviction that the races should remain separated.

Still one of South Africa's best loved authors, Herman Charles Bosman (1905–1951) was a short-story writer of genius. His tales of life in the Groot Marico district of northwestern South Africa, featuring a crusty old Afrikaner narrator, Oom (Uncle) Schalk Lourens, are at once ironic, satirical, humane, and extremely funny. Early in life, Bosman spent four years in jail for murder. He wrote a fascinating memoir of the experience in *Cold Stone Jug* (1949). Anyone who wishes to understand white South Africa should read him.

Almost contemporary with Bosman, though much longer lived, was Alan Paton (1903–1988), liberal politician and author of biographical, autobiographical, and fictional works. Paton's novel *Cry, the Beloved Country* (1948) is perhaps the best known of all South African novels. The work tells the tragic story of a rural black man's search for his son in violent Johannesburg.

During the post-Sharpeville apartheid years, South Africa produced a number of writers who would portray to a worldwide readership the injustices being perpetrated in their country. The dramatist Athol Fugard (b. 1932) wrote many plays, such as *Boesman and Lena* (1969) and *Sizwe Banzi Is Dead* (1972) that exposed the evils of apartheid.

Nadine Gordimer (b. 1923), longtime political activist and recipient of the 1991 Nobel Prize for literature, has published many short stories and novels, all of which take the condition of South Africa as their theme. Her works were sharply critical of the apartheid regime, which banned several of them. Also much banned was novelist André

Brink who started out writing in Afrikaans, but then went on to publish his many novels both in that language and in English. South Africa's other Nobel laureate, novelist J. M. Coetzee (b. 1940), has cultivated a more indirect, allegorical way of representing his country's shortcomings in works such as *Waiting for the Barbarians* (1980) and *Life and Times of Michael K* (1983).

Visual Arts

The days when South African critics drew a sharp distinction between fine art and craft are long over. Today local artists work with whatever means they choose—wire, beads, feathers, cement, rubber, digital media, or the traditional media of painting, graphic art, and sculpture. As in most cultural domains, South African art has a divided past, with the work of white and black artists occupying mainly separate worlds.

Traditional homesteads and traditional crafts, Lesedi Cultural Village

Local artwork, Lalibela Game Reserve

White Artists: Colonial artists of European origin, most famous of whom is Thomas Baines (1820–1875), saw themselves as reporters, giving a detailed account of the exotic peoples, animals, plant life, and landscape of South Africa to a fascinated public back home. South African art begins only in the late 19th and early 20th century to focus on local subjects for their own sake, through the bronzes of Anton van Wouw (1862–1945) and the paintings of Hugo Naudé (1869–1941). The canvasses of J. H. Pierneef (1886–1957), one of South Africa's finest painters, capture the light and landscape of the highveld in a style that tends to the geometric.

Successive artistic movements in Europe found distinguished South African followers. Irma Stern (1894–1966) developed her own distinctly African brand of expressionism, while Maggie Laubscher (1886–1973), like Stern, used bright color in her post-impressionist images of the countryside. The stylized forms and bold colors of fauvism appeared in the art of Maurice van Essche (1906–1977), applied to local subjects. An entire school of abstract expressionism developed in Johannesburg around the artist Bill Ainslie (1934–1989); and Italian-born Edoardo Villa (b. 1915) produced many abstract metal sculptures that adorn South Africa's public spaces.

In the 1950s and 1960s several artists drew their inspiration directly from the art of Africa. Cecil Skotnes (b. 1926) became the country's undisputed master of the woodcut, representing indigenous subjects in a range of blacks, reds, and browns. Walter Battiss (1906–1982) developed a uniquely playful and colorful style of painting inspired by Bushman rock art. Alexis Preller (1911–1975) painted subject matter derived from Africa in a dreamlike, surreal manner.

During the decades of open struggle against apartheid, protest art flourished. The most iconic piece to emerge from this period is the *Butcher Boys*, by Jane Alexander (b. 1959). In her sculptural group three horned, naked, partially flayed figures sit in silence, creating an eerie sense of evil.

Black Artists: Indigenous artists in South Africa have expressed themselves for centuries through rock painting, ceramics, and brightly colored beadwork. In the 20th century, however, to gain access to the art market, black artists began to work in Western forms such as oil painting, sculpture, and graphic art. For many years the work of these artists was simply ignored by the art establishment, but increasingly since the late 1980s this art is reclaimed, exhibited, and its history written. A major exhibition at the Johannesburg Art Gallery, "The Neglected Tradition," in 1988, displayed the work of scores of black artists whose names had been all but forgotten.

One such is the painter Gerard Sekoto (1913–1993), whose oils broke with tradition by representing not tribal subjects, but instead vibrant scenes of life in the townships. Sekoto lived the second half of his life in exile, in Paris. George Pemba (1912–2001) spent his whole life in Port Elizabeth, painting urban scenes and portraits.

Two centers set up in the 1950s and 1960s helped to promote black creativity. From 1952 Johannesburg's Polly Street Art Center established the career of several artists, among them sculptors Sydney Kumalo (1935–1988), whose work was exhibited in Venice in 1966, and Ezrom Legae (1937–1999). In KwaZulu-Natal, the Rorke's Drift Art School taught especially etching and screen-printing techniques. Well-known artists to emerge from Rorke's Drift include John Muafangejo (1943–1987), Paul Sibisi (b. 1948), and Dan Rakgoathe (1937–2004).

Several individualistic, largely self-taught artists made their mark, such as the religious sculptor-in-wood Jackson Hlungwane (b. 1923) and Dumile Feni (1942–1991) who, for economic reasons, worked mainly in ballpoint pen on paper.

Many artists between 1960 and the early 1990s used their art as a means to protest against apartheid. One of the most striking of these is the self-taught Willie Bester (b. 1953), who incorporates scrap materials to make powerful statements on injustice and human rights. Bester's works are exhibited widely in South Africa and internationally.

> ## Keep an Eye On:
> **Other contemporary artists whose work you should look for include William Kentridge (b. 1955), a graphic artist, videomaker, and film and stage director whose work has been exhibited worldwide; playful postmodern sculptor in metal, Brett Murray (b. 1961); artist Kevin Brand (b. 1953), with his strong sculptural forms; and Walter Oltmann (b. 1960), creator of weird and wonderful sculptures in copper and steel wire.**

Architecture

In South Africa's cities and suburbs you will find public and domestic architecture similar to that all over the English-speaking world—high-rise, glass-faced towers, concrete shopping malls, apartment blocks, and single-story dwellings. But the country has developed two unique types of domestic architecture: elegant Cape Dutch and colorful Ndebele.

Cape Dutch Architecture: Multiple influences went into the making of Cape Dutch architecture: building styles imported by Dutch and French Huguenot settlers at the cape in the late 17th century and the skills in decorative plasterwork of Indonesian slaves.

Cape Dutch buildings served agricultural needs. Originally farmhouses in this style were built on a simple rectangular plan with a steeply raked thatched roof and floors either of bare earth or of peach pits pressed into the ground. But with increasing prosperity in the 17th century, houses grew larger, and the unique feature of Cape Dutch architecture appeared, the large central gable—often elaborately molded—on the long side of the house, above the front door. Wings were added to the basic rectangle, to create U-, T-, or H-shaped floor plans. The owners also constructed outbuildings, such as barns, wine cellars, or a *jonkershuis* for the eldest son.

Whitewashed Cape Dutch houses of the Western Cape, often surrounded by vineyards and set against a backdrop of soaring mountains, still remain stunningly beautiful. Outstanding examples can be seen in Stellenbosch, and at the estates of Groot Constantia, near Cape Town, and Vergelegen, in Somerset West.

Ndebele Architecture: Since the late 19th century, the Ndebele people in the north of South Africa have developed a strikingly decorative style of building for their homesteads. The basic layout consists of a cylindrical house topped by a conical thatched roof, with a bare, clean courtyard around the house. A low wall pierced by an elaborate gateway surrounds the yard.

Unique to Ndebele dwellings are the elaborate, polychrome, geometric designs that cover the white gateway and walls of the house. The designs were originally derived from shapes seen in nearby towns, such as Union Jack flags and elements of European domestic architecture. Today the red, green, blue, yellow, and ocher patterns, each outlined strongly in black, remind the visitor of the abstract paintings of Piet Mondrian.

> South Africa has a proud history of music, its distinctive contribution being various musical styles that fuse imported jazz with indigenous African melodies and rhythms.

Music

South Africa has a proud history of music, its distinctive contribution being various musical styles that fuse imported jazz with indigenous African melodies and rhythms.

Black South African jazz arose among urbanized workers in the mining cities of the Witwatersrand. The first local jazz music to come to prominence in the 1920s was a form of swing known as *marabi*, combining the sounds of piano with the rattling of pebble-filled cans. Marabi was later followed by *kwela*, in which the high-pitched sound of the tin pennywhistle predominated. The heyday of local jazz arrived during the 1950s, the *Drum* Era (from *Drum* magazine), when all races swung to the rhythms of outstanding musicians in Johannesburg's Sophiatown. These musicians combined marabi and *kwela* to create the hugely popular, new *mbaqanga* style.

Major songstresses of the time included Miriam Makeba (b. 1932), who would later achieve worldwide fame, and Dolly Rathebe (1928–2004). An important focus of Sophiatown music in the 1950s was the Sophiatown Modern Jazz Club, influenced by musicians such as Dizzy Gillespie (1917–1993) and Charlie Parker (1920–1955). Born out of the club, the Jazz Epistles band produced such luminaries as pianist Dollar Brand (b. 1934), later known as Abdullah Ibrahim, saxophonist Kippie Moeketsi (1925–1983), and trumpeter Hugh Masekela (b. 1939). Like so many other aspects of South African culture, music was hard hit by the apartheid repression of the 1960s. Sophiatown was razed to the ground, and all the best jazz musicians of the time, among them Makeba, Masekela, and

Joseph Shabalala, Paul Simon, and the Ladysmith Black Mambazo

Brand, left the country to return only in the 1990s after the coming of democracy.

The major musical success of the 1970s was a Zulu a cappella group, Ladysmith Black Mambazo, lead by Joseph Shabalala (b. 1941). The group came to international attention when it worked with singer Paul Simon, on the album *Graceland*. A few years later, Johnny Clegg (b. 1953), dubbed the White Zulu, with Sipho Mchunu (b. 1951), created a fusion of Western pop with Zulu music and dance. Clegg's bands Juluka, and then Savuka, achieved great popularity in South Africa and Europe. A new phenomenon of the 1980s was the rise of successful "alternative" white musicians, both English and Afrikaans, opposed to the apartheid regime. Locals in the 1980s thrilled to the sounds of the blues band Cherry-Faced Lurchers, led by the outstanding James Phillips (1959–1995), aka Bernoldus Niemand, and singers such as Johannes Kerkorrel (1960–2002) and Koos Kombuis (b. 1954). From the early 1990s on, South African popular music has been dominated by *kwaito*, a local adaptation of house and hip-hop.

Classical music has a presence in South Africa's larger cities, several of which support a symphony orchestra and smaller chamber groups. Opera has rapidly transformed itself since 1994 from an all-white art form to one dominated by black singers, many of whom trained at the University of Cape Town's opera school. ∎

A historical port of call with buzzing cosmopolitan flair, set on a dazzling blue bay in the shadow of rugged mountains

Cape Town & the Peninsula

Cape Point, where the waters of the Atlantic and Indian Oceans are said to meet

Cape Town & the Peninsula

Cape Town is full of contrasts. In summer it's all palm trees, blue sea, and white beaches. In winter it's a rain-softened mezzotint of meadows, bare vineyards, and log fires. Cape Town is truly blessed: a mild Mediterranean climate, the soaring improbable bulk of Table Mountain that cradles the city between granite and sea, and a natural beauty that surprises the eye.

Perched on the fringe of a bay that stretches from horizon to horizon, Cape Town grew around a cosmopolitan seaport. Vasco da Gama, the Portuguese explorer who first dropped anchor in Table Bay, named this deceptively placid crescent of white sands the Cabo de Boa Esperanza—Cape of Good Hope. But when northwesterlies unleash wrecking waves, the calm mirror of the bay turns into a storm-lashed maelstrom. That's when the other name comes into play: Cabo Tormentoso, Cape of Storms.

The city of Cape Town is tucked into its own bay on the western side of a peninsula that juts out into the southern oceans, terminating in the craggy Cape Point. Nature built the backbone of the peninsula from granite peaks. The Twelve Apostles, a succession of almost identical knuckles that stretch from Camps Bay to Hout Bay, grip the cold sea. In the secluded bays between the digits closest to the city, you'll find the beaches and cosmopolitan areas of Clifton, Camps Bay, and Llandudno. Here international sybarites have invested in mansions that cling to the cliffs above the sea, protected by a mountain buttress from the ceaseless blast of the summer southeasters.

Almost opposite the Twelve Apostles lies False Bay, so named because early mariners confused it with Table Bay. The sea there, cuddled by the warm Agulhas Current, supports a different underwater flora and fauna from that of the cold side. Snorkel here, and you'll find Indian Ocean fish, sea stars and anemones, sea urchins and octopuses. Whales come into the gentle waters each year to calve.

Multicultural Influences

Like all great seaports, Cape Town is a palimpsest of cultural influences. The nomadic Khoikhoi and San (also known as Bushmen) peoples inhabited these shores for untold centuries before the Europeans. The Portuguese, seeking a trade route to the East, recorded their discovery of the anchorage in 1492. The Dutch followed in

NOT TO BE MISSED:

1652, establishing a supply station for their galleons that plied the spice routes to the East. Then came French Huguenots, fleeing religious persecution, and finally the British, who ruled without interruption from 1806 until South Africa's independence in 1961.

In between came Malays, Germans, American sailors serving on the Confederate raider *Alabama,* Chinese, and Indians—both Muslim and Hindu. These diverse cultures left their marks in the form of foods, music, turns of phrase, dress codes, and, more tangibly, in architecture. The British bequeathed the neoclassical late-Georgian buildings; the Malays an affection for intense color that enlivens their 18th-century homes; the Muslims their mosques; the Hindus their temples; the Dutch the swirls of Cape Dutch farmhouse facades.

Today Cape Town is a bustling city, boasting superb restaurants and outstanding music, contrasting 18th-century facades with towering glass-and-chrome business blocks and vineyards folded around whitewashed 17th-century barns, equipped with ultramodern vinicultural machinery. Many of the streets are still paved with ballast stones almost three centuries old. ∎

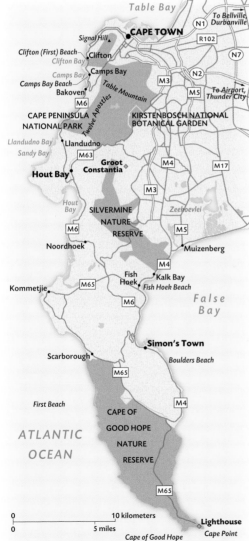

Area of map detail

Pretoria

South Africa
color-coded by region

Cape Town

Perched at the southwesternmost tip of Africa, Cape Town hums with the energy of two cultures and unmatched natural beauty. From the brightly colored Bo-Kaap quarter to the regality of the Victoria & Alfred Waterfront, from the cape to the monolithic Table Mountain, it is rare that so many remarkable sights are found in such tight quarters.

The Victoria & Alfred Waterfront—with its mix of shopping and entertainment venues, world-class hotels and marina—is South Africa's most visited destination.

Cape Town

🅰 Map p. 57

Visitor Information

✉ Cape Town Tourism Information Center, Burg & Castle Sts.

☎ 021/487-6800

💲 $

www.castleofgood hope.co.za

Castle of Good Hope

If you want to get to the heart of Cape Town, where it all began, the place to start is the Castle of Good Hope. Built at the behest of the Dutch East India Company (VOC) in the 17th century, it's a stolid pentagonal structure, grim and forbidding, squatting uncomfortably near a modern main road at the seaside of the city. Yet it has endured for more than three centuries and is a testament to uncertain times.

When Jan van Riebeeck first landed at the cape in 1652, he encountered the Khoikhoi (men of men) and the San people. These people had inhabited the cape for some centuries before the arrival of the European explorers and understandably regarded the interlopers with some distrust.

Van Riebeeck began to trade livestock in good faith with the locals, but to the Khoikhoi, sheep and cattle were important symbols of status within their society; the elders were reluctant to trade what was effectively their wealth, in return for trinkets that had no symbolic or material value within their culture. In addition, in laying out a garden, the newcomers had effectively annexed Khoikhoi grazing land. Relations soured. To protect his livestock from raids by daring Khoikhoi and to prevent the English or French East India companies from hijacking the outpost, van Riebeeck ordered a small fort to be built at the beach.

This original fort (Fort de Goede Hoop) was a simple four-bastion mud-clay-and-timber structure with a protective moat. Within ten years it had proved inadequate, and, with war between the Dutch and the British a constant fear, the Dutch decided to build a stronger fort. The present castle, the oldest such structure in South Africa, is the result.

The site selected was 60 *roods*—about 720 feet (219 m)—to the east of the original fort. The cornerstone of the castle, as it came to be known, was laid in 1666 by Governor Zacharias Wagenaar, and first habitation started eight years later although the building was only completed in 1679. Based on the general design, later known as the Vauban model, the castle has five bastions, each named after one of Willem, the Prince of Orange's main titles—Leerdam, Oranje, Nassau, Catzenellenbogen, and Buuren. The building was made of stone, mortar, and wood, and much of the unskilled work was undertaken by Dutch East India Company servants, soldiers of the garrison, sailors commandeered from passing ships, convicted criminals, and such Khoikhoi as were willing to undertake manual labor. The resulting imposing testimony to Dutch craftsmanship stands to this day. The waves of Table Bay no longer break on its outer walls (the foreshore of reclaimed land has pushed the sea back some miles), but as a historic site, the castle is well worth a visit. Guided tours are available.

Visiting the Castle: You enter the castle through a gate crowned by the **Bell Tower,** completed in 1684. The huge bell—rung to sound the hours of day and night and to toll for VIP funerals—was cast in Amsterdam, and its voice was not heard until 1697.

Be sure to also venture into the frightening blackness of the **Torture Chamber** and the Donker Gat (the Black Hole), which are reputed to be haunted. Modern-day guards at the castle have reported

Castle of Good Hope

✉ Buitenkant St.
☎ 021/464-1260
$ $
www.castleofgood hope.co.za

INSIDER TIP:

Cape Town is one of the best places in the world to do an ocean-going bird-watching trip. Majestic seabirds as well as many marine mammals can be seen best in winter.

—CAGAN H. SEKERCIOGLU
National Geographic field researcher

Footsteps to Freedom Walk

When Cape Town was founded by Jan van Riebeeck, he was part of a world in which slavery was endemic, torture accepted, and public execution commonplace. This history is reflected in the sites you can visit on this walk.

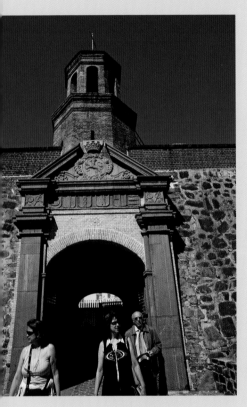

Bell Tower entrance to the Castle of Good Hope

Begin with a visit to the **Castle of Good Hope ❶** (see pp. 58–59 & 62) and its **William Fehr Collection** of oil paintings, furniture, and decorative arts. After exiting the castle and crossing Buitenkant Street, a short walk along Darling Street will take you to the **Grand Parade ❷**, flanked by tall date palms, opposite **City Hall.** This was once a military parade ground and the site of public executions and floggings under the

rule of the Dutch East India Company (VOC). Retracing your steps to Buitenkant Street and heading toward Table Mountain will lead you by the **Old Customs House ❸**. Built in the early 1800s, it has been used variously as a grain storage depot, a female prison, and a magistrate's office.

Just down the road you will find the **District Six Museum ❹** (25A Buitenkant St., tel 021/466-7200, closed Sun., $), which commemorates one of the worst and most arrogant social crimes of apartheid. Defined as Municipal District Six, this picturesque area once housed a vibrant "Coloured," predominantly mixed-race community. The district of 66,000 people was systematically bulldozed and evicted when the area was proclaimed "White."

Continue along Buitenkant Street to No. 78, the **Rust en Vreugd Museum ❺** (78 Buitenkant St., tel 021/464-3280, closed Fri.–Mon.). This 18th-century building houses the Fehr Collection's art on paper: prints, drawings, and watercolors covering the period of Dutch colonization to British rule. Next, backtrack on Buitenkant and turn left on Albertus Street. Turn right on Corporation Street, and a short dogleg will land you on Spin Street. The traffic island halfway up this street displays a simple plaque commemorating the **Slave Tree,** under which slaves of the Dutch East India Company were sold. Walk 20 paces straight ahead to the corner of Bureau and Parliament Streets, and you will see the **Groote Kerk ❻** (43 Adderley St., tel 021/422-0569), the oldest church of the Dutch Reformed denomination in existence (it was established in 1704) and the mother church of that faith in South Africa, as well as the oldest church in South Africa. The **Slave Lodge** (Bureau & Adderley Sts.) was built in 1679 to

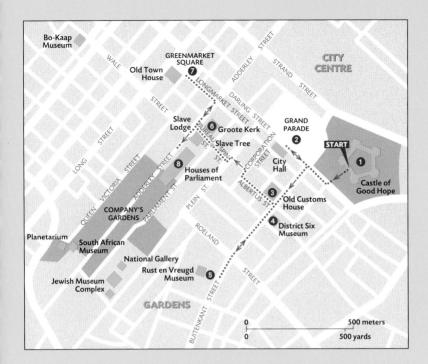

house the slaves of the VOC, as well as lunatics and convicts. Since then it has functioned as a post office, an "unofficial" house of ill repute, and the Supreme Court.

A right turn on Adderley Street, then a first left on Longmarket Street will reveal **Greenmarket Square ⑦**, which served as a produce market since 1696. Today it is a lively crafts market of African goods and curios. The **Old Town House** (*Greenmarket Sq., tel 021/481-3933, closed Sun.*), also on Greenmarket Square, completed in 1761, holds the important Michaelis Collection of 16th- to 18th-century Dutch and Flemish art. For refreshments on the square, the traditional Tudor Hotel or the Park Inn offer drinks and fine restaurant fare, including cigars at a cigar bar.

Retrace your steps to Adderley Street, head toward Table Mountain, and when the road turns right, you will find the **Houses of Parliament ⑧** (see pp. 63–64), home of the legislative authority of South Africa. Parliament

◪ Also see area map p. 57
► Castle of Good Hope
⟷ 1.7 miles (2.7 km)
◷ 1 hour
► Houses of Parliament

NOT TO BE MISSED:

Castle of Good Hope • District Six Museum • Greenmarket Square • Houses of Parliament

sits for six months, from January to June, in Cape Town and is a tribute to South Africa's three great Nobel Peace Prize winners: Nelson Mandela, F. W. de Klerk, and Archbishop Desmond Tutu, who liberated the country from its apartheid past. Guided tours are available during the week, and visitors can buy tickets (*foreign visitors must present a passport*) to attend sessions.

**Michaelis School
of Fine Art**

✉ 32–37 Orange
St.

☎ 021-480-7111

www.michaelis.uct
.ac.za

National Gallery

✉ Government
Ave., Adderly &
Wale Sts.

☎ 021-467-4660

🕐 Closed Mon.

💲 $, free on Sat.

www.iziko.org.za/
sang

Jewish Museum

✉ 88 Hatfield St.

☎ 021/465-1546

🕐 Closed Sat.

💲 $

www.sajewish
museum.co.za

ghostly screams and echoing foot-steps, and levelheaded soldiers are convinced that these mysterious noises are made by victims of the grisly tortures of yesteryear.

The **Cellar Museum** houses relics found during excavation of a pit in the cellar. The artifacts include bones, paintings, and antique cutlery.

More enchanting is the elegant **Lady Anne Barnard Room** named after the English noblewoman who lived in the castle from 1797 to 1802. Equally interesting is the restored **Dolphin Pool,** which was named after a statue of a Mediterranean-

---

Heart Throb

The world's first heart transplant occurred in Cape Town on December 3, 1967, when a team of 30 led by Dr. Christiaan Barnard replaced the failed heart of local grocer Louis Wash-kansky with that of a young woman who had died in a car accident the day before. The Heart of Cape Town Museum in Groote Schuur Hospital (Main Rd., Observa-tory, tel 021/404-1967, www .heartofcapetown.co.za), displays photos and instru-ments from the operation.

---

style dolphin. The restoration, completed in 1982, follow the competent sketches by Lady Anne Barnard herself.

Het Bakhuys (the Bake House or Bakery) has also been restored and houses the De Gouwerneur

Restaurant (tel 021/461-4895, closed Sun.), with a stylish tearoom.

Some years later, Commission-er van Rheede van Oudtshoorn ordered the **Kat** to be built, a tall, thick stone cross wall, for defensive purposes. Buildings were added later, extending across the width of the courtyard. One building houses the **William Fehr Collection** of documents, old paintings of the cape, and a superb sculpture by Anton Anreith (1754–1822). Legal judgments and announcements were read from the **Kat Balcony—**surely the finest aspect of the castle.

Company's Gardens

They're known simply as the Gardens, tranquil and quiet, with oak-flanked walkways. Originally tended by Jan van Riebeeck as vegetable gardens and fruit orchards to supply the VOC's ships with fresh produce, meat, and water, they're now a public park and botanical garden, in the heart of the city center. Today you are likely to see parliamentarians locked in debate there, exotic-looking art students from Hiddingh Hall, which hosts the University of Cape Town's **Michaelis School of Fine Art,** or budding thespi-ans from the University of Cape Town's Drama School at the Little Theatre.

Right after you enter, on your left, you will catch a glimpse of the **Houses of Parliament** (see opposite), superb examples of neoclassical architecture. In the center of the gardens, you will not want to miss the **National**

Houses of Parliament, completed in 1885

Gallery, the earliest art museum in South Africa. Completed in 1931, the National Gallery was built around an initial bequest of paintings acquired in 1871. The collections include important British, French, Dutch, Flemish, and South African artworks. In 1990 the acquisition policy of the gallery called for efforts to redress an imbalance that had made hierarchical distinctions between "high" and "low" art. The current exhibitions therefore include more precolonial and recent African and South African artworks, including traditional beadwork, sculpture, and smaller objects such as snuffboxes. Exhibitions change regularly.

Close to the National Gallery you'll see the breathtakingly modern architecture of the **Jewish Museum Complex** clad in Jerusalem stone, incorporating the **Old Synagogue** (1863), the **Great Synagogue** (1905), and the **Holocaust Centre.**

At the upper end of the gardens you will discover the **South African Museum** with a fine natural history exhibit and the local **Planetarium,** which hosts spectacular audiovisual shows.

Houses of Parliament

The Houses of Parliament are the site of the legislative capital of the Republic of South Africa and are of considerable historical interest, not least because of the miracle of the peaceful transition from a racist regime to a representative democracy.

Since their construction in the late 1800s, the Houses of Parliament have served successive administrations: from the British colonial rulers, through the fledgling Union of South Africa's first parliament following the devastating Boer War, which united both Boer republics, plus Natal and the Cape Colony, the apartheid years of the Nationalist

South African Museum

✉ 25 Queen Victoria St.

☎ 021/481-3800

$ $

www.iziko.org.za/sam

Planetarium

✉ 25 Queen Victoria St.

☎ 021/481-3900

🕐 Closed 1st Mon. of month

$ $

www.iziko.org.za/planetarium

Houses of Parliament

✉ Parliament Ave. (visitor center entrance, 120 Plein St.)

☎ General information: 021/403-2911 Guided tours: 021/403-3683

www.parliament.gov.za

EXPERIENCE: Cooking Cape Malay Cuisine

As a true "rainbow nation," South Africa's cuisine has been influenced by a myriad of cultures. From exotic delicacies such as fried mopane worms, crocodile steaks, and chicken feet, to the less adventurous stews and curries that warm up most kitchens, there is a host of gastronomical treats in store. Two unique cooking classes offer insights on Cape Malay food. In the Bo-Kaap quarter, where the food originated, a class will progress leisurely from the Bo-Kaap Museum through the colorful, hilly streets to shop for ingredients for the upcoming meal. The cooking class takes place in a local home, where participants will learn how to combine spices, make

curries, and fold samosas. Finally the cooks can sit back and enjoy the meal while being regaled with Bo-Kaap stories by the hostess. Contact **Andulela Experience** (tel 021/790-2592, www .andulela.com) for bookings.

Alternatively, Cass Abrahams, who is the unchallenged doyenne of Cape Malay cuisine, offers cooking demonstrations in Paarl, just outside Cape Town, at her vineyard restaurant. Here you can sip a glass of wine while learning about the history, culture, and food of the Cape Malay people, after which you can enjoy a vineyard tour. Contact **Cape Fusion Tours** (tel 021/461-2437, www.capefusion.co.za) for reservations.

Government from 1947 to 1994, and the African National Congress (ANC) dominated democratic government chosen as a result of the first free elections in 1994.

The British ideal of a democratic government elected by universal adult suffrage, with a firm separation between the legislature and the state, finds daily expression here during the parliamentary sittings from January to June. South Africa is a young democracy and democratic principles are precious, so the proceedings of the Houses of Parliament, and their recording in Hansard, the transcripts of debates, are matters of great moment for South Africans.

The buildings, completed in 1885, are fine examples of English neo-Palladian civil architecture, with impressive Corinthian columns, spacious porticos, and a soaring cupola. The construc-

tion was not without setbacks. The original architect, Charles Freeman, was dismissed for misjudging the foundations, and Henry Greaves completed the project. In 1910, Sir Herbert Baker, British imperial architect par excellence, built the addition of the **House of Assembly** in high neoclassical style. The parliament building also houses the **Library of Parliament** with its patrician central dome and pavilions. In the **parliamentary gardens,** visitors will find a statue of Queen Victoria, erected in 1887 to commemorate her Jubilee.

Tickets for parliamentary sessions and guided tours are available. Foreign visitors must bring their passports to book a tour.

Bo-Kaap Quarter

Bo-Kaap means "above the cape" in Afrikaans and refers to the location of this delightful area tucked into the slopes of

Signal Hill above Wale Street. This area is best reached by taxi, and there are guided tours every Saturday from 8 a.m. to 2 p.m. by Monique le Roux of Andulela Experience (see sidebar opposite). Tourists are advised not to walk the streets of the Bo-Kaap alone.

Bo-Kaap is inhabited by descendants of Sri Lankan, Indonesian, Indian, and Malaysian slaves who paintwork. The old mosques (the Auwal Mosque was built in 1768), the soaring minarets, and the voice of the muezzin calling the faithful to prayer all add to the charm of the place. Gregoire Boonzaaier (1909–2005), one of South Africa's best loved artists, spent many hours recording the beauty of the streets. His deft pigment-loaded brush captured

The historical Bo-Kaap quarter, formerly known as the Malay quarter

were brought to the cape by the VOC from the Dutch colonies in the 17th and 18th centuries. The community is largely Muslim, interspersed lately with unconventional students, and the steep streets, narrow alleys, and interesting architecture make it one of the most vibrant attractions of Cape Town.

The plain artisans' houses are a blend of Cape Dutch, Georgian, and Edwardian styles. The colors are bright and brazen—pink, turquoise, lime green, and orange—in enchanting flaking the summer heat and the riot of color in memorable paintings; some of his work can be seen in the Bo-Kaap Museum.

The **Bo-Kaap Museum** *(71 Wale St., 021/481-3939, closed Sun., $)*, on Wale Street, was originally the home of Abu Bakr Effendi (1835–1880), a well-known Turkish scholar and prominent leader of the Muslim community. Built between 1763 and 1768, the present house was declared a museum in 1978 and is furnished as a typical Muslim home of the 19th

Koopmans-De Wet House

✉ 35 Strand St.

☎ 021/481-3935

🕐 Closed Fri.–Mon.

www.iziko.org.za/ koopmans/

Gold of Africa Museum

✉ 96 Strand St.

☎ 021/405-1540

🕐 Closed Sun.

$ $

www.goldofafrica .com

century. The Muslim community on the cape contributed enormously to the development of the unique culture and played a prominent role in the development of Afrikaans, which evolved from High Dutch as a new language. The Bo-Kaap Museum has plans to evolve into a center that locates the Bo-Kaap and Muslim heritage in a wider sociocultural and political context.

In 1914, when the **Koopmans-De Wet House,** a few blocks northwest, was declared a museum, it became the first home to be opened to the public. The facade of this exquisite 18th-century house, several blocks east of the Bo-Kaap Museum, is attributed to French architect Louis Michel Thibault (1750–1815) and sculptor Anton Anreith. The museum houses a fine collection of cape furniture, Chinese and Japanese ceramics, delicate blue Delftware, and a superb range of glass and silverware.

Cape Malay Cuisine: The unique Cape Malay cuisine of Cape Town, which originated in the Bo-Kaap Quarter, is perhaps the only positive outcome of the 18th-century slave trade (see sidebar p. 64). The slaves brought their skills with them: The men were often fine tailors, coopers, and carpenters, and the women brilliant cooks.

Louis Leipoldt, one of South Africa's greatest Afrikaans poets, was also an amateur chef. His book *Cape Cookery* traces the roots of Cape Malay cooking to these 18th-century women who were responsible for the spicy *bobotie* (a delicately spiced, baked mince-

meat dish in a rich egg custard) and *breyani* dishes (rice-and-meat delights with lentils, suffused with home-ground masala), the cooling *sambals* and the piquant fruit *atchars* that turned local cookery into a cultural sense-trip. The spices for this cuisine were first brought to South Africa by the galleons of the VOC to market,

INSIDER TIP:

Don't miss the Gold of Africa Museum, which presents the history of gold and displays intricate works. There is also a workshop where you can watch a modern-day goldsmith.

—ERIN MONRONEY
NG Kids writer–researcher

but later, demanding housewives placed their orders directly with the galleons' captains.

A remnant of this spice trade survives at **Atlas Trading** (*94 Wale St., tel 021/423-4364, closed Sun.*). This almost Dickensian store is rich with tantalizing smells: a heady stew of garlic, chili, fenugreek, cumin, turmeric, cardamom, and cinnamon. A long counter runs the width of the room, and in the queue you'll be flanked by housewives from the Bo-Kaap, chic restaurateurs, keen foodies, and travelers simply bent on inhaling the aromas. Behind the counter toil a multitude of salespeople who are happy to give advice—you select and pay, then collect your spices.

You can sample this cuisine in several restaurants patronized by the locals. At Biesmiellah Restaurant *(2 Upper Wale St., tel 021/423-0825, closed Sun.)*, for example, you'll not only enjoy the finest boboties and curries, but be exposed to a fund of local history. Similar is the Noon Gun Tea Room & Restaurant *(273 Longmarket St., tel 021/424-0529, closed Sun.)*, owned and run by the Misbach family and serving traditional three-course dinners that include a main course of bobotie, chicken breyani, or a tender lamb curry pulsing with intense flavor.

Nearby Sites

In the myriad antique shops that line nearby **Long Street,** just outside the Bo-Kaap district, you might find anything from a fine pair of solid silver George III candlesticks to a yellowwood relic from a farmhouse kitchen. There are also fine antiquarian bookshops (Clarke's) and other musty and dusty repositories of books both valuable and curious.

The **Mount Nelson Hotel** *(76 Orange St., tel 021/483-1000, www.mountnelson.co.za)*, opened in 1899, is a Cape Town institution. The exterior of the "Nellie," as it is affectionately called, is still painted in its original rose-tinted pink, but the public rooms and guest suites are restrained in English country-house style. Go for afternoon high tea: Smoked salmon and cucumber sandwiches plus a spread of cakes and pastries to tempt the most die-hard dieter.

Victoria & Alfred Waterfront

The Victoria & Alfred Waterfront is both a historical site and a social gathering place, offering everything from shopping malls to arts and crafts markets, theaters, live music, and entertainment, within a working harbor.

The name relates to Prince Alfred, Queen Victoria's second son, who in 1860 dropped the first rock into the sea to signal construction of Cape Town's much needed breakwater. But in the burgeoning age of steam, the Alfred Basin soon couldn't

Jazz musicians, Victoria & Alfred Waterfront

John H. Marsh Maritime Research Centre

✉ Union Castle House, Dock Rd.

☎ 021 405 2880

www.iziko.org.za/maritime

accommodate the increased shipping volumes, and the larger Victoria Basin was built.

In 1988 renewal work began, incorporating several designated national monuments, offering waterfront walks, tours, boat trips,

Loggerhead turtle, Two Oceans Aquarium

helicopter flights, seaplane rides, a working brewery, and numerous fine restaurants that serve seafood as fresh as you can get anywhere.

The recently revamped **John H. Marsh Maritime Research Centre,** in the waterfront's Union Castle Building, features a collection of ship models and objects associated with shipping, in particular the era of the Union Castle mail ships. Its research

center houses an archive of shipping logs dating back to the 19th century and more than 19,000 negatives and photographs of 9,200 ships, dating from the 1920s to the 1960s.

Other sights include the Victorian Gothic **Historic Clock Tower** of 1882, where the original port captain's office was located. The top floor held the clock mechanism. From the second floor the captain was able to observe all activities in the harbor via a number of mirrors. On the lower floor a tide-gauge mechanism monitored the level of the tides.

Next to the Dock House Hotel is the **Time Ball Tower** of 1894, with an instrument that dropped a ball at a given time, to which all the ships in port set their clocks.

The **dragon tree** (*Dracaeno draco*) growing nearby is a species from the Canary Islands. The original tree was said to have been planted by a sailor passing through. Legend claims its blood red sap, the "dragon's blood," was spilled by a dragon thrashing against ships passing through the Pillars of Hercules, and the tree grows only where some of the drops fell around the Mediterranean and a few islands beyond.

Ever since the early days of the Dutch East India Company, **Robben Island** (see opposite) functioned as a prison and was, most notoriously, recently used for political prisoners, including Nelson Mandela. You can buy tickets at the **Robben Island Exhibition and Information Centre**—near the clock tower—for a 30-minute catamaran ride to the island and a guided tour by bus and on foot.

A colony of cape fur seals are a familiar sight resting on the landing next to the original Bertie's Landing Restaurant and on old tires on the quay.

Around the corner from the marina complex awaits the former **Breakwater Prison,** constructed in 1860 to house the convicts working on the breakwater. Ironically, this severe punitive institution now houses the University of Cape Town's Graduate School of Business and the comfortable Breakwater Lodge.

Opposite, the **Two Oceans Aquarium** is Africa's largest. It reveals the fascinating web of life supported by the cape's oceans. More than 3,000 marine creatures, including seals, turtles, and penguins, are on view. Besides adventure diving with sharks, the aquarium offers educational activities for kids and environmental education programs. The aquarium is also involved in shark conservation and sunfish research. A personal favorite is the tropical fish exhibit in the first gallery. The shark tank is awe-inspiring and gets you as close to these predators as you'll want to be.

Robben Island

Author Lawrence G. Green described Robben Island as the "Island of Exiles." It was a prescient comment, for Green wrote this before Robben Island had played host to its most famous prisoner of all, Nelson Mandela.

Besides Mandela, who spent 27 years at Robben Island, a large number of other antiapartheid

leaders were imprisoned here, among them the late ANC leader Walter Sisulu (1912–2003) and Govan Mbeki (1910–2001), the father of current president Mbeki of South Africa. Political prisoners played a vital role in shaping the resistance movement against apartheid. And the prison became a symbol of the oppressive apartheid regime to the world.

At some 7 miles (12 km) off the waterfront, Robben Island has always been inaccessible. The Portuguese exiled prisoners to this desolate place as early

INSIDER TIP:

Go for Namibian oysters and crayfish at Willoughby & Co., a seaside favorite, sandwiched between shops and jazz clubs on the Victoria & Alfred Waterfront.

–DAVID CASE
National Geographic writer

as 1525, and this history was to continue. Between the 17th and the 20th centuries Robben Island was successively a criminal and political prison, a "hospital" for socially unacceptable people like lepers and the criminally insane, and a military base. The 9.2-inch guns of the World War II battery still stand sentinel over the entrance to Table Bay. Today the maximum security prison on Robben Island is a tourist

Robben Island Exhibition & Information Centre

✉ Buy tickets at Robben Island Exhibition and Information Center, near clock tower, Victoria & Alfred Waterfront. Tours depart from Nelson Mandela Gateway

☎ Reservations: 021/413-4200

💲 Tours: $$–$$$

www.robben-island. org.za

Breakwater Prison

✉ Portswood Rd.

☎ 021/406-1911

www.breakwater lodge.co.za

Two Oceans Aquarium

✉ Victoria & Alfred Waterfront

☎ 021/418-3823

💲 $$

www.aquarium.co.za

Treasure Wrecks

The Cape of Storms is aptly named. Open to the southern oceans, cursed by savage winter storms, the bay that is a haven in summer becomes a deadly lee shore when northwesters blow. Records list more than 350 wrecks in Table Bay alone.

A 17th-century painting of Dutch galleons off Table Bay

The clumsy Portuguese caravels and carracks with their high poops, overloaded on their return from the East, were easy prey for the cape storms. So were the lumbering Dutch trading vessels, packed with pepper and silks, cinnamon and cloves. On a single night—May 17, 1865—18 oceangoing ships and 30 smaller craft became total losses between midnight and dawn.

The chronicler of the sea, Lawrence G. Green, wrote that in his opinion the cape's winter gales had drowned more men than those of any other coast in the Southern Hemisphere. And one of Cape Town's most fanatical treasure hunters, the late George Austin (a salvage engineer), estimated from archival records that more than 22 million pounds sterling lay scattered across the sands of Table Bay.

Here are some of the wrecks:

In 1694, the little **Dageraad** was dispatched to St. Helena Bay to pick up treasure chests salvaged from the VOC's East Indiaman **Gouden Buys,** which had run ashore, her hapless crew and passengers—except for two—dead from scurvy. On her way back the *Dageraad* herself ran aground off the west coast of Robben Island. Sixteen of her crew died. Eight of the seventeen money chests went down with her and are still safe in Davy Jones's locker.

On May 26, 1698, the fast new ship **Het Huijs te Crayesteijn** was wrecked during fog on a reef, about 3 miles (4.5 km) south of Camps Bay. Of the treasure chests she was carrying 16 were transferred to the shore soon after the accident. One was broken open while still aboard the wreck and the contents removed, while

INSIDER TIP:

Great white sharks cruise the South African coast like nowhere else, and between the town of Gansbaai and Dyer Island, they squeeze into a narrow channel called Shark Alley—it's quite an amazing sight.

—CERIDWEN DOVEY
National Geographic writer

two chests sank to the bottom. The chests that were salvaged were sent by ox wagon to the governor in Cape Town. Sport divers often swim out to visit the wreck. A few of the ship's cannon are tumbled in among the rocks, and large stone mill wheels, used as ballast, lie nearby. The sandy bottom sometimes reveals glimpses of cannonballs and fragments of wood, but the millions stay hidden.

On April 3, 1702, the **Meresteijn,** a Dutch East Indiaman, outward bound from Amsterdam and flush with silver specie, headed for Cape Town. The ship sighted land and stood in toward the coast. But the master misjudged his approach, and the ship wrecked off Jutten Island. More than a hundred people lost their lives there. There were no survivors. Hints of the tragedy can be found in the silver coins washed up occasionally on the island. The coins are ducatoons—easily confused with Spanish pieces of eight—bearing the head of Philip IV and the inscription: "By the Grace of God King of Spain and the Indies." They were minted in Brussels, the chief city of the Spanish Netherlands.

In June 1722, a winter storm drove five Dutch merchantships—the **Zoetigheid, Standvastigheid, Lakenman, Schotse Lorrendraaier,** and the **Rotterdam**—onto the beaches of Table Bay and pounded them to bits. Most of them were outward bound to trade in the East and carried a substantial amount of money to finance the company's purchases. The coins were never found.

EXPERIENCE: Shark-Cage Diving

Great white sharks, although villainized as ruthless killers by movies such as *Jaws,* ironically faced extinction after years of being brutally and unnecessarily killed. Since they have become a protected species, these elusive and magnificent creatures are thriving again, especially in **Gansbaai,** a two-hour drive from Cape Town, which is known as the "great white capital of the world." While the sharks in this area can easily be spotted from the comfort of a boat, a more adventurous option is to cage dive with them. During such an excursion your boat will travel to **Shark Alley,** a 20-foot-deep (6 m) channel between Dyer and Geyser Islands, and you will be lowered, in diving gear, into a floating steel cage, which is kept next to the boat, in case you want out.

Although it may be argued that this activity could lead sharks to see humans as food, that is not the case, if such diving is performed responsibly. Tour operators should never feed the sharks red meat, taunt, harm, or unduly disturb them. In fact, rather than tip the natural balance, the knowledge gained from this peaceful experience can go a long way toward dispelling the myth that almost led to the extinction of these fascinating creatures. For reservations and further information contact **Marine Dynamics** (*tel 028/384-1005, www.sharkwatchsa.com*); **White Shark Projects** (*tel 021/405-4537, www.whitesharkprojects.co.za*); or **Shark Diving Unlimited** (*tel 028/384-2787, www.sharkdivingunlimited.com*). Average R1,300 cost includes transport from Cape Town.

Visiting Robben Island prison

destination that offers insights into the nature of political repression and the brutality of the apartheid regime. It is a salutary reminder that bigotry of any form degrades the bigot as much as the victim.

But time heals. As Nelson Mandela wrote in his Robben Island series of 2002: "Today, when I look at Robben Island, I see it as a celebration of the struggle and a symbol of the finest qualities of the human spirit, rather than as a monument to the brutal tyranny and oppression of apartheid. It is true that Robben Island was once a place of darkness, but out of that darkness has come a wonderful brightness, a light so powerful that it could not be hidden behind prison walls."

More Robben Island Sites:

The political significance of Robben Island obviously overshadows its other attractions, but these should not be overlooked. *Robbe Eiland* is a Dutch name meaning "seal island." In the

early days, thousands of seals and other sea mammals, as well as penguins and tortoises, lived on Robben Island. The waters around the island were then a safe breeding ground, and hundreds of years ago whales in great masses swam and bred here.

Jan van Riebeeck wrote in 1652: "Noticed many whales in the bay, and especially this month they were so near the ship that one could easily jump onto them from the yacht."

But during the late 1800s, whaling became a big industry, and the southern right whales visiting these waters were reduced to 10 to 30 adult females by the time commercial whaling was stopped in 1940. The same fate befell the seals and penguins, which were also seen as commercially exploitable.

In 1999 the island was declared a World Heritage site, and much has been done to restore the island's ecology to its pristine state. In 1991 Robben Island was included in the SA Natural Heritage program, and the northern parts of the island were declared a bird sanctuary. Rabbits, a wide variety of gazelles including springbok, and 132 species of birds are found here.

Despite its austere natural assets, Robben Island will be remembered as a memorial to the indomitability of the human spirit and the innate human desire for freedom. Daily tours to the island include the ferry trip (the capricious cape weather permitting), an island tour, including the limestone quarries

INSIDER TIP:

On the official bus trip round Robben Island, be sure to alight when the bus stops at the coastline. From here you can get superb photos of Table Mountain.

—RICHARD WHITAKER
National Geographic contributor

where the prisoners toiled, and a tour of the prison. A former prisoner leads the tour, which also includes **Garrison Church** (1841), the **lighthouse** (1863), **Lepers' Church** (1895), the **guesthouse** (1895), and a **Muslim shrine.** Most moving are the "cell stories" in the 40 isolation cells, each cell with a story by one of the inmates.

Allow 3.5 hours and make reservations in advance. Ferries leave at regular intervals from the Nelson Mandela Gateway near the clock tower at the Victoria & Albert Waterfront (see pp. 68–69).

Thunder City

If jet fighting is your dream, this civilian operator of extreme flight adventures, located near the airport and featuring the world's largest and most diverse military fighter-jet and bomber-jet squadron, is for you. You can climb 60,000 feet (18,288 m) straight up in a Mach 2 English Lightening, roar across the Atlantic at 650 mph (1,046 kph) in a Buccaneer, or do aerobatics in a Hawker Hunter. ◼

Thunder City
✉ Site 10, Tower Rd., Cape Town International Airport
☎ 27 21 934 8007
💲 $$$$$
www.thundercity.com

EXPERIENCE: Deep-Sea-Fishing Charters

With 1,860 miles (3,000 km) of coastline, South Africa is any fishing afficionado's dream destination. Whether you're more comfortable knee-deep in the waters of a lagoon with a fishing net, or in the middle of the ocean pursuing game fish, the country holds a host of opportunities. Because of the diversity in ocean life and fishing levels, the best way to go about choosing a fishing experience is to go by particular species. South Africa is renowned for its yellowfin tuna fishing, which is best tackled off Cape Point. In season the average tuna caught in this area weighs a whopping 120 pounds (55 kg), and the latest craze is to catch them with fly rods.

There are many tour operators in the area who can organize full-day offshore charters. Try **Two Oceans Sport Fishing** (tel 021/782-3681 or 082/469-8280, www.tosf.com) in Simon's Town. Alternatively, contact **Toledo Charters** (tel 021/790-407 or 072/907-3443, www.toledo-charters.com) in Hout Bay. Most charters will take on about six people for a 12-hour excursion.

Marlin fishing is another exciting opportunity, offered by Natal's warmer waters, where these giants can weigh up to 150 pounds (68 kg). To book a tour, contact **Sport and Safaris** (tel 086/010-4800, www.sportandsafaris.com) at Chaka's Rock.

The Peninsula

From the rugged wilderness of Table Mountain and the vineyard-covered hillsides of Groot Constantia, the peninsula stretches in scenic sandstone outcrops to the southwesternmost tip of Africa, to Cape Point of the Cape of Good Hope. The Atlantic Ocean surf batters the peninsula on the western side, while gentler, warmer waters in False Bay bathe its beaches on the eastern side. Little towns and beaches galore beckon.

Dias Cross, Table Mountain National Park

The Beaches

Cape beaches range from the hectically trendy to the utterly deserted. Beach culture is as well entrenched in Cape Town as it is in southern California, and the rippling six-packs and golden curves of the sun addicts could have been transplanted from Venice Beach. But there are also miles of white sand free of footprints, inhabited only by the albatross and the tern, and occasional fishers casting from a surf rod into the green water. The cape beaches are traditionally divided into "cold side" and "warm side." The cold side is anywhere not embraced by the warm curve of False Bay, and the temperature differences are acute; five minutes in the icy water of Clifton Beach without a wet suit will bring an ache to your bones, whereas summer temperatures in False Bay range from 68°F to 72°F (20°C–22°C), not tropically warm but pleasant for swimming and surfing.

Clifton Beach on the cold side

is the most stylish and fashionable of Cape Town's many beaches, a ten-minute drive from the city center. It is, in fact, not one beach but five, all accessible at low tide, separated by rocky promontories at high tide. The distinctions, subtle and rigid, between each of the beaches (First to Fourth, with tiny Moses Beach a favorite of the monokini'd cognoscenti) is understood only by sophisticated initiates. But **First Beach** is considered to be the chosen venue of the young, beautiful, tanned-to-the-toenails South African equivalent of *les mimis de St. Tropez*. Don't set foot on Clifton's sands without an umber tan and a perfect body. You'll do irreparable damage to your self-esteem.

A five-minute drive from Clifton, **Camps Bay Beach** is a long white curve of palm-tree-flanked sand, backed by a main road with glitzy restaurants and fast food places. Hunky models and their girlfriends drive around in ultrachic convertibles. The stylish habitués of Camps Bay Beach are likely to be young millionaires from Moscow, hedge-fund traders from New York, or rock stars on holiday.

Fish Hoek Beach is different. Situated on the warm side on False Bay, this exquisitely beautiful half-moon of soft sand stretches for nearly 2 miles (3 km). It is a family beach, and bathing in the warm Indian Ocean is safe and exhilarating. Beautiful People patronize this beach, too, but they are not the hard-edged international set you find at Clifton and Camps Bay. Along the rocky walkway, there are numerous

safe areas (notably **Skellie Pool**), where neophyte snorkelers can investigate the underwater world. Here you will find electric rays and spiny sea urchins, brilliant sea anemones, scurrying rockfish, and darting blacktail dassies.

An occasional, seasonal sight at Fish Hoek is the traditional fishing technique of "treknetting." The local fisherfolk, having fished since early childhood, sometimes put out from the beach in two longboats. They take with them

Adventures

If you're seeking more hardcore athletic pursuits, here are some outfitters that will help provide that rush: **Abseil Africa** (*tel 021/424-4760, www.abseilafrica.co.za*) specializes in rappelling off Table Mountain. **Cape Xtreme** (*tel 021/788-5814, www.cape-xtreme.com*) organizes shark-cage diving, cycling, surfing, and climbing. **Downhill Adventures** (*tel 021/422-0388, www.downhilladventures.com*) offers cycling, sand-boarding, paragliding, abseiling, cage diving, and quad biking.

a long, shallow, much drained purse net and row in a half-moon, lowering the net into the deep water beyond the break line. Both boats return to the beach some 200 yards (183 m) apart. Then the *trek,* the pull, begins, as teams of fishermen, aided by small boys, retirees, muscled young surfers,

Table Mountain Cableway

✉ Lower Cable Station, Tafelberg Rd.

☎ 021/424-0015

$ $

and curious onlookers haul in the bulging net. Slowly the catch is pulled onto the beach, and when the net reaches the shallows, the sea writhes with captive sea life. There are delicious bream and mullet, locally known as *haarders,* along with eagle rays, the odd red roman, baby sharks, and

Camps Bay Beach

sometimes even stingrays, which are always greeted by applause.

Table Mountain

When you approach Cape Town from the ocean, the first thing you see above the horizon is the imposing bulk of Table Mountain. This mountain of granite and sandstone, 3,562 feet (1,086 m) high, has inspired endless legends. With rapid changes in the weather, the mountaintop is often covered by clouds, the proverbial "tablecloth." At other times it is too windy for an ascent. But in good weather, you can enjoy the easy walks or longer hikes of the Table Mountain National

Park (see opposite) and ride to the summit of the flat tabletop via the **Table Mountain Cableway** that leaves from the Tafelberg Road. The cableway rotates as you ascend, allowing for a spectacular view of the rugged cliffs and the blue ocean beyond.

Since the opening of the cableway 79 years ago, more than 16 million people have taken the trip to the top of Table Mountain, including King George VI, Queen Elizabeth II, Oprah Winfrey, Sting, Steffi Graf, Arnold Schwarzenegger, Margaret Thatcher, Prince Andrew, and Tina Turner. Standing on the top of this extraordinary mountain you can see the curvature of the Earth as you look across the ocean and down on the bowl of the city nestled in the mountain's embrace. A café and some souvenir shops offer other inducements.

The **Table Mountain National Park** encompasses the scenic Table Mountain chain that stretches from Signal Hill in the north to the Cape Point of the Cape of Good Hope in the south. The park's biodiversity is so unusual it was declared a Natural World Heritage site with the most common plants being fynbos, consisting of four major groups: protea, a flowering, broad-leaved bush; Erica, a heatherlike plant; restio, a reedlike plant; and geophyte, a wetland bulb.

Activities in the park will engage even the most jaded traveler, including spectacular hiking, mountain biking, hang

INSIDER TIP:

Walk up Table Mountain! Carry a detailed map, and don't take shortcuts. Weather can change in a few minutes to complete whiteout conditions. Don't attempt Skeleton Gorge if it's raining.

—THURE CERLING
National Geographic field researcher

gliding, and parasailing (see sidebar below).

There is no entry fee to the park, except at three points—Cape of Good Hope, Boulders, and Silvermine—which require conservation fees. Several activi-ties do require permits; inquire at the Table Mountain Head Office.

Kirstenbosch National Botanical Garden

One of the finest botanical gardens in the world, Kirstenbosch on the eastern slopes of Table Mountain couldn't have a more dramatic setting. Established in 1913, the landscaped gardens of 89 acres (36 ha) display South Africa's diverse flora.

On the slopes in a 1,300-acre (528 ha) natural area grows *fynbos* (fine bush), the predominantly small-leaved and hardy complex of plants unique to the mountains and coastal plains of the south-western cape, and Afromontane forest, dominated by broadleaved evergreen trees. Most beautiful in spring, between August and

Table Mountain National Park

☎ 021/701-8672 or 021/465-8515

www.hhoerigwa ggatrails.co.za or www.tmnp.co.za

Kirstenbosch National Botanical Garden

✉ Rhodes Dr., Newlands

☎ 021/799-8899

$ $

www.sanbi.org/frames/kirstfram

EXPERIENCE: Hiking, Biking, & More

The many hiking trails within the Table Mountain National Park appeal to a wide audience. If you are an avid hiker, the **Hoerikwaggo Trail** is for you. The excursion, organized by the park, is a luxury three-day guided, portered, and catered hike that links the cityscape of Cape Town with the natural environment of Table Mountain.

The **Platteklip Gorge hike** is one to do on your own. The trail will take you straight up the mountain from the lower cableway station, leading from the Tafelberg Road on a zigzag path steeply to the top in about two to three hours.

Once on top, there are a number of easy hikes to different observation points. **Maclear's Beacon hike,** for one, will take about 35 minutes from the top of Platteklip Gorge across the "front

table," where you will overlook False Bay.

From the Kirstenbosch gardens (see p. 78) you can hike up Skeleton Gorge, beginning at **Smuts' Track,** the trail used by J. C. Smuts, the former Boer general and prime minister, to the top of Table Mountain. **Nursery Ravine trail** also begins at the Kirstenbosch. The round-trip will take about five hours.

Mountain-biking trails within the park can be reached from Tokai Forest, Silvermine, Kloofnek, Mowbray Ridge, and at the Cape of Good Hope. Rock climbing includes world-class routes such as Africa Face. Contact the Mountain Club of South Africa for further details *(tel 021/465-3412).*

Hang gliders and paragliders can be launched from designated areas at Lion's Head and Silvermine.

Groot Constantia

✉ Groot
Constantia Rd.,
off M41

☎ 021/794-5128

💲 Wine tasting: $$

**www.grootco
nstantia.co.za**

October, when the Namaqualand daisies and many other plants are in bloom, the gardens feature 6,700 of the estimated 20,000 species of indigenous plants of South Africa. On the upper slopes the unusual cycad species, called living fossils, are growing in the **Cycad Amphitheatre,** and the **Protea Garden** features a

INSIDER TIP:

From Kirstenbosch, hike up Skeleton Gorge and down through Nursery Ravine. You'll likely find stunning red disa orchids in the former and king protea, South Africa's native flower, in the latter.

—RES ALTWEGG
National Geographic field researcher

profusion of proteas, pincushions, and the rare and endangered silver trees.

Facilities at Kirstenbosch include a restaurant, book shop, and garden shop, as well as a visitor center and information desk.

Groot Constantia

Snuggled into the fertile Constantia Valley, the gracious Cape Dutch homestead of Groot Constantia is a testimony to the elegance of a past age. Granted to Governor van der Stel in 1685, the farm became famous in the 19th century for its sweet dessert wine. Rigorous production standards and the happy combination of sun, soil, and sea produced a wine so luscious it was loved by members of the British royal family, Napoleon Bonaparte, Frederick the Great of Prussia, and King Louis-Philippe of France. In 2003, the winery resumed production of the sweet dessert wine, Grand Constance (red and white muscadel), last made over 200 years ago, which seems to echo its former essence.

The Cloete family inherited part of the estate from Simon van der Stel and commissioned French architect Louis Michel Thibault in the 18th century to design and construct additions, among them a two-story wine cellar, embellished with a rococo-style stucco relief featuring Ganymede, the classical cupbearer to the gods, surrounded

Concerts in the Garden

Every Sunday afternoon in the summer, you can enjoy an open-air concert in the beautiful **Kirstenbosch National Botanical Garden.** The program incorporates all kinds of music, from jazz to classic, rock to folk, and the ambience is always relaxed and friendly, with picnickers lounging in the park partaking of the music, the sunset, and a good

bottle of local wine. Call for program information and reservations *(tel 021/761-2866, www.sanbi.org).*

If you happen to be traveling the country in the winter, Johannesburg's **Walter Sisulu National Botanical Garden** hosts jazz and classical concerts every Sunday afternoon. Call for more information *(tel 011/958-1750, www.sanbi.org).*

Horseback riding at Noordhoek beach

by frolicking cherubs.

The Cape Dutch entries usually have ornately carved front doors with a scrolled architrave. Yet the doors at Groot Constantia are unusually restrained, rectilinear, and neoclassical. The gable is another thing entirely. Extravagant, almost double the usual height, it bears in a niche a sculpted female figure symbolizing Abundance, thought to be the work of the prolific sculptor Anton Anreith. The main house is a well-preserved and authentically furnished example of a Cape Georgian manor.

In 1993 the estate was bought by the Groot Constantia Trust, which has mounted a permanent exhibition there on rural slavery, curated by the South African Museums. Visitors can visit the wine museum, enjoy wine tastings, or dine at either Simon's or Jonkerhuis restaurant; both offer breakfast, lunch, or even picnics during the daytime and sumptuous dinners at night.

Kalk Bay

Walk along the Main Street of Kalk Bay, the picturesque fishing harbor near Fish Hoek, and you will find a treasure trove of antique shops, coffee bars, restaurants, poky emporiums selling objets d'art, junk shops with bric-a-brac, bookshops, and shrines of fine dining. A number of seaside restaurants are inviting, including the Brass Bell *(waterfront, tel 021/788-5455)* and Harbour House *(Kalk Bay Harbour, tel 021/788-4133)*. You can watch the fishing boats amble into harbor with their catch, while you savor your mussels in garlic, grilled spiny lobster, or fresh line fish. A great way to start your day is at Olympia Café and Deli *(34 Main St., tel 021/788-6396)* for coffee and freshly baked goods.

Simon's Town

A bit farther down on the Cape Point, this charming Victorian town owes its existence to the original British naval base, built when the British Navy ruled the world's oceans, and the sea route to India needed constant protection from the fleet. The beach itself is just outside the town and is a gentle bathing beach with views of False Bay as far as Cape Hangklip.

Boulders Beach, on the road from Simon's Town to Cape Point, is famous not only for its safe bathing within sheltering boulders but also for its penguin population. These birds roost and live around Boulders' many beaches. There are also scuba opportunities for the more adventurous.

Cape Point & Cape of Good Hope

To many visitors, getting to Cape Point is a highlight similar in impact to that of seeing Victoria Falls: There is the same acknowledgment of the magnificence of the scene, the sheer height of the cliffs, the ruggedness, the untamed wildness of the water. Sir Francis Drake (1540–1595), who circumnavigated the globe and knew a thing or two about ocean beauty, saw Cape Point in 1580 and called it the "fairest cape in all the world."

A number of routes lead to Cape Point, each of them providing a different kind of scenic beauty. For the most spectacular drive, take the winding, awe-inspiring route between Noordhoek and Hout Bay, along **Chapmans Peak.** Cut into the mountainside several hundred feet above the sea, this picturesque, 5-mile (8 km) route will make you stop regularly to admire the views of the rocky coastline, with sheer drops down to the sea. Numerous designated lookout points allow visitors to park and take in the vistas.

Or you can drive to Fish Hoek and along the coast to historical Simon's Town and continue along

EXPERIENCE: Kalk Bay Fishing Community

Kalk Bay's charismatic and quick-witted fishermen, with their brightly colored wooden boats and even more colorful stories, make a trip to the harbor an essential cultural experience. The fishermen are proud of their heritage, rightly so, considering that they were the only South African community to successfully oppose the apartheid government and avoid relocation. They have fished these waters for centuries and still launch their wooden boats before dawn every day, defiant of the larger trawler vessels that prowl farther out at sea.

Make sure to stroll down to the harbor at about lunchtime, when you can watch the fishermen returning, freshly stocked and ready to haggle and heckle. For next to nothing you can pick up a whole snoek, a tender and flavorful silver fish notorious for its razor-sharp teeth. To this day it's caught using a hand-line method passed down through generations, and if you decide to buy the fish, it will be sold to you wrapped in newspaper with free cooking advice. Forget lemon butter—rather, try cooking up a traditional dish such as "snoek with apricot jelly and onion," or whichever recipe happens to pop into the fisherman's mind that day.

If the lure of the ocean calls, you can experience the fishing firsthand, with a local fisherman who will take you out on his wooden boat.

the coastal road to the entrance of the **Cape Peninsula National Park.** Here you will find the cape's unique fynbos—and Cape Chacma baboons, with the alarming habit of jumping onto your vehicle.

Drive on and you will be greeted by one of the Earth's greatest views: the long, craggy snout of Cape Point stretching into the South Atlantic. The sea here is turbulent and famously stormy. Stories persist that this is where the Indian and Atlantic Oceans meet, but that is a bit of folklore. The actual meeting place is a less dramatic spot, at Cape Agulhas several miles farther south.

You can hike up to the lighthouse or ride on the funicular in a scenic trip to the observation point near the old Cape Point lighthouse. Two cars of the funicular travel from the parking lot 780 feet (238 m) to the observation point, just below the lighthouse.

The **lighthouse** is one of many that have been placed on the Cape Point peaks to warn unwary mariners of the treacherous seas and rocks. One, built in 1857, proved almost worthless because it was built too high and was often wreathed in clouds. The latest lighthouse is considerably more effective and the most powerful one on the whole South African coast; it has a range of 39 miles (63 km) and every 30 seconds beams out a group of three flashes each of ten million candlepower.

Stop for a meal at Two Oceans Restaurant *(tel 021/780-9200)*, perched on the side of a cliff at Cape Point, with breathtaking views of False Bay.

Cape Point lighthouse

Dining on local seafood, you may catch sight of a Bryde's whale or another denizen of the deep. Or stop for a picnic at the store and take a slow stroll along the many walkways.

Scarborough

On the return trip from the point, just north of the Cape of Good Hope Nature Reserve, lies Scarborough. This suburb of Cape Town is tucked into the steep hills of Slangkop and Red Hill, but the beaches are a fine stretch of sand. Here fishers and surfers, windsurfers and kayakers outnumber the swimmers, who must be careful of rip currents. The surfers prefer the rocky point break on the left-hand side of the beach. In summer, especially during the December holidays, the beach gets crowded. A restaurant, high above the waves, allows for dining with incredible views. ■

An austere, sometimes desolate coastline along the cold Atlantic north of Cape Town, famed for springtime wildflowers, winery tours, and crayfish *braais* on the beach

West Coast

A field of wildflowers near Citrusdal

Langebaan Lagoon, the epitome of a water-sport enthusiast's paradise

West Coast

If Cape Town is like a good Champagne—all fizz and elegance—the West Coast is an austere and restrained white Burgundy. This area has its own reserved and pared-down beauty that explodes in a burst of color when the wildflowers bloom in springtime, September and October.

NOT TO BE MISSED:

Darling's wildflowers and fine wine route 86–87

Flamingos and penguins in the West Coast National Park 90–91

Whale watching in Saldanha Bay 91

Lobster-pot crayfishing in Paternoster 93

A dive among the shipwrecks in the Brittania Bay area 93

A walk in Steenberg's Cove with eccentric local, Oom April Snyders 94

Stargazing from the Cederberg Astronomical Observatory 95

An alfresco beach meal with freshly caught seafood 97

The West Coast is quintessentially South African. The area is not beautiful in the accepted sense of the word. Yet when you've spent a little time here you remember later with affection the dense Prussian blue of the sea and the clear pale brilliance of the beaches. Isak Dinesen, author of *Out of Africa,* described the African coastline succinctly: "The scenery was of a divine, clean, barren marine greatness...."

North of Cape Town and stretching more than 250 miles (400 km) from south to north, the region and its people offer the visitor an austere, and at times desolate, coastal region with the magnificent Langebaan Lagoon and numerous small fishing villages of modest cottages; the far-flung wheat fields and vineyards of the Swartland and Sandveld; and rooibos tea plantations and citrus orchards. There are also the wineries of the Swartland and the Olifants River Valley, and the spectacular magnificence of the scenic and remote Cederberg range.

Nature Abounds

Even the arid beauty of the land is transformed in midwinter until the end of spring when the world-renowned wildflowers burst overnight into brilliant color. The white daisies herald the beginning of the new season, followed by orange, pink, yellow, and purple as the cape fynbos blossoms in all its glory. Various wildflower reserves can be found in Darling, Langebaan, Paternoster, and Saldanha, or along the roads around St. Helena Bay, and from Vredenburg and Velddrif to Hopefield.

Some of the most popular hiking trails in the area follow the coastline from Swartriet to Tietiesbaai and from Paternoster to Stomp-

neusbaai. The West Coast National Park and Rocherpan Nature Reserve also have hiking trails to choose from. Off-road enthusiasts head to Elandskloof farm at St. Helena Bay, Langebaan, and Pasternoster.

The Cederberg Wilderness Area offers unsurpassed opportunities for contact with the natural world. In this wilderness, with its fantastic rock formations, away from the city bustle, you can find space and peace for your soul. But if you're an active explorer, you'll also find more energetic things to do such as racing down 4WD trails, or hiking and rock climbing. Hiking trails of varying difficulty crisscross the wilderness and offer adventurers a simple way to explore the area. Rock climbing is permitted throughout most of the wilderness area. ■

Darling & Its Wine Country

A spectacular drive north from Cape Town on the R27, between the Cape Fold Mountains and the glittering Atlantic, to the village of Darling is the perfect weekend getaway. Visitors can explore the sights and wineries of this delightful town, spend time lolling on the beach in nearby Yzerfontein, or travel along the Swartland Wine Route.

At the Evita se Perron restaurant and cabaret, Darling train station

Darling

Map p. 85

Visitor Information

www.darlingtourism.co.za

Only 47 miles (75 km) north of Cape Town, Darling dozes among undulating vineyards and golden wheat fields. For most of the year, the small town has the tranquil look of a storybook village with tree-lined streets and small Cape Dutch and Victorian-era cottages. But in spring— September to October—the town explodes with visitors who come to revel in the profusion of wildflowers, when more than a thousand species of flowering plants cover every hillside and meadow. The dazzling colors make for a sensory overload.

The astonishing variety of plants led to the founding of the town's Wildflower Society in 1915, and the village organized its first wildflower show in 1917. Since then, the flower show is held every year during the third weekend in September. At the same time, an exceptional orchid show takes place there.

Several nearby private nature reserves, nurseries, and farms that are also very much in bloom are open to visitors. The **Tienie Versfeld Wildflower Reserve** *(R315, 7 miles/12 km W of Darling),* for example, is brilliant during flower season; and the

Rondeberg Nature Reserve
(R27, 15 miles/25 km from Darling, tel 022/492-3099, www.rondeberg.co.za, $) features guided tours of its lowland sandplain fynbos.

Beginning around 1853, the farms near the Dutch Reformed Congregation on Langefontein farm gathered into this community. Eventually called Darling,

INSIDER TIP:

During the Darling wildflower festival, the third weekend in September, several nature reserves provide an opportunity to see some of the world's most beautiful and rare bulb plants.

—ANTON PAUW
National Geographic field researcher

after Sir Charles Henry Darling (1809–1870), the lieutenant governor of the cape, the town did not become a municipality until 1955. The town is still an agricultural center for dairies, wheat farming, sheep farming, and, lately, wine growing.

The Darling Creamery, founded in 1902, was once one of the town's important businesses. Exhibits showcasing early buttermaking are found at the **Darling Museum** (Pastorie St., tel 022/492-3361). Housed in the old city hall of 1899, the museum also offers displays on Victorian life, agriculture, and other aspects of early Darling.

Since 2004, Darling also features its own **wine route** (tel 022/492-3361, www.darlingtourism.co.za), which includes the **Cloof** and adjoining **Darling Cellars, Groote Post,** with a country restaurant, **Ormonde Vineyards,** and **Oudepost Estates,** all within a few miles of the village. The vineyards offer wine tastings by reservation.

Housed in the old train station, **Evita se Perron** is a cabaret and restaurant venue owned by and showcasing the one and only Pieter-Dirk Uys, aka his cross-dressing alter ego, Evita Bezuidenhout, a white Afrikaner socialite and political activist. The restaurant features *boerekos,* farmer's food. Next to the restaurant is one of the many local arts-and-crafts markets. ∎

Art Scene

Darling is full of arts and crafts galleries that capture the Western Cape's eclectic, Euro-African feel. At the **!Khwa Ttu Arts & Craft Shop** (off the R27, W of town, tel 022/492-2998), for example, you'll find an assortment of crafts made by the San people (ostrich egg necklace, anyone?). The **Darling Original Art Supermarket** (18 Long St., tel 082/718-9373) showcases local paintings and sculptures. A walk down Main Street or Pastorie will reveal others.

Cloof
- Map p. 85
- From Darling Cellars, turn left and follow signs to Cloof
- 022/492-2839
- Closed Sun.
www.cloof.co.za

Darling Cellars
- Map p. 85
- R315, Mamre Way Station
- 022/492-2276
www.darlingcellars.co.za

Groote Post Vineyard
- Map p. 85
- Darling Hills Rd., off R307
- 022/492-2825
www.grootepost.com

Ormonde Vineyards
- R27, NW of Darling
- 022/492-3540
- Closed Sun.
www.ormonde.co.za

Oudepost Estate
- R307
- 022/492-2368
- By appt.

Evita se Perron
- Arcadia St.
- 022/492-2831
- Closed Mon.; shows Fri., Sat. afternoon & evening, & Sun. afternoon
www.evita.co.za

Swartland Wine Route

The Swartland, or "black country"—named for the endemic renosterbos, a shrub that turns black in winter—stretches east between Darling and the villages Riebeek West and Riebeek Kasteel and from Malmesbury in the south to Piketberg in the north.

Cloof Wine Estate

Much of the renosterbos land has been turned into wheat fields that make this area the breadbasket of South Africa. Since 1986 the land has also become known for its fine Shiraz-producing vineyards of bush vines that thrive in the dry land. The bush vines grow a smaller grape than the conventional trellised vines and have a more concentrated flavor. The vineyards are spread out over scenic hillsides with the Perdeberg and Kasteelberg mountains in the distance, usually with a grand estate building in the white-gabled Cape Dutch architecture.

Driving east from **Darling** (see pp. 86–87)

to Malmesbury via the R315 and R45, begin with the **Swartland Winery ❶** (tel 022/482-1134, www.swwines.co.za) on the Swartland Wine Route. This estate has been in the grape-growing business since 1948.

Continue on the R45, turn off onto the R46, and you come to the **Meerhof Wine Cellar ❷** (tel 022/487-2524, www.meerhof.co.za). This estate used to be a wheat and sheep farm, but since 1961 the owners have concentrated on wine.

A short distance farther on the R46 awaits the **Kloovenburg Vineyards ❸** (tel 022/448-1635, www.kloovenburg.com), which the owners describe as "hanging like a swallow's nest below Kasteel Mountain." Although grapes were grown on the estate since the mid-18th century, the serious winemaking began with the first Shiraz in 1998. The estate also offers olives and other olive products for sale.

Turning onto the R311 you will see in the distance the white church steeples rising above the villages **Riebeek-Kasteel** and **Riebeek-West.** At Riebeek-Kasteel the town square is surrounded by a number of artist's galleries and a great choice of restaurants and cafés. On the first Saturday of the month the **Riebeek Valley morning market** takes place in Riebeek-West with fresh regional produce and other specialties such as farm butter.

Here, too, **Het Vlock Casteel** ❹ *(tel 022/448-1488, www.hetvlockcasteel.co.za)*—with a castlelike building at the entrance to the estate that looks similar to the old castle in Cape Town—is the producer of wines, olives, and fruit. You can purchase your wine and peaches, grapes and oranges, and a large range of preserved products during the season. Three-hour grape tours are conducted from shortly after Christmas until March. Throughout the year there are also olive oil–tasting tours, which include demonstrations on preserving olives. Reservations are required.

North on the R311 you'll come to **Allesverloren** ❺ *(tel 022/461-2320, www.allesverloren .co.za)*, which translates to "all is lost," relating to the estate's early history, when in 1704 the settler family returned from an outing to Stellenbosch, a long trip by wagon, to find the house burnt to the ground and the farmland devastated. Nonetheless, the family rebuilt the farm, and today the estate celebrates 200 years of winemaking.

Continue on the R311 and return via the N7 to Malmesbury and the R315 to Darling.

NOT TO BE MISSED:

Swartland Winery • Riebeek Kasteel & the Riebeek Valley morning market• Het Vlock Casteel • Allesverloren

---

🅰 Also see area map p. 85

▶ Darling

↔ 90 miles (145 km)

⏱ 3–4 hours depending on stops

▶ Darling

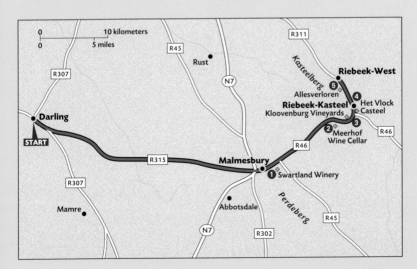

Along the West Coast

The West Coast, with its long beaches and simple fishing villages, flocks of birds on a still lagoon and windswept hills, makes for a peaceful retreat, yet there is much to see and do.

The harbor at Saldanha Bay

West Coast National Park

- Map p. 85
- ✉ Off R27, 7 miles/11 km N of the R315
- ☎ 022/772-2144 or 022/772-2145
- 💲 $

www.sanparks.org /parks/west_coast

West Coast National Park

About 75 miles (120 km) north of Cape Town, south of Saldanha Bay, the West Coast National Park was established as a nature reserve and marine protected area in 1985 and is protecting unique environmental niches. Encompassing 88,500 acres (29,700 ha), this wetland is of global importance because it is the end point of wading-bird migrations coming from the Arctic. The birds arrive exhausted in September, feed and recover, and congregate noisily again in March before taking off on the reverse journey. Besides the thousands of migrating

birds, the wildflowers in an unbelievable range of colors are another attraction in spring.

Footprints and other traces of prehistoric life have been found in and near the park dating from some 120,000 years ago.

Inside the park at Kraalbaai you can rent a houseboat for a day or longer. At the Geelbek Information Center, a tearoom serves light meals, and a few paces away a bird blind is set up for the many birders. The park also has accommodations at Churchhaven, notable for the many pink flamingos feeding in its bay.

Langebaan Lagoon: The heart of the park is the clear,

blue Langebaan Lagoon, filled twice daily by the ocean tides, which bring nutrient-rich water from the Antarctic. Without the influx of fresh water from a river, the lagoon is purely a saltwater pool. On the islands at the mouth of the lagoon, breeding colonies of penguins, gannets, cormorants, gulls, oystercatchers, and many other birds find undisturbed shelter.

Birders come here for the jackass penguin, pink flamingo, waders harrier and black harrier, black-shouldered kite, cape francolin, kelp gull, and the endangered African black oystercatcher and white-fronted plover.

In the **Postberg section** of the park, which is open from August to September when the spring wildflowers are in bloom, a number of antelope species and zebra can be spotted.

The lagoon is flanked on the Atlantic coast by golden, sandy beaches as far as the eye can see. But the water is cold; the Benguela Current brings its icy waters from the Antarctic, and wetsuits are a necessity for any contact with the water. Nonetheless, water sports are a favorite activity here, and the resort of Langebaan offers a plethora of choices such as paragliding, windsurfing, sailing, and guided canoe and kayak trips. Without ocean waves, the lagoon's flat surface is particularly well suited for neophytes trying out windsurfing.

Saldanha Bay: Just north of the lagoon, Saldanha Bay was named after Antonio de Saldanha, captain of a Portuguese vessel in Alfonso d'Albuquerque's fleet, which visited South Africa in 1503. Because of its isolated location and lack of fresh water, development happened only gradually. Saldanha Bay is a deep natural bay and one of the best natural harbors in the world, where a Naval Training Base sends out its young recruits for basic training. The fishing fleet still goes out for mussels, oysters, spiny lobsters (called crayfish here), calamari, hake, mullet, and snoek—a silvery, fang-toothed, rather bony fish, distantly related to mackerel, and unique to South Africa.

Saldanha Bay offers deep-sea diving around shipwrecks, sea

INSIDER TIP:

The West Coast National Park comes alive with color during the spring flower season. Spectacular displays can be found in the Postberg section, open to visitors in August and September

—JON MINSTER
travel journalist

kayaking, and game fishing—yellowtail and tuna are said to be easy catches. Cape fur seals hang out on the small islands, and southern right whales can be seen from August to November, humpback whales from October to November, and Bryde's whales year-round.

Jacobsbaai

Jacobsbaai, midway between Saldanha Bay and Paternoster, is an isolated, traditional West Coast village. The roads are largely unpaved, keeping the town remote and yet making it an ideal

---

EXPERIENCE:
Gone Fishing

The West Coast is celebrated for its fish—the question is, how to get them out of the water and onto your *braai* (see p. 97). Besides fish, the area is famous for its crayfish, mussels, and abalone. **Anker** *(contact André Kleynhans, tel 083/480-4930)*, a local company in Paternoster, provides traditional fishing tours, arranging for spear fishing, diving for crayfish, or just catching fish from a boat.

Hotels also offer fishing trips, such as the **Blue Dolphin** on Warrelklip Street in Paternoster *(tel 022/752-2001, www .bluedolphin.co.za)*, which will take you out looking for crayfish.

Or, simply go fishing the old-fashioned way: Buy a pole and some worms.

Jacobsbaai
🅼 Map p. 85

Britannia Bay
🅼 Map p. 85

Paternoster
🅼 Map p. 85

spot for an unregimented vacation. Jacobsbaai has seven smaller bays: **Kwaibai** is a good surfing spot; **Jacobsbaai, Smalbaai,** and **Moerie** are ideal for launching boats; **Bamboesbaai** and **Toothrock** invite snorkelers, scuba divers, anglers, and crayfishers. The long coastal trails invite dune riding and hiking.

The town's history is one of waning fortunes in this stark land. Since the early 1800s, farmers from the area traded with the Stefan Brothers Company, and

a number of indebted farmers ceded their farms' 99-year lease in payment to the company. In the end, the company owned much "private" land and effectively kept other businesses out. In 1990 an employee at the deeds office in Cape Town found that the 99-year leases had expired and land could be bought again, bringing about new development, including some choice tourist accommodations.

Britannia Bay

Traveling farther north along the coast, you come to Britannia Bay. The town is yet named for another shipwreck, the *Britannia,* which struck a reef 3 miles (5 km) out on October 22, 1826. Fortunately the crew made its way safely to shore. A local farmer bought the wreck and recovered some of its cargo, much of it consisting of wine and copper sheets. The wreck was salvaged again under the supervision of the National Monuments in 1998 with serendipitous finds of porcelain and crystal glassware.

The area is littered with sunken vessels. Statistics list more than 240 shipwrecks between Britannia Bay and Dassen Island. Divers regularly search for treasures. Local dive shops offer a number of choices from easy to advanced scuba diving, and a good person to contact is André Kleynhans *(tel 083/480-4930)*, who organizes and leads dives on many of these wrecks.

Britannia Bay's beaches attract more swimmers because the

icy Benguela Current does not reach the bay, and the water is somewhat warmer. From June to September southern right whales and humpback whales swim near the shore, and dusky dolphins and the endemic heavisides' leap around the small boats.

Paternoster

A few miles up the coast awaits Paternoster, another idyllic fishing village. Colorful wooden boats lie on the beach, and whitewashed cottages are set into the dunes and built above the boulders. Some of the older

fishing is the main occupation. One of the major catches between November and April is snoek. There is also crayfishing, abalone diving, and fishing for sardines and anchovies in the spawning grounds.

A few artists' and potters' studios add to the colorful street life with their exhibits, and beachfront restaurants and bars beckon for a break.

The **lighthouse** on Cape Columbine, about 3 miles (5 km) out from Paternoster, was the last manned lighthouse on the coast of South Africa. A campsite on

A restaurant in Paternoster

homes have extravagant external chimneys for indoor wood-fired ovens. At the pub in the hundred-year-old **Paternoster Hotel** *(Main Rd., tel 022/752-2703, www.paternosterhotel.co.za),* people gather in the evening to talk over the day's events and "the one that got away." Among the 1,500-strong population,

the beach between the granite boulders makes for a true refuge in the wild.

The cape is named for the vessel *Columbine,* which foundered on the rocks in 1829. The few surviving Portuguese sailors thanked God with the Paternoster, the Lord's Prayer, and the village was thus said to be named.

St. Helena Bay

St. Helena is positioned on the bay in such a way that you can watch the sun rise over the sea, which is unique on the West Coast. A number of fishing villages are tucked into the bay's sheltered arms. More than half the fish processed in South Africa are handled in the communities of **Stompneus Bay, West Point, Sandy Point,** and **Steenberg's Cove.**

Portuguese navigator Vasco da Gama dropped anchor in the bay on November 8, 1497, for eight days and reported: "The bay was found to be very clean and to afford shelter against all winds, except those from the NW.... We named it St. Helena."

The calm waters of the bay appeal to the southern great whales that come into the bay to calve in August and stay until November. Humpback whales also come through, between October and November, on their migration from West Africa to their feeding grounds in the Antarctic.

Berg River Estuary

The great variety of wading birds along this coast finds another sanctuary at the **Berg River Estuary** in Velddrif, where blinds overlooking the mudflats are set up for birders (get key at Flamingo Restaurant across the street). More than a quarter of all bird species found in South Africa can be seen here. Among the great flocks of waders, birders will also spot bar-tailed godwit, common whimbrel, grey plover, South African shelduk, and purple heron. For special tips, birders should check in with the local cape bird club at www .capebirdclub.org.za.

Rocherpan Nature Reserve

Lying 14 miles (25 km) north of Velddrif, between the area known as the sandveld, or "sandy field," and the Atlantic Ocean, the Rocherpan Nature Reserve is another birders' paradise, with two blinds and picnic sites. One visitor described the birds in the reserve: "Some were stacking on ordered flight paths, others were landing, refueling or taxiing through reed

Oom April Snyders

To hear some stories of the region, 80-something Oom (for Uncle) April Snyders from Steenberg's Cove is the one to seek out. He is known as one of the most colorful characters of the small villages on the bay. The former boatbuilder with a phenomenal memory relates the region's history better than any monograph. He can point out any number of old wells that have long been covered by wind and sand and tells of ancient potsherds and ostrich eggs that could be found near his home when he was a boy. You will have to sit down to listen to one of his fish stories.

INSIDER TIP:

Bokkoms Alley in Velddrif is a step back in time. Spend some time strolling along the lagoon mouth, meeting the local fishermen. It's active on weekdays but not weekends. Don't forget your camera!

—SAMANTHA REINDERS
National Geographic photographer

channels. Islands in the stream were crowded with Egyptian geese, yellow-billed ducks, and coots, while reed cormorants and gray herons flew nest-building sorties overhead. A lone fish eagle played air-traffic controller from his perch."

The reserve is the most important breeding and molting site for the cape shoveler. Birders will also find the rare African black oystercatcher and white pelican, and greater and lesser flamingos shown as endangered on the red list of the International Union for the Conservation of Nature.

Olifants River Valley

The route inland from the West Coast takes you through scrubby fields north on the N7 to the green valley of the Olifants River with extensive vineyards. The scenery changes to manicured rooibos tea plantations and tidy orange groves near **Citrusdal.** Visitors come here to hike in the rugged **Cederberg range** with trails for all levels of fitness. Mountaineers should head off to the strange rock formations of Wolfberg Arch and Cracks, the Maltese Cross, Tafelberg, or Sneeuberg. Easier options include the Maalgat rock pool and the Stadsaal (City Hall) caves, with San rock art nearby depicting shamans and elephants, which once must have roamed in the valley.

An evening at the **Cederberg Astronomical Observatory** (*www.cederbergobs.org.za/index*), a private 16-inch (40.6 cm) telescope on the Dwarsrivier farm, is an ideal way to look into the unpolluted dark skies. Except on full moon evenings, when it's too bright to see anything, the observatory is open to the public on Saturdays for views of the southern skies. To reach the observatory from the N7 north toward Clanwilliam, turn at the sign to Algeria Forest Station (gravel road). It's 30 miles (48 km) farther, about 0.6 mile (1 km) before you reach the Dwarsrivier farm on the Maltese Cross Road.

The nearby **Cederberg Cellars** (*tel 027/482-2827, www.cederberg wine .com*), at 3,400 feet (1,036 m) the highest vineyards in South Africa, where the slogan is "wine with altitude," offers food and wine, with the dramatic setting of the weathered sandstone formations in the background.

You won't want to miss a soak at **The Baths hot springs**—ideal for soothing aching muscles from a strenuous hike or to cure a hangover from imbibing too much good wine. ∎

The Baths

✉ Take the N7 turnoff to Cistrusdal; after 0.6 mile (1 km), turn right again. Follow signs for 10 miles (16 km).

☎ 022/921-8026

www.thebaths.co.za

Seafood Paradise

The entire West Coast is a seafood lover's heaven. What can you expect? Crayfish are found everywhere—and celebrated at an annual festival at Lambert's Bay—as are succulent abalone, West Coast oysters, mussels, snoek, and salted dry fish, for starters. Here are some ways to prepare—or order—these delectable local specialties.

Catch of the day at Lambert's Bay

Go into any pub and ask the barman a little too loudly about ways of preparing seafood and within minutes any number of locals—fisherfolk, lawyers, scuba divers, housewives, secretaries, trawler captains, and tramps—will tell you in great detail how to prepare any seafood dish. The problem is that no two of them ever really agree.

The locals have many idiosyncratic ways of preparing crayfish (spiny lobster). Connoisseurs simply wrap the freshly caught crustacean in fresh brown kelp fronds and *braai* (barbecue) them over an open fire of driftwood on the beach. When the kelp turns green and the crayfish shells are as red as hibiscus blossoms, the meat will be cooked through and very tender. Other devotees simply boil them in seawater.

Abalone (known locally as *perlemoen*) is another favorite, rated as the most seafoody of all seafoods. This is the large single-shelled, crusty-surfaced shellfish known elsewhere in the world as ormer, which is a corruption of the French *oreille de mer*, or sea ear.

Those in the know say that pounded steaks of perlemoen, dredged in egg, dipped in breadcrumbs or batter, then very quickly fried and served with a slice of lemon cannot be bettered. One very old Cape Dutch recipe worth trying is *Paarl Lemoen*. You dice the pounded steaks of a perlemoen fairly small, then add it to a pot in which you've boiled a cup of salted water, a glass of white wine, a good cube of butter, a squeeze of lemon juice, and a grind or two of black pepper. Simmer the dish very

Paternoster fishermen

slowly for about two hours, add a cup of soft breadcrumbs and a good grating of nutmeg, and serve as an hors d'oeuvre on fresh toast.

For the ultimate taste of oysters, you need to eat them on the West Coast. They are best prepared with the addition of a little raspberry vinegar into which you've finely diced a touch of red onion or the milder flavored shallot.

The mussels available on the West Coast are at least as good as those you'll find, say, in Normandy, simply served with a variety of sauces, from plain garlic butter to cream and scallions.

Another local delicacy is *bokkoms,* salted dry fish that you see hung out in the sun to dry along Bokkums Alley on the banks of the Berg River in Velddrif, but that is an acquired taste.

EXPERIENCE: Beach *Braai* Bash

Any country with a coastline has its own version of a beach cookout. In South Africa they're called braais, and organizing one is no more complicated than gathering some friends, some seafood, and heading down to the water.

A firm fish will not fall apart on the grill or coals, so choose something like swordfish or tuna. Prawns and shrimp are another good choice, though cape crayfish are world famous for a reason.

While you can easily procure a store-bought grill, you really don't need one. Make a circle of rocks, and fill it with charcoal that can be bought anywhere. Don't use wood; it's unreliable and burns more quickly than charcoal.

Depending on the supplies at hand and ingenuity, there are several cooking methods. A grate can be placed about

4 to 6 inches (10–15 cm) over the coals depending on the heat; a spit for kebabs can be erected easily enough; or the food can be wrapped in aluminum foil and tossed on the coals. Recipes vary, so the best bet is just to wing it.

Use a lot of butter, or white wine if you're feeling ambitious. Coat every cooking surface with olive oil. It's important to baste anything that isn't sealed in foil. A tried-and-true basting sauce can be made with olive oil, lemon juice, garlic, and a pinch of salt.

A great crayfish dish involves stuffing the tail with crushed garlic, apricot purée, soy sauce, lemon juice, black pepper, and cayenne. Since this is wine country, after all, a few bottles of Chardonnay should be present, or a case of local beer. As always, don't litter.

Exquisite wildlife, noble vineyards, the Garden Route's botanical gems—easily South Africa's most popular destination

Western Cape

Limestone formations, the Cango Caves

Western Cape

The Western Cape stretches from Cape Town along the Garden Route to Plettenberg Bay and up into the Winelands: two regions that give South Africa much of its allure.

Vineyards near Franschhoek

The Western Cape has a classic natural beauty: a rich montage of craggy mountains, deserted beaches, and undulating countryside, making it without doubt the most conventionally beautiful province in South Africa.

Bordered by two oceans—the Indian to the south and the Atlantic to the west—the Western Cape coastline stretches from Lambert's Bay on the west all the way to Plettenberg Bay in the east. Here you'll find the lovely Cape Winelands, where acres of manicured vineyards dotted with gabled Cape Dutch houses look like picture-postcard scenes dreamed up by a romantic art director. Here, too, is the scenic Garden Route, the breathtaking, fertile, 130-mile (370 km) stretch of coastline from Mossel Bay to Storms River, with its rich botanical treasure of forests and mountains, lonely beaches and rivers. Whale- and dolphin-watching, hiking, swimming, and

NOT TO BE MISSED:

Wine tasting in picturesque
 Franschhoek   **103–105**

A meal at Franschhoek's legendary
 Tasting Room Restaurant   **104**

A leisurely drive through the
 Winelands   **106–107**

The spectacular Cango Caves   **108**

An ostrich farm visit in
 Oudtshoorn   **109**

A ride on the Outeniqua
 Choo-Tjoe   **111**

A sundowner and oyster tasting on
 the Knysna Lagoon   **112–113**

A hike through Tsitsikamma
 National Park   **114**

surfing are all popular pursuits here. While most people explore the Garden Route by car, you can also hop aboard the Outeniqua Choo-Tjoe, Africa's last remaining passenger steam train, for some old-fashioned exploration between George and Knysna.

To the North

Northward lies the Klein Karoo, a nearly-but-not-quite desert landscape of wide-open spaces, undulating hills, and the vast ostrich farms of Oudtshoorn, a legacy of the early 20th-century craze for oversize feathers. Here you'll also find the limestone Cango Caves, at the foothills of the Swartberg range, with magnificent halls and narrow chambers. A little-known fact: The Klein

Karoo is the country's easternmost wine-producing region.

Here, too, you can explore the Cederberg mountains. This extensive, little-visited range is home to some spectacular rock formations. On a clear day, you can see the ocean from the top of the Sneeuwberg.

Every season brings its own riches in the Western Cape: the wildflowers of spring, ripening orchards in summer, the sunburned gold of deciduous leaves in autumn, and the snow-capped mountain peaks in winter. In the Boland (Uplands), golden wheat fields and fragrant orchards abound.

Note that South Africans take their summer vacation in December, a time when the area becomes packed with visitors. ■

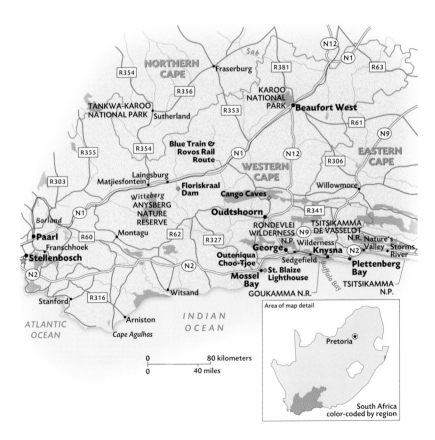

Cape Winelands

Less than an hour's drive northeast of Cape Town via the N1 highway, visitors will discover an area that produces wines as noble as its natural beauty.

The Cape Winelands—fanned out around three historic towns and their valleys, Stellenbosch, Franschhoek, and Paarl—are an oenophile's Eden, cradled in a region of dramatic mountains and fertile valleys. The soil is so rich, it's said the farmers need only a tenth of the fertilizer used by European farmers for the same acreage.

The area is a combination of small historic towns and technically modern wine estates that produce wines in a variety of Old and New World styles (including the interesting Chardonnay-and-Pinotage blend from Haute Cabrière, a delicious pink summer wine that will remind cognoscenti of the rosé wines of Anjou in France) plus sherries and brandies. There's even a succulent Ratafia to delight those who know and

The figure in the Huguenot Memorial holds a broken chain in one hand, a Bible in the other, symbolizing religious freedom.

INSIDER TIP:

Fairview Winery near Paarl is worth a visit for award-winning cheeses and great wine.

—RES ALTWEGG
National Geographic field researcher

covet the lushness of this unusual wine, originally drunk to celebrate the ratification of treaties (hence the name, derived from the Latin *rata fiat*, consider it done) but now perfect for drinking with foie gras or cheese or desserts.

Above the wine estates and award-winning restaurants, there

are vineyard hiking trails and fine golf courses. Helicopter rides, aerobatic flights, hot-air balloon rides, and tandem paragliding can also be arranged through the local visitor centers. Or take an invigorating hike through one of the many indigenous fynbos nature reserves in the area: Mont Rochelle Nature Reserve in Franschhoek and Paarl Bird Sanctuary, for starters. Whether you enjoy the thrill of tearing down a hillside on a mountain bike, relaxing next to a tranquil river catching trout, or savoring the beauty of the setting sun on horseback, the Winelands will not disappoint.

See pp. 106–107 for a leisurely drive through the region.

Stellenbosch

At the heart of the Winelands, Stellenbosch was founded in 1679, making it the second oldest town in the country. With its picturesque Cape Dutch buildings, Dorp Street feels like a museum piece, yet Stellenbosch (pop. 100,000) buzzes with activity.

In the old town, the **Village Museum** (18 Ryneveld St., tel 021/827-2902) consists of four restored buildings that each highlight a stylistic period from the past 300 years. Stellenbosch also boasts the oldest music school in the nation, the **Conservatoire** of 1905.

Boschendal Wine Estate

The Boschendal winery, set against the Drakenstein mountains between Franschhoek and Stellenbosch, produces some of South Africa's best known

wines. Its gabled Cape Dutch Manor House, dating from 1812, is a museum today. Visitors should make reservations for the **Boschendal Wine Tasting Centre Cellar Tour,** which explains Boschendal's viticultural heritage. At the **exhibition vineyard,** wander through a working vineyard and see the estate's viticultural practices at close range.

Franschhoek

This gustatory capital of South Africa, famed for its food and wine, attracts gourmands from many parts of the world.

The small town is tucked into a fertile valley, originally settled in 1688 by French Huguenot refugees. Once called Olifants Hoek,

---

EXPERIENCE:
Tasting Wine

Although South Africa may not seem the most obvious choice for wine courses, three centuries of successful winemaking surely qualify the region. If your passion lies in wine-tasting, the Cape Wine Academy (tel 021/889-8844, www.capewineacademy.co.za, $$$$$) **has a variety of short courses, including an introductory course focusing on South African wines. If you're up for the challenge, why not try a "garagiste" (small-scale) winemaking course. Under the tutelage of a professor from the University of Stellenbosch, you will taste a variety of "homemade" wines, gain a basic understanding of the various cultivars, and learn how to perfect a bottle in your own home. For more information visit** www.garagiste.org, **or for reservations contact Professor Wessel du Toit** (tel 021/808-4545, e-mail: wdutoit@sun.ac.za, $$$$$).

Stellenbosch
🅰 Map p. 101
Visitor Information
✉ 36 Market St.
☎ 021/883-3584
www.stellenbosch tourism.co.za

Boschendal Wine Estate
✉ 10 miles (16 km) W of Franschhoek via main road to Paarl & the R310
☎ 021/870-4279
💲 $
www.boschendal .com

Franschhoek

Map p. 101

Visitor Information

Franschhoek Vallée Tourisme, 28 Huguenot Rd., Franschhoek

021/876-3603

www.franschhoek
.org.za

Huguenot Monument

Lambrecht St., Franschhoek

021/876-2532

www.museum.co.za

or Elephants' Corner, for the vast herds of elephants that roamed the area, the valley saw its last elephants—a mother and calf—in about 1850 on what is today the Franschhoek Pass.

Given the origin of the settlers and the fierce national pride of the French, the area's name inevitably changed to Franschhoek, or French Corner, with some settlers naming their new farms after the regions in France from which they came. Many of these farms have grown into renowned wineries and most of them offer guided tours of their wine cellars, accompanied by a leisurely tasting. La Motte, La Cotte, Provence, Chamonix, Dieu Donné, and La Dauphine were among the first vineyards established here, and most of them retain their original farmhouses.

The valley's vineyards and the region's culinary reputation have attracted some of South Africa's greatest chefs. Not surprisingly, eight of South Africa's Top 100 restaurants are established in the town—in particular, the innovative and award-winning cuisine of executive chef Margot Janse of the **Tasting Room** at Le Quartier Français Hotel (16 Huguenot Rd., tel 021/876-2151, www.lequartier.co.za; see p. 286).

The village's architecture is largely in the Cape Dutch style, looking snug and well kept. A host of shops and galleries on the main street and a wonderful choice of antiques, artworks, and bric-a-brac provide an excuse for a little retail therapy before you confront the challenge of which restaurant

to go to and what to eat. Guided tours in Franschhoek are available through the tourism office; or hop on one of the carriage rides that sway around the town or out to some of the wine estates.

Be sure to stop by **Oom Samie se Winkel** (84 Dorp St., tel 021/887-0797), an old-fashioned general store; the **Van Ryn Distillery and Brandy Cellar** (Van Ryn Rd., outside

INSIDER TIP:

Make reservations for lunch at La Petite Ferme, a country inn and winery southeast of Franschhoek, with expansive views of the Franschhoek Valley.

—ERIN MONRONEY
NG Kids writer–researcher

town off R310, tel 021/881-3875, closed Sun.), which distills the famous 12-year-old single pot-still brandy; and the hillside cellars of **The Bergkelder** (Pappagaaiberg, Adam Tas Rd., tel 021/809-8582, closed Sun.), a wine center offering wine tastings and wine tours.

In the summer, the **Oude Libertas Amphitheatre** (Oude Libertas Centre, Adam Tas & Oude Libertas Rds., tel 021/809-7473) sets the stage for open-air entertainment, preceded by a picnic on the lawns.

For nature lovers, the **Mont Rochelle Nature Reserve** (tel 021/876-3062) offers hilly terrain in the shadow of Table Mountain.

Huguenot Monument:

Standing at the top end of Franschhoek, the Huguenot Monument commemorates the cultural influence of the Huguenots in South Africa. Inaugurated on April 7, 1948, it celebrates a quarter millennium of cultural contributions by the French. Huguenots began to arrive in 1685 when the revocation of the Edict of Nantes unleashed a wave of aggressive anti-Protestant religious fervor in France. Refugees settled in South Africa from as early as 1671, and a large-scale emigration took place during 1688 and 1689.

A policy instituted in 1701 by the Dutch East India Company dictated that schools should teach exclusively in Dutch so that by the middle of the 18th century the French Huguenots lost much of their native language. The **Huguenot Memorial Museum** *(two blocks from the Huguenot Monument on Lambrecht St., tel 021/876-2532, www.museum.co.za, $)* chronicles the history of the first settlers, with each of the original Huguenot farms telling its own story.

Paarl

A modern, functioning city, as opposed to cozy Stellenbosch and Old World Franschhoek, Paarl spreads along the banks of the Berg River for 6.8 miles (11 km).

At the edge of town, the **Afrikaans Language Museum and Monument** *(11 Pastorie Ave., tel 021/872-3441, closed Sat.–Sun.)* commemorates Afrikaans as an official language in South Africa with exhibits that span its history.

For nature lovers, the **Paarl Mountain Nature Reserve** offers panoramic views, while the **Paarl Bird Sanctuary** *(Drommendaris St., tel 021/868-2074)* showcases more than 140 different species flitting among five island-dotted ponds. ∎

Paarl

🅰 Map p. 101

Visitor Information

✉ 216 Main St.

☎ 021/872-3829

www.paarlonline.com

Paarl Mountain Nature Reserve

✉ Jan Phillips Mountain Dr., Paarl

☎ 021/872-3658

La Petite Ferme

✉ Franschhoek Pass

☎ 021/876-3016

www.lapetiteferme.co.za

EXPERIENCE: Learn Zulu Beadwork in a Township

To a teenage girl from a Zulu tribe, a blue beaded bracelet will cry out to her distant lover that she will wait for him to return. Yellow speaks of envy and anger, while red simply says "I love you."

For centuries, the Zulu people, as well as many other southern African cultural groups, have adorned themselves with pieces of bone, horn, wood, or stone, and with the arrival of the Europeans came a penchant for colorful ceramic and glass beads, and later plastic. Despite modernization, beadwork remains an important aspect of traditional life.

The work serves not only as an aesthetic treat but also as a glimpse into the colorful labyrinth of traditional life. Because the colors have specific meanings, they are used to create "love letters," intricately woven to relay intimate messages. Each piece of jewelry speaks about a person's background. People in a community can tell a woman's age, marital status, or the sex of her children simply by eyeing her jewelry.

Andulela Experience *(tel 021/790-2592, www.andulela.com, $$$$$)* offers a township tour, in Kayamandi, near Stellenbosch, which begins with a guided walk and ends with a workshop on beading in the community center.

The Winelands Drive

Less than an hour's drive from Cape Town, the Winelands route leads through
green valleys and dramatic mountain ranges with the neatly staked patchwork of
vineyards along the slopes.

Le Quartier Français restaurant, Franschhoek

This area holds some of the oldest South
African vineyards planted by early European
settlers. The wine estates look impressive
with grand manor houses and beautifully
laid out gardens. Stellenbosch is the starting
point of the scenic **Stellenbosch Hills Wine
Route** *(www.wineroute.co.za)*, which includes
numerous wine estates within a 7-mile
(12 km) radius.

From Cape Town, proceed east along the N2
to the R310 to **Stellenbosch ❶** (see p. 103),
the capital of the Winelands. Its oak-lined streets,
whitewashed Cape Dutch buildings, and lovely
setting along the Eerste River give it a storybook
aspect, with students from University of Stellenbosch adding a youthful tempo.

The long-established estates here are known
to produce some of the finest wines. **Lanzerac
Manor & Winery** *(off Jenkershook, tel 021/887-*

*1132, www.lanzerac.co.za, tours Mon.–Fri. 11 a.m.
& 3 p.m.)* sits in the heart of Stellenbosch, a
few blocks east of the train station. Famed for
producing the world's first Pinotage, the estate
has bottled wine since the 1920s (though the
land has been lived on since the 1600s). It also
offers luxurious accommodations, with rooms
overlooking the vineyards.

Stop by some of the town's other long-
standing estates, including **Uiterwyk** *(Kloof Rd.,
tel 021/881-3711, www.uiterwyk.co.za)*, producing
limited release wines; and **Eikendal** *(6 miles/9.5
km S of Stellenbosch on R44, tel 021/885-1422, www.
eikendal.com, tours Mon.–Sun.)*, with its barrel-
vaulted cellar buildings.

From Stellenbosch, drive northeast via the
scenic **Helshoogte Pass** on the R310 to the
R45, past the **Boschendal Wine Estate** (see p.
103), to the charming village of **Franschhoek**

❷ (see pp. 103–105). Just before entering town, be sure to stop by **La Motte Wine Estate** *(tel 021/876-3119, www.la-motte.com, closed Sun.).* Dating back to the late 1600s, La Motte has evolved into much more than a vineyard. It has recently become a producer of ethereal oils; and it plays an important role in the local community through a large outreach program that centers on its employees. La Motte is open for wine and wine-sorbet tasting in its luxurious wine-tasting room.

Just 2.5 miles (4 km) beyond the Huguenot Monument off the main road, another great stop is the family-run **Stony Brook Vineyard** *(tel 021/876-2182, www.stonybrook.co.za),* which currently harvests ten wines. It's open on mornings Monday through Saturday; otherwise, call ahead for an appointment.

From Franschhoek backtrack on the R45, continuing north to the town of **Paarl** ❸ (see p. 105) via the R45. Among its many wineries, **KWV Wine Emporium** *(Kohler St., tel 021/807-3007, www.kwvwineemporium.co.za, $),* one of the larger vineyards in the Winelands, is right in town. KWV has played an important role in the history of Paarl's winemaking, as it began in 1918 as a cooperative of local wine farmers

joining forces to combat an insect outbreak. It's an internationally traded company, yielding nearly a hundred wines and six brandies. Winery tours are offered daily.

The **Fairview Wine Estate** *(tel 021/863-2450, www.fairview.co.za),* just outside of town on Suid-Agter-Paarl Road, is a multigenerational family-owned winery on a sprawling 741-acre (300 ha) estate at the foot of the Paarl Mountains. It boasts more than 30 varieties of wine and dozens of cheeses.

This is just a sampling of Western Cape's fabled wineries. No doubt you'll want to tarry in this beautiful countryside and visit some more.

NOT TO BE MISSED:

Picturesque Stellenbosch • Lanzerac Manor & Winery • La Motte Wine Estate • Stony Brook Vineyard

---

🗺 Also see area map p. 101
▶ Stellenbosch
🛣 100 miles (160 km)
🕐 Half day or more, depending on stops
▶ KWV Wine Emporium, outside Paarl

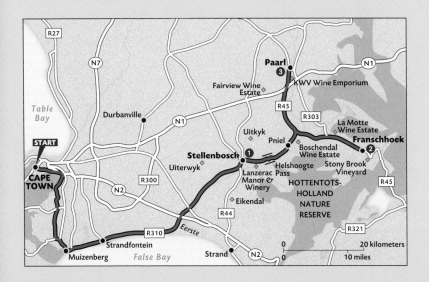

Oudtshoorn & Around

The Klein (Small) Karoo, the eastern rim of the Western Cape, is a region of fertile valleys, turning into semidesert farther north as the Great Karoo. Small 18th-century towns offer outings to mineral springs and backpacker trails.

Oudtshoorn and the surrounding area are home to the world's largest ostrich population.

When ostrich feathers were an attribute to high fashion at the turn of the 20th century, the wealthier merchants trading in feathers built some grand mansions in the town, lending it a degree of elegance.

The **Klein Karoo National Arts Festival** *(tel 044/203-8600)* is celebrated in March each year, when Afrikaans-speaking art lovers gather for a week of dancing, films, cabaret, classical music, comedy, contemporary music, open-air concerts, plays, literature, art, and poetry. This event now enjoys international sponsorship.

At the **Cango Wildlife Ranch,** just outside town, you can come face-to-face with chee-tahs, the fastest animals on land. This highly successful breeding station for the threatened spe-cies is one of the two oldest in

Oudtshoorn

🅐 Map p. 101

Visitor Information

✉ Baron van Reede St.

☎ 044/279-2532

www.oudtshoorn. com

Oudtshoorn

Oudtshoorn lies 40 miles (65 km) inland from the coast and is famous for three things: its ostrich farms, the Klein Karoo Arts Festival, and the mysterious Cango Caves.

Tours of the Cango Caves

A visit to the Cango Caves can be as serene or adventurous as you choose. You should arrive at least ten minutes early, because you are led into the caves five minutes before the actual tour starts. There are two tour options:

Standard Tour *($$):* A moderate walk through the first two magnificent halls, continuing to the African Drum Chamber. Several stairways are included in the standard tour.

Adventure Tour *($$):* A challenging tour, with exciting passages and narrow chimneys. The tour lasts about 1.5 hours; this is only a 0.7-mile-walk (1.2 km), but 416 stairs must be negotiated.

The tunnel section at the back of the caves (Devil's Chimney) comes close to an extreme adventure, which is best attempted only if you're fit. It is not advisable for small children, or heavy-weight adults.

EXPERIENCE: Oudtshoorn's Ostrich Farms

The first commercial ostrich farm in South Africa was established in 1860. By the turn of the 20th century, when severe droughts affected the Oudtshoorn area, farmers noticed that their ostriches were thriving in the dry conditions, which led several farms to turn solely to ostrich farming. Today there are as many as 400 ostrich farms in and around Oudtshoorn, three of which have been named show farms and are open to the public. Want to ride an ostrich under careful surpervision? At 7.8 feet (2.4 m) tall and weighing more than 220 pounds (100 kg), the birds can be a challenge. And be warned, although their soft beaks are harmless, an ostrich kick can be life threatening. Don't leave without tasting the newly trendy (for its health benefits) ostrich meat, or an ostrich egg omelette. With each egg weighing 3.3 pounds (1.5 kg), you may want to share. The three show farms are: **Cango Ostrich Farm** (Cango Valley, 9 miles/14 km from Oudtshoorn, tel 044/272-4623, www.cangoostrich.co.za, $$); **Chandelier Game Lodge & Ostrich Show Farm** (4.3 miles/7 km) from Oudtshoorn on the N12, tel 044/272-6794, www.chandelier.co.za); and **Safari Ostrich Show Farm** (4.3 miles/7 km from Oudtshoorn on the R62, tel 044/272-7311, www.safariostrich.co.za, $$).

the Southern Hemisphere. You'll also have the opportunity to be photographed while cuddling a cheetah cub.

Cango Caves

About 18 miles (29 km) north of Oudtshoorn, the Cango Caves, a national monument, consist of a series of colorful limestone formations. Only one main section is open to the public, and in some sections you will have to get down on all fours or slide on your stomach—at the Devil's Chimney, for example—to get to all the viewable areas (see sidebar opposite).

For thousands of years, the caves were unknown. About 10,000 years ago the Khoisan used the entrance area of the cave as a shelter; they don't seem to have wandered deeper into the caves because of certain superstitions. The entrance area to the caves was originally rich in Khoisan paintings, but over time these have been damaged. The Khoisan left this area about 500 years ago.

Since the late 17th century, the caves have been a tourist attraction, with the first official tour taking place in 1891. Over the years, more and more chambers and tunnels have been discovered. Between 1972 and 1975 Cango 2, 3, 4, and 5 were found. The present tourist route extends for 0.7 mile (1.2 km) into the cave, with another 2.5 miles (4 km) closed to the public for conservation reasons.

The temperature in the Cango Caves is a somewhat warm and humid 65°F (18°C), so light clothing is recommended. Ample lighting makes uneven pathways and stairs easy to negotiate and provides opportunities for memorable photographs. The tours are led by knowledgeable guides. ■

Cango Wildlife Ranch
✉ 2 miles (3 km) outside of Oudtshoorn on the R62 toward Cango Caves
☎ 27 44 272 5593
$ $$$

www.cango.co.za

Cango Caves
⚠ Map p. 101
✉ 19 miles (29 km) N of Oudtshoorn on the R328
☎ 044/272-7410
$ $$

www.cangocaves .co.za

Garden Route

The Garden Route stretches from Mossel Bay to the Storms River in the far eastern reaches of the Western Cape. Wedged between mountains covered by the largest continuous Afromontane forest and the coves and beaches of the Indian Ocean coast, the region rightfully takes pride in its scenery.

The historic Dutch Reformed Mother Church in George

George

⊠ Map p. 101

Visitor Information

✉ 124 York. St., George

☎ 044/801-9295

www.georgetourism.org.za

Garden Route Botanical Garden

✉ 49 Caledon St., George

☎ 044/874-1558

$ $

www.botanicalgarden.org.za

George

George lies roughly midway between Cape Town and Port Elizabeth and is the gateway to the Garden Route. The town is also the center of **South Africa's golf route** (George Golf Club, tel 044/873-6116, www.georgegolfclub.co.za), with world-class courses designed by golfing greats, among them Oubaai and Le Grand George. The Fancourt Golf Estate hosted the President's Cup in 2003 and holds other high-profile golf tournaments. Besides golf, top national rugby sevens teams from around the world come to Outeniqua Park for the South Africa Sevens leg, one of the tournaments in the IRB Sevens World Series.

Among George's historic landmarks is the **Outeniqua Transport Museum** (2 Mission Rd., tel 044/801-8288, closed Sun.), which houses a large collection of steam locomotives and old carriages. At the corner of Hibernia and York Streets, an ancient English oak planted by the Landdrost (magistrate) van Kervel in 1811 is known as the **Slave Tree**, because of the large chain and lock embedded in the trunk—

today, it's a national monument. Among the colonial buildings, the **King Edward VII Library** is one of the best examples of Edwardian architecture in town. The **Garden Route Botanical Garden** at the end of Caledon Street shows off the local flora, including cape reeds, daisies, and Afromontane forest.

George lies some 5 miles (8 km) from the beach, and visitors stay here mostly in transit to explore the Tsitsikamma National Park (see p. 114) or to take the Outeniqua train (see sidebar this page).

Mossel Bay

Twenty-five miles (40 km) southeast of George on the N2 Garden Route, Mossel Bay is named for the mussels (*mossels* in Dutch) the first European settlers found here. In the 1980s industrial development of offshore oil rigs and natural gas processing plants marred this Eden. But the beaches and the town's historic center still make this a worthwhile visit.

Many explorers' ships anchored in the bay: Bartolomeu Dias stopped here in 1488, followed by Vasco da Gama in 1497 and Admiral João da Nova in 1501. Not until 1787 did a permanent settlement begin.

To celebrate the 500th anniversary of Dias's landing, the town opened the **Bartolomeu Dias Museum Complex,** where a reproduction of the caravel in which Dias rounded the cape in 1488 is on exhibit. Seeing and touching this ridiculously small vessel, you understand the extreme courage it took to set out into the wilds of the Atlantic Ocean. Here you'll also find the **Maritime Museum,** housed in what once was a grain mill and sawmill; and the **Shell Museum,** which displays shells from around the world and aquarium tanks with live shellfish.

The **St. Blaize Lighthouse,** built in 1864 on Cape St. Blaize, is a great spot from which to watch

Mossel Bay

🅰 Map p. 101

Bartolomeu Dias Museum Complex

✉ 1 Market St.

☎ 044/691-1067

www.diasmuseum.co.za

EXPERIENCE: Riding the Outeniqua Choo-Tjoe

The Outeniqua Choo-Tjoe is South Africa's last fully operating steam train, and the 32-mile (52 km) scenic trip from George to Knysna and return offers tourists a unique way of experiencing the Garden Route. The first stretch of the railway opened in 1907, and the train continues service as a "preserved line."

The train stops in many small towns, as well as at several museums and places of historical interest, including an aquarium and a railway workshop.

The railroad tracks wind their way through amazing scenery that can't otherwise be seen from the road. The views present some awesome photo opportunities of dense forests, fern-covered hills, tranquil lakes and rivers, the famous Knysna lagoon, and dramatic aspects of the Indian Ocean.

These days the train still transports an estimated 115,000 passengers per year, 70 percent of whom are foreign tourists. For train reservations contact Outeniqua Choo-Tjoe (*2 Mission St., George, tel 044/801-8288, www.onlinesources.co.za, $$$*).

The round-trip does not have to be completed the same day and offers the possibility of spending the night in Knysna.

Sedgefield

⚠ Map p. 101

Visitor Information

✉ 30 Main St., Sedgefield

☎ 044/343-2007

tourismsedgefield.co.za

Wilderness

⚠ Map p. 101

Visitor Information

✉ Beacon Rd., Millwood Village

☎ 044/877-0045

www.tourismwilderness.co.za

Knysna

⚠ Map p. 101

Visitor Information

✉ 40 Main St., Knysna

☎ 044/382-5510

www.tourismknysna.co.za

whales and dolphins. The **St. Blaize Trail** to Dana Bay, running for 8 miles (13 km), starts at the Bats' Cave below the lighthouse.

Sedgefield & Wilderness

The seaside resorts of Sedgefield and nearby Wilderness on the Kaaimans River, east of George on the N2 Garden Route, are surrounded by a string of lakes—Langvlei, Rondevlei, Swartvlei,

INSIDER TIP:

Don't miss the outstanding fresh food and products at the Farmers Market and Scarab Craft Market, every Saturday, just west of Sedgefield off the N2.

—RICHARD WHITAKER
National Geographic contributor

and Groenvlei—separated from the Indian Ocean by a narrow strip of dunes, with a backdrop of densely forested mountains. The estuaries and beaches teem with birdlife of marine, estuarine, and evergreen forest species, including the famous Knysna lourie.

Midway between Sedgefield and Knysna, **Buffalo Bay,** with its safe areas for swimming and slightly wilder stretches for surfing, is known for its family beach. Some stables offer horseback riding through the surf; try G.R.E.A.T. Horseback Riding & Horse Trails

(tel 082/835-9110 or 082/824-1248, www.great.co.za).

Groenvlei, the only freshwater lake on the Garden Route, is a favorite bass fishing spot and forms part of the **Goukamma Nature Reserve** *(off the N2 at Buffalo Bay, tel 044/383-0042 or 021/659-3500, www.capenature.co.za).* The reserve attracts birders and hikers. Safe beaches for bathing, fishing, and spearfishing and a choice of nature trails make this area a favorite vacation spot.

Knysna

Knysna, 15.5 miles (25 km) east of Sedgefield on the N2 Garden Route, lies at the edge of a beautiful lagoon, which opens between two high sandstone cliffs, called the Heads, to let the ocean rush in. On the **Eastern Head,** an observation point provides a grand view over the surroundings. The town is lively with bars and restaurants, souvenir shops and boutiques along the main road.

Knysna's history began in 1804 with the arrival of a mysterious man, who called himself George Rex—apparently a royal name. He surrounded himself with much pomp and circumstance, and lived in such style that he was rumored to be the illegitimate son of King George III. He neither confirmed or denied these stories. George Rex bought the estate known as Melkhoutkraal on the shores of the lagoon and settled his family and considerable entourage in Knysna.

The **Millwood House Museum** *(Queen St., tel 044/302-6320, closed Sun.)* holds items relating to

Knysna Oyster Festival

As the official oyster capital of South Africa, Knysna naturally has its own annual Oyster Festival (www.oysterfestival .co.za). Every year in July, gourmands from around the country flock to the Garden Route for the ten days of the festival to sample the town's oysters. Knysna oysters are ranked as some of the tastiest in the world. Typically, more than 200,000 oysters are eaten during the festival.

To alleviate any culinary guilt, revelers can sign up and participate in many sporting events during the festival, including a mountain-bike race, a road race, a marathon, and an angling competition. And with a program second to none, including a whiskey and jazz festival, helicopter jaunts, and a host of courses and classes, the festival is bound to satisfy even the fussiest visitor.

the town's history and includes many objects once owned by George Rex.

The surrounding **Knysna Forest** is the largest indigenous forest in South Africa with Afromontane species—stinkwood, yellowwood, white pear, terblans beech, and assegai—as well as blackwood, ironwood, white alder, Cape chestnut, and fynbos. There are several places to enjoy the beauty of this wilderness, including **Diepwalle Forest** (10 miles/16 km outside Knysna on R339, tel 044/382-9762).

Knysna Elephant Park

Knysna Elephant Park, 14 miles (23 km) west of Knysna on the N2, is a private park, opened in 1994 to settle the last remaining elephant in Knysna, together with orphaned elephants rescued from culling operations at the Kruger National Park. The park's 148 acres (60 ha) make for a controlled, free-range environment, where guides allow close contact with the animals.

Plettenberg Bay

A 20-minute drive farther east along the N2 brings you to this peaceful village, which bursts at

the seams during December as vacationers flock from all over the country to enjoy the beaches. The largest, **Robberg Beach,** is a 2.6-mile (4.2 km) stretch of uninterrupted, dramatic coastline, with two family areas protected by lifeguards. You're likely to spot dolphins showing off in summer or whales lolling in the surf in winter. At the far end of the beach lies the **Robberg Peninsula,** with a 6.8-mile (11 km) trail that leads along the rugged coastline with rock pools and views of seal colonies. **Central beach,** alongside Robberg, is home to the iconic **Beacon Isle Hotel** (tel 044/533-1120), the most popular postcard image of Plettenberg Bay.

Nature's Valley

This small village on the Groot River estuary is part of the **De Vasselot** section of the Tsitsikamma National Park. Its forest is dense with yellowwoods and fern trees, the coast a narrow strip with unspoiled beaches and rocky cliffs. Visitors come to swim, sail, canoe deep into the estuary, or look for the colorful Knysna lourie.

Knysna Elephant Park

🛆 Map p. 101

✉ 14 miles (22 km) W of Knysna on N2

☎ 044/532-7732

💲 $$$$

www.knysna elephantpark.co.za

Plettenberg Bay

🛆 Map p. 101

Visitor Information

✉ Tourism Bureau, Melville's Corner Center, Main St., Plettenberg Bay

☎ 044/533-4065

www.plettenbergbay .co.za

The beautiful setting of the Fancourt Golf Estate

**Tsitsikamma
National Park**

 Map p. 101

✉ On N2 E of
George, 5 miles
(8 km) W of
Storms River
Bridge

☎ 042/281-1607

$ $$$

www.sanparks.org
/parks/tsitsika
mma/

Tsitsikamma
National Park

This is the third most frequently
visited national park in South
Africa, and it's easy to see why.

"Tsitsikamma," a Khoisan word,
means "place of much water." On
some 50 miles (80 km) of rugged
coastline, the park stretches about
3 miles (5 km) out to sea, protecting
intertidal life, reef, and deep-sea
fish. This combination makes it one
of the world's largest single marine
protected areas (MPA), conserving
11 percent of South Africa's temper-
ate south coast shoreline. It was
proclaimed a marine national park
in 1964, the first of its kind in Africa.

The dense forest of mountain
fynbos and evergreens, ferns and
flowering plants, is home to mon-
keys and small antelopes, otters
and many species of birds. Daring
visitors can take a tour through the
treetops on a system of platforms
and cable slides. Numerous trails
extend into rocky paths to the sea,
including the 26-mile (42 km), five-
day **Otter Trail** from the Storms

River Mouth to Nature's Valley. A
number of cultural heritage sites in
the park range from Khoisan cave
and rock art to ruins of small fishing
villages and former forestry sites.

The park is safe enough to be
explored without a guide, yet for
a small fee guides are available for
groups of ten or more.

Farther Afield

Laingsburg is located in the
semiarid Karoo, 175 miles (280
km) northeast of Cape Town.
The small town has an old stone
Dutch Reformed Church and
the Library Hall's **Wolfaardt
Collection** (Van Riebeeck St., tel
023/551-1019). Exhibits feature
artifacts from both the Khoisan
and Dutch, including musical
instruments, farm equipment, and
household items.

Geologists also find this area of
interest. A bed of white quartz-like
stone extends from Matjiesfontein
to Laingsburg and on into the
Eastern Cape. The Khoisan may
have chipped off this hard rock

to shape into ax heads. Strange rock formations, and marine and terrestrial fossils can be found on the **geological walk** laid out at Geelbeksbrug farm, next to the **Anglo-Boer War Blockhouse.** Tours to San rock-art sites in Springfontein can be arranged through Laingsburg Tourism.

The village of **Matjiesfontein** lies 18 miles (30 km) west of Laingsburg via the N1. The community was established in 1884 by James Logan, a train porter on the route from Cape Town to Pretoria, who found the dry air of the Karoo good for his lungs. He settled in the area and advertised the curative aspects of the air. The town soon became a popular stop on the train route and attracted prominent people, among them the Sultan of Zanzibar, Lord Randolph Churchill (Winston Churchill's father), Cecil Rhodes, Edgar Wallace, Rudyard Kipling, and the South African author Olive Schreiner.

During the South African War (1899–1902), Matjiesfontein served the British as a military stronghold, and its elegant Victorian **Lord Milner Hotel** (on the N1 at Matjiesfontein, tel 023/561-3011, www.matjiesfontein.com) became a war hospital. In 1970 the village and hotel were restored and declared a national monument—and it's the main reason people visit today.

The station building houses the **Matjiesfontein Museum,** aka the Marie Rawdon Museum. This collection of David Rawdon, an enthusiast of all things Victorian, includes elaborate dresses of bygone days and a fully stocked apothecary. The **Transport Museum** (behind Lord Milner Hotel, tel 023/561-3011, $) exhibits a collection of vintage cars, from the era of the historic gas station where gas is still being sold.

Two trains make special stops to allow visitors to tour the town: the luxury **Blue Train** (tel 021/334-8459, www.bluetrain.co.za, e-mail: bluetrain@transnet.co.za) and **Rovos Rail** (tel 021/323-6052, www.rovos.co.za, e-mail: reservations@rovos.co.za). ∎

Bungee Jump

The Garden Route offers an unrivaled opportunity for thrill seekers the world over. The area is home to the highest commercial bungee jump in the world. Spanning a whopping 710 feet (216 m) over the Bloukrans River (Face Adrenalin, tel 042/281-1458, www.faceadrenalin.com, $$$$$), the jump boasts spectacular views, although we're willing to bet you'll fail to notice them on your way down. For the less adventurous, there is a smaller jump, a three-hour drive to the west along the N2, at the Gourits Bridge (Face Adrenalin, tel 083/414-2380, www.faceadrenalin.com, $$$$$). The drop may only be 213 feet (65 m) down, but it holds its own record of being the oldest bungee jump in the country. The venues are open daily.

Laingsburg
🗺 Map p. 101

Visitor Information
✉ Laingsburg Library, Voortrekker & Meiring Sts.
☎ 023/551-1868

Anglo-Boer War Blockhouse
✉ 7.5 miles (12 km) N of Laingsburg on N2
☎ Call Die Blokhuis, inn next door to blockhouse, tel 023/551-1774, for entry

Matjiesfontein
🗺 Map p. 101
✉ 18 miles (30 km) S of Laingsburg on N1
☎ 023/561-3011
www.matjesfontein.com

BIKO

18/12/1946 - 12/9/1977

Perhaps South Africa's most diverse province, with lonely beaches and surfing hot spots, elephants and migratory whales, the homeland of Nelson Mandela, Steve Biko, and other national heroes

Eastern Cape

A bronze statue of black consciousness leader Steve Biko outside East London's City Hall

Eastern Cape

The Eastern Cape, pinned between South Africa's two most popular provinces (Western Cape and KwaZulu-Natal), is an undiscovered jewel. The shoreline extends from the Umtamvuna River in KwaZulu-Natal to the Storms River mouth on the Garden Route in the west and stretches north to the Lesotho border. The province also incorporates the apartheid-era homelands of the Ciskei and Transkei of predomiantly Xhosa culture.

If you travel east from Cape Town, beyond the popular Garden Route, it is here that you feel for the first time that you really are in Africa—right at the edge of the wilderness. The Eastern Cape offers 500 miles (800 km) of untouched coastline. Port Elizabeth alone has 25 miles (40 km) of sandy beaches and is known as one of the best sailing venues in the world. Jeffrey's Bay is a top surfing spot; and the Wild Coast, an eco-haven between East London and Port Edward, is one of the country's least developed regions. Many

ships have foundered on the reefs off this coastline, but its lone beaches and estuaries invite hikers and campers to roam. The Eastern Cape is malaria free and ideal for safaris.

Western Region

The western region stretches along the coast from the Tsitsikamma National Park, through Port Elizabeth to Port Alfred. This region boasts South Africa's greatest concentration of elephant herds, especially in the Addo Elephant National Park, and, on a smaller scale, on the private Shamwari Game Reserve and Lalibela Game Reserve.

Farther inland, rolling hills give way to the dry grasslands plateau of the Karoo, which spreads to the sandstone formations and sheer cliffs of the Sneeuberg range. The highest point, Mount Kompas, reaches 8,215 feet (2,504 m). The range forms the watershed between the Sundays River and the Great Fish River. Formerly known as Settler Country, the area was colonized in the 1820s by the British to farm vast tracts of land and to defend the eastern frontier against the Xhosa people. The land is only good for irrigated farming. To this day, mostly sheep and game farms carve out an acceptable living.

Eastern Region

The beaches along the Sunshine Coast, between St. Francis Bay and East London, bask in nature's splendor, with a profusion of flora and fauna and teeming birdlife. From East London north to Port Edward, the Wild

Coast extends along untamed shoreline,
with rugged cliffs, towering sand dunes,
and unexplored beaches. It's a backpackers'
paradise, where few roads are paved
or even marked on a map. Hikers
follow sandy paths from
village to village. ■

LESOTHO

KWAZULU-NATAL

EASTERN CAPE

N2

R56

Port Edward

R61

Rouxville

N6

R396

Maclear

Port St. Johns

R58

EASTERN CAPE

Mthatha

Qunu

Coffee Bay

R61

Mvezo

Umzimvubu

MANDELA ROUTE

Queenstown

Great Kei

N2

Mazeppa Bay

To Richmond

N6

Kei Mouth

R61

NELSON

Morgan's Bay

Haga-Haga

Gonubie

To Nieu-Bethesda

R344

King William's Town

Bhisho

Bonza Bay

R63

Buffalo

EAST LONDON

MOUNTAIN ZEBRA
NATIONAL PARK

Kidd's Beach

Cove Rock

Gulu Beach

Igoda Beach

N10

GREAT FISH RIVER
NATURE RESERVE

To Graaff-Reinet &
Valley of Desolation

R63

R72

Great Fish

Darlington
Dam

Lalibela
Game
Reserve

Grahamstown

Bathurst

SHAMWARI GAME
RES.

Kowie

Port Alfred

ADDO
ELEPHANT
N.P.

Zuurberg

Sibuya Game Reserve

Kirkwood

AMAKHALA
PRIVATE
RESERVE

Kenton-on-Sea

R75

Colchester

INDIAN OCEAN

WILD COAST

Apple
Express

Algoa Bay

PORT ELIZABETH

Loerie

Seaview Game & Lion Park

St. Francis Bay

Jeffrey's Bay

St. Francis Bay

N

To
TSITSIKAMMA
NATIONAL PARK

Seal Point

0   80 kilometers

0   40 miles

Area of map detail

Pretoria

South Africa
color-coded by region

Port Elizabeth

Known for its sunshine and safe, sandy beaches, Port Elizabeth stretches out along beautiful Algoa Bay of South Africa's southeastern coast, about 500 miles (800 km) east of Cape Town. In 1820 some 4,000 British settled in Port Elizabeth (or PE, as the locals call it), and built graceful period homes, many of which still enhance the city center. Since that time, the settlement has grown into the fifth largest city in South Africa and become a major port.

Monument to the mythical king-priest Prester John and the Portuguese explorers of southern Africa

Port Elizabeth

◪ Map p. 119

Visitor Information

✉ Donkin Reserve
Lighthouse
Complex,
Belmont Terr.,
Central

☎ 041/585-8884

www.portelizabeth.co.za

Vacationers flock here mostly for the water sports—scuba diving, surfing, and windsurfing—but the city also has some notable sights.

The British left their unmistakable stamp on Port Elizabeth's architecture, as a stroll around the central **Market Square,** with several historic buildings, will show. Centered on the square, the **City Hall** with its clock tower dates from 1858. At the corner of Whites Road and Main Street, the original courthouse, built in 1835, is now the **City Library,** with an imposing stained-glass dome.

Nearby awaits **St. George's Park,** covering 180 acres (73 ha) of wooded parkland, with the world-famous Port Elizabeth Cricket Club (promising the possibility of an exciting test match) and the oldest bowling green in South Africa.

No. 7 Castle Hill Museum *(Castle Hill Rd.)* is housed in the oldest surviving settler cottage, dating back to 1827. It displays Victorian furniture and household items.

Climb hilly **Donkin Street** with its well-maintained Victorian houses. At the top of the street, Sir Rufane Donkin, the cape's acting governor, had a strange **memorial** built to his wife, Elizabeth, who died in India before the town was built. A plaque on the stone pyramid pays tribute to her: "One of the most perfect human beings, who has given her name to the town below."

The city's **information center** is set up in the old lighthouse, built in 1861. Maps and information on the region are available; of particular interest is a map of a 3-mile (5 km) walking tour, the **Donkin Heritage Trail,** through the hill area and central city, taking in 47 historic sites.

At the entrance to the harbor, a **Campanile** with a carillon stands guard, commemorating the land-ing of the British settlers of 1820. Visitors can climb the 204 steps for a great view over the city.

The **St. Croix Motor Museum** in Newton Park has more than 80 cars on display, dating from the 1900s to the 1960s. Call founder Even de Vos to arrange a visit.

By the Shore

Port Elizabeth's most visited site on the beachfront is probably **Bayworld,** one of the best and largest museum complexes in South Africa, with an ocean-

INSIDER TIP:

For Port Elizabeth history, try the Donkin Heritage Trail, vintage cars in the St. Croix Motor Museum, and the Campanile and its view of the city.

—CAGAN H. SEKERCIOGLU
National Geographic field researcher

arium, a snake park, and a museum. The **Oceanarium** is home to two Indian Ocean bottlenose dolphins that perform mornings and afternoons for the crowds. In two other large aquariums, cape fur seals and large Southern Ocean elephant seals swim along with game and reef fish, sharks, and turtles.

The **Snake Park** allows strollers to safely view tortoises and terrapins, lizards and iguanas, crocodiles and mambas in landscaped enclosures.

St. Croix Motor Museum
- ✉ Mowbray St., Newton Park
- ☎ 083/463-5286
- 🕐 Call for appt.
- **www.bayworld.co.za**

Bayworld
- ✉ Beach Rd., Humewood
- ☎ 041/584-0650
- 💲 $–$$
- **www.bayworld.co.za**

Apple Express
- ☎ 041/583-2030
- 💲 $$$$$ (for weekend)
- **www.apple-express .co.za**

Apple Express

The Port Elizabeth Apple Express is the only narrow-gauge steam train still operating in southern Africa, traveling the 44 miles (72 km) from Port Elizabeth to Loerie with 16 stops in between.

Near the end of its scenic route, the train crosses the Van Stadens River Bridge, about 254 feet (78 m) above the gorge, the highest narrow-gauge viaduct in the world. With only three public trips each month, be sure to make reservations ahead of time.

Dolphins and trainer, Bayworld Oceanarium

**Seaview Game &
Lion Park**

🅰 Map. p. 119
✉ Off N2, W of
   Port Elizabeth
☎ 041/378-1702
💲 $$
www.seaview
gamepark.co.za

The **museum** displays range from prehistoric dinosaur bones to recent artifacts and extensive ethnic arts and beadwork.

The Beaches: Port Elizabeth's clean, absolutely gorgeous beaches, protected by gentle Algoa Bay, boast water temperatures that remain invitingly warm year-round. Among the best: Famous **Kings Beach** has 1.3 miles (2 km) of white sand; **Hobie Beach** is located right next to Shark Rock Pier; while **Humewood Beach** is a constant Blue Flag winner.

Surfing spots include the wild **Bluewater Bay,** just north of Port Elizabeth; **the Fence, the Pipe,** and **Millers Point,** to mention just a few.

Watching for Wildlife

Several wildlife reserves exist within easy reach of Port Elizabeth. The closest one is

the **Seaview Game & Lion Park,** 15 miles (25 km) west of the city center. Lions, giraffes, zebras, wildebeests, impalas,

INSIDER TIP:

Shamwari, Amakhala, and other private reserves have reclaimed unproductive farmlands, restored native vegetation, and reintroduced native animals. They offer day-tour programs, including game drives.

—JOHN SEATON CALLAHAN
National Geographic contributor

duikers, and some 40 other species roam free in the reserve. The park offers a self-drive tour to let you observe the animals in their natural habitat.

The park's main draw here is the chance to play with lion cubs that are between four-to-nine-months old. After a brief explanation of how to safely interact with the cubs (*$*), you can pet the cubs. Or, you can watch a lion feeding at noon on Sundays. Several white lions were born at the park and still roam free.

The private **Shamwari Game Reserve** is tucked into a lush setting along the Bushmans River, halfway between Port Elizabeth and Grahamstown. Shamwari prides itself on conserving a vanishing way of life, and the 62,000-acre (25,000 ha) reserve boasts five of South Africa's seven biomes, supporting many forms of plant, animal, and bird life.

Visitors can explore the terrain through game drives and visit the **Born Free Foundation Centers**—a sanctuary for abused large wild cats. The reserve features the Big Five—elephant, lion, leopard, buffalo, and the endangered black rhino—as well as hippos, giraffes, black wildebeests, and cheetahs. For its conservation efforts and responsible tourism work, the reserve has received international awards, including the "World's Leading Conservation Company and Game Reserve" for several years. Each of its six luxurious lodges offers a distinctive ambience.

The nearby **Amakhala Private Reserve** is playing an equally important role in returning 20th-century grazing lands to their original natural state, and overseeing the reintroduction of animals into the lands they once roamed freely. Lodging ranges from comfortable to luxury. ■

Shamwari Game Reserve
- Map. p. 119
- 40 miles (65 km) E of Port Elizabeth on N2 toward Grahamstown
- 041/407-1000 or 877/354-2213 (toll-free from U.S.)

www.shamwari.com

Amakhala Private Reserve
- Map p. 119
- 40 miles (65 km) E of Port Elizabeth via N2 toward Grahamstown
- 046/636-2750

www.amakhala.co.za

EXPERIENCE: On the Boardwalk

Centuries after 4,000 English immigrants landed at Port Elizabeth, the British influence can still be felt throughout the coastal town. Whereas the City Hall and the City Library evoke thoughts of ivy-and-brick Victorianism, the Boardwalk (www.boardwalk.co.za), overlooking the city's beautiful beaches, is a lot flashier, along the lines of England's Brighton.

Halfway between anachronistic and just plain weird, embraced by tourists and locals alike, this artifice of a coastal strip mall is something to be seen. Its classic red-and-white buildings, lit brilliantly at night, contain shops, restaurants, entertainment arcades, and plenty of things for children to do.

In this shopper's paradise, stores cater to every demographic: Head to the Billabong store for the latest surfwear, for example, or go to EzamaXhosa for handmade crafts.

Hang out at **Brooke's Pavilion,** on the corner of Brooke's Hill and Beach Drive, with its many pubs and restaurants serving everything from spaghetti to sushi.

And for the gamblers, the **Casino** is a destination in itself, with 802 slot machines and 21 casino tables.

And should you tire of the Indian Ocean's pristine views, head over to the man-made lake and feed the ducks. Make sure you have plenty of time to stroll, gawk, and partake in this most eccentric of South African venues.

Around Port Elizabeth

The Eastern Cape around Port Elizabeth flattens out along the Sunshine and the Shipwreck Coasts with endless, undisturbed beaches. But travel inland just a few dozen miles and the landscape becomes hilly again with the Zuurberg mountain range and the Sundays River Valley, where malaria-free game reserves and a choice of scenic hiking trails vie for visitors.

Mothers and calves, Addo Elephant National Park

Addo Elephant National Park

 Map. p. 119

✉ Off N2 toward Grahamstown, 45 miles (72 km) E of Port Elizabeth

☎ 042/233-8600

💲 $$–$$$

www.sanparks.org/ parks/addo

Addo Elephant National Park

The park stretches for 413,000 acres (164,000 ha) along the densely forested valley of the Sundays River. In 1931, when just 11 elephants remained in the area, the original elephant section of the park was proclaimed a national park. Today the park teems with more than 480 elephants, as well as cape buffalo, black rhino, and a variety of antelope. Addo is home to the Big Seven: elephant, lion, buffalo, leopard, rhino, plus the

southern right whale and the great white shark.

Five of South Africa's seven major vegetation biomes are found throughout the park. In the subtropical thicket, called valley bushveld, you'll be able to view the elephant population and an abundance of antelope, such as red hartebeest, eland, kudu, and bushbuck. Other game species, found in the outlying areas of the park in the Great Karoo, include gemsbok, black wildebeest, springbok, buffalo, and black rhino. The cape mountain zebra, mountain reedbuck, baboon, blue duiker, and red rock rabbit are found in the Zuurberg mountain range.

For bird lovers, the **SASOL Red Bishop Bird Blind,** located opposite the water hole in the main rest camp, offers a chance to spot weavers, herons, coots, and, true to its name, red bishops. The main game area features some 170 bird species; the expanded park may contain as many as 450 species, from brown-hooded kingfisher and greater double-collared sunbird to Denham's bustard and African penguin; it's also one of the few spots in South Africa for roseate terns to breed.

In the future, Addo proposes to turn 300,000 acres (120,000 ha) along the shore east of Port Elizabeth into a marine-protected area. Offshore islands in this area that are home to the world's largest breeding populations of cape gannets and the second largest breeding population of African penguins are already incorporated into the park.

Two rest camps are located within the park: **Addo Rest-Camp** (tel 042/233-8600, e-mail: addoenquiries@sanparks.org; see p. 293), near the entrance gate, has some 60 accommodations of various types. Activities include day and night guided game drives and guided horseback rides, along with a pool, a restaurant, and a store.

Camp Matyholweni (tel 041/468-0916 or 041/468-0918, e-mail matyholweni@sanparks.org; see p. 293) is a second rest camp near the town of Colchester on the N2 highway. The camp is accessible by car and is about a 45-minute-drive from the main camp.

How to Visit Addo: You can either do a self-drive along the park's paved and gravel roads (a 4WD is not necessary unless you take the specific 4WD route), or take a game drive. A number of game drives of about two hours are conducted by qualified guides in open Land Rovers or trucks. Reservations are required (tel 042/233-8621).

Addo's Private Lodges

Darlington Lake Lodge (tel 042/243-3673) in the park's Darlington Dam area is an intimate lodge in colonial African style.
Gorah Elephant Camp (tel 011/679-2994) in the park's main Addo section is a five-star operation with luxury, tented camps and elephants to view while sipping tea.
Nguni River Lodge (tel 042/235-1022, www.ngunilodges.co.za) offers eight luxury suites built high on a ridge overlooking a water hole with views on the Zuurberg.
River Bend Lodge (tel 042/233-8000, www.riverbendlodge.co.za) in the park's Nyathi area is a five-star accommodation in the shadow of mountains with a wellness center.

Surfing at Jeffrey's Bay

Surfing in South Africa began to grow in popularity in the 1960s, and the Beach Boys' music became emblematic of the beach culture of the country. Since then, surfing has grown hugely, and some places in South Africa are famous among surfers worldwide. For top surfers, there are few better places to go than Jeffrey's Bay.

Surfing at Jeffrey's Bay

Most surfers have heard about the surf at Jeffrey's Bay and smile at the thought of that swell, those tubes, and the most consistent wave formations in South Africa. The waves can get big, sometimes as high as 10 feet (3 m) or so, but surprisingly the bay is also renowned for its safety. Surfers make a pilgrimage to beaches with names as diverse as Magnatubes, Boneyards, and the Albatross. Some places provide surfers with a ride as long as three minutes.

Every July the world-famous Billabong Pro takes place at the aptly named **Supertubes** beach. Although often delayed because of

sharks in the area, the tournament attracts the world's top surfers. Here is perhaps South Africa's longest and most consistently good wave.

Best of the Best

Around the corner from Supertubes, in front of the Beach Hotel, **Magnatubes' Reef** is famed for its fast and hard-breaking swell. It closes out often; otherwise, it's simply perfect.

At **Boneyards,** you must negotiate a fast wall that comes down toward the main takeoff zone at Supertubes. You might even take off outside Boneyards, fly through some heartstopping barrels, and exit at Supertubes. Boneyards

EXPERIENCE: Learn to Surf

South Africa's epic surf spots were epitomized in the 1966 cult surf movie *Endless Summer*, making it a definite "to-do" point on any serious surfer's dream list of finding the perfect wave. For curious novices, surf schools have been established in most coastal towns, the oldest being **Gary's Surf School** in Cape Town. There you can experience the rush firsthand in Muizenberg's relatively warm water, where constant waves make for the perfect classroom. Single lessons are available, and all equipment can be rented through the school. Day and week surfing trips are also available. Contact Gary Kleynhans *(34 Beach Rd., Muizenberg, Cape Town, tel 021/788-9839, www.garysurf.com, 2-hour lessons, including equipment, $$$$$).*

For lessons in the iconic Jeffrey's Bay, contact the **J-Bay Surf School** *(Island Vibe Backpackers, 10 Dageraad St., Jeffrey's Bay, tel 042/293- 4214, www.islandvibe.co.za, 2-hour lessons, including equipment, $$$$$).*

And surfing in Durban's warm waters is yet another experience. Try **Jeep uShaka Surf and Adventure** on the Durban beachfront *(tel 084/823-9470, www.surfadventures.co.za, 1-hour lessons, including equipment, $$$$).*

INSIDER TIP:

The right-breaking tubes at Jeffrey's Bay's famous Supertubes beach are the world's finest. Rent a board at Billabong and step into the blue.

—THOMAS BERENATO
National Geographic writer

can get a few 10-foot (3 m) waves when there is not much swell elsewhere.

Albatross is the last stop in a long line of sections along the point at Jeffrey's Bay, which allows some surfers to surf all the way from Boneyards to, and through, Albatross. This ride could last for nearly a mile.

More Surfing at Jeffrey's

Oyster Bay has a fickle, exposed beach break with a clean, medium-size groundswell. It's best to surf in light north-northeast winds there.

Seal Point has two distinct sections: an outside and a full stop rock, from where the inside breaks. The inside is a more common phenomenon, except during peak surfing season between April and September. The inside is a walling point break, running along a rock shelf for a good 260 to 320 feet (80–100 m). The outside swell often has to refract around the outside point before it hits Seals Point.

A lone surfer, Big Bay Beach, near Cape Town

Among the choices are a sunrise tour, when you may spot hunting lions, buffalos, and kudos; a day drive, when you will undoubtedly spot herds of elephants, zebras, and ostriches; and a nighttime drive.

Another choice is to hire a local guide who will hop in your vehicle and guide you through the game area. These guides are typically extremely well informed and will show you exactly where to find that elephant calf or blue duiker that you've been dying to see.

Another option is to tour on horseback. Trail rides at Addo move from the main camp to the **Nyathi** section of the park, where large game can be seen, including elephants, cape buffalos, black rhinos, zebras, and antelopes—don't

Kenton-on-Sea

INSIDER TIP:

Addo is compact and one of the best places in Africa to photograph elephants. Do not bring any citrus fruit in your car, as elephants love it and will damage your car trying to get it.

—JOHN SEATON CALLAHAN
National Geographic contributor

worry, there are no lions or hyenas. All trail rides are conducted by experienced guides. There's a two-hour morning ride for beginners and a three-hour afternoon ride for more experienced riders. You can also ride in the **Zuurberg** section of the park; though it offers no big game, it promises gorgeous fynbos and forest scenery. Trails are suitable for riders of all skills. One-, three-, and five-hour tours are available.

Hiking is also extremely popular at Addo, with options ranging from a one-hour stroll along the **Cycad Trail** to the four-hour **Doringnek Trail** in the Zuurberg to a glorious water hole. The routes are clearly marked;

pick up a map at the Zuurberg offices, which are located 10 miles (16 km) from the park's main entrance. For the truly adventurous, there's the two-day, 22-mile (36 km) **Alexandria Hiking Trail,** which crosses the largest dune field in the Southern Hemisphere, as well as beach and forest. Huts along the way provide overnight shelter. You must make a reservation through Camp Matyholweni. Finally, the **PPC Discovery Trail** is a short walk through the valley thicket where you can learn more about the plants and animals of the region.

Eastern Cape's Beaches

The Eastern Cape coastline, called the Sunshine Coast, is a mecca for all water-sports enthusiasts and maintains a thriving surfing culture. The world-famous **Jeffrey's Bay** (see pp. 126–127), west of Port Elizabeth, offers a long stretch of pristine beaches with amazing waves and swells. The town hosts the annual **Billabong Pro** surfing competition in July when surfers from all over the world come to enjoy the rolling surf. The safe beaches are also perfect for bathing and other water sports.

The **St. Francis area,** west of Jeffrey's Bay, includes Port St. Francis, St. Francis Bay, Cape St. Francis, and Oyster Bay. The town of St. Francis Bay lies on Cape St. Francis where the winding Kromme River flows into the estuary and is often called "little Venice" because of its man-made canals and waterways. The white beaches offer some of the safest bathing and fishing on the coast.

Skimboarding

Dating back to 1920s California, skimboarding, one of the tamer extreme sports, has recently caught on in South Africa.

A skimboard is a thin, oval-shaped piece of varnished wood or Plexiglass. To ride one, you just need good balance and a flat, sandy beach. Run parallel to a crashing wave, board in hand, and as the water ebbs to nothing more than a film, toss the board down and jump onto it. A great way to impress the kids unless, of course, you fall.

Most of the Eastern Cape beaches are good for skimboarding, but the best places are probably Kenton-on-Sea and Jeffrey's Bay.

North of Port Elizabeth, **Kenton-on-Sea** has beaches as far as the eye can see. Its **Kariega Beach** was voted the best beach in South Africa in 2000.

Just a bit farther east of Kenton-on-Sea, on the R72 coastal road, lies **Port Alfred.** Once a sleepy fishing village at the mouth of the Kowie River, Port Alfred today boasts a modern yacht harbor, with man-made islands and canals. Boat owners can either put out to sea or explore the river, which is navigable for some 17 miles (28 km). Several reefs along the coast offer excellent diving; Keryn's Diving School offers its services to novices.

Keryn's Diving School

✉ Small Boat Harbour, Port Alfred

☎ 082/692-6189

Cape buffalo, Lalibela Game Reserve

Lalibela Game Reserve

🅰 Map p. 119

✉ 56 miles (90 km) E of Port Elizabeth on N2

☎ 041/581-8170

💲 $$$$$

www.lalibela.co.za

Sibuya Game Reserve

🅰 Map p. 119

✉ Kenton-On-Sea, 80 miles (130 km) E of Port Elizabeth via R343

☎ 046/648-1040

💲 $$$$$

www.sibuya.co.za

Sibuya Game Reserve

Sibuya, meaning "we will return," is a 5,900-acre (2,400 ha), Big Four game reserve (minus the lion) and is accessed exclusively by riverboat. The ride will evoke scenes straight out of the film *The African Queen* with Humphrey Bogart and Katharine Hepburn.

Park in the reception area in Kenton-on-Sea. You'll be brought to the reserve and river camp by boat, a 7-mile trip (12 km) up the Kariega Estuary. The reserve is a luxury camp with tents on raised wooden decks in **River Camp;** and **Forest Camp,** considered slightly more upscale.

The region's East Cape valley bushveld, grasslands, and coastal areas play host to a myriad of animals, showcasing antelope (including the rare bontebok and oribi), giraffe, zebra, in addition to the Big Four. Sibuya is also a birder's paradise with nearly 300 species. Keep a special lookout for the elusive Narina trogan and rare bard owl.

You can go in search of all of them with the help of a professional guide, via game drive, river cruise, or guided bush walk. If it's rest and recreation you're after, you can also swim, canoe, take beach walks, and simply enjoy the lush surroundings.

Lalibela Game Reserve

Five of South Africa's seven ecosystems are found at the Lalibela Game Reserve, explaining its breathtaking diversity of flora and fauna. All kinds of animals, including the Big Five, spotted hyena, zebra, giraffe, antelope, hippo, and cheetah, roam free here on some 18,500 acres (7,500 ha). It's completely private; there are no public roads running through the property.

Lalibela has three game lodges: **Lentaba Lodge,** located on a hillside; **Mark's Camp,** with stone-and-thatch chalets; and **Tree Tops,** a camp with luxurious safari tents on high platforms overlooking the valley.

INSIDER TIP:

Don't be shy to go to game blinds in the heat of day—you may be surprised how many animals do come out then, and you are in the shade anyway.

—KEVIN HALL
National Geographic field researcher

Nearby Places

Located about 37 miles (60 km) inland from the coast in Settler Country, **Grahamstown** was founded in 1812 as a military stronghold for the protection of British settlers on the surrounding land from the Xhosas. But repeated Xhosa raids on British farms made many settlers give up their land and move to town. As a result, the population increased considerably. Today, Grahamstown has a population of 100,000. Its city center is attractive with many Victorian and Edwardian buildings, enlivened by a dynamic student crowd from Rhodes University.

The city celebrates many festivals each year. The **National Arts Festival** *(www.nationalartsfestival .co.za)* in July attracts more than 50,000 visitors from all over the country for the best of indigenous and other arts.

Bathurst, 25 miles (40 km) southeast of Grahamstown on the R67, is a small farming village founded in 1820 that has become a favorite artist haven. With its many preserved settler buildings, it still resembles a small English town of the early 19th century. Here you can buy handicrafts and art or attend the annual *oxbraai* (barbecue; *www.oxbraai.co.za*) in December, an all-day event. The town is also the hub for one of South Africa's main pineapple-growing areas. ∎

Grahamstown
⌖ Map p. 119
Visitor Information
✉ 63 High St., Grahamstown
☎ 046/622-3241
www.grahamstown .co.za

EXPERIENCE: Pray

A walk around Grahamstown, nicknamed the "City of Saints," will bring overwhelming rapture to the spiritually inclined, and confusing awe to the secular traveler. Within city limits you'll spy more than 40 places of worship, ranging from the more common (Roman Catholic, Presbyterian) to the lesser known (Pinkster Protestante, Apostolic). There are churches for Scientologists, Mormons, Baptists, Ethiopian Episcopalians, and others. The town's largest church is the **Cathedral of St. Michael and St. George** *(High St. at Church Sq.)* with South Africa's tallest spire, at 176 feet (54 m); Sunday services are at 7:30 and 9:30 a.m. Even if you aren't religious, the cathedral, built in 1824, is an undeniably beautiful and historically important monument. This and the many other churches, most of which are Christian, recall the age of the missionary.

Into the Karoo

Between the aptly named Valley of Desolation and the Sneeuberg range, the terrain begins to stretch into the vast and dry Karoo.

A silhouetted greater kudu, Mountain Zebra National Park

Mountain Zebra National Park

⧆ Map p. 119

✉ N of Port Elizabeth via N10 & R61

☎ 048/881-2427 or 048/881-3434

$ $$

www.sanparks.org/parks/mountain_zebra/

Karoo, a Khoisan word meaning "land of thirst," describes South Africa's immense central plateau, a land of wide-open skies, rugged mountains, and arid plains. It covers nearly one-third of South Africa, divided into the Klein Karoo in the south and the Great Karoo in the north. Once great herds of springbok trekked through the Karoo on annual migrations; today it is a semidesert, supporting little wildlife or livestock. For the visitor, though, mysterious rock art and ancient fossils, together with some of the world's best stargazing, make this a magical place.

Mountain Zebra National Park

North of Port Elizabeth, the Mountain Zebra National Park has become a much needed preserve for the cape mountain zebra. Only 11 of this species remained in the area when it was proclaimed a national park in 1937. These zebras differ from the plains or Burchell's zebras in that they have narrower stripes, an absence of shadow stripes, and a light orange facial coloration. Their population now stands at 350 animals.

Other mammals found here include eland, black wildebeest, red hartebeest, kudu, springbok, gemsbok, and two of the park's more recent reintroductions, the African buffalo and the black rhino. Game viewing takes place from your own car; guided game drives *(reservations are required, $$$)*, and short nature hikes can be arranged. You can stay in a guesthouse, cottage, or campsite.

Graaff-Reinet

The Eastern Cape's oldest town and the fourth oldest in South Africa, Graaff-Reinet lies in the heart of the Karoo along the Sundays River. It was founded in 1786 as an administrative center for the surrounding Boer farms by Governor Cornelius Jacob van de Graaff and his wife, Cornelia Reinet. More than 200 buildings remain from that early period and are listed as national monuments—ranging from gabled Cape Dutch houses and Victorian mansions to slave cottages. The **Reinet House** *(Naude & Murray Sts., tel 049/892-3801, $)*, originally a Dutch Reformed parsonage, is now a period museum depicting early life on the cape. The **Hester-Rupert Art Museum** *(Church St., tel 049/586-1030, $)*, a former Dutch mission church, showcases contemporary paintings and sculptures. The **Old Library** *(Church & Somerset Sts., tel 049/892-3801, $)* functions as a museum as well, with photographs, rock paintings, and fossils from the area.

Although Graaff-Reinet lies in the sandy plains with incredibly hot summers, it is surrounded by the green belt of **Camdeboo Park** *(tel 049/892-3453, $)*, located 5 miles (8 km) from Graaff-Reinet on the N9/Murraysburg Road. Within the park lie the **Nqweba Dam** and the **Valley of Desolation** with some spectacular rock formations. You'll likely spot antelope and communities of meerkats along the trails.

Nieu-Bethesda

Some 29 miles (50 km) north of Graaff-Reinet in the valley of the Sneeuberg mountains, this little hamlet has become a retreat for artists and other creative people, including Athol Fugard (b. 1932), whose play, *The Road to Mecca,* is based on the town.

Nieu-Bethesda itself is toured quickly: It has only a couple of main streets, no street lights, a few guesthouses, restaurants, a pub, and some art galleries.

The main draw is **Owl House** *(River St., tel 049/841-1733)*, home of eccentric recluse Helen Martins until her death in 1976. With the help of Koos Malgas, the untrained visionary artist transformed her house and surroundings into a gallery of unique glass and cement sculptures. ■

Graaff-Reinet
🗺 Map p. 119

Visitor Information
✉ Church St.
☎ 049/892-4248

www.graaffreinet.co.za

Nieu-Bethesda
🗺 Map p. 119

Visitor Information
✉ Martin St., Nieu-Bethesda
☎ 072/558-4883

www.nieubethesda.info

Afrikaans Phrases to Get You By

ja	Yes
nee	No
dankie	Thank you
asseblief	Please
totsiens	Goodbye
gesondheid!	Cheers!
lekker dag!	Have a nice day
Verskoon my! Jammer!	Excuse me

East London & Around

A rugged coastline and sandy beaches frame the former homeland of the Ciskei and Transkei, an area that has spawned many important black leaders.

Residents and visitors, East London Aquarium

East London

Map p. 119

Visitor Information

✉ Shop 1 &
2 King's
Entertainment
Center,
Esplanade

☎ 043/733-6015

**www.tourism
buffalocity.com**

East London
Museum

✉ 319 Oxford St.
(entrance on
Dawson Rd.)

☎ 043/743-0686

$ $

East London

East London is South Africa's only river port, set on the broad Buffalo River and often referred to as Buffalo City. The town of 250,000 boasts a population of more than 700,000 in the metropolitan area. During the Frontier Wars between the British, the Dutch, and the Xhosa, East London served as a supply base. The port also brought in droves of new settlers. Between 1858 and 1862, for example, some 3,400 German immigrants arrived in East London and were settled in already established villages in the Xhosa-speaking area. On the centennial of their arrival, the city fathers erected memorials to the German settlers in East London and King William's Town.

Today the city presents its past with a number of well-preserved examples of 19th-century architecture, such as **City Hall** (*Cambridge St.*), erected in 1899; and the **Daily Dispatch Building** (*Caxton & Cambridge Sts.*), which has printed newspapers since 1897.

Among the sights is the **East London Museum,** where an exhibit of a coelacanth is the big draw. This species of fish has lived in the Indian Ocean for 400 million years and was thought to be extinct, until it was rediscovered in 1938. The catch of a live coelacanth in the East London harbor was seen as the most significant zoological find of the century. Other exhibits include what may be a dodo egg, fossils, and trace human footprints.

The **Queen's Park Botanical Garden,** west of the city center, has a small zoo of some 250 animals, including a white lion. Pony rides are offered for children.

On the Esplanade, the small **East London Aquarium,** built in 1931, prides itself of being the oldest public aquarium in the country with displays of African penguins and denizens of the deep. A wooden boardwalk that protrudes from the foyer of the aquarium over the intertidal zone offers fantastic whale-watching

INSIDER TIP:

East London is the gateway to the largely undeveloped Eastern Cape. African Heartland Journeys (www.ahj.co.za) leads five-day tours to the region's green hills, coastal bluffs, and desolate beaches.

–DAVID CASE
National Geographic writer

during whale season along this point of the official **MTN Cape Whale Route** *(tel 083/910-1028).* Each year hundreds of southern right whales migrate here between June and November, and humpback whales between May and December. Best viewing opportunities are posted by a set of blue flags immediately after whales are sighted.

East London's long stretch of sandy beaches appeals to swimmers, sun worshipers, and especially surfers. In addition, visitors can easily reach other vacation destinations from here going to the Sunshine Coast (see p. 127) and the Wild Coast (see pp. 138–139) and make excursions inland to the Amatola Mountains that still hold some of the original Afromontane rain forests.

Nahoon Beach, north of the Nahoon River mouth, features miles of mostly uncrowded and unpolluted sand with excellent waves. The reef is challenging enough for skilled surfers that national surfing and waterskiing competitions are held there.

Just past the aquarium opposite Marina Glen, **Eastern Beach** has fast food restaurants, changing rooms, and impressive waves for surfers. It is so popular that on New Year's Eve as many as 400,000 people descend on this shore.

On the eastern side of the Buffalo River, **Orient Beach** used to be known as the Sandy Beach until the Russian vessel, the SS *Orient,* ran aground here in 1907. The beach is extremely safe because the breakwaters of the harbor make for a gentle surf. Visitors stroll on the Orient Pier, ride the Water Tube, and enjoy a filtered children's pool, changing facilities, and a refreshment stand.

More Nearby Beaches:
Bonza Bay's beach lies off the Quinera Lagoon, allowing for fishing, birding, and swimming. The high dunes keep areas well hidden,

Queen's Park Botanical Garden

✉ Turnberry Ave., Bunkers Hill

☎ 043/705-2637

East London Aquarium

✉ Esplanade

☎ 043/705-637

$ $

www.elaquarium.co.za

King William's Town

⚑ Map p. 119

Visitor Information

✉ Public Library,
Alexandria Rd.

☎ 034/642-3391

giving the beaches a private feel.

It's not a good swimming beach, but **Cove Rock,** west of the Buffalo River along the coastal road, attracts surfers and divers. Visitors come for the remarkable sandstone formations—a suitable cover for breeding seabirds. It is also a perfect fishing spot and whale-watching point. A beachfront walk from Cove Rock to Lagoon Valley takes about 45 minutes.

Gulu Beach, 2.5 miles (4 km) west of East London, is mostly visited by recreational anglers, but the beach at the Gulu River mouth offers safe swimming areas and is set up with life guards.

At **Igoda Beach,** 10.5 miles (17 km) west of East London, the safest areas for bathing are the river banks. The beach with its forested sand dunes and the nearby nature reserve each have trails for leisurely walks. The village of **Winterstrand** has secure parking for the beach.

King William's Town

Established in 1834 by the London Missionary Society as a mission station on the banks of the Buffalo River, King William's Town today boasts a population of mostly Xhosa from the former Ciskei homeland. Many of the town's buildings date back to the Frontier Wars.

The **Amathole Museum** *(Alexandria Rd.)* has a large collection of African mammals and excellent exhibits on the Xhosa culture. The **Missionary Museum** *(Berkeley St.)* was a former church and school where many of South Africa's profes-

Steve Biko

One prominent native of the area was Steve Biko, born in 1946 in the black township of Ginsberg just outside King William's Town, and leader of the black consciousness movement in the 1960s and early 1970s.

He was involved in the antiapartheid protests and strikes, which culminated in the Soweto Uprising of 1976. Frequently arrested, Steve Biko died while in police custody in 1977, after being held for 26 days under the Terrorism Act.

sional blacks were first educated. King William's Town, together with the nearby town of Bhisho—the administrative capital of the Eastern Cape and the former capital of the Ciskei—is closely associated with the struggles and protests of the apartheid era. Nelson Mandela and Thabo Mbeki, the former president and his successor, hail from the area.

Steve Biko (see sidebar above) is buried at King William's **Ginsberg Cemetery,** renovated as a Garden of Remembrance.

Nelson Mandela Route

The son of a Thembu chief, Nelson Mandela was raised in a traditional community and groomed to become a tribal leader himself. As the first child in his family to attend school, he eventually earned a law degree and, with Oliver Tambo, opened South Africa's first black law firm. At university he became involved in politics and later helped form the youth league of the African National Congress. Always at the forefront of the civil disobedience campaign against apartheid, Mandela, after various arrests, was brought to trial in 1964 for sabotage and fomenting revolution and sentenced to life imprisonment. Released in 1990, he continued to protest against apartheid. In 1994, in the first fully representative, democratic

Mandela studied, and moves on to the **Healdtown Institution** in Alice, where he completed his schooling. The route also visits **Bhisho,** home of the provincial government, and three sites that comprise the Nelson Mandela Museum.

Nelson Mandela Museum:

The museum opened on February 11, 2000, on the tenth anniversary of Mandela's release from prison. He insisted that the museum should not be a tribute to him, but should serve as a

Steve Biko Garden of Remembrance

✉ Cathcart St. S, turning left onto 1st road past bridge

☎ 043/642-1177 (Steve Biko Foundation)

www.sbf.org.za

Nelson Mandela Museum

✉ Nelson Mandela Dr. & Owen St., Mthatha

☎ 047/532-5110

🕐 Closed Sun.

💲 Donation

www.nelson mandelamuseum .org.za

At the Nelson Mandela Museum, Mthatha

elections, he was elected president of South Africa. He retired from government service in 1999.

For anyone wanting to learn more about this great man, who was born in the area and has made it his home, the Nelson Mandela Route *(mandela.wildcoast.org.za/ man)* has been established, linking sites related to his life.

The route begins at the **University of Fort Hare,** where

catalyst to uplift and develop the local community. The museum's three sites are: **Mvezo,** the tribal village where he was born; **Qunu,** the cluster of rural settlements where he grew up; and the magnificent **Bhunga Building** in Mthatha, the former capital of the Transkei. At the latter, an exhibit outlines the story of Mandela's life, as told in his autobiography, *A Long Walk to Freedom.* ■

Wild Coast

North along the Eastern Cape, between East London and Port Edward, stretches the largely unpopulated and beautifully untamed Wild Coast for some 218 miles (350 km). The shores with forested hills and plunging cliffs, wooded dunes and sandy beaches invite exploration. Along footpaths you will discover traditional Xhosa settlements and beachside villages.

Fishing off the rocky coastline of East London's outskirts

The village of **Gonubie,** a Xhosa name meaning "bramble berry," lies on the estuary of the Gonubie River about 5 miles (8 km) north-east of East London on the N2. When the tide is out, the lagoon's tidal pools disclose their little sea creatures. A long wooden walkway invites strolling, while protecting the primary dunes from human traffic. There's a flea market every first and last Saturday on the main road.

About 49 miles (75 km) north of East London, the village of **Haga-Haga** is surrounded by green hills and deep river valleys that descend onto the long, white beaches. From here, hikers can take the lower **Wild Coast Trail** south to Cintsa or north to Qora Mouth. The full trail of 53 miles (86 km) of scenic coastline is usually walked, with overnight stops, in six days.

Farther up the Coast

Moving up the coast, the beach resort of **Kei Mouth** lies on the bank of the Great Kei River. A few miles inland awaits **Morgan's Bay,** a village surrounded by steep cliffs separated from Kei Mouth by a nature reserve with a good swimming beach and protected lagoon. An old-fashioned pontoon ferry transports hikers and drivers with their cars across the Kei River to travel on to Coffee Bay or the legendary Hole in the Wall.

The **Strandloper Trail,** a 37-mile-long (60 km), five-day hiking trail, lets you relish the feeling of solitude on unspoiled beaches. The trail starts at Kei Mouth and wends its way down to Gonubie.

Mazeppa Bay, 25 miles (40 km) up the coast from Morgan's

Bay, is famous for its excellent fishing. The largest fish caught in the bay was a 1,744-pound (791 kg) great white shark, in 1981. The most popular beach is **First Beach;** from here you can walk across a 328-foot-high (100 m) suspension bridge to reach Mazeppa Bay's island. The other two main beaches lie to the south of the lagoon and are ideal for long walks and beachcombing.

Hole in the Wall

This towering cliff at Coffee Bay, up the coast some 50 miles (80 km) from Mazeppa Bay, has a large opening carved through its center by the waves. The Xhosa call it "place of thunder." During high tide in stormy conditions, the waves thud so loudly that the impact can be heard throughout the valley.

Xhosa legend attributes the hole to the "sea people" who look like humans but have flipperlike limbs. Once a beautiful girl from the village was wooed by one of the sea people. Her father objected, but the sea people enlisted the help of a big fish that battered its way headfirst through the rock wall. The sea people spilled through the wall and swept the Xhosa girl away.

Port St. Johns

On the coast 35 miles (56 km) east of Coffee Bay, the Thesiger and Sullivan mountains along the Umzimvubu River mouth are

called the gates of Port St. Johns. The laid-back town is a magnet for hippies, eccentrics, and backpackers. Three good beaches, excellent fishing, and a rather colorful history, involving smuggling in colonial times and illicit growing of cannabis more recently, might be the draw.

In town you may hear the thumping of the *kwaito* rhythms of the local Xhosa or meet a *sangoma* (traditional healer) in full dress on the street. ∎

Wild Coast

🗺 Map p. 119

Visitor Information

☎ 043/722-2203; e-mail: info@ wildcoast.org.za

www.wildcoast .org.za

Port St. Johns

🗺 Map p. 119

Visitor Information

✉ Main road in town

☎ 047/564-1187

www.portstjohns .org.za

Wacky Point

Wacky Point, to the right of the main beach at Kei Mouth, is a great surfing spot where the annual Wacky Point Surf Competition is held.

For landlubbers, the folks at Sunray Farm arrange horseback rides along the beach to Morgan's Bay cliff top or along the Kei River mouth.

Contact **Sunray Farm** *(Key Mouth Rd., Haga Haga, tel 043/831-1087).*

INSIDER TIP:

Spend two days in a village of Xhosa tribesmen, where you'll learn their rituals, sleep in thatched huts, and toast the trip with a glass of home-brewed corn beer.

—DAVID CASE
National Geographic writer

Rich in Zulu tradition, bustling with Durban city life, a region of spectacular mountains, surfing beaches, and wildlife-rich wetland parks

Durban &
KwaZulu-Natal

A Zulu woman weaving hats and baskets

Durban & KwaZulu-Natal

KwaZulu-Natal (kwah zoo loo nuh-TAL), simply referred to by the locals as KZN, is the most northerly east coast province of South Africa, extending from the Eastern Cape in the south to the country of Mozambique in the north.

The Amphitheater in the northern Drakensberg

This subtropical paradise gives visitors a taste of the true Africa. The red soil, the flat-topped acacias, the heat, and humidity all combine to give KZN the look and feel of more distant and exotic parts of Africa such as neighboring Mozambique, or Kenya.

Between the Tugela and the Pongola Rivers, traditional Zulu settlements dominate. You'll see a landscape dotted with thatched-roof woven rondavel homes placed around cattle kraals and enclosed by stick fencing.

The narrow lowlands along the Indian Ocean in the south widen in the northern region, giving way to a hilly plateau in the central region, the Natal Midlands. Two mountainous areas distinguish the landscape: the Drakensberg in the west and the Lebombo Mountains in the north. The Drakensberg is actually a jagged wall of basalt that rises to 11,422 feet (3,482 m) near the border with Lesotho. The Lebombo Mountains form long ranges of volcanic rock, running southward from Swaziland.

Along the deep ravines of the coastal region grows Afromontane forest, changing to moist grasslands and rolling hills from the area of the Valley of a Thousand Hills to the Midlands. Vast savannas reign in the north, and the Drakensberg region largely consists of alpine grasslands.

The coastal region has a humid, subtropical climate, becoming increasingly more tropical farther north along the coast toward the border with Mozambique.

Visiting KZN

The province's cosmopolitan heart is Durban, the country's third largest city and one of the busiest ports. Since the end of apartheid, people from the far corners of the provinces and the rest of the world have streamed to Durban, making the city center a hub of modern architecture, shantytowns, Victorian

NOT TO BE MISSED:

Durban's Golden Mile   146–147

A spice-filled Indian bazaar in Durban   148, 151

A dive in Aliwal Shoal, where you can spot coral, sponges, and the ragged-tooth shark   152

The warm waters of the beautiful South Coast beaches   154–155

A Zulu village visit   156

Seeing San rock art in the Drakensberg   158–159

The eeriness of Golden Gate Highlands   160–161

The hippos, crocodiles, and loggerhead and leatherback turtles of the St. Lucia wetlands   164–166

buildings, mosques, temples, and bazaars.

Nearby await glorious beaches, Widenham, Scottburgh, Ramsgate, and Marina Beach among them. The Valley of a Thousand Hills is home to the Zulu who carry on in a traditional way of life.

Just beyond beckons a taste of wild Africa: the uKhahlamba-Drakensberg National Park, encompassing the striking Drakensberg mountains, selected as a UNESCO World Heritage site for their exceptional natural beauty and diversity of habitats. Some 600 rock faces and caves in the park harbor ancient rock paintings made by the San people some 4,000 years ago. Here, too, is the Hluhluwe-iMfolozi Park, one of the country's oldest reserves.

North along the coast, the iSimangaliso Wetland

Park encompasses several protected areas, including the Maphelane and Kosi Bay Nature Reserves, where subtropical coastline, wetlands, and tropical forest support an enormous diversity of species.

This northeastern niche along the coast is nicknamed the Elephant Coast, for the herds of elephants that reside here. See them up close at the Mkhuze Game Reserve, along Zululand's northeastern corner, and nearby Tembe Elephant Reserve; both offer wildlife drives. ■

Durban

Durban was named after the 19th-century English governor Sir Benjamin D'Urban. Until construction of the Suez Canal, England's ships traveled the long way around the cape, and Durban was a desirable stopover for civil servants and army officers heading toward or away from India. At one time Durban was nicknamed "the last outpost of the British Empire," and the colonial influence is evident in its Victorian cityscape.

The imposing Durban City Hall, modeled on the city hall in Belfast, Northern Ireland

Durban

⚠ Map p. 143

Visitor Information

✉ 160 Pine St., Ste. 303

☎ 031/366-7500

www.durban.kzn .org.za

Durban is the third largest city in South Africa, with a population of 3.5 million that is rapidly expanding to ever farther outlying suburbs. The city is a thriving industrial center and the busiest seaport in Africa.

Durban moves to a modern African beat with a great racial mix of people, many of whom flooded into town after suspension of apartheid's population influx controls. The defining culture is that of the Zulus, the warrior tribes of the "Sons of Heaven" who dominated

the area until the British subdued them in the late 19th century. Today about 63 percent of Durban's residents speak Zulu at home. A high percentage of Indian immigrants has left its stamp on the city as well, with Hindu temples, Muslim mosques, and bazaars. Many Indians arrived more than a century ago as indentured servants to work in the sugarcane fields.

Golden Mile

The main draw in Durban is its beachfront and promenade,

the several-mile-long Golden Mile (see pp. 146–147), with its high-rise hotels and tony and funky restaurants.

Sea World, at the enormous **uShaka Marine World** theme park, located at the foot of the Golden Mile, will give you a fore-taste of what can be found in the quieter bays and coves along the outlying beaches. The displays in-clude a saltwater aquarium, dolphin stadium, seal stadium, and penguin rookery. The **Offshore Rocky Reefs Exhibit** presents rare reef fish of the KwaZulu-Natal coast, and the **Rocky Touch Pool** allows visitors to touch sea stars and sea cucumbers. **Exhibits of the Deep Zone** show off creatures of the darkest deep. You can even experi-ence sharks up close in Sea World's **Xpanda Shark Cage** (*$$$$*).

Here, too, you'll find the typical theme park attractions, including wa-terslides and rides. The Village Walk teems with restaurants and shops.

City Center

In the city center, the neo-baroque **City Hall,** a copy of the city hall in Belfast, Ireland, domi-nates Francis Farewell Square. The **Natural Science Museum** (*City Hall, 1st fl., Smith St., tel 031/311-2256*) is in the same building, showcasing an array of African mammals, birds, and insects. On the second floor, the **Durban Art Gallery** exhibits works by contemporary South African art-ists, including Andrew Verster (b. 1937) and Penny Siopis (b. 1953), and has a significant collection of Zulu arts and crafts, besides European traditional

and contemporary arts. Every Wednesday at 1 p.m., musical, song, and dance performances are held on the steps of City Hall.

Alongside City Hall is Durban's **Old Court House Museum** (*Smith & Aliwal Sts., tel 031/311-2229*), housed in the first public building erected in Durban, in 1866. Exhibits highlight the Natal region's colonial history, as well as some of Durban's most famous figures (keep an eye out for Zulu King Shaka; see p. 27).

INSIDER TIP:

Sunrises over the Indian Ocean from Durban are a photographer's favorite, with fisher-men on the piers and great views of surfers and the fantastic Golden Mile skyline.

—JOHN SEATON CALLAHAN
National Geographic contributor

A block away on Church Square sits the neo-Gothic **St. Paul's Church** (*Pine St., tel 031/305-4666*)—and its vicarage—built in 1853 and rebuilt in 1906 after a fire. Plaques commemorate many of the early settlers. The church served also as a mission to seamen.

Around Victoria Embankment

Along Victoria Embankment, **Wilson's Wharf,** a new development, is thronged with youthful crowds, charter boats,

uShaka Marine World

✉ 1 Bell St.
☎ 031/328-8000
$ $$$
www.ushakamarine world.co.za

Durban Art Gallery

✉ City Hall, 2nd fl., Smith St.
☎ 031/311-2264/9
🕐 Contact one week before visit to schedule a tour.

The Golden Mile

The Golden Mile—a glitzy stretch of beach and promenade in Durban that's actually 3.7 miles long (6 km)—runs from the Bay of Plenty and North Beach to South Beach, parallel to the business district. Behind the golden sands sprawl row upon row of luxury high-rise hotels.

Bright lights along Durban's Golden Mile

The name derives from Portuguese explorers who referred to the sea sand along the coast in this areas as "sands of gold."

The beaches are separated by a number of piers and protected year-round by lifeguards. Nets placed in the deep water prevent sharks from coming near the swimmers. The Golden Mile is also popular among surfers, especially North Beach, Dairy Beach, and the Bay of Plenty, with South Beach considered a perfect spot for neophytes. Dozens of swimming and splash pools, fountains,

waterslides, souvenir stands, and merry-go-rounds line the beachfront. All along the way, you'll find vendors and hawkers with Zulu arts and crafts.

Begin your stroll at **Natal Command ❶**, at the corner of Argyle and Snell Parade, at the Golden Mile's north end, which turns into Marine Parade.

Nearby, **Minitown ❷** (*114 Snell Parade, Lower Marine Parade, North Beach, tel 031/337-7892, closed Mon., $*) presents Durban's most interesting buildings in miniature form, with

Zulu Rickshaws

Hop aboard a gaudily painted Zulu
rickshaw, driven by a colorfully cos-
tumed puller, for a truly unique ride
along the beachfront.

▲ Also see area map p. 143
► Natal Command
↔ 0.5 mile
🕐 2 hours
► uShaka Marine World

models scaled down to ¹⁄₂₅ their size, including
a small working train and an airport.

As you amble farther south, the **Bay of
Plenty** is to your left, a world-famous surfing
beach, home to the famous Gunston Surfing
Contest in July; it also holds the world's only
night surfing contest.

Wander through the **Sunken Garden and
Amphitheatre ③** opposite the North Beach
Garden Court to Central Marine Parade. The
sunken garden has pretty flowers, ponds, and
fountains; at night, it's illuminated. If you're
lucky, you'll catch a concert at the open-air
amphitheater. On Sundays a flea market is
usually underway.

At the junction with Old Fort Road, a stat-
ue honors Bartolomeu Dias, the Portuguese
explorer who in 1488 sailed his ship as far as
Algoa Bay. He is said to have inspired Vasco da
Gama to sail onward. Da Gama reached the
Natal Coast on Christmas Day 1497.

Backtrack to the Lower Marine Parade
and proceed farther south along the
beachfront.

At the end of the Golden Mile on South
Beach lies the **uShaka Marine World ④** (see
p. 145), Africa's largest marine theme park,
with a Sea World exhibit complete with an
aquarium and other water displays. It also runs
a rehabilitation program for injured marine life.

NOT TO BE MISSED:

**Bay of Plenty • Sunken Garden
and Amphitheatre • uShaka
Marine World**

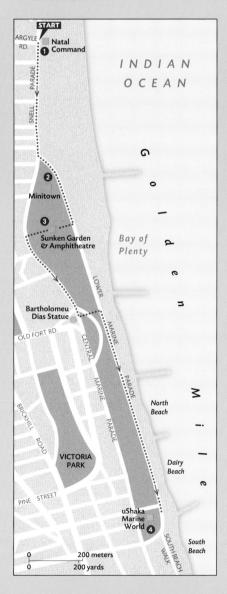

**Bartel Arts
Trust Centre**

✉ SAS Inkonkoni
Bldg., 45
Maritime Place,
Small Craft
Harbour, Victoria
Embankment

☎ 031/332-0468

www.batccentre
.co.za

**Durban Botanic
Gardens**

✉ Sydenham Rd.,
off M8 in Berea

☎ 031/201-1303

www.durbanbot
gardens.org.za

restaurants, theaters, and stores. A vibrant community art center, the **Bartel Arts Trust** (BAT) focuses on local arts and crafts that reflect the heritage of KwaZulu-Natal. Open studios, upscale art galleries, and hip restaurants enliven the scene.

Bluebottles

Beware of gelatinous blobs stuck in the sand along Durban's Golden Mile. They might be blue-bottles, Durban slang for a Portuguese man-of-war. This nasty little inverte-brate is not a jellyfish, as commonly thought, but actually a colony of miniscule siphonophora. The sting of a man-of-war is particularly painful, frequently resulting in death. The peculiar name comes from the organ-ism's air bladder, used to aid tidal propulsion, which resembles the sail of an old Portuguese galleon.

Durban Botanic Gardens

Spreading across 35.8 acres (14.5 ha), Durban Botanic Gardens are a treasure house of Africa's indigenous plants. Established in 1851, the well-maintained gardens are the city's oldest natural attrac-tion and the oldest surviving botanic garden in Africa. The collection of some 150,000 different plants focuses on orchids, cycads, and palms, but there is also an impressive

bromeliad collection and a mixed arboretum of African, American, and Asian trees. Of particular concern are plants threatened with extinction.

A lake area, a sunken garden, a fern dell, and a teahouse make the visit a tranquil excursion.

Located between Sydenham and St. Thomas Hill Roads, at the foot of the Berea (a ridge above the city), the gardens are easily reached from downtown; it is only a few minutes' walk from the Warwick Triangle.

Indian District

Indians account for close to 20 percent of Durban's population, composing the largest Indian population outside of Asia, and their cultural impact clearly marks this section of town. The **Juma Masjid Mosque** (Grey & Queen Sts., tel 031/306-1774, closed Sun.) towers above the lively neighbor-hood with two gilded minarets. It is the largest mosque in the Southern Hemisphere and can hold up to 4,500 worshipers. Call ahead for a tour.

Around the corner from the mosque, in the narrow alley between Grey Street and Cathedral Road, the crowded **Madressa Ar-cade** bazaar is arrayed with mounds of spices, colorful fabrics, and other Indian ware. A few stalls also sell African music and mysterious bits pertaining to African magic.

Along Grey Street, several Indian food stores specialize in the unique Durban sandwich called "bunnychow," which is half a scooped-out loaf of bread filled with meat or vegetarian curries.

Carefully measuring out spices in the Victoria Street Market

Killie Campbell Museum & Africana Collection

✉ 220 Marriott Rd.

☎ 031/260-1720

🕐 House tours by appt. only

$ $

http://campbell.ukzn.ac.za

On the corner of Queen and Victoria Streets, the 160 stalls of the brightly painted **Victoria Street Market** offer a pungent whiff of India redolent from meat and fish, fruits and vegetables, and spices and incense. You'll also find woven baskets, carved wooden objects, and many other South Asian goods.

Durban boasts more than 20 Hindu temples. The imposing **Shree Ambalavaanar Alayam Hindu Temple** (*Bellair Rd., Umkumbaan, Cato Minor, tel 031/311-1111*) lies a bit beyond the Indian quarter, but it is well worth a visit. Built in 1883, it is the oldest and largest Hindu temple in South Africa.

Killie Campbell Museum & Africana Collection

The Killie Campbell Collection presents three major research sources on the history and culture of KwaZulu-Natal. Housed in **Muckleneck,** the neo–Dutch Cape estate of Natal sugar baron and politician Sir Marshall Campbell (1848–1917),

the collections consist of the Killie Campbell Africana Library, the William Campbell Furniture and Picture Collection, and the Mashu Museum of Ethnology.

INSIDER TIP:

You can't leave the Indian District without having tried bunny-chow, a local fast food dish of curry served in a hollowed-out bread loaf.

—ROBERTA COCI
National Geographic contributor

The collections were established by Sir Marshall's daughter, well-known Africana collector Dr. (Margaret) Killie Campbell. Her brother William donated Muckleneck as a repository for his sister's collections, which have been administered by the University of KwaZulu-Natal since her death in 1965.

The **Killie Campbell Africana Library**'s main subject areas broadly cover holdings on the socioeconomic, political, and cultural history of KwaZulu-Natal. Areas of specialization include early exploration and travel in Africa, Christian missions, the Anglo-Zulu War, the Anglo-Boer War, the 1906 Bhambatha Uprisings, and the James Stuart Archives,

Helena. The Cape Dutch furniture is considered to be among the finest in a public collection ouside of the cape. The extensive picture collection includes both contemporary black art by such artists as Azaria Mbatha (b. 1941), Trevor Makhoba (b. 1956), and George Msimang (b. 1948), as well as topographical

Inside the Campbell Furniture and Picture Collection

which cover Zulu oral histories. The collections are used by national and international researchers as well as the general public.

The **William Campbell Furniture and Picture Collection** showcases the furnishings of Muckleneck during the time when the family still lived there. Some items are interesting for the historical importance of their former owners: for example, a stool carved by Dinizulu, the Zulu king, while detained on the island of St.

views of 19th-century South African flora and fauna by Africana artists like William John Burchell (1781–1863), Thomas Baines (1820–1875), and Samuel Daniels (1775–1811).

The **Mashu Museum of Ethnology** contains a fine collection of Zulu cultural artifacts, wood carvings, sculpture, pottery, costumes, and beadwork. The costume studies of indigenous African dress by artist Barbara Tyrrell (b. 1912) are considered a highlight of the collections.

It is possible to observe more than 200 bird species around Durban. Pelagic birding trips from the Umgeni River Bird Park are offered, providing a relaxed opportunity to enjoy the birds.

—CAGAN H. SEKERCIOGLU
National Geographic field researcher

Umgeni River Bird Park

Just a ten-minute drive from the city center, the Umgeni River Bird Park rates among the world's top aviaries and refuges. About 1,000 birds of more than 240 different species from all over the world nest along the thickly vegetated Umgeni River, about 0.7 mile (1 km) from the river mouth. The Umgeni River Bird Park is also involved in the breeding of rare and endangered bird species.

The many pathways winding through lush subtropical vegetation, past sparkling waterfalls, make it easy for visitors to spot louries (touracos), cockatoos, various parrot species, and other indigenous birds. Walk-through aviaries and open paddocks allow for views of macaws, kookaburras, toucans, flamingos, and critically endangered species such as the wattled crane. At the free-flight bird shows (*daily 11 a.m. & 2 p.m.*), you can observe owls, storks, hornbills, and cape vultures in unrestricted flight. During breeding season, a window allows views into the "baby room," where young chicks are fed hourly by the staff.

The Cockatoo Café in the tea garden offers breakfast and light meals in a surrounding of brilliantly plumaged birds and echoing birdcalls. ∎

Umgeni River Bird Park

🅰 Map p. 143

✉ 490 Riverside Rd., off M4, Durban north

☎ 031/579-4600

💲 $

www.umgeniriverbirdpark.co.za

Spice Nation

When the British came to Durban in the 19th century, they brought an Indian workforce. And with the Indians came spices—after all, India produces 86 percent of the world's spices.

Historically, Durban was the largest port in Africa, and naturally it had a major role to play in the spice trade. Before the Suez Canal was completed in 1869, all ships coming from Europe went around Africa and stopped in Durban before heading to the East Indies.

For all these reasons, you'll find amazing spices in Durban and tantalizingly hot and spicy dishes made with those spices. Among the most famous dishes is Durban curry, made of red chilies and cayenne pepper (making it more red than its Indian counterpart).

If you want to do some spice shopping, **Victoria Street Market,** on the corner of Victoria and Queen Streets, is the place to go. Stalls and stalls display their wares of exotic spices in granular pyramids out in the open. Some are pure—saffron or cayenne pepper—and some are local blends, such as the oddly named "mother-in-law exterminator" and "honeymoon BBQ."

For an on-the-spot spicy snack, pick up some samosas (pastries filled with curry) or bunnychow.

Underwater Delights

South Africa's east coast along the Indian Ocean, warmed by the Aghulas Current, has the perfect environment for all kinds of water sports. But the shore, reefs, and rocky coves of the KwaZulu-Natal are perhaps most famous for their supreme snorkeling and diving. Here are some of the best places to take the plunge.

Scuba diver and Devil firefish, Sodwana Bay

Kosi Bay (see pp. 166–167), an estuary on the Mozambique border, consists of four inter-linked lakes, part of the iSimangaliso (a Zulu word for "marvel") Wetland Park, formerly known as Greater St. Lucia Wetland Park, a UNESCO World Heritage site. The park is renowned for its diverse marine flora and fauna, including the endangered leatherback and loggerhead turtles, crocodiles, and hip-popotamuses. There's good snorkeling in the coral reefs in the Kosi River mouth, where you might spot poisonous stonefish.

Slightly farther south, but still part of iSimangaliso, is **Sodwana Bay** (see sidebar opposite). Here the coral reefs, the southern-most in Africa, are named after their distance from the beach: 2-Mile to 9-Mile. Perhaps the

most scenic one is 7-Mile Reef. Conditions at Sodwana are suitable for diving year-round but are best in summer from November to May.

Divers from around the world have named **Aliwal Shoal** (see sidebar opposite) one of the world's top 10 dive sites. It's a 40-minute drive south of Durban, near Umkomaas. The shoal is a fossilized sand dune and lies 2.5 miles (4 km) offshore. Named for the shipwrecked *Aliwal*, which ran aground here in 1849 (with several others to follow), the area is full of ledges and caves where divers can find a variety of sponges, soft and hard corals, both warm-water reef fish and cold water fish, besides the ragged-tooth shark.

Farther south at the Eastern Cape on **Pro-tea Banks,** about 5 miles (8 km) offshore from

Shelly Beach, divers find another world-class site. Starting at a depth of 82 feet (25 m), divers may spot Zambezi, tiger and hammerhead sharks in summer, ragged-tooth sharks in winter, along with copper sharks, threshers, and great whites. The caves are filled with hard and soft corals.

At the very end of the Eastern Cape, at the **Tsitsikamma National Park** (see p. 114), the first proclaimed marine national park in South Africa, snorkelers find tidal pools covered with sea stars, sponges, and mollusks. Deep-water species include ragged-tooth sharks and eagle rays.

Beyond KZN

Cape Town offers excellent diving opportunities year-round because the peninsula has the cold Atlantic Ocean on one side (better in summer) and the warmer Indian Ocean on the other side (better in winter). Diving on the cold side, means chilly waters but beautiful kelp forests. The west coast is uniformly cold except for the slightly milder **Langebaan Lagoon** (see pp. 90–91), about an hour's drive north of Cape Town on the west coast.

Near Mafikeng in the North West Province,

Wondergat (Wonder Cave) is a water-filled sinkhole, a popular inland diving site. At about 4,800 feet (1,460 m) above sea level and descending to a depth of 130 feet (40 m), divers can find rare cave shrimp and a unique species

known as the banded tilapia. Wondergat is periodically closed for clean-up, so be sure to check beforehand.

There are diving schools in almost every center in the country, offering day dives, short courses, and rental equipment.

EXPERIENCE: Diving at KZN's Best Spots

Sodwana Bay and Aliwal Shoal offer some of the most exciting diving opportunities in South Africa. Divers flock from all over the world to experience the rich diversity of the marine life on display. Here's where to go:

SODWANA BAY
7-Mile Reef: Full of drop-offs and pinnacles offering views of the rich marine life. More than 1,200 species of fish have been identified here. Expect to see scorpionfish, pufferfish, rays, and the rare paper fish.
Anton's Reef (2-Mile Reef): A phenomenal variety of tropical fish and corals can be found here.

Pinnacles: A shallow dive featuring a labyrinth of cavelike coral formations. Not to be missed: Loggerhead and leatherback turtles come out of the sea on summer nights to nest on the beaches. Contact Elephant Coast tourism *(tel 035/562-0353)*.

ALIWAL SHOAL
Cathedral: An amphitheater in the reef, filled with

rays, eels, and ragged-tooth sharks.
The Nebo: A shipwreck fairly covered in soft corals and sponges.
Raggies Cave: A cave teeming with ragged-tooth sharks. Contact Aliwal Shoal Dive Centre *(tel 039/973-2233, www.aliwalshoal.co.za)* or South Coast tourism *(tel 039/312-2322)*.

Around Durban

Durban is the ideal hub for exploratory forays in all directions. The beaches north and south of the city boast miles of undisturbed sand and surf. To the north await traditional rural Zulu villages and extensive national parks showcasing unique wildlife far beyond the Big Five.

The award-winning beach at Margate

Umdoni Coast

🅰 Map p. 143

Visitor Information

✉ Scott St.,
   Scottburgh

☎ 039/976-1364

**www.scottburgh
.co.za**

Hibiscus Coast

🅰 Map p. 143

Visitor Information

✉ Panorama
   Parade,
   Margate

☎ 039/312-2322

**www.hibiscuscoast
.kzn.org.za**

South Coast Beaches

The South Coast is a 100-mile-long (160 km) run of beaches and cheek-by-jowl seaside resorts leading from Durban to Port Elizabeth. The coast once called Ugu—the "edge of the great water"—by the Zulu, now has its share of beach hotels and developments and is lush with banana trees, palms, thorn trees, and lianas. Many of the beaches are attracting visitors from as far away as Johannesburg.

About 28 miles (45 km) south of Durban and just beyond the town of Umkomaas lies a sheltered surfing and bathing beach at **Widenham,** with quaint and upscale vacation homes above the beach.

A bit farther south, **Scottburgh** is a thriving resort town. Its bathing beach is manned by lifeguards and fully equipped with shark nets. The waves allow for great surfing, windsurfing, and body-boarding. The former fishing port is still a paradise for sport fishers.

Pennington incorporates the quiet beaches and beautiful bays of Umdoni Park, Ocean View, Kelso, Sezela, Bazely Beach, Ifafa, Elysium, and Mtwalume.

The area from Hibberdene to Port Edward is called the **Hisbiscus Coast,** for the profusion of those blooming shrubs, and includes Port Shepstone, Shelly Beach, Margate, Southbroom, and Port Trafalgar, all with wonderful beaches and the facilities of full-fledged resorts.

A great hub of beach resorts, **Margate** beckons 13 miles (20 km) southeast of Port Shepstone. The mile-long (1.6 km) beachfront won blue flag status for the town, ranking it among the world's finest. Fashionable boutiques and arty little shops abound, and by sundown "the Strip" comes alive with crowds and music along sidewalk cafés, restaurants, bars, and clubs, belting out the latest dance tunes for all-night raves.

By contrast, **Ramsgate** is a small village south of Margate. Its beaches along a parklike setting provide a peaceful getaway.

Marina Beach, at the southern end of the province, boasts a long sandy beach and a lovely tidal pool between Southbroom and San Lameer. Its proximity to the Trafalgar Marine Reserve and Mpenjati River mouth and lagoon makes it a particularly attractive destination.

Valley of a Thousand Hills

Halfway between Durban and Pietermaritzburg, the poetically named Valley of a Thousand Hills lies on the edge of densely folded hills that stretch as far as the eye can see. Here, Zulu people still live in traditional villages.

The valley's beauty and tranquillity have long attracted artists and

Valley of a Thousand Hills

⬛ Map p. 143

Visitor Information

✉ 690 T1

☎ 031/777-1874

www.1000hills.kzn .org.za

EXPERIENCE: Hit a Hole in One

KwaZulu-Natal's divine subtropical coastline sets the scene for one of South Africa's most coveted golf destinations. Here are some of the best courses to play.

Amanzimtoti (1 Golf Course Rd., Athlone Park, tel 031/902-1166) is a slicer's paradise because so many holes favor a fade. The last three holes are tough when the wind is up.

Durban Country Club (101 Walter Gilbert Rd., tel 031/313-1777, www.dcclub .co.za) has two courses: the Country Club and the Beachwood. Ranked fourth in South Africa, they are carved into the dunes and both are demanding.

Kloof Country Club (26 Victory Rd., Kloof, tel 031/764-0555, www .kloofcountryclub.co.za), in the hilly mist belt, provides a welcome retreat from coastal humidity. An attractive parkland course with lovely trees, Kloof integrates natural beauty with challenging hazards.

Margate Country Club (Wingate Rd., Margate, tel 039/317-2340, www.mar gategolf.co.za) looks easy but is extremely challenging; it's a delightful course, with water features. The five par-3s are striking and highly regarded.

Royal Durban (16 Mitchell Crest, Durban, tel 031/ 309-2581, www.royaldurban .co.za) is flat, but one of the most demanding courses in the country. It looks easy, but there's little protection from the wind.

San Lameer (Main Rd., Lower South Coast, San Lameer Estate, tel 039/313-5141, www.sanlameer.co.za) is rated in South Africa's top 30. Set in a nature conservation area with rich bird- and animal life, the course features plenty of water. Play conservative golf.

At **Scottburgh's** (Taylor & Williamson Sts., Scottburgh, tel 039/976-0041, www. scottburghgolf.co.za) undulating course, the Indian Ocean is in the background. The course has narrow fairways with out-of-bounds on the right and coastal forest on the left. Many a golfer's heart has been broken by the wind.

Umgeni Steam Railways

🅐 Map p. 143

✉ Kloof Station

☎ 031/303-3003 or 082/353-6003

$ $$$–$$$$

www.umgenisteam railway.co.za

Isithumba Village

🅐 Map p. 143

✉ Isithumba Adventure Tourism, District, Road D1004, Botha's Hill

☎ 031/777-7167 or 073/303-6288

www.isithumba.co.za

artisans, who still ply their crafts today producing pottery and leather sandals, hand-painted fabrics, wooden furniture, and intricate beadwork. Stalls along **Old Main Road** in the Hillcrest and Botha's Hill areas sell these craft items, as well as fresh farm produce, homemade jams, and pickles.

For a nostalgic tour of the valley—and one of the most scenic train rides in South Africa—hop aboard the **Umgeni Steam Railways.** The one-hour trip from Kloof Station to Inchanga Station heads up some of the steepest railway gradients in South Africa, through one of the oldest tunnels. Dating from 1893, Inchanga Station sits in the tranquil surroundings of the lower Midlands.

Two Zulu cultural villages are set up to receive tourists in the Botha's Hill area of the valley. At **Isithumba Village,** in the KwaXimba Tribal Authority, experienced guides take you into Zulu homes, the thatched-roof rondavels. Share a traditional meal, attend dances, watch a *sangoma* (traditional healer) perform, and spend the night in modern chalets with en suite bathrooms at the Adventure Tourism Center.

To reach the village, turn off Old Main Road past Monteseel onto District Road D1004. Follow the road into the valley; the center is on the banks of the Umgeni River.

Or head to the nearby **Phezulu Safari Park** (*5 Old Main Rd., Botha's Hill area, tel 031/777-1000, www .phezulusafaripark.co.za),* where you can attend traditional Zulu dances and visit the kraals. You can also visit a snake farm and crocodile farm. ∎

EXPERIENCE: Consult a *Sangoma*

The idea of sitting across from a beaded, feathered man, who chants, blows, and waves a leather whip while throwing bones in your direction, may be intimidating but makes for a unique cultural experience. *Sangomas,* or traditional healers, are an integral part in Nguni culture, as they are said to possess the power to communicate with ancestral spirits, who are revered and believed to guide daily life. Although Nguni people make regular sacrifices to keep their ancestors happy, the desired result is not always achieved. That's when a sangoma will step in. Armed with the voices of the ancestors and the help of a herbalist, or iNyanga, a sangoma is able to predict the future and diagnose and cure illnesses. While the questionable activities of

several sangomas have cast the tradition in a negative light in recent years, "good" sangomas still abound, often being hailed as more effective than Western doctors.

If you are looking for spiritual guidance on a tough decision or a unique experience, make reservations to see **Dr. Elliot Ndlovu** at the **Fordoun Spa Hotel** in the Midlands (*Nottingham Rd., tel 033/266-6217, www.fordoun.com, $$$$$ per session).* In the Cape Town area, contact **Zibonele Tours** (*tel 021/511-4263, www.ziboneletours.com, $$$$$ for tour),* which runs a half-day township tour daily, including a consultation with a sangoma by the name of Ndaba. In Johannesburg, contact **A Taste of Africa** (*tel 011/482-8114, www.tasteofafrica .co.za, $$$–$$$$).*

The Real Africa

The untamed Africa with its rugged mountains, wide savannas, and beautiful wildlife begins here. Long-established farmers and tribal people live a simple life, set to nature's rhythm.

The spectacular Drakensberg

The Drakensberg

Tracing South Africa's Eastern Escarpment for some 600 miles (965 km), dividing KwaZulu-Natal from Lesotho, the Drakensberg mountains—"dragon mountains," in Afrikaans—are a stunning, unpopulated wilderness of alpine grasslands and forests, waterfalls and rivers. You could hike for days on end and not come across a soul.

The variety in topography of this wall of rock, ranging from 4,200 feet (1,720 m) to nearly 11,500 feet (3,500 m), makes for the flora's great diversity. In the higher altitudes, endemic and endangered species of alpine flora predominate, and in the valleys, proteas, cycads,

fern trees, cabbage trees, and yellow-woods prevail.

The breadth of wildlife that you'll see here is breathtaking as well, ranging from baboons to several species of antelope—eland, rhebok, reedbuck, bushbuck, blue duiker, klipspringer, and oribi—and jackals, lynx, and otters.

Of the 299 species of birds, 43 species are endemic, with 10 species of global conservation importance, including the whitewinged flufftail, cape parrot, corncrake, lesser kestrel, wattled crane, and yellow-breasted pipit. Among the more common birds here are kingfishers, storks, secretary birds, nightjars, shrikes, and weavers.

Activites run the gamut, with

The Drakensberg
M Map p. 143

Visitor Information
☎ 036/448-1557 or 036/448-2455 or 083/485-7808

www.drakensberg .co.za

Kamberg Game Reserve

◭ Map p. 143

✉ Giant's Castle exit off N3, Central Berg

☎ 033/267-7251 or 031/845-1000

💲 $

Royal Natal National Park

◭ Map p. 143

✉ N. Berg Rd., 8 miles (19 km) off R74

☎ 036/438-6303

💲 $

Giant's Castle Game Reserve

◭ Map p. 143

✉ Giant's Castle exit off N3, Central Berg

☎ 036/353-3718

💲 $, Cave tours: $, Blind tours: $$$$$

Vulture Restaurant at Giant's Castle

✉ Lammergeyer Hide

☎ Call Giant's Castle

💲 $$$$$ (includes transportation to blind)

INSIDER TIP:

Vulture Restaurant at Giant's Castle is a fantastic place to see majestic but declining vultures up close. You can marvel and know that your dollars help their conservation.

—CAGAN H. SEKERCIOGLU
National Geographic field researcher

everything from hiking to fly-fishing, bird-watching, horseback riding, and rock climbing. Even skiing is offered in the southern Drakensberg at Tiffindell (in the Eastern Cape) from late May to early September.

uKhahlamba-Drakensberg National Park

Much of the Drakensberg mountains and the surrounding area compose the 600,000-acre (243,000 ha) uKhahlamba-Drakensberg National Park. The park was established as a UNESCO World Heritage site in 2000; the Zulu name of the extensive range means "battlement of spears," which quite accurately describes the sweeping basalt peaks and buttresses of the surrounding mountains.

Several existing parks were joined together in 1993 to create the larger uKhahlamba-Drakensberg National Park, including Royal Natal National Park, Giant's Castle Game Reserve, and Kamberg Game Reserve.

There are 15 entrance gates

to the park, but they are not connected to one single road, so visitors must select a particular area for hiking or camping. **Tendele** in Royal Natal National Park and **Giant's Castle Game Reserve** have overnight accommodations.

Rock Art in the Drakensberg: The Drakensberg is also one of the most important archaeological regions of South Africa, with traces of human occupation from 20,000 years ago. Beginning with the Late Stone Age, San people lived here in caves and shelters and over the last 4,000 years left behind some 600 sites of rock art in about 35,000 images.

This is the most concentrated group of rock paintings in Africa south of the Sahara. The images are of high artistic quality. The sensitive rendering of animals and human beings suggests the San's complex connection with nature and seems to link some of the art to San shamanic religion. Not all rock art is prehistoric—the most recent paintings date from the 19th century, and some tell of clashes with early settlers holding guns.

Rock art sites can be visited in the Royal Natal National Park, Giant's Castle Game Reserve (at least 50 sites), and Kamberg Game Reserve. Some art sites can be seen on a self-guided trail, others only with a tour.

The **Kamberg San Rock Art Trail and Interpretative Centre** gives such tours with a trained community guide. It was here that archaeologists found the San "Rosetta Stone"—the key with which they were able to unlock the symbolism of the paintings' spiritual content, enabling them to understand how San hunters believed to gain magical power from the animals they hunted. A video documentary on the world of the San can be viewed at the center, which also provides contact with San descendants who still live in the area.

Royal Natal National Park: One of the most striking geographical features of the northern Drakensberg is the **Amphitheatre,** located in Royal Natal National Park; its impressively large cliff face makes it one of the most daunting and thrilling

mountain-climbing destinations in the world. Here, too, the Tugela River drops some 3,000 feet (914 m) in a series of five falls that compose **Tugela Falls,** South Africa's longest. A popular walk here winds up the Tugela Gorge.

Giant's Castle Game Reserve: Enormous peaks, breezy grasslands, and a magnificent collection of San paintings are the draws to this 85,000-acre (34,398 ha) reserve, located south of Monk's Cowl.

Park Permits: Permits are provided by KwaZulu-Natal

EXPERIENCE: Riding in the Drakensberg

The Drakenberg mountains offer a unique equine experience. The mountains themselves of this World Heritage site offer views of picturesque peaks, cascading waterfalls, and wide open spaces, and a rider on horseback can ramble through the nearby game reserves, catching glimpses of giraffes, rhinos, and countless buck species.

If you are interested in history, you can take a guided tour with your horse, trotting through the historic battlefields to visit sites such as the **Battle of Blood River,** where the Voortrekkers fought off the Zulus in 1838.

And with more than 600 sites of San rock art dating as far back as 4,000 years ago, there's no shortage of trails in the area to transport you back to the early ages of these intriguing hunters.

Tours on horseback will also take you to modern Zulu villages, where you can observe the lifestyles of rural South Africans. You may even take time out for a consultation with a practicing *sangoma* (traditional healer).

The entire mountain range is navigable by horse, providing trails for experts and novices alike. The trails range from pony rides for the little ones, to two-hour scenic trails around the mountains. Multiple-day tours, complete with chef and guide, can also be organized through almost all the resorts in the Drakensberg.

For an experience with a twist, hikers can rent llamas to carry up to 88 pounds (40 kg) of their camping equipment and other baggage.

For reservations contact your resort, or try one of the following venues: **Khotso Horse Trails** (*tel 033/701-1502, www.khotsotrails.co.za*); **The Northern Horse** (*tel 082/337-8770, www.drakens berghorseriding.co.za*); or **Sengani Horse Trails** (*tel 036/352-1595*).

Golden Gate Highlands National Park

🗺 Map p. 143

✉ 165 miles/265 km S of Johannesburg

☎ 058/255-0012; e-mail: goldengate@sanparks.org

www.sanparks.org/parks/golden_gate

Hluhluwe-iMfolozi Park

🗺 Map p. 143

✉ Off N2 at Hluhluwe exit; cross over freeway, following road for 9 miles (14 km) to entrance

☎ 033/845-1000

NOTE: Hluhluwe–iMfolozi Park is in a malarial area; anti-malaria precautions are necessary.

Wildlife in Pietermaritzburg (tel 033/845-1000) or Durban (tel 031/304-4934); or at the Central Drakensberg Information Centre (tel 036/488-1207, www.cdic.co.za); the Ukhahlamba-Drakensberg Tourism (tel 036/448-1557, www.drakensberg.org.za); or the Southern Drakensberg Escape Tourism Centre (tel 033/701-1471, www.drakensberg.org).

Golden Gate Highlands National Park

Wedged between the northwestern edge of KwaZulu-Natal and Lesotho lies Free State's only refuge, the Golden Gate Highlands National Park. The

---

Operation Rhino

It was at Hluhluwe-iMfolozi that Operation Rhino, an initiative to save the white rhino from extinction, was started in the 1960s. The rescue teams successfully captured and relocated many white rhinos within South Africa and abroad. As a result, South Africa's white rhino population has grown to around 6,000: 12 times the 1960 count of 500.

Today the park also focuses on saving the endangered black rhino, the numbers of which have shrunk from 14,000 to 2,550 animals in the last decade. At least one-fifth of the world's black and white rhino population is now found in the reserve.

---

scenic beauty of the towering buttresses—still part of the Drakensberg mountains—make this a park well worth exploring. The highest peak, the Ribbokkop, rises to 9,281 feet (2,829 m). The Little Caledon River forms the southern border. The highland habitat covers 28,700 acres (11,600 ha) of unique protected environment and is rich in highveld and montane grassland flora, Afromontane forests and high-altitude Austro-Afro alpine grassland. Ouhout (old wood, Leucosidea sericea), an evergreen species, is the most common tree in the park. This is a bird-watcher's paradise with 140 species, including cape vulture, bearded vulture, bald ibis, martial eagle, lammergeier, and rock kestrel. Game includes black wildebeest, gray rhebok, springbok, duiker, steenbok, oribi, mountain reedbuck, hartebeest, eland, blesbok, and zebra. It's also an area rich in fossils. The oldest dinosaur embryos ever discovered—from the Triassic period (220 million–195 million years ago)—were found in the park in 1978.

Inside the park the small **Basotho Cultural Village** features aspects of traditional Basotho life. Hiking trails to rock-art sites, guided walks to explore medicinal plants, and more strenuous two-day hikes to various peaks and lookouts are just a few of the activities.

Accommodations include Glen Reenen Rest Camp, Protea Hotel Golden Gate (www.proteahotels.com/goldengate); Highland Mountain Retreat, Brandwag

Hotel *(closed through March 2010);* and Qwa Qwa Rest Camp. Call *(tel 012/428-9111 or 082/233-9111)* for reservations and information for all.

Hluhluwe-iMfolozi Wildlife Park

Between the northern end of Zululand and the Elephant Coast lies the spectacular Hluhluwe-iMfolozi Wildlife Park. Named for the Hluhluwe and iMfolozi Rivers, the reserve was established in 1895 and is the oldest one in South Africa, covering 230,000 acres (96,000 ha). The area's diverse topography— from mist-shrouded hills to sun-bleached savannas, with its yellow fever trees *(Acacia xanthophloea)* and umbrella acacias *(Acacia tortillis),* the many traditional Zulu villages and sugarcane plantations—makes for picture-perfect postcard views.

Here you'll find the Big Five— elephant, lion, leopard, buffalo, and rhino—as well as the Nile crocodile, hippo, cheetah, hyena, blue wildebeest, jackal, giraffe, zebra, waterbuck, nyala, eland, kudu, impala, duiker, reedbuck, warthog, bushpig, mongoose, and baboon.

For the Birds: The park
is one of the prime birding destinations in South Africa; more than 300 species of birds have been recorded. The Hluhluwe River floodplain is one of the few areas in South Africa where yellow-throated, pink-throated, and orange-throated long claw species can be seen together. Other noteworthy species in the

park include African finfoot, Delegorgue's pigeon, cinnamon dove, white-eared barbet, yellow-spotted nicator, Rudd's apalis, and yellow-billed and red-billed oxpeckers.

Walking in the Hluhluwe-iMfolozi Wildlife Park

Game Viewing: Game-
viewing drives are organized by **Hilltop Camp** *(tel 035/562-0848),* with morning and evening drives. Hilltop Camp in the Hluhluwe section of the park is one of the newer camps and sits high on the edge of a steep forested slope with views of Zululand's hills and valleys. **Mpila Camp** *(tel 035/550-8477),* which is centrally located at the iMfolozi section, offers only evening drives.

A network of well-maintained roads throughout the park, with rest stations in between, allows visitors to explore the reserve by car on their own. In addition, two self-guided foot trails, one at the

Maloti Mountains Drive

This drive takes you through the attractive scenery of the eastern Free State, along South Africa's border with Lesotho.

Golden Gate Highlands National Park

For most of the drive, crossing and recrossing the Klein (Little) Caledon River, you will pass through farmlands with the often snowcapped Maloti (aka Maluti) Mountains of Lesotho on your left.

Expect to see spectacular sandstone formations, yellow, gold, brown, pink, and gray in the varying light; stands of bushy gray poplars and towering Lombardy poplars; fields bright green with corn and wheat from spring through summer, tawny brown in winter. You can also make a short detour to visit fine San rock paintings.

Start from the **Golden Gate Highlands National Park** ❶ (see pp. 160–161), the imposing sandstone cliffs towering above you to the left and the right as you drive out of the park.

A drive of 11 miles (18 km) on the R712 across undulating countryside brings you to the small town of **Clarens** ❷, named after the place in Switzerland where Paul Kruger, exiled president of the old Transvaal Republic, died in

1904. Positioned among low hills, Clarens has developed enormously as a tourist destination in the last few decades, becoming crowded on weekends. A grassy square forms the center of town, and is surrounded on all four sides by art galleries, restaurants, cafés, bars, and shops. In a corner of the square you will find **Clarens Destinations** (Shop 8, Market St., tel 058/250-1189), which has information about the town and region. If you intend to visit the San rock paintings at Schaapplaats (see below), make reservations here ($) and inquire about the state of the gravel road.

Leave Clarens the way you came in, and turn right onto the R711 toward Fouriesburg. After 1.2 miles (2 km), turn left where you see a large sign pointing to Kgubetswana in the opposite direction and smaller signs indicating Schaapplaats. A ten minutes' drive (4 miles/6 km), at first on tar but mainly on gravel, will bring you to the farm **Schaapplaats** ❸ (tel

058/256-1176, www.ashgarhorses.co.za). Ask at the farmhouse about the San rock paintings. A guide will lead you on a ten minutes' walk up a valley to a large overhanging cave. Here you can view superb rock paintings, some of them thousands of years old, of antelope and strange animal-headed shamans, wrapped in skins. You should tip the guide R5–R10.

Return to the R711 and continue left toward Fouriesburg. When you have crossed the Little Caledon again, drive up a steep hill, and just over the brow of the hill you will see a sign to **Surrender Hill ❹**. Park and walk uphill. A bronze plaque gives the history of the place: Here, in July 1900, during the South African War (1899–1902), more than 4,300 Boers surrendered to British forces, one of the greatest setbacks to the Boer side during the war.

A mile farther, an observation point on the left offers a magnificent view of the Little Caledon Valley, with Lesotho and the Maloti Mountains beyond.

Twenty-two miles (36 km) from Clarens, turn right into **Fouriesburg ❺**. As you reach the town, you will see on your left **Matsoho Arts & Crafts** *(tel 072/230-3206),* which sells good local work. Take a few minutes to drive around Fouriesburg. This is a typical, small, eastern Free State town, with a school, municipal buildings, and a church built from the local golden-brown sandstone. A good place to have lunch is the old Fouriesburg Country Inn *(Reitz at Theron Sts., tel 058/223-0207),* with its pressed steel ceilings and low sandstone rooms in back.

NOT TO BE MISSED:

Golden Gate Highlands National Park • Clarens • Schaapplaats farm • Fouriesburg

◪ Also see area map p. 143
➤ Golden Gate Highlands National Park
↔ 34 miles (54 km)
🕒 Half-day with stops
➤ Fouriesburg

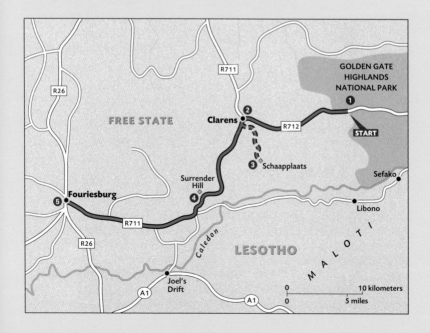

iSimangaliso Wetland Park

 Map p. 143

Visitor Information

✉ Visitor center accessed from Mtubatuba on R618. After bridge, leave traffic circle on right, McKenzie St. Follow to St. Lucia tourist center and park entrance.

www.isimangaliso.com

Hilltop Camp, another in the iMfolozi section, give access to the wildlife.

Guided walks, led by a trained and armed ranger, are also available. These short day walks of approximately two hours are conducted from Mpila and Hilltop Camps. The walks may be reserved at the reception desk in either camp.

The Hluhluwe-iMfolozi Park is also famous for its rugged **Wilderness Trails** established by Ian Player (the brother of golfer Gary Player) in the 1950s. Hikers can choose from four guided hikes from two to five days on the vast trail system.

Lodging: Ezemvelo KwaZulu-Natal Wildlife (the agency responsible for managing KwaZulu-Natal's biodiversity and natural resources) offers lodge or self-catering accommodations at Mthwazi, Hilltop, Muntulu, and Munyawaneni Camps in the

Hluhluwe area. In the iMfolozi area similar accommodations are provided at Masinda, Mpila, Sontuli, Gqoyeni, and Hlathikhulu Camps. Camping is not permitted in the park.

iSimangaliso Wetland Park

Previously known as the Greater St. Lucia Wetland Park and recently renamed the iSimangaliso (the Zulu word for "marvel") Wetland Park, this pristine ecosystem is South Africa's third largest protected area and its first World Heritage site. The 810,000-acre (328,000 ha) reserve stretches for 125 miles (200 km) of coastline, from the borders of Mozambique in the north to Maphelane south of the St. Lucia estuary.

The park unites a number of well-known destinations, including Maphelane Nature Reserve, St. Lucia Marine Reserve, Cape

Hoping for hippos on the St. Lucia Estuary

Vidal, Mkuze Game Reserve, Sodwana Bay, Lake Sibaya, Rocktail Bay, and Kosi Bay Nature Reserve, making for a vast and safe range for all its creatures.

The combined park protects five individual, but interdependent ecosystems: the marine system of the Indian Ocean; the

Zulu Handshake

Sharing a Zulu handshake with a local is sure to gain you favor. It is a three-part shake, beginning with a traditional handshake, shifting into an arm wrestling position, and returning to the first position. The three shakes, which move smoothly on from each other, cover the usual conversation: "Hello." "How are you?" and "I am fine."

coastal dune system consisting of high linear vegetated dunes and subtropical forests, coastal grasslands, and wetlands; the estuary-linked lakes of St. Lucia and Kosi Bay, with the four freshwater lakes of Sibaya, Mgobezeleni, Bhangazi North, and Bhangazi South; the Mkhuze and iMfolozi Swamps and extensive reed and papyrus marshes; and the Western Shores—ancient shoreline terraces and dry savanna woodlands.

What sets this park apart is this combination of subtropical coastline, wetlands, and tropical forest, which supports a greater diversity of species than some of the larger reserves such as the Kruger National Park, or the Okavango Delta in Botswana, and the area has suffered minimal human interference. Besides leopards, thick-tailed bushbabies, Samango monkeys, jackals, hyenas, wildebeests, impalas, reedbuck, buffalo, wild dogs, cheetahs, zebras, crocodiles, and white and black rhinos, the park holds the largest population of hippopotamuses in South Africa. Lake St. Lucia alone is home to more than 800 hippos and 1,200 crocodiles. Elephants were reintroduced in 2001.

The vast array of birds includes 521 different species. Some 200 species of waterbirds nest and feed along the shores.

The park from Sodwana Bay northward includes not only beaches but also offshore coral reefs, extending for the length of the park.

Humpback whales migrate along the entire KwaZulu-Natal section of the coast in winter, between June and November. Giant leatherback and loggerhead turtles lay their eggs on the beaches in the summer from November until March.

Another rarity, the coelacanth, an aquatic species known to scientists from fossil records and once presumed extinct, is found here. In fact, in November 2000 three coelacanths were sighted and photographed in a submarine canyon off the coast near Sodwana Bay inside the marine reserve.

The park can be entered from nine different entrance gates and offers wilderness trails, guided walks, a network of roads for

A Tsonga girl

St. Lucia
Map p. 143
Visitor Information
☎ 083/584-7473
www.stluciasouth
africa.co.za

Maphelane
Nature Reserve
Map p. 143
✉ Southern border
of iSimangaliso
Wetland Park
☎ 033/845- 1000

Cape Vidal
Map p. 143
✉ N of St. Lucia
☎ 035/590-
9012 or
082/841-5953;
Reservations:
033/845-1000;
E-mail: info@
kznwildlife.com
$ $$

viewing game, whale-watching, turtle tours, boat tours, and canoeing. The **Crocodile Center,** near the town of St. Lucia, serves as interpretive center for crocodiles and shows off all three African species: the Nile, long-snouted, and dwarf crocodile.

A number of accommodations are available throughout the park and are run by various operators. You can reserve them at *www.elephantcoast.kzn. org.za.*

St. Lucia: St. Lucia town, the southernmost entrance to the wetlands park and its resort town, has been well known as a wildlife and fishing destination since 1822 and was proclaimed a reserve in 1895. This is where visitors can get their bearing and plan the various forays into bush

and veld, estuary and tidal pool. In high season the town is a tourist hub with busy restaurants and souvenir shops, but the atmosphere is easygoing with monkeys or the occasional hippopotamus wandering down the single main street. Visitors come for both onshore and offshore game fishing and catch-and-release charter tours.

You can take a boat trip on the southern section of the 86,000-acre (36,000 ha) **St. Lucia Lake** *(KZN Wildlife Office, St. Lucia, tel 035/590-1259; reservations required)* itself—called the Narrows—which makes for close encounters with fish eagles, pelicans, flamingos, spoonbills, herons, and kingfishers, as well as other waders and waterfowl. Crocodiles and hippos wallow in sight of the pristine shoreline.

Maphelane Nature Reserve: The Maphelane section of iSimangaliso, lying across from the St. Lucia Estuary, hugs the south bank of the iMfolozi River where the river enters the sea. This remote sanctuary offers splendid walks through forest and bush. Along the beaches surf fishing is also a popular activity. **Maphelane Camp** has ten fully equipped log cabins, each with two bedrooms, bathroom, kitchen, and dining area. There are also 45 trailer and camp sites with modern bathroom facilities. More upscale lodges are available as well.

Cape Vidal: Cape Vidal is a magnificent coastal camp set in a sheltered bay north of St. Lucia. The cape with its shallow pools and rock ledges for snorkeling, forested sand dunes, and fine beaches is a favorite getaway within the iSimangaliso Wetland Park.

Its camp has a launch site for fishing kayaks, fishing Jet skis, and deep-sea fishing boats. Anglers regularly catch game fish, such as marlin, sailfish, bonito, and dorado. The camp has a gas station, souvenir shop, and small grocery store. Self-catering accommodations include cabins, as well as fishing cabins, and camp sites.

Mkhuze Reserve: Mkhuze, the northeastern corner of Zululand, flanked by the Lebombo Mountains in the west, the Indian Ocean in the east, and Mozambique in the north, is in an area that was inhabited by Shangaan people on both sides of the Mozambique border. This section of iSimangaliso has an astonishing diversity of habitats, including high mountains, broad stretches of acacia savanna, swamps, a variety of woodlands, and riverine forests, including a rare type of sand forest.

This topographic diversity accounts for the wide variety of animal species that inhabit the park, including black rhino; white rhino; elephant; giraffe; nyala, a spiral-horned antelope; blue wildebeest; warthog; hippo; impala; and kudu. Cheetah, hyena, leopard, and the wild dog are more rarely seen.

About 420 species of birds are recorded and three game-viewing blinds have been set up near the Kubube, Kamasinga, and Kwamalibala Basins. During the winter months, large concentrations of game also can be seen at these water holes. Two beautiful basins, **Nhlonhlela** and **Nsumo,**

INSIDER TIP:

The tented safari camps in Mkhuze are a great value, but close the tents tightly to keep monkeys out of your food and clothes! Do NOT underestimate the hippos: They can easily outrun you!

—KEVIN HALL
National Geographic field researcher

are home to hippos, crocodiles, pink-backed and white pelicans, and ducks and geese.

There are 60 miles (86 km) of roads to drive in search of wildlife. Day walks and night drives can be arranged through the manager of **Mantuma Camp** *(tel 038/845-1000).* The camp offers self-catering safari tents and chalets.

Sodwana Bay: Most popular for its sportfishing, scuba diving, and snorkeling, Sodwana Bay is a truly remote tract of South Africa within the iSimangaliso Wetland Park. The bay offers deep drop-offs close to shore and magnificent underwater

Mkuzhe Game Reserve
🔺 Map p. 143
✉ iSimangaliso Wetland Park
☎ 035/573-9004
💲 $$–$$$$$

Sodwana Bay
🔺 Map p. 143
Visitor Information
✉ Off N2 at the Hluhluwe exit, to SDI road to Mbazwana for 50 miles (80 km)
☎ 035/590-1633

seascapes of marine flora and fauna, including branching coral, table and plate coral, beautiful overhangs, drop-offs, and mushroom rocks.

Divers and snorkelers will find an abundance of tropical fish, hard and soft coral, sponges, moray eels, large schools of pelagic fish, potato bass, hawksbill turtles, loggerheads, green and leatherback turtles, and, depending on the time of year, southern right and humpback

Park *(tel 035/571-0284, www.mseni .co.za)* rents cabins. **Ezemvelo KZN Wildlife** *(www.kznwildlife. com)* has 20 five- and eight-sleeper self-catering log cabins.

Driving along this coast requires four-wheel-drive vehicles. Malaria precautions are necessary.

Lake Sibaya: Lake Sibaya, South Africa's largest freshwater lake, lies close to the northern coast with sandy beaches and

Kosi Bay

whales, whale sharks, and dolphins.

This pristine location guarantees quiet walks on the dunes with a 3-mile (5 km) self-guided trail for hikers and bird enthusiasts to **Lake Mgoboseleni.** Guided turtle tours are also available between November and March.

Accommodations can be found at **Coral Divers** *(tel 033/ 345-6531, www.coraldivers.co.za)* in huts and safari tents. The lodge at Coral Divers has a diving school. Scuba and snorkeling equipment can be rented there. **Mseni Lodge** in Sodwana Bay National

high sand dunes. The lake's white beaches and marshes soon make way for dense forest and farmland with traditional homesteads bordering the park in this area. The lake provides a habitat for birds, mammals, and aquatic life, including the second largest concentration of hippos and crocodiles in KZN. Other species include white-tailed and water mongoose, reedbuck, Samango monkey, and red and blue duiker.

The sheltered bays provide for 279 recorded bird species, including red- and white-breasted

INSIDER TIP:

If you want to avoid the masses at Sodwana, head up to Kosi Bay for the best snorkeling and diving South Africa has to offer.

—KATE PARR
National Geographic field researcher

cormorants; pied, giant, and malachite kingfishers; fish eagles; herons; darters; and egrets.

Located at Mabibi, close to Lake Sibaya, is the **Thonga Beach Lodge** *(off N2, 3 miles/5 km from Lake Sibaya, tel 035/475-6000, 4WD only, call ahead to arrange 2WD pickup)*, which nestles into beautiful coastal dune forest with sweeping views of the beach below. The thatched bush suites provide complete privacy.

Rocktail Bay: An exclusive beach resort, Rocktail Bay lies on a string of lakes, marshes, coral reefs, and secluded beaches midway between Sodwana Bay and Kosi Bay Nature Reserve.

With 25 miles (40 km) of unspoiled coastline, Rocktail Bay offers a very private beach experience. The warm sea attracts a large diversity of marine life including leatherback and loggerhead turtles that lay their eggs in the soft sand during summer. Ragged-tooth sharks congregate off rocky reefs and bottlenose dolphins play in the waves. Whale sharks often come close to investigate the boats, and humpback whales migrate here in winter.

Halfway between Sodwana Bay

and Kosi Bay, **Rocktail Bay Lodge** *(tel 011 883 0747, www.rocktailbay .com)* is built within the forest canopy of vegetated dunes.

Kosi Bay Nature Reserve: Kosi Bay, the northernmost area in KwaZulu-Natal, consists of a system of deep, clear, interconnected lakes covering

Kosi Bay Nature Reserve

⛰ Map p. 143

✉ Off N2 at Hluhluwe to R22 toward Sodwana Bay; continue to KwaNgwanase, Kosi Bay's main town

☎ 035/592-0204

Too Sweet

When flying above KwaZulu-Natal, you can't miss the green sugarcane fields that sprawl across the countryside. Sugar is big business in this part of the country, with the industry bringing in R4.2 billion per year. While supplying thousands with jobs, the sugar business has been tough on the environment, causing deforestation and erosion. A few years ago, it was estimated that 68 to 114 gallons (257–432 l) of water were needed to make a pound of sugar. Recently, however, the industry has made strides in becoming more eco-friendly.

---

56 square miles (37 sq km), separated by reedbeds. A narrow estuary empties into the ocean at Kosi Mouth. The lakes harbor crocodiles and hippopotamuses and are separated from the ocean by high forested dunes.

This part of the iSimangaliso Wetland Park consists

Tembe Elephant Reserve

Map p. 143

Visitor Information

N2 to turnoff past Mkuze, paved road leads to entrance gate

031/267-0144

www.tembe.co.za

of marshland and mangrove swamps, date and palm trees, and sycamore fig forests, which are home to 250 species of birds, many of which are at their most southerly limits of distribution, among them crab plover, flufftail, palmnut vulture, white-backed and night heron, and purple and reed kingfisher.

Kosi Bay offers superb fishing and snorkeling over offshore coral reefs with a multitude of brightly

Lodge. A four-wheel-drive vehicle is recommended.

Kosi Bay is in a malaria area and special precautions are necessary.

Tembe Elephant Reserve

The Tembe Elephant Reserve, on the border with Mozambique, was established in 1983 to protect the elephants that were once able to wander freely back and forth between KwaZulu-Natal and southern

EXPERIENCE: Inselo!

Although you probably won't hear that directed at you, the Zulu invitation to a stick fight—the ceremonial sparring match—is fun to watch.

While Zulu stick fighting has existed since at least the 1780s (the oral tradition only goes this far back), it has evolved over the years from a war game to a symbolic cultural gesture. Stick fighting is key to several rites of passage, such as Thomba, the male puberty ceremony, and Umgangela, an organized intertribal contest, complete with ornate costumes.

It is also widely used to settle disputes. The combatants are each allowed two sticks, one for offense and one for defense. There is no stabbing allowed, and the fight is over once blood is drawn. Afterward, to ensure no bad blood, the victor helps nurse the loser's wounds.

There has been a recent effort to make organized stick fighting into a professional sport. Nelson Mandela himself practiced it as a youth. You can witness the vicious, yet seemingly choreographed fighting at any authentic Zulu village tour.

colored tropical fish. Bushbuck, duikers, and monkeys inhabit the forested parts. Accommodations are available at **Kosi Forest Lodge** (tel 035/474-1473 or 072/227-5860), a luxury lodge with thatched bush suites and camping and self-catering log cabins, run by Ezemelo KZN Wildlife. Each of the lodges overlooks the third of the four lakes making up the Kosi Lake system. When making a reservation, be sure to obtain a detailed map at the camp to find your way to the Kosi Forest

Mozambique. During the Mozambican civil war, the elephants suffered severely from poaching, and the Tembe Elephant Reserve was established to shelter them. The park opened to the public in 1991. Today the 190-square-mile (300 sq km) park is home to some 220 very large elephants.

Tembe's varied habitats include dense sandveld forests, woodlands, grasslands, and swamplands, which provide an ideal habitat for the elephants and many other

The lodge at the Tembe Elephant Reserve

INSIDER TIP:

At the beautiful Tembe reserve you may see elephants with tusks so large they drag on the ground. Mahlasela blind has water year-round so you are guaranteed to see elephants even in winter.

—GABRIELLA FLACKE
National Geographic field researcher

species. More than 340 bird species have been recorded, including the rare Rudd's apalis, the rufous-bellied heron, the Natal nightjar, and the Woodward's batis.

Lions were reintroduced in the park in 2002, and besides the Big Five, visitors will encounter hippos, serval cats, hyenas, giraffes, jackals, warthogs, bush babies, and a number of the more common antelope species.

Once in the park, you should leave your car parked at the conference center. You'll be picked up in an open four-wheel-drive vehicle for transfer to Tembe's small luxury tented camp. Each en suite tent is surrounded by bush, and you'll get the true feel of Africa around the communal campfire in the evenings.

Trained guides lead morning and afternoon game drives in an open four-wheel-drive vehicle. Afternoon drives often turn into evening drives with stops at elephant blinds. Particularly rewarding is the **Mahlasela blind. Ponweni blind** overlooks a basin in the Muzi Swamp. For safety's sake, a picnic area at **Manungu** and a walking trail are closed off from large animals by an electric fence, and a viewing tower in the **Gowanini** section of the park offers a panoramic view over the reserve. ∎

A single province possessing some of South Africa's most celebrated gems, the Kruger National Park the most prominent among them

Kruger & Mpumalanga

Cheetah family at one of South Africa's game reserves

Kruger & Mpumalanga

Mpumalanga Province has much to offer tourists, with four attractions ranked on South Africa's top 20: the Kruger National Park, the Blyde River Canyon, Pilgrim's Rest, and, collectively, the province's private game reserves.

It goes without saying that the Kruger National Park is one of the world's best spots to view wildlife. Here, at South Africa's flagship national park, you're guaranteed sightings of the Big Five—lion, leopard, Cape buffalo, elephant, and rhino—on the quintessential African safari. But there's so much more to do here, including bush walks, astronomy excursions, bush barbecues—not to mention, simply relaxing at your luxury lodge where, most likely, you can spot big game without even having to budge from your chair.

Northwest of Kruger, the Blyde River Canyon—the world's third deepest canyon, after the Grand Canyon in the western U.S. and Namibia's Fish Eagle Canyon—is spectacular in its own right. Recently renamed the Motlatse, its cliffs rise spectacularly above the river bed, with more impressive views at every turn.

On a different note, Pilgrim's Rest, south of the canyon, stirs up the memories of the 1870s, when gold was discovered in this frontier town. Now the whole village is a national museum, with much of its original architecture remaining intact. You can attend the National Goldpanning Championship, or try your own luck at panning for gold.

Lay of the Land

The Drakensberg escarpment divides Mpumalanga into a western half (consisting mainly of high-altitude grassland called the highveld) and an eastern half (situated in low-altitude subtropical lowveld/bushveld), featuring predominantly savanna. The Lebombo Mountains in the east forms the border with Mozam-

bique. The lower-lying Waterberg mountains are a UNESCO biosphere reserve, offering malaria-free Big Five game viewing.

The drier highveld and the humid lowveld habitats produce corn, wheat, sorghum, barley, sunflower seed, soybeans, groundnuts, sugarcane, vegetables, coffee, tea, cotton, tobacco, and citrus, subtropical, and deciduous fruit. Forestry is extensively practiced around Sabie in the far north. Natural grazing is a large industry in Mpumalanga, the main products of which are beef, mutton, wool, poultry, and dairy. Mining is also important, and local minerals include gold, platinum, silica, chromite,

---

NOT TO BE MISSED:

Spotting the Big Five in the Kruger National Park   176–177, 181–182

A journey through time at the Sudwala Dinosaur Park   187

Fly-fishing in Dullstroom   187–188

A colorful Ndebele village in Siyabuswa   191

Reliving the past in Pilgrim's Rest   188–189

The awe-inspiring Blyde River Canyon   189–191

The world-famous view from God's Window   190

The ruins of the Kingdom of Mapungubwe   191–193

vanadiferous magnetite, argentiferous zinc, antimony, cobalt, copper, iron, manganese, tin, coal, andalusite, chrysotile asbestos, kieselguhr, limestone, talc, and shale.

The capital of Mpumalanga, Nelspruit, is located in the lush valley of the Crocodile River. The town lies in the lowveld, about 225 miles (360 km) to the east of Johannesburg. The best time of the year to visit Nelspruit is in spring and early summer when colorful flowering bauhinia and bougainvillea light up the town. Attractions include the Lowveld National Botanical Garden along the banks of the Crocodile River, with its riverine forest and tumbling cascades, and the adjacent Crocodile Farm.

Kingdom of Mapungubwe

Farther afield, the Kingdom of Mapungubwe is a sight not to be missed. The remains of an ancient society—a flourishing Iron Age metropolis, ruled by an African king nearly a thousand years ago—were discovered in 1932. It's now a national park and a World Heritage site, providing poignant insight into another life and time. ■

Kruger National Park

In the heart of the lowveld nestles the largest game reserve in South Africa, the Kruger National Park. Nearly 4.8 million acres (2 million ha) of wilderness, the Kruger stretches for 220 miles (352 km) along the Mozambique border, from the Crocodile River in the south to the Limpopo River in the north. It is 40 miles (64 km) wide and comprises an area of some 7,700 square miles (20,000 sq km).

Big game in the lowveld, Kruger National Park

Kruger National Park

◭ Map p. 175

✉ Entrance through 9 different gates, 255 & 375 miles (410 & 600 km) from Johannesburg via N1 or N4

☎ 012/428-9111 or 082/233-9111

www.sanparks.org/parks/kruger

Kruger is considered by many to be the greatest of South Africa's national parks. It has more species of mammals than any other African game reserve (147 in all) and is reportedly the most biodiverse on Earth. The excellent infrastructure in Kruger includes picnic sites, rest camps, water holes, and blinds.

Here you'll feel the magic of Africa's enigmatic stillness. You'll see firsthand the untouched primal beauty that so entranced early hunters and explorers. You'll experience hills shrouded in haze

and land dotted with trees—acacia, knob thorn, green fever trees, and, in the drier north, mopane and majestic baobabs. If you are lucky enough, you may spot all of the Big Five—elephant, lion, leopard, buffalo, and rhino—in their natural habitat. And also perhaps the so-called Little Five—leopard tortoise, elephant shrew, buffalo weaver, rhino beetle, and ant lion. If you're an avid bird-watcher, you'll probably see birding's "Big Six," too—the ground hornbill, kori bustard, lappet-faced vulture, martial eagle, Pel's fishing owl, and saddle-billed stork.

The Kruger National Park is still very nearly pristine. But it could so easily have been different. In the 19th century, the rule of law did not extend into the wilderness areas; this was the heyday of indiscriminate hunting and unbridled ivory poaching, and much of the game that roamed the present Kruger area was being shot out. In 1902, after the Second Boer War, Maj. James Stevenson-Hamilton was appointed the first warden of this territory. In 1926, in a gesture of reconciliation, the British (who had defeated Paul Kruger's regime in the wars against the Boers) renamed the reserves after Paul Kruger, and the Kruger became South Africa's first national park.

Visiting the Park

Nine different entrance gates access the park, with Phalaborwa being the best to access the northern section, Orpen Gate recommended for the central section, and Paul Kruger and Malelane Gates for the southern region.

There are many, many ways to experience the park, some of the most popular being bush drives and walks (see sidebar below). You can drive yourself through Kruger or contract one of the many professional guided tour operators. A convenient 1,615-mile (2,600 km) road network winds through the national park, 435 miles (697 km) of which are tarred.

A host of rest camps, most of them scenically positioned throughout the park, provide comfortable and, often, luxurious accommodation after sundowner time (note that within the park boundaries you're only allowed to explore between sunrise and sunset). The dry winter season is the best time to watch game. The

---

EXPERIENCE: Seeing the Best of Kruger

Most camps offer the following must-do activities. Or contact the park office (tel 012/428-9111, www.krugerpark.co.za , e-mail: reservations@sanparks.org).

Adventure Trails: For those wanting to really get off the beaten path, Kruger has four 4WD trails.

Bush *Braais*: A game drive ends at a lantern- and fire-lit camp, where you feast on barbecued meat amid the sounds of wild animals. **Game Drives:** Morning, late afternoon, and nighttime drives through the bush.

Guided Walks: Armed guides share their expertise on early morning and late afternoon walks (see sidebar p. 185).

Lebombo Overland Trail: The 310-mile (500 km) eco-safari spans the length of the park, best experienced on a five-day 4WD trip. The trail is rated the best in southern Africa for its diversity of fauna and flora.

Olifants Stargazing: Game astronomy drives are offered at Olifants Camp, including an overview of the southern sky, telescope viewing, and a nighttime game drive on the way back.

Overnight Wilderness Trails: For the most adventurous visitor, who wants to stay in rustic, primitive camps and experience the bush on foot. Remoteness and tranquility guaranteed.

The Big Five

The Big Five of Africa are the lion, the leopard, the elephant, the rhino, and the buffalo. Their ferocity when cornered, allied to their power and courage, earned them the respect of early hunters, who gave the animals their famous nickname.

A leopard asleep in a tree, also a favorite place for eating

Their beauty is also completely captivating. You only clearly understand the allure of these magnificent animals when you see them in their natural habitat. Sighting a leopard in a riverine fig tree at dusk, coming across a pride of lion feeding on a kill, or seeing a herd of elephant file with massive majesty across the savanna: These precious experiences will stay with you for a lifetime.

The **African elephant** (Loxodonta africana), the largest land mammal, is unmistakable. You can't help but be awed by the power and grace of these sensitive and compassionate animals, with their tight family ties.

The elephant measures 10 to 15 feet (3–4.5 m) tall at the shoulder and weighs between 8,000 and 13,200 pounds (3,630–5,990 kg). Elephants walk at 4 mph (6 kph) but can speed up to 25 mph (40 kph) when angry or alarmed. You can't outrun a charging elephant! Highly intelligent, elephants use seismic vibrations at infrasound frequencies to communicate over vast distances.

Elephants consume an average of 100 pounds (45 kg) of vegetation daily as a consequence of their highly inefficient digestive system. Over time the elephant's molars wear down, and a new set moves forward to replace them. The last set of teeth lasts until the elephant is 65 to 70 years old. When they wear out, the elephant dies of starvation.

Herds consist of related females and their young. All decisions are made by the eldest of them, the matriarch. Males sometimes accompany family herds, but most old bulls wander off on their own, only joining the herds to mate. After 22 months the female gives birth to a single 35-inch-tall (90 cm) calf that weighs about 45 pounds (20 kg). A few days after birth the calf is able follow the herd on foot.

The **lion** (*Panthera leo*) is a big meat-eating cat with a tawny coat. Males have a darker heavy mane around the neck and shoulders. Not surprisingly, humans respect and fear them: When our ancestors roamed the African plains they were easy prey for these powerful hunters. The complex feelings we have for the lion—and the leopard—no doubt are locked deep in the ancestral vaults of our psyche.

Lions live for 10 to 14 years and inhabit savanna and grassland. A pride consists of related females and offspring and a smaller number of dominant males. Lions begin to hunt from the age of two. Their prey consists mainly of wildebeest, impala, zebra, buffalo, warthog, kudu, hartebeest, gemsbok, and eland. Female lions hunt together, encircling a herd and targeting the closest prey. The attack is short and quick, with a powerful final leap.

Lionesses reproduce at about two years and give birth to a litter of between one and

INSIDER TIP:

Winter is the best time for game photography in South Africa—when the bush is a little less dense than in summer. Early mornings and evenings are the best time to catch the animals on camera.

—SAMANTHA REINDERS
National Geographic photographer

four cubs. The gestation period is around 105 days. Lionesses raise cubs cooperatively, and cubs suckle from any placid lioness. In the wild, competition for food is fierce—more than three quarters of all lion cubs die before reaching the age of two.

The **leopard** (*Panthera pardus*) is probably the most efficient of all land predators, with a fearsome set of killer's tools: powerful muscles, razor-sharp claws, and strong curved canines.

The agile and graceful leopard has dark rosette-like markings on a tawny yellow hide and is found in habitats as diverse as rain forest and desert. Some of them have even been found living on the outskirts of modern cities! Shoulder height is 17 to 31 inches (42–79 cm). Males are much larger than females and weigh 74 to 198 pounds (34–90 kg). Leopards are very stealthy, nocturnal predators and stalk closely before making a fast final rush, grabbing their prey by the throat and suffocating it with their powerful jaws.

White rhino *(Ceratotherium simum)*

Although they've been known to prey on humans, leopards usually shun contact with people. Still, they are regarded with fear and dread by rural Africans. The animals are immensely strong, and watching a leopard leap up into a tree carrying a big dead prey animal like a wildebeest (to protect it from scavengers) is an inspiring and humbling experience. Little wonder the leopard is known as "the prince of darkness" and "the silent killer."

The **African** or **Cape buffalo** (*Syncerus caffer*) is thought to be the most dangerous of the Big Five—when wounded by careless hunters.

Elephants at a private game reserve near the Kruger National Park

Novelist Robert Ruark once said that buffalo look at you like you owe them money. He's right. Heads raised, their small eyes mean and untrusting, their horns shining dull black, their hides solid anthracite, old bulls stare at you with disapproval and suspicion. But they have their own massive iron-hard solidity and grandeur. The buffalo is a powerful beast. Even lions treat them with respect and they have few other natural enemies. Lions do kill and eat buffalo, but it takes more than a single lion to bring down a big bull.

A buffalo herd consists of females and their offspring. Males form bachelor groups, and old males (*kakulis* or dagga boys) normally live alone. After 11.5 months' gestation, cows produce their first calf when they are five years old. They hide the newborns away in the bush before allowing them to join the herd. The adults then surround and protect the young by keeping them in the center of the herd. After two years, males leave their mothers and join the older bachelor groups.

Two species of **rhinoceros** live in Africa; the black (*Diceros bicornis*) and the white (*Ceratotherium simum*). The names refer not to color but to the width of the nose and mouth. The black, a browser, has a narrow prehensile lip; the white, a grazer, has a wide (*wyd* in Afrikaans, which is pronounced vait) mouth, hence its name. Both species have a pair of horns on the snout. The animals are similar in height, about 5.5 feet (1.6 m) at the shoulder, but the white weighs twice as much as the black.

In the past, poaching almost wiped out Africa's rhino populations. Their horns are highly prized. Black rhinoceros horn is used in the Middle East to make ceremonial dagger handles and in the Far East as an aphrodisiac.

Black rhinos (said to be aggressive) usually attack simply because they have very bad eyesight. They've even been said to charge tree trunks. Adults are solitary, coming together only for mating. Mating does not have a seasonal pattern, but young are usually born at the end of the rainy season.

Gestation is 15 to 16 months. The single calf weighs 75 to 110 pounds (35–50 kg) at birth, and can follow its mother around after just three days. Mother and calf stay together for two to three years, until the next calf is born.

grass is low then and the trees and bushes largely leafless. There's very little rain, and you can easily spot thirsty animals when they come down to water holes in the morning and at evening to drink.

Skukuza

Skukuza, largest of the Kruger camps, offers a wide range of facilities: a restaurant, ATM, shop, Internet café, fuel station, and library.

Skukuza—literally, "he who sweeps clean"—was the Tsonga nickname for Maj. James Stevenson-Hamilton, the first warden of Kruger, who is remembered

In addition to Wolhuter's knife, the skin of the lion that he managed to kill is among the objects of interest on display in the museum.

Letaba Elephant Hall

Equally fascinating is the elephant museum at Letaba Rest Camp. Thirty years ago seven huge elephant bulls with tusks of more than 100 pounds (45 kg) were often spotted making their leisurely way through Kruger. The chief warden at the time decided to use these giants to publicize the park's outstanding conservation work. He gave

Skukuza

- Map . 175
- ✉ Via Paul Kruger Gate
- ☎ 013/735-4153 or 082/802-1204

www.sanparks.org /parks/kruger /camps/skukuza

Stevenson-Hamilton Memorial Museum

- Map p. 175
- ✉ Skukuza Rest Camp, S bank of Sabie River
- ☎ 012/735-4152

www.sanparks.org /parks/kruger /camps/skukuza

Letaba Elephant Hall

- ✉ Letaba Rest Camp, in N of Kruger National Park, 30 miles (48 km) from Phalaborwa entrance gate
- ☎ 013/735-6636

www.sanparks.org /parks/kruger /elephants

Shangana Cultural Village near the Kruger that seeks to preserve the heritage of the local Shangaan people

for translocating many of the local people when the park was first established. The **Stevenson-Hamilton Memorial Museum** houses a collection of interesting historical artifacts—including the sheath knife with which ranger Harry Wolhuter single-handedly killed a lion that attacked him way back in 1903.

each of the bulls a name and called them collectively the Magnificent Seven.

When these great elephants died, their tusks and skulls were retrieved and they are now displayed in the Letaba Elephant Hall. The tusks—an echo of an age before poaching destroyed Africa's population of giant tuskers—are

Sabi Sands Private Game Reserve

⚠ Map p. 175

✉ Via Paul Kruger Gate

www.sabisands.co.za

Singita Lebombo

✉ 22 miles (36 km) from Paul Kruger Gate, left on gravel road for 17 miles (28 km)

☎ 021/683-3424

www.singita.com

Singita Sweni

✉ 22 miles (36 km) from Paul Kruger Gate, left on gravel road for 17 miles (28 km)

☎ 021/683-3424

www.singita.com

Singita Ebony

✉ 22 miles (36 km) from Paul Kruger Gate, left on gravel road for 17 miles (28 km)

☎ 021/683-3424

www.singita.com

Singita Boulders

✉ 22 miles (36 km) from Paul Kruger Gate, left on gravel road for 17 miles (28 km)

☎ 021/683-3424

www.singita.com

magnificent to behold. Dzombo, Joao, Kambaku, Mafunyane, Ndlulamithi, Shawu, and Shingwedzi will not be forgotten.

Kruger's Private Lodges

The Kruger National Park contains a number of private lodge concessions that combine five-star luxury with spectacular game viewing. Top among them are the pair, **Singita Lebombo** and **Singita Sweni** (see p. 300).

INSIDER TIP:

Stay at the Exeter River Lodge in Sabi Sands, overlooking the Sand River. You'll see the Big Five out in the game drives, dine on Karoo lamb in the wooden boma, and dip in your private plunge pool.

—ERIN MONRONEY
NG Kids researcher–writer

Lebombo, set high on a hillside, is the larger lodge, providing superbly designed glass-and-steel accommodation units, screened with narrow wooden poles, blending seamlessly into the surrounding bush. The smaller Sweni, with fewer units and set closer to the river, has a more intimate feel. At both lodges you can enjoy outstanding game viewing from your own balcony.

Expert game rangers take you out on game drives in the morning and evening, while guided

walks, and even mountain-bike rides, through the bush are offered. Unlike in Kruger proper, in this concession the game-viewing vehicles are allowed off-road, so that you can follow elephants, or a pride of lions, almost within touching distance.

See p. 300 for additional options.

Sabi Sands Game Lodges

The 160,000-acre (65,000 ha) **Sabi Sands Game Reserve,** on Kruger's southwestern boundary, is South Africa's most exclusive private game reserve. Many of South Africa's most luxurious game lodges lie within Sabi Sands, including **Singita Ebony** (see p. 300), set among giant ebony trees, with nine luxurious suites; and **Singita Boulders** (see p. 300), along the Sand River, with 12 luxury suites.

The highly recommended **Londolozi** is a justly famous safari lodge in Sabi Sands, said to provide the best game experience in all of southern Africa. The animals are accustomed to 4WD vehicles, and your chances of seeing the Big Five—including the normally elusive leopard—are excellent. Birders will be spoiled by Londolozi's 40-plus species of raptors, and along the Sand River you'll find paradise flycatcher, Heuglin's robin, collared sunbird, and green pigeon.

Moonlit alfresco dining, customized breakfasts in the bush, guided stargazing trips, and a glass of late-night port on the airstrip will be typical of your stay.

Among Londolozi's accommodations options are **Tree Camp,** perched above the Sand River; **Founder's Camp,** tucked away in dense riverine forest on the Sand River; and the newly renovated **Pioneer Camp,** steeped in the aura of Londolozi's bygone days.

MalaMala Game Reserve

Internationally acclaimed, the award-winning MalaMala Game Reserve is one of the region's oldest

graphic safaris, nighttime stargazing, and day and night game drives. Walking safaris with an armed ranger can be arranged on request.

Three different tent camps offer accommodations: **MalaMala Main Camp,** its unpretentious, traditional style and spectacular views making it a top choice; intimate **Rattray's,** its main building featuring a viewing deck with telescope and a convivial

One of the private game reserves adjacent to Kruger

established private reserves. The MalaMala experience is characterized by peerless attention to detail and seemingly effortless elegance.

After an early game drive in open 4WD vehicles conducted by MalaMala's renowned guides, you can relax at the pool or laze on the viewing deck until lunch.

MalaMala's chefs make every mealtime a temptation, and you'll be lured to dinner—served under the stars in a reed-enclosed *boma*— by the sound of African drums. MalaMala offers specialist photo-

bar area; and luxury **Sable Camp** *(tel 013/735-9200, www.malamala .com/sable),* at the southern end of the MalaMala main camp.

Camp Jabulani

Camp Jabulani combines luxurious accommodation with an unforgettable wildlife experience. The camp is built in a Big Five reserve incorporating the **Hoedspruit Endangered Species Centre,** known for its contribution to the conservation of wildlife and where you can visit

Londolozi
- ✉ 22 miles (36 km) from Paul Kruger Gate, left on gravel road for 17 miles (28 km)
- ☎ 013/735-5653

www.londolozi.com

MalaMala Game Reserve
- 🗺 Map p. 175
- ✉ From Paul Kruger Gate, 23 miles (37 km) to MalaMala sign, left on gravel road for 18 miles (29 km)
- ☎ 013/735-9200

www.malamala .com

Rattray's on MalaMala
- ✉ MalaMala Game Reserve, 2.4 miles (4 km) down Sand River from main camp
- ☎ 013/735-3000

www.malamala.com/ rattrays

Camp Jabulani
- 🗺 Map p. 175
- ✉ Kapama Game Reserve
- ☎ 012/460-5605

www.campjabulani.com

Hoedspruit Endangered Species Centre
- ✉ R40 between Klaserie & Hoedspruit
- ☎ 015/793-1633
- 💲 $$$

www.wildlifecentre .co.za

Timbavati Game Reserve

Map p. 175

✉ From Hoedspruit, right on R40 for 5 miles (8 km), left at Timbavati signpost to gate, right at Kings Camp sign; follow road 4 miles (6 km) to reserve

☎ 015/793-2436

💲 $$$

www.timbavati.com

Kurisa Moya Nature Lodge

✉ N1 to R71 toward Univ. of Limpopo and take left at lodge sign. After 16 miles (26 km) the road becomes dirt just before lodge entrance on right.

☎ 015/276-1131

www.krm.co.za

INSIDER TIP:

Kurisa Moya Nature Lodge in Magoebaskloof Forest Reserve provides a great rainforest experience in a very serene setting. A must for bird, outdoors, and healthy-living enthusiasts.

—CAGAN H. SEKERCIOGLU
National Geographic field researcher

cheetahs and other endangered species up close.

You can go on an elephant-back safari—an absolutely unforgettable experience—or even a night safari on elephant back (Jabulani is the only camp offering such night safaris). The Jabulani elephants are all rescued and

rehabilitated African elephants, and you'll have the opportunity to tuck them into their stables at night. Other activities include game drives and hot-air balloon flights. Back at camp, relax in the main dining area with its stylish African furnishings.

Timbavati Game Reserve

This private game reserve adjoining Kruger, just to the north of Sabi Sands, promises an excellent chance of spotting the Big Five (40 mammal species in total). Among its many lodging options is **Kings Camp** (see p. 301), offering colonial-style accommodation. The camp faces a water hole that is visited 24 hours a day by many different species of animals.

Walking safaris through the bush take place just after breakfast on request, and are the best way of experiencing the finer aspects of the bushveld. ∎

Guests at family-run Londolozi, one of the original pioneering lodges of the ecotourism industry

EXPERIENCE: Walking in the Bush

There is no better way of experiencing the sights and smells of the African bush than to traverse it on foot. While a game drive involves chiefly your sense of sight, a bush walk engages all five senses.

On foot you will see few larger animals, since they tend to melt away into the shrubs and long grass at the approach of humans. However, an expert ranger will be able to point out all sorts of smaller things that you might miss from a game-viewing vehicle. Things such as the distinctive tracks of predators and the various types of antelope; the round spoor of elephant, the three-toed spoor of rhino, and the four-toed marks of hippopotamus. The ranger may show you where a mass of spoor, broken bushes, and blood stains indicate a desperate struggle and a kill in the night; or where horns and sun-bleached bones bear witness to the work of vultures and hyenas.

A bush walk gives you the chance to learn about birds, insects, and smaller reptiles, and about the many species of shrubs, trees, creepers, flowers, and grasses that grow in the bushveld. Discover the practical uses of indigenous plants—how to make strong rope from plaited strips of bark of the silver cluster-leaf tree, and which plants will cure headache or upset stomach.

Up close and personal on a guided bush walk, in Singita Lebombo

Part of the excitement of a bush walk is the slight element of danger. If predators and large mammals are present, you will always be accompanied by an armed ranger. Speak to the rangers, though, and you will find that they have seldom, if ever, had to fire their gun in anger. However, you must obey to the letter their instructions about how to behave on the walk and what to do if a dangerous animal is encountered.

For the full bush experience, go on a multiday walking trail. **Siyabona Travel** (tel 021/424-1037, www.siyabona.com) offers a variety of bush walks in Kruger, as well as in private game reserves in the area, ranging from five to two days.

At the luxury Kruger National Park lodges, **Singita Lebombo** and **Singita Sweni** (see p. 182) rangers will take you on one- or several-hour bush walks, tailored to your wishes.

The **Kruger National Park** offers morning and afternoon walks from most of its camps, a variety of three-night wilderness trails, as well mountain biking from Olifants Camp. For full details and useful advice about what equipment and clothing you need on a bush walk, click on Activities on the Kruger National Park page of the South African National Parks website, www.san parks.org.

Beyond Kruger

Beyond Kruger await countless manifestations of Africa: Big game sprint or waddle, depending on their mood. The land is terse and dry, or verdant. Shrouded in mist, historic towns stand witness to a history that passed them by.

Some 240 million years old, Sudwala Caves are the world's oldest caves.

Sudwala Caves

 Map p. 175

✉ R539 (Sabie) turnoff from N4 toward Pretoria and go 5 miles (8 km) toward Sudwala Caves. After getting off R539, cross Houtboschloop River and go 1 mile (1.6 km) up mountain.

☎ 013/733-4152

💲 $

www.sudwalacaves. co.za

Sudwala Caves

The Sudwala Caves were formed some 240 million years ago, making them the oldest known caves in the world. It is still a mystery as to who discovered them. Early, Middle, and Late Stone Age tools have been found there, indicating that the caves were used as a shelter by humans thousands of years ago. In more recent times, about 200 years ago, they were used as a refuge by the Swazi people under the leadership of Somquba, one of the sons of King Sobhuza I when he was

fleeing for his life from his brother Mswati.

Some 3.5 miles (5.5 km) of the cave passages have been surveyed at Sudwala, and exploration is ongoing. Only 650 yards (594 m) are presently open to tourists. The biggest chamber is the circular **Owen Hall**—19 yards (18 m) high and 71 yards (65 m) in diameter—named after the man who developed and opened the caves as a tourist attraction in 1965.

There are a number of calcium structures in the caves, with names like the **Lowveld Rocket, Sam-**

son's Pillar, and the **Screaming Monster.** Owen Hall has natural air-conditioning and this—plus the cave's remarkable acoustics—make it a spectacular venue for stage productions. Attending an operatic or dramatic performance here is an exhilarating experience.

The Sudwala Caves are privately owned and can only be visited on guided tours. One-hour tours through the underground world are offered several times a day. On the first Saturday of

....

The Sudwala Caves were formed some 240 million years ago, making them the oldest known caves in the world.

....

every month, the five-hour Crystal Tour takes place. The Crystal leads adventurous visitors more than a mile (1.6 km) through the caves to the spectacular **Crystal Chamber** and its aragonite crystals. In parts of the chamber you'll have to climb through narrow tunnels, sometimes filled with water. Tough shoes and clothing are required, and the minimum age is 16 years. Visitors should register two weeks ahead.

Located next to the caves, the **Sudwala Dinosaur Park** uses life-size, scientifically accurate models of prehistoric animals—like the ancient amphibious and mammal-like reptiles, dinosaurs, extinct mammals, and prehis-

toric man—to graphically and grippingly tell the story of the evolution of life on Earth. A fun-filled edutainment experience for the whole family.

Dullstroom

Dullstroom, which is just a three-hour drive from Johannesburg en route to Kruger, has become a tourist haven for its idyllic countryside, countless antique and bric-a-brac stores, quaint pubs and coffee shops, and laid-back friendly atmosphere. But the small town remains most famous as South Africa's premier fly-fishing

Boer War

During the Second Boer War (1899–1902), Dullstrom was decimated by British soldiers, as part of their scorched-earth campaign. The men who weren't killed went underground, attempting to fight a guerilla war against the better equipped English. The woman and children suffered worse; they were forced into concentration camps in the nearby town of Belfast, where many died in captivity. In town, a statue and garden memorialize those who died. In the cold mornings (Dullstroom is at 6,446 feet/1,964 m), take a walk through town and listen to your shoes crunching the same dry earth where the Boer soldiers walked.

Sudwala Dinosaur Park
- Map p. 175
- Next to Sudwala Caves parking lot
- 013/733-4152
- $

Dullstroom
- Map p. 175

Pilgrim's Rest

🅰 Map p. 175

Visitor Information

✉ Main St.

☎ 013/768-1060

**www.pilgrims-rest
.co.za**

Young woman in traditional Ndebele beads and dress

Pilgrim's Rest

The whole town of Pilgrim's Rest is a national monument. In a sense Pilgrim's Rest is a living fossil, because a visit takes you back in time to the days of the old Transvaal gold rush.

The town allegedly got its name in a picturesque way. Legend has it that in 1873 a gold digger named Alec Patterson was destination. Professionals and amateurs alike flock to the town for weekend getaways, lazing around any of the numerous trout dams, where catching your dinner is almost guaranteed.

prospecting in the hills around the area. At a place called Pilgrim's Creek he saw huge nuggets of gold shining up at him through the clear water of the stream. Delighted, he shouted: "At last the pilgrim can rest!"

Word spread, with predictable results. The alluvial deposits of gold at Pilgrim's Rest turned out to be the finest in South Africa. Diggers from all over the world flocked there. But when the deposits finally ran out, the town became deserted. In 1972 the settlement was bought by the South African government and declared a national monument. The unique nature of Pilgrim's Rest was preserved by a thorough program of restoration and refurbishment of its old buildings, including the town's characteristic tin-roofed cottages.

Many of the original buildings, built from corrugated metal and timber, are still standing on the main street, including businesses, museums, and the late Victorian **Royal Hotel** *(tel 013/768-1100),* one of South Africa's best known hotels. You can explore houses such as **Alanglade** *($),* appointed with good period furniture of the 1920s, which housed the manager of the Transvaal Gold Mining Estate Ltd.

The **House Museum** *($),* a typical Pilgrim's Rest building, exhibits furnishings and examples of decorative style from the late Victorian era. The **War Memorial** *(Main St.)* commemorates soldiers from Pilgrim's Rest and the surrounding region who fought and died in the two World Wars.

EXPERIENCE: Gold Crazy

Not to say that Pilgrim's Rest isn't without its charms, but far-flung outposts beg the question, "Why?" Just what is it that drew people to this remote, dusty locale?

The answer is in the soil. Since the discovery of gold in 1873, not much has happened that doesn't revolve around the ever elusive AU. The town hosts the **South African Gold Panning Championships** in September. You can pan for gold at the **Diggings Museum** (R533, 1 mile/2 km S of town, $), or do it

yourself. To do so, take a gold pan to a slow-moving stream (not too swift, but not stagnant) about 6 inches (15 cm) deep. Fill up the pan with gravel and shake it in a circular motion under the water, dislodging bits of moss and mud with your fingers, until all that is left is fine silt. Gold is heavier than most other sediments, so it will sink to the bottom of the pan. Carefully feel around for gold. You probably won't get rich, but it will be fun.

At the **Information Centre** (Main St.), you'll find brochures and maps, and you can purchase tickets for the town tours and museums. Displays here feature geological specimens, photographs, and items related to gold mining at Pilgrim's Rest; the staff can tell you how to try your own luck at panning for gold (see sidebar above).

Blyde River Canyon

Blyde River Canyon (recently renamed the Motlatse) is one of the great wonders of the African continent and a must-see for visitors. Its natural beauty is rare and its vistas awe-inspiring.

Some 31 miles (50 km) in length, the canyon is the second largest in Africa and the third largest—after the Grand Canyon in the United States and the Fish River Canyon in Namibia—in the world. It was formed when Gondwanaland, the ancient supercontinent, tore apart some 200 million years ago and Madagascar and Antarctica were ripped away from Africa by tectonic forces. The mass

of the vast shallow sea that then stretched west beyond present-day Pretoria slowly tilted the shattered edge of the continent to form the canyon.

The R532, which is clearly signposted, parallels the most dramatic parts of the canyon. Commonly known as the **Panorama Route,** the R532 is one of the most beautiful thoroughfares in South Africa, running as it does through the untamed northern reaches of the Drakensberg.

The route starts at the town of Graskop and includes Bourke's Luck Potholes, God's Window, and the Three Rondavels. Where the swift-flowing Blyde River is joined by the Ohrigstad River from the west, eco-conscious engineers have built the unobtrusive **Blyde Dam** in a bottleneck below the confluence. The vicinity of the canyon abounds in wildlife. Near the canyon opening, down on the lowveld plain, look out for zebra, blue wildebeest, waterbuck, and kudu. In the lake formed by the Blyde Dam, crocodile and hippo can be seen, and on the escarpment,

Blyde River Canyon

🗺 Map p. 175

✉ E of Vaalhoek, off R532

Bourke's Luck Potholes, at the head of the Bourke River Canyon

the forest itself.

Just a few miles north of Graskop a small loop road leads to the aptly named **God's Window,** where you will find one of the world's greatest views. The spot derives its name from the stunning panoramas of the bushveld stretched out 3,000 feet (900 m) below. Rare indigenous forests cling to the sides of the ravine, and vertiginous cliffs plummet down to the lowveld and its enormous game reserves.

Bourke's Luck Potholes *(22 miles/35 km N of Graskop on R532, tel 013/769-6019)* were named after Tom Bourke, a 19th-century gold prospector who staked a claim nearby. Although Bourke was right in his forecast that abundant deposits of gold would be discovered in the vicinity, his own claim was utterly unproductive.

The **Bourke's Luck visitor center** *(R532, tel 031/761-6019)* details the interesting natural and sociohistorical attributes of the area and is the starting point of the comfortable 750-yard (685 m) walk to the potholes.

Incalculable millennia went into the making of the potholes. Where the Treur River plunges into the Blyde the resulting swirling whirlpools of water, sand, and rock ground great cylindrical potholes into the very bedrock of the river. A network of pathways and footbridges allows visitors to explore the potholes, some of which are 18 feet (5.5 m) deep. A 150-yard (137 m) circular trail, usable by the physically challenged, starts at the visitor center and showcases

mountain reedbuck, while dassies scuttle about the canyon walls.

You'll find viewing sites along the length of the canyon, and there are numerous trails for hiking, horseback riding, and mountain biking. For the best lookout points and the most exotic forest plants, the more adventurous visitor should avoid the crowds and hike up through the clouds into the misty rain forest. Take refreshments with you on the hike because the area can be very humid and reaching the rain forest involves an extremely steep and strenuous walk. Once you get there, you'll be delighted by the beauty of the scenery and the lichens found in the area.

The **Three Rondavels,** 9 miles (14 km) north of Bourke's Luck Potholes, are a very popular and picturesque site at Blyde River. Massive round rocks that look surprisingly like the huts (rondavels) of the indigenous people stand silently here, like sentinels guarding the spectacular views.

INSIDER TIP:

The Blyde River slices through redrock that separates Drakensberg from lowveld jungles. Raft its Class III–IV rapids past dramatic amphitheaters and emerald bluffs.

—CERIDWEN DOVEY
National Geographic writer

The Blyde River Canyon is located in northern Mpumalanga, and the best way to get there is to fly to Phalaborwa and drive the last leg. Even better, combine a visit to Kruger with a self-drive option. *(Leave Kruger at the Phalaborwa Gate, head first to Mica, then to Ohrigstad, taking Abel Erasmus Pass and then the R532 turnoff to Graskop.)*

Siyabuswa

In the cultural heartland of Mpumalanga lies a small township that was established in the 1970s and remains of great importance to the Ndebele people, who still practice their traditional way of life here.

Three different groupings of Ndebele live in the north of South Africa and across the border in Zimbabwe. A welcoming people, the Ndebele are famous for their polychrome designs, used on both houses and clothes, as well as for their outstanding arts and crafts.

At Siyabuswa, you'll find many authentic Ndebele villages and shops selling arts and crafts. Tours that help illuminate the local culture are also available, including a visit to a royal kraal (village).

Farther Afield: Kingdom of Mapungubwe

Mapungubwe lies in the far north of South Africa, on the borders of Zimbabwe and Botswana in Limpopo Province. The spreading plains are full of noble baobab trees, many of them hundreds of years old, and great soaring sandstone inselbergs. On the very top of one of these buttresses is the Kingdom of Mapungubwe, which is among South Africa's most important archaeological and cultural sites. Mapungubwe was declared a national heritage site in 2001 and added to the World Heritage List in 2003.

Between A.D. 1000 and A.D. 1300, Mapungubwe was a key link in the Indian Ocean Arab dhow trade. Alluvial gold from the Empire of Monomotapa in Zimbabwe was transported overland via Mapungubwe to the coast near Sofala, where it was bought by Arab merchants from the Persian Gulf.

Before its abandonment at some point during the 14th cen-

Siyabuswa

🅰 Map p. 175

Visitor Information

✉ 6 miles (10 km) E of Marble Hill

The Golden Rhino of Mapungubwe

Most famous of all the finds at Mapungubwe is the Golden Rhino. In its manufacture, gold foil was attached with tiny pins to a very carefully crafted wooden model or template underneath. The artifact, now widely regarded as representative of this civilization, has given its name to the Order of Mapungubwe, one of South Africa's newly created national orders.

The rhino is beautifully crafted and the artist has captured the weighty mass of the rhino with great deftness. It is an astonishingly modern-looking piece of art and can be viewed at the University of Pretoria's Mapungubwe Museum *(Old Arts Bldg., Lynwood Rd., Pretoria, tel 012/420-3146)*. The same technique was used to make the Golden Bowl and the Golden Sceptre, which were discovered at Mapungubwe in the same grave as the rhino.

By analyzing the contents of a nearby ancient rubbish dump (known as K2), archaeologists have learned in considerable detail about the diet and way of life of Mapungubwe's inhabitants.

The short-legged, single-horned gold rhino was discovered in 1933.

tury, Mapungubwe had grown to be the biggest kingdom in sub-Saharan Africa. Thereafter, climate change inspired migrations to Great Zimbabwe. The remains of the palace sites and the entire settlement area, as well as two earlier sites, survive almost untouched. The precious artifacts, including the famous **Golden Rhino** (see sidebar above) are breathtakingly beautiful and of great historical importance. When Mapungubwe was first discovered, archaeologists initially kept its precise whereabouts a secret to prevent the looting of its abundant gold ornaments. The artifacts date from the period of the dhow trade and also include pottery, glass trade beads, Chinese celadon ware, ceramic figurines, organic remains, crafted ivory and bone, and refined copper and iron.

Mapungubwe testifies to the existence of an African civilization that flourished before Western colonization. The archaeological evidence indicates that the population numbered about 5,000, supported by successful agricultural production, and that the settlement had trade links with

....

Mapungubwe testifies to the existence of an African civilization that flourished before Western colonization. Supported by successful agricultural production, it had trade links with India and China.

....

places as far away as India and China. This was one of the first societies in southern Africa to be stratified by class, with a wide gap between rich and poor, who occupied different areas of the site.

Mapungubwe was discovered in 1932 and excavations continue to this day, with a rich collection of artifacts made of gold and other materials housed at the University of Pretoria. Evidence of differentiation by class was found in some of the 23 graves so far excavated. Luxury items of copper and gold, as well as imported glass

beads, accompanied the bodies of three individuals who were buried like royalty, seated upright and facing west. What these discoveries also show is that gold was being worked and smelted at a very early date in southern Africa. Findings in the area of Mapungubwe and the neighboring K2 site are typically Iron Age. Smiths created objects from pottery, wood, ivory, bone, ostrich eggs, the shells of snails and freshwater mussels, iron, copper, and gold for trade and decoration.

Visiting Mapungubwe:

Mapungubwe lies within a game-rich national park with fine accommodation in self-catering air-conditioned suites. The **Leokwe Camp,** Mapungubwe's main camp, in the park's eastern section, is located in what was once the natural stone-encircled kraal where the king's cattle were kept.

A good **visitor center** provides detailed information on Mapungubwe. Knowledgeable guides take visitors to the sandstone rise on which Mapungubwe sits and explain the archaeological digs. The climb to get there, up wooden steps, can be quite strenuous.

The park also offers game drives, treetop walks to a blind, and a picnic spot at the confluence of the Shashe and Limpopo Rivers, where South Africa meets with Botswana and Zimbabwe.

To gain more perspective, drive the **Route of Lost Kingdoms,** from inside the Kruger National Park through Mapungubwe to the small town of Allydys, following a trail of myths and legends. ∎

Kingdom of Mapungubwe National Park

🏕 Map p. 175

✉ N1 to R572 at Musina, 42 miles (68 km) to entrance

☎ 012/428-9111

$ $$

www.sanparks.org/ parks/mapungubwe

Fast-paced, cosmopolitan Johannesburg and South Africa's genteel capital, Pretoria, set against a vast, untamed interior

Johannesburg & the Interior

A resident of the Lesedi Cultural Village in traditional garb

Johannesburg & the Interior

Johannesburg, provincial capital of Gauteng (Sotho for "place of gold"), ranks among the 40 largest of the world's metropolitan areas. In the surrounding region, a mix of sites—from Soweto Township to wildlife-filled national parks to shopping meccas to rustic towns—provide alluring reasons to visit South Africa's interior region.

Johannesburg was built on dreams of fabulous wealth, and even today the greed inspired by the 19th-century discovery of gold still drives this most rapacious of African cities. There's a ruthlessness about Johannesburg that manifests itself not only in cut-throat high-level business deals but also in the stratospheric crime statistics. Today, Gauteng is by far the richest of South Africa's provinces, boasting the largest economy in Africa south of the Sahara.

Johannesburg—known as Jo'burg by older whites, Egoli or Jozi by blacks and the vibey white young—is a cosmopolitan African city. After the ANC came to power in 1994, South Africa opened up to the rest of Africa, and immigrants from all over the continent—Nigeria, Mali, the Ivory Coast, Cameroon, the Central African Republic, the Congo—flocked to Johannesburg to make their fortunes. As the downtown part of the city began to change, big business predictably moved away from what was once the CBD (Central Business District) and out to the northern suburbs in order to escape the chaos of urban decline. But the inner city is slowly reviving and will no doubt become a thriving environment once again. The cross-cultural Newtown Cultural District, along with the Market Theatre and MuseuMAfrika, is a precursor of this urban revival.

If you're a shopper, pack your plastic and head for Johannesburg's largest shopping center, Sandton City. Nearby Hyde Park is perhaps the most prestigious, and between them they host outlets for many of the ultra-luxury goods brands.

The Interior

Not far from Johannesburg lies the township of Soweto, originally created during the apartheid era as a place where migrant workers were forced to live, but now a vibrant cultural hub. The administrative and official capital of South Africa, Pretoria, with its art and natural history museums, lovely architecture by Sir Herbert Baker, and fine restaurants, is just a 40-minute drive away along a modern highway.

NOT TO BE MISSED:

Live music in a Johannesburg nightspot   202–203

The cultural hub of Newtown   205–206

Johannesburg's Chinatown and Indian districts   206–207

Traditional medicine shops on Diagonal Street   207

Learn about gold mining in Gold Reef City   208–209

The imposing Apartheid Museum   209–210

A Soweto tour   214

An archaeological dig at the Cradle of Humankind   229

An overnight at the Lesedi Cultural Village   232–233

A night of gambling in Sun City   233, 236

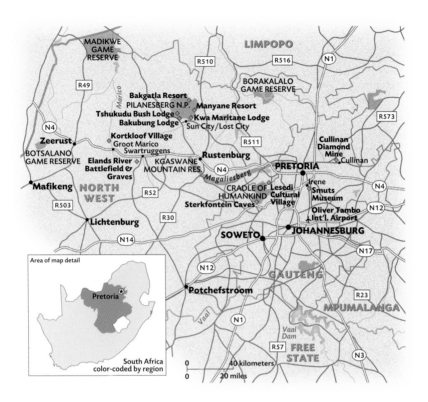

Johannesburg is also close to the Cradle of Humankind, where you can investigate the origins of humans—some of the world's most amazing paleonthological discoveries have taken place here—or visit the austerely beautiful Magaliesberg area.

Glitzy Sun City is a two-hour drive from Johannesburg. Not far from the resort's hotels, restaurants, casinos, and golf courses are the Pilanesberg National Park, an extinct volcano with a central lake that attracts the Big Five; and the Lesedi Cultural Village, where you can glean an informed appreciation of the cultural nuances between South African tribes.

For a complete change of pace, visit the quiet, dusty towns of Groot Marico and Zeerust, replete with the spirit of bygone days.

Word of Caution

Johannesburg is, unfortunately, known for its crime; always pay attention to your surroundings. Listen carefully to advice on where to go. Central Improvement District (CID) security guards, in green-and-yellow uniforms, are stationed on nearly every corner in targeted areas. Even so, downtown Johannesburg is best visited on a tour. Avoid looking like a tourist (e.g., don't fumble with a map on a street corner). Stay away from areas such as Hillbrow, Berea, and Yeoville. Carjackings are fairly common, but car crashes much more so; drive carefully with the windows up and the doors locked. Never pick up anyone. If you are stopped at a red light and someone runs up to the car, be prepared to break a traffic law or two in order to get away. ■

Johannesburg

Sitting on the highveld 5,700 feet (1,737 m) above sea level, Johannesburg is South Africa's most transformed city. Fighting a reputation of crime and danger, this largest of the country's cities (six million residents) boasts a melange of cultures and languages, the result of apartheid's end as well as an influx of immigrants and refugees.

The Central Business District reflected in the plate glass of a downtown office building

Johannesburg

📍 Map p. 197

Visitor Information

✉️ Rosebank
   Mall, Upper
   Level, Baker &
   Craddock Sts.

☎ 011/327-7000

www.gauteng.net

Central Business District

There are two Central Business Districts: the old CBD, which is situated in the center of the city of Johannesburg, and the new, properly functioning CBD, which is in Sandton, one of Johannesburg's most affluent suburbs to the north.

This strange proliferation of CBDs is a result of the vast social revolution presently engulfing South Africa. Under apartheid, the old CBD was classified as a whites-only area, meaning that black people could work in the city but were forbidden to live there. When the Group Areas Act was abolished in 1991, disadvantaged black people flooded into the city center, often taking over whole buildings. Many of the new arrivals were unemployed and desperately poor, and, almost inevitably, the crime rate rose.

The old CBD and the surrounding area had formerly been highly desirable real estate, but the large-scale migration of business and commerce away from the old CBD to the northern suburbs—fueled by the sharp rise in crime, serious traffic congestion, and inadequate public transport—lowered property prices.

The provincial government of Gauteng is based in the old CBD, and initiatives are under way to redevelop this part of the city. The Johannesburg municipality has installed a number of CCTV cameras there, and the presence of these silent monitors is said to have cut crime rates dramatically—but not completely. Several of the historic buildings have also been turned into condominiums, and developers hope that this will help draw new, more affluent residents into the area. The process of gentrification and redevelopment continues.

Despite the ups and downs of the CBD, Johannesburg remains the hub for radio and television in the country, and a number of magazines and newspapers are still located in the center of the city or nearby. Some stations, though, have already, or are in the process of, moving northward. Just outside the Johannesburg CBD, in Auckland Park, is the headquarters of the South African Broadcasting Corporation (SABC).

The old CBD has a very vibrant African charm and offers visitors a typically brash and sometimes bizarre set of contradictions. Glassed skyscrapers rise above aromatic Indian bazaars, sweet with the scent of fenugreek and cardamom. Busy retail outlets hawk flashy suits beside African *muti* (medicine) shops where traditional healers dispense advice, herbal remedies, and the occasional highly prized baboon paw. Street vendors sell fresh fruit, and the unmistakable smell of "Russians" (a popular spicy and very fatty sausage) grilling over charcoal braziers rises into the sky—where international jets soar overhead en route from Oliver Tambo International Airport to destinations right across Africa and the world.

Diagonal Street (see p. 207) and the **Newtown Cultural Precinct** (see p. 205) are

EXPERIENCE:
Watch a Rugby Match

One of South Africa's proudest moments came on June 24, 1995, when Nelson Mandela, dressed in a Springbok rugby shirt, presented the Rugby World Cup trophy to the South African team. South Africa—a new democracy, the first single-country host of the tournament, and the world champions—had finally come together as a nation, the whole country celebrating a sport that for so many years had been reserved for the white minority. Rugby is undoubtedly an important part of South African culture, and watching a live match at the now-famous **Ellis Park Stadium**, where the 1995 World Cup final was played, is an unforgettable experience for any fan. To view match schedules and for information on booking tickets, visit *www.ellispark.co.za*. Ellis Park is situated on the corner of Currey and Staib Streets in Doornfontein, Johannesburg. For larger matches, free park-and-ride facilities are available, in order to avoid traffic jams and ensure you get to your game on time. Inside the stadium, you can purchase refreshments at a number of food and beverage stalls, as well as at eight licensed pubs.

Carlton Centre

✉ 50 Commissioner St.

☎ 011/308-1331

💲 $

Standard Bank's African Art Collection

✉ Simmonds & Frederick Sts.

☎ 011/631-1889

🕐 Closed Sun.

www.standard bankgallery.co.za

colorful, cross-cultural areas and combine the best of the multi-ethnic present with a distinctly optimistic and upbeat attitude about the future.

It's this surprising contiguousness—supernatural cheek by jowl with the super-fashionable—that gives the old CBD its unique attraction. Urban decay notwithstanding, it boasts Africa's densest collection of skyscrapers—including the 730-foot-tall (223 m) **Carlton Centre,** still the continent's tallest, with a wonderful panoramic view of the city from its observation deck, **Top of Africa.** For a viewing of a

Sandton & Rosebank

The new CBD is situated in upmarket Sandton, high-intensity nouveau riche territory—an energetic, fun, ultramodern cosmopolitan business district full of vitality and ambition, fueled by unabashed conspicious consumption. Decidedly Euro- and Amerocentric, this corporate, commercial, and residential district, located in the northern part of the greater Johannesburg area, is considered the "richest square mile in Africa," the economic hub of the continent. The Johannesburg Stock Exchange moved

The Johannesburg skyline, dominated by the Hillbrow Tower

different kind, the Carlton Centre also houses the **Standard Bank Gallery,** where you can see the cream of contemporary South African artworks; Irma Stern, Gerard Sekoto, and Cyprian Shilakoe have all exhibited here.

to Sandton several years ago, to be followed by major financial institutions and information technology companies, many of which have their headquarters here. In Sandton fortunes can be won or lost in a single afternoon.

INSIDER TIP:

Don't miss a stroll through Parkhurst's quaint Fourth Avenue, with its eclectic antique stores and wide choice of restaurants. Breakfast or lunch at Nice is a must, with the egg basket being my Sunday weakness.

—ROBERTA COCI
National Geographic contributor

Sandton is pure glitz and glamour. It has superb hotels (the Michelangelo, for example; see p. 301), fine restaurants that cater for every taste from Thai through French classical to Cantonese and Punjabi, and glittering shopping centers (Sandton City, Hyde Park) that stock everything for those with five-star tastes and a penchant for displaying their wealth.

Sandton also abounds with nightclubs, music venues, spas, bookshops, galleries, antique shops, and luxury car showrooms showing off the latest from Aston Martin and Rolls Royce. In the surrounding quiet leafy suburbs like **Hyde Park,** newly built mansions and their well-manicured gardens are safely tucked away behind their high security walls, their driveways lined with gleaming luxury vehicles.

Nearby **Rosebank** is equally lively, though as a place for tourists to visit and locals to do business, this northern suburb has a more multicultural feel than Sandton.

It has effectively combined a successful commercial business area with very pleasant working, shopping, and entertainment environments. In compact Rosebank everything is within easy reach, walkable for visitors, residents, and workers alike.

In addition to being a place of business, Rosebank offers a wide range of leisure facilities and entertainment: sidewalk cafés, excellent restaurants, mime artists and street performers, nightclubs, art galleries, movie theaters, luxury hotels (including the Grace; see p. 301), and shopping malls that also feature weekly flea markets. There's a particularly good **African Crafts Market** *(Baker St. & Craddock Ave.),* which houses dreadful tourist junk alongside genuine antiques from Mali and Senegal. One of the finest malls in the northern suburbs, the **Zone@Rosebank** *(177 Oxford St, tel 011/788-1130, www.thezone atrosebank.co.za),* features a sizable movie theater as well as a number of expensive stores stocked with luxury shopping items.

There's always a buzz in Rosebank. Whatever your tastes —viewing art in some of the best galleries in South Africa, spending money on designer clothes, watching a foreign-language movie, or simply going for a walk through the leafy streets— Rosebank can satisfy them all. The suburb used to be home to outstanding art deco architecture and although, regretably, some of the best of it has been demolished to make way for redevelopment, you still catch surprising glimpses of deliciously formal facades.

Nice restaurant

✉ 14th St. & 4th Ave.

☎ 011/788-6286

🕐 Closed Mon. L, Sat.–Wed. D

Music in Johannesburg

The variety of musical traditions at play in Johannesburg today is unprecedented. Africa is vast, its cultures diverse, and most of its music forms are in evidence here. Outside any restuarant you might hear a Zanzibari street performer reel off complex guitar riffs that echo with the cadence of the Indian Ocean islands, while farther down the street, the sounds of Kenya, Nigeria, or Mali dominate the night.

The African folk music of Vusi Mahlasela was an inspiration to many in the antiapartheid movement.

There are numerous venues where you can enjoy live music as well as indigenous disco and toe-tapping *kwaito*, a local, driving township hip-hop.

Carfax *(39 Pim St., Newtown, tel 011/834-9187)* is a magnet for the cultural and artistic avant-garde of Johannesburg. The vivid kaleidoscope of musical styles and art forms showcased at this club testify to the fact that for all kinds of artists today Johannesburg is the hottest place in Africa to be. Carfax isn't just about music. It's typical of a wider South African cultural revolution. For good reason it touts itself as South Africa's most progressive arts scene venue.

Just a ten-minute ride away from Carfax is **Bassline** *(10 Henry Nxumalo St., tel 011/838-9145)*, in the Newtown Cultural Precinct—which is billed as Africa's Cultural Hub. Bassline's logo declares "In Music We Trust," and it's this faith in the integrity of good music and dedicated musicians that has driven the venue's continued success. It's a deeply held belief in the power of melody, lyrics, and composition to bond, soothe, and inspire that is one of Bassline's core values. Most nights here you can catch hip-hop, kwaito, or any of the other mutant musical genres.

In Melville you'll find **Roxy's Rhythm Bar** *(20 Main St., Melville, tel 011/726-6019)*, a Johannesburg musical institution that has been pumping out live music for around 20 years. Roxy's, as it's known affectionately by its regulars, has showcased neophyte South African musical talent since its launch, and continues to do so today. There's a youngish student population living in the Melville area whose taste in music is eclectic and sophisticated, honed as it is by Internet access and pop videos but jaded by constant exposure. Its boredom threshold is also notoriously low. As a result, Roxy's rapidly became a nursery for young groups with groundbreaking musical ideas that satisfied an audience eager for new sounds.

Go north to fashionable Sandton and you'll find **The Blues Room** *(Village Walk at Rivonia Rd. & Maud St., Sandton, tel 011/784-5527)*, a fashionable musical nightclub. This very cool venue is a magnet for the glamorous musical elite of Johannesburg. You'll see more Prada here than at Carfax or at Bassline, and the picky clientele demands—and gets—not just great music but great food, too.

INSIDER TIP:

Oppikoppi Music Festival— which takes place in August just two hours from Jo'burg—is the best place to experience a good mixture of South African music. It is a truly South African cultural experience.

—SAMANTHA REINDERS
National Geographic photographer

The atmosphere is sophisticated and laid-back at The Blues Room, and the music styles range from really good blues through jazz fusion to plain old rock. The vibe here isn't raw or edgy or rough; it's more about achieved perfection and virtuoso skill. This is a real professional musician's venue, where refinement, technique, and subtlety of interpretation are paramount. You'll find music lovers of every color and creed tapping their feet in time to the beat here—an audience that shares both a discerning ear and an appreciation for trans-cultural brilliance.

Popular Johannesburg venue Bassline and its musical credo

Johannesburg Art Gallery

✉ Klein St.,
   Joubert Park
☎ 011/725-3130
🕐 Closed Mon.

Johannesburg Art Gallery

The Johannesburg Art Gallery is situated in Joubert Park, on the edge of the old Central Business District. Although the neighborhood around the JAG isn't the best, there is a secure parking lot nearby.

The originator of the JAG's collection was the keen connoisseur and art collector, Lady Florence Phillips, wife of the landlord and mining magnate Lionel Phillips, known to all as Florrie. When she and her husband resided at the Arcadia estate in Johannesburg in the

Visiting the Museum: Upon entering the graceful three-story building, designed by Sir Edward Lutyens, you have the pick of 15 exhibition halls. The gallery's collection is so large, it can only display a tenth of it at once, but that fraction will still keep you out of the sun for hours—unless of course, you stay in the sculpture gardens.

The museum's **African art collection** is unbeatable, with paintings, sculpture, photography, prints, new media, video, and installations ranging from the 19th century to contemporary times. You'll find masterpieces by Gerard

Exhibits from African artists at the Johannesburg Art Gallery

early 1900s, she promoted local handicrafts and culture, and she was an important benefactor to both famous and struggling artists. She tirelessly worked for the creation of the JAG, a dream that became reality in 1916. Using funds donated by her husband, she established the museum's first collection.

Sekoto (1913–1993), a pioneer of urban black art; Alexis Preller (1911–1975), whose works diffuse surrealism with the African art of Swaziland and Zaire; and sculptor and painter Sydney Kumalo (1935–1988), inspired by Henry Moore and Marino Marini, as well as by African traditions.

Here, too, you'll find a vast array of traditional items, including

Market Theatre

One of the Newtown Cultural Precinct's highlights is the Market Theatre, where you'll experience some of the best theater, dance, and music in South Africa. The hall that houses the complex was once an indoor Indian fresh produce market (hence the name). Restoration began in 1975 when a group of committed thespians raised funds to save the old building with its fancy twin Edwardian entrance towers, doing much of the restoration work themselves.

The complex contains the **Main Theatre,** the **Barney Simon Theatre,** and the **Laager Theater.** It hosted protest theater during the years of struggle against apartheid and many great names appeared here—Athol Fugard, Mbogeni Ngema (writer of "Sarafina"), Barney Simon, John Kani, Winston Ntshona, and Pieter-Dirk Uys among them.

Tours of the Market Theatre are offered by appointment.

---

the **Brenhurst** and **Jacques Collections** of headrests, sticks, beadwork, and snuff containers. Such work was neglected during the colonial and apartheid eras, at a time when a more narrow definition of "high art" reigned.

You'll also discover an impressive array of **works by Europeans:** names like Picasso, Degas, Pissaro, and Monet. There was an El Greco, but that was stolen in 2002. Here are 17th-century Dutch paintings, European and British works of the 18th and 19th centuries, 19th-century and contemporary art from South Africa, and a representative selection of international 20th-century art.

Newtown Cultural Precinct

Situated in what was once a run-down area, the Newtown Cultural Precinct (also known as the Newtown Management District) is being developed into a grittily chic cultural hub that pulses with a uniquely African combination of energy and bursting artistic talent. It is a showcase for the vibrant renaissance of Afrocentric arts and crafts, theater, and a whole mix of hybrid art forms that have no real collective name in English. "Street art" probably comes closest.

Every Saturday a colorful **flea market** with a unique African atmosphere bustles into life next to the Market Theatre. Stallholders sell crafts and curios, clothing, antiques, printed fabrics, sculptures, and beadwork.

The precinct covers an area that stretches from the marshalling yards and railway lines to the north, the M2 highway in the south, West Street in the east, and Quinn Street in the west. Remember to always be alert to matters of personal safety, avoid excessive alcohol, and don't walk through the streets alone at night.

MuseuMAfrica: Adjoining the Market Theatre complex, in the former fruit and vegetable market, MuseuMAfrica is a premier history and cultural museum. It takes a good look at South Africa's complex

Market Theatre

✉ 56 Margaret Mcingana St.
☎ 011/832-1641
www.markettheatre .co.za

MuseuMAfrica

✉ 121 Bree St.
☎ 011/833-5624
🕓 Closed Mon.

geological, social, political, and economic history, including geological specimens, as well as reproductions of huts, tools, arts and crafts, and clothing of South African peoples and tribes. There's a permanent exhibition on the **"Treason Trials"** (1956–1961), in which radio announcements, newspaper headlines, and video interviews take you through these famous trials that put Nelson Mandela, among others, behind bars on Robben Island (see pp. 69, 72–73). Another exhibition, **"Johannesburg Transformations,"** includes a walk-through shack, a miner's dorm room, and a 1950s shebeen (illegal bar).

The museum also houses the **Bensusan Museum of Photography,** concentrating on the advances in the photography industry; and the **Museum of South Africa Rock Art,** providing insight into San Rock art.

Chinatown

Just as there are two Central Business Districts, so there are two Chinatowns in Johannesburg: one on Commissioner Street near the old CBD, the other on Derrick Avenue in Cyrildene.

In the 1900s the "First Chinatown" grew up at the western end of **Commissioner Street,** where Chinese immigrants from Guangdong Province lived and ran general stores, laundries, greengrocers' shops, teahouses, and wonderful restaurants, some of the best of which are right in the shadow of John Vorster Square police station.

There are still excellent restaurants and shops here, but as a result of urban decay (and despite the fact that local government is doing everything to renew the CBD) the Chinese community has progressively moved to the "Second Chinatown," in **Cyrildene.**

Cyrildene was once a predominantly Jewish area, but Mandarin has long since replaced Yiddish as the lingua franca, and the strip of Chinese restaurants and exotic shops

INSIDER TIP:

Make sure to pop by the specialist tea store called Chinese Tea, at 28 Derrick Avenue, where you can pick up unique gifts and recharge with a freshly brewed cuppa.

—ROBERTA COCI
National Geographic contributor

along **Derrick Avenue** is the result. Both sides of the avenue are crammed with beauty salons, flashy video-rentals, traditional herbalists, Asian food shops, and simple authentic eateries (formica tabletops, plastic bowls). You can enjoy delicacies from Canton and Shanghai, and sample dim sum and crispy roast duck breast, spicy slices of fried pork, dressed noodles, and a mouthwatering vareity of prawn and fish dishes.

One of the many restaurants along Derrick Avenue in Chinatown

Eating in Chinatown:

Eateries in Cyrildene's China-town include the well-estab-lished **Long Men** *(41 Derrick Ave., Cyrildene, tel 011/622-6861),* which uses fresh ingredients that vary daily to create a basically Cantonese cuisine. The dim sum is recommended. Down at the southern end of Derrick Avenue are two excellent restaurants that specialize in steamed dump-lings: the **Ching In** *(35 Derrick Ave., Cyrildene, tel 082/502-6456)* and the **Northern Dumpling Shop** *(S end of Derrick Ave.).*

The food is great. Be warned, though: If you don't speak Chinese, you may be reduced to sign language to place your order.

Diagonal Street & Fordsburg

Diagonal Street in the CBD could only exist in Africa. In the shadow of the former home of the old **Johannesburg Stock Exchange**—a beautiful modern blue-glass-and-steel construction that soars above the low rises of the old street—you'll find a jumbled array of African herbalist shops. You can browse among the merchandise—dried leguan skins, horns, bits of bark from muti (medicine) trees, skulls, bones, beads, and "magical" wristlets and anklets—before buying traditional medicine that (the shop owner will assure you) is an infallible and sovereign remedy for anything from asthma to tuberculosis. There might even be a *sangoma* (traditional healer) on hand who'll promise to predict the future by "throwing the bones" for you. And all this at midday on a 21st-century urban street.

Typical of the neighborhood is the **Museum of Man & Science**—not a museum at all, in fact, but a dark, aromatic, and musty shop that styles itself "The King of Muti, Herbal and Homeo-pathic Remedies." The "museum" is visited constantly by tourists

Museum of Man & Science

✉ 14 Diagonal St.

☎ 011/836-4470

🕐 Closed Sun.

Oriental Plaza

✉ Bree & High Sts., Fordsburg

☎ 011/838-6752

🕐 Closed Sun.

www.orientalplaza-fordsburg.co.za/

who tend to opt for good walking sticks and other curios rather than the dried vervet monkey skins.

The Fordsburg neighborhood has become a major center of South Asian culture, and if you like Pakistani curries this is the place to go for an authentic halal meal. The vegetarian Indian fare is equally

taken for granted that the shopper must bargain.

Walking in the plaza, your sense of smell is teased by delicious scents. The spice shops (a particular favorite is **Akhakwaya Spice Centre,** *Shop S263, tel 011/836-9280*) sell fresh ground curry ingredients troweled from big bins.

Fordsburg is home to many South Asian grocery stores and food outlets.

Gold Reef City

✉ Shaft 14, Northern Pkwy., Ormonde

☎ 011/248-6800

🕐 Closed Mon.

💲 $$$

www.goldreefcity .co.za

good. At the **Oriental Plaza** *(enclosed by Bree, Malherbe, Lilian, & Main Sts., tel 011/838-6752),* Muslim and Hindu coexist in enviable harmony, driven by their common goal of fair profit. This complex houses some 300 shops where you can buy anything from proper Sperry boat shoes to shoddily made junk from the Far East. Here you can find genuine designer merchandise that is priced 30 to 40 percent lower than at the Rosebank or Sandton malls. The plaza has long been famous for its fabrics: cottons, gaudily colored synthetics, and genuine silk cloth. All the prices marked are only a suggestion—at the plaza it is

Eating in Fordsburg: There's also a huge range of restaurants in Fordsburg and the plaza. Two of the best are **Al Makka** *(28 Mint Rd., tel 011/838-2545)* and **Just Samoosas** *(Shop 186/7 Oriental Plaza, tel 011/833-1139)* in the plaza. **Jimmy's Killer Prawns** *(41 Central Rd., tel 011/836-7237, www.jimmyskiller prawns.com)* is popular among seafood cognoscenti.

Gold Reef City

Gold Reef City (like the famous Lost City at Sun City; see pp. 233 & 236), 3 miles (5 km) from the city center on the

Northern Parkway, is really a theme park. True, it was rebuilt on the site of a former gold mine (No. 4 shaft of Crown Mines); entire streets, true to the originals, have been reconstructed, complete with furnished miners' houses. The employees even dress in authentic costumes from the 1800s. But its Disneylike theatricality is more showy than living history.

The attractions are many and varied. Kids and adrenalin junkies can try the **Anaconda, Flintstones, Miners' Revenge,** and **Golden Loop** rides. If you're curious about how gold is mined, take a trip down one of the city's deepest mines. Or view gold-containing veins in an old mine, and see how gold is poured into ingot molds. There are also a casino, nostalgic steam-train ride, a 4-D movie theater, and the Apartheid Museum.

Apartheid Museum

You cannot properly understand present-day South Africa unless you have a clear grasp of the impact that apartheid has had on the entire country. This is exactly what the Apartheid Museum sets out to do.

Opened in 2001, the museum

INSIDER TIP:

For an inside glance into Jo'burg's checkered history, join one of the Parktown Heritage Trust's *(www.parktown heritage.co.za)* **fascinating historical walks. Different routes cover various parts of the city.**

—ROBERTA COCI
National Geographic contributor

sits within the grounds of Gold Reef City, on a 17-acre (7 ha) site. The museum was designed by a consortium of architects, and its exhibitions by an interdisciplinary group of curators, filmmakers, historians, and designers. It is located within a garden landscaped to look like the indigenous South African bush.

Visitors may gain a small glimpse of the reality of apartheid as they first enter the building, where museum staff begin to classify each of them by race and the color of their skin. An enlightening

Apartheid Museum

- ✉ Gold Reef City, Northern Pkwy. & Gold Reef Rd., Ormonde
- ☎ 011/309 4700
- 🕐 Closed Mon.
- 💲 $

www.apartheid museum.org/

Arts for Sale

As people from across the continent are drawn to Johannesburg for economic reasons, they bring with them their diverse arts and crafts, which many make and sell. Masks, beaded dolls, wire baskets, and wooden carvings are among the prized pieces you may find at markets and shops around the city.

Visit the huge flea market in **Bruma** *(closed Mon.)* for a sampler. **Market Theatre's** Saturday flea market (see p. 205) is considered the original. There's also the **Rooftop Market** at Rosebank Mall on Sundays, frequented by locals and tourists alike. And these are just for starters ...

One of the exhibition areas at the Apartheid Museum

and slightly disturbing process, indeed. Once they "recover," visitors will appreciate the skillful use of documentary film footage, photographs, text panels, historical artifacts, and personal accounts of life in the old South Africa.

The displays, located in 22 exhibition areas, depict everyday apartheid scenes, while television monitors show images of "The Struggle" against the regime. The exhibitions lead the visitor on a deeply affecting emotional journey that tells the story of this state-sanctioned system of racial oppression, concluding with a look at post-apartheid South Africa.

One particularly powerful display consists of 131 nooses hanging from the roof, each noose representing one of the political prisoners who was hanged or "died in detention" during the apartheid era. Other displays capture iconic events in apartheid history: the notorious Sharpeville Massacre, the Rivonia Treason Trial, the Soweto Uprising, and the razing of District Six. They also depict the antiapartheid movements in exile and the widespread international sporting boycotts.

The key personalities are all there, too: "Grand Apartheid" architect H. F. Verwoerd, South Africa "strong man" B. J. Vorster, and P. W. Botha—as well as Desmond Tutu, F. W. de Klerk, martyr Steve Biko, and, of course, Nelson Mandela.

The museum experience culminates in the birth of a new democratic country in 1994 and the inauguration of Mandela—"the prisoner who became a president." An experience not to miss.

Museum Tours: Official four-hour tours to the museum depart Tuesdays, Wednesdays, Thursdays, and Fridays year-round—including pickup at your Johannesburg hotel, or other designated pickup point. ∎

EXPERIENCE: Help Fight AIDS

Africa is facing a formidable foe when it comes to the HIV/AIDS pandemic. This tragic disease is an insatiable killer, and despite efforts to prevent its spread, the rate of HIV infection is still rising in many African countries. Added to the poverty and malnutrition already rampant in much of the continent, AIDS is crippling the lives and economies of many nations, and South Africa is no exception.

The disease is leaving millions of children orphaned, and the number of child-headed families in South Africa is a growing concern for the government. There simply are not enough resources to give these children the education and care that they need. What's more, unlike in North America and Europe, people suffering from AIDS in South Africa often do not have access to the drugs that could enable them to live a relatively healthy, normal life.

One of the largest problems facing the country is the lack of a highly skilled health and development workforce equipped to fight the pandemic. This is largely due to the impact of AIDS itself, which has claimed the lives of many such trained workers and scared off their still healthy colleagues. Recent years have seen a mass exodus of doctors from the country. Many nations in Africa now have an average life expectancy of less than 40 years, with all kinds of negative consequences for health care and economic development.

Another challenge is educational. Efforts have been made by the government to increase awareness of the dangers of contracting AIDS and of the ways of preventing it. But more has to be done. Transmission rates are still too high.

The role of individuals is crucial in the battle against AIDS in South Africa. Volunteers can help in a variety of ways, whether it be in health care, education, or child care. Many programs help raise public

INSIDER TIP:

AIDS is a real problem in South Africa, especially in heterosexual relationships. So remember "the A-B-C rule": Abstain—Be faithful—Condomize.

—RICHARD WHITAKER
National Geographic contributor

awareness by sending out volunteers into communities and schools to help inform people about the pandemic. Individual volunteers can help in any stage of this process, from making posters to speaking to groups in the community.

Directly helping families affected by AIDS is another way that you can help. Volunteers can deliver food and clothes, talk to families about ways to stay healthy, and provide much needed moral support. Medical professionals are in particularly high demand for the treatment of patients, and those motivated individuals who have a science background can help in laboratories.

In addition, there are many programs that provide education, health care, and social welfare to the millions of AIDS orphans in the country, as well as programs that involve the HIV testing and counseling of adults. Volunteers are not required to have any special skills or qualifications to help in these efforts, although they must have a level of compassion, patience, and flexibility. Many of those affected by AIDS need care and encouragement to help them deal with the situation and make progress.

For information on how you can get involved, contact the **Nelson Mandela Foundation** (tel 011/728-1000, www.nelsonmandela.org), the **Treatment Action Campaign** (tel 086/136-3448, www.tac.org.za), or **Greater Good South Africa** (tel 021 794 0580, www.myggsa .co.za).

Soweto

Though it sounds like an African word, Soweto is actually an acronym of South Western Townships. Situated south of Johannesburg, Soweto was designed and built in the 1950s by the apartheid government as a dormitory suburb for black migrant workers on whose labor the city so heavily depended.

Well-manicured homes of Soweto's emerging middle class

Soweto

🅰 Map p. 197

Visitor Information

✉ Walter Sisulu Square of Dedication, Kliptown

☎ 011/982-8034 or 082/962-6776

www.sowetotourism
.co.za

Once started Soweto grew, without planning, into a sprawling collection of townships. Despite government attempts to stop them, impoverished black workers in search of work began to move to Johannesburg—from dead-end rural areas (the "homelands"), from the so-called Bantustans (which were economically unviable), and even from neighboring African countries.

Soweto is now really a city in its own right, where more than two million people live—the largest black urban concentration on the continent. Soweto is home to the only black-owned private clinic in South Africa and its public hospital, Chris Hani Baragwanath, is the biggest in Africa. Increasingly, Soweto is also becoming known for its nightlife, featuring such jazz and *kwaito* (Soweto-style hip-hop) venues as **The Rock** and the **Back Room.**

A wide spectrum of dwellings exists in Soweto, ranging from shacks of corrugated metal to the luxurious mansions of the newly rich. Black migrant workers were originally housed in tiny four-roomed "matchbox houses," and these structures are still everywhere to be seen. Soweto also comprises wealthier, middle-class areas like **Diepkloof,** just beyond Orlando West, and neighboring **Diepkloof Extension,** where trees line the well-maintained roads, and good schools and nursery schools are available.

An unfortunate social reality are the shack areas (politely known as "informal settlements") that have grown up around the township. Sadly, many South Africans are still poor and unemployed, and have little choice but to seek shelter in these makeshift dwellings.

Fight Against Apartheid

The reason most people visit Soweto is to try to obtain some insight into the township's past political struggles—and triumphs. It has a proud history as the place where the politics of resistance to the apartheid regime flourished. Among the places associated with the freedom struggle are **Kliptown** and **Freedom Square** (*near Union St. & Boundary Rd., Kliptown*). Here

EXPERIENCE: Drinking in a Shebeen

To the majority of the South African population, shebeens (traditionally unlicensed drinking holes in the townships) are glorious, magical places. They're a symbol of power, of unity, of rebellion—and of a great night out. The apartheid government tried to exclude black South Africans from any kind of independent economic activity, but resourceful township men and women (the latter affectionately known as "shebeen queens") opened up their houses to the community, serving up all sorts of backyard-brewed concoctions.

The prohibition, intended to rein in and humiliate the township folk, instead led to the development of a new cultural expression. Shebeens became go-to spots where all-night parties were held, political meetings run, and legendary singers like Miriam Makeba got their start. However, shebeens were risky business, constantly subjected to police raids that always led

to confiscation of alcohol and often arrest. Not that this deterred the shebeen owners, who always stepped straight back into their trade.

In 1984 the apartheid government realized that the shebeens were a force to be reckoned with, and agreed to hand out 27 licenses. Nowadays there are several hundred licensed shebeens in the country. However, unlicensed ones are still rumored to rule the roost.

For a true shebeen experience, visit **Wandies Place** (*618 Makhalenele St., Dube Village, tel 011/982-2796, www .wandies.co.za*), a success story. Wandi Ndaba opened his illegal shebeen in 1981 and had to endure the threat of police raids for a full decade before finally being licensed in 1991. Now able to ply his trade legally, Wandi offers a full restaurant and bar experience not to be missed.

Most township tours offer visits to shebeens; see sidebar p. 214 for details.

EXPERIENCE: Visiting a Township

During the apartheid era, blacks (as well as Indians and other nonwhites) were forced to live in townships, which are located on the outskirts of urban areas. A large proportion of the urban population still live in these separate entities, many of them in dwellings that lack electricity and other basic facilities. Many visitors can spend a month in South Africa without stepping foot in one of its townships. However, a township tour offers the chance to gain an appreciation of the South African reality, to see how the majority of South Africans live.

Your time will be filled with a wide variety of activities. Whether you browse herbalist stores, drink in a shebeen, shop at home-based *spaza* shops, listen to live music, or just chat with local residents, a township tour is bound to provide insight into a different culture.

One of the most established companies to take you on a one-day tour of Soweto is **Themba Day Tours & Safaris** *(contact Pat Duxbury, tel 011/463-3306, e-mail: nik@global.co.za, www.sowetotour .co.za/index.html)*. This company offers you a new perspective and personal insight into the largest and most vibrant black city in Africa.

For other tours in the Johannesburg area, contact **Soweto Tours** *(tel 011/326-1700, www.soweto.co.za)* or **Vhupo Tours** *(tel 011/936-0411, www.vhupo-tours.com)*. For tours in Cape Town, contact **Camissa Travel and Tours** *(tel 083/392-8588, www.gocamissa.co.za)* or **Inkululeko** *(tel 021/433-2322, www.inkululekotours.co.za)*.

Tours range in price between R300 and R800.

---

the Congress Alliance adopted the Freedom Charter. (The Congress Alliance was a group of like-minded organizations that met in 1955 to chart a future for all the people of South Africa.) The ANC subsequently adopted the Freedom Charter as policy.

Another important institution is the **Regina Mundi Church** *(1149 Khumalo St., Rockville, tel 011/986-2545, closed weekends, doncation)*. Within its walls took place many protest meetings, gatherings of people passionately opposed to apartheid, and funerals of slain resistance leaders.

The **Orlando West** quarter is the world's only neighborhood that two Nobel Peace Prize winners have called home:

> The Orlando West quarter is the world's only neighborhood that two Nobel Peace Prize winners have called home: Nelson Mandela and Anglican Archbishop Desmond Tutu.

Nelson Mandela and Anglican Archbishop Desmond Tutu. **Nelson Mandela's first house** *(Vilakazi St., Orlando West, tel 011/936-7754, $)*, where the future president lived before his arrest in 1962, contains personal artifacts including honorary degrees. Nearby stands **Desmond Tutu's residence** (*Vilakazi St., Orlando West, closed to public),* near **Holy Cross Church,** his home parish.

One of Soweto's most poignant sights is the **Hector Pieterson Memorial Site & Museum** *(Khumalo & Pela Sts., Orlando West, tel 011/536-* fusillade, 12-year-old Hector Pieterson among them. This tragic event put into motion the momentum that eventually led to apartheid's demise.

The memorial and museum were built in 2002, near the spot where young Hector was shot. The memorial is an inscribed stone slab, while the

An "informal settlement" in Kliptown, the oldest residential district of Soweto

0611, $), opposite Holy Cross Church. On June 16, 1976, many schoolchildren came together in Soweto to protest the government's insistence that Afrikaans should be used as the language of choice by teachers in township schools. Apartheid regime police were out in force, and as children began to sing the banned ANC anthem "Nkosi Sikelel' iAfrika," the police opened fire on them. Twenty children died in the museum has photos and films.

Soweto is a vibrant, cacophonic, endless sprawl that, once you're in the middle of it, is difficult to navigate your way out. Given that, along with the fact that safety can be an issue, the best way to visit is by guided tour, usually offered by half day or one day. Special interest tours are also available, including ones that focus on the arts, restaurants, or traditional medicine. ∎

Pretoria

Just a half hour away from Johannesburg, elegant, tranquil Pretoria is the official administrative and de facto national capital of South Africa. Located in a rich valley ringed with hills, it's affectionately called Jacaranda City for the clouds of purple-blossomed trees that line its thoroughfares in summer.

A statue of Paul Kruger at Church Square, downtown Pretoria

Pretoria

🗺 Map p. 197

Visitor Information

✉ Old Nederlandsche Bank Bldg., Church St.

☎ 012/358-1485

In all probability, the valley in which Pretoria is situated was first settled by the Ndebele people, and later by refugees from the Zulu *mfecane* (literally "the crushing" of rival tribes) induced by Shaka's military adventures in and around what is now KwaZulu-Natal. The town of Pretoria, founded in 1855, was named after the famous Voortrekker leader, Andries Pretorius, the hero of the Battle of Blood River (1838).

Pretoria is a particularly pretty city, with wide, jacaranda-lined boulevards and a settled, placid air. As the country's administrative capital, it boasts many foreign embassies and consulates, bringing a cosmopolitan and urbane atmosphere. Home to a variety of higher education institutions—the large University of Pretoria, the (correspondence-course) University of South Africa, the Tshwane University of Technology, and the Council for Scientific and Industrial Research—it is also the country's unofficial academic capital. The presence of so many students promises a vibrant

La Madeleine

Celebrities, diplomats, and lovers of good cooking flock to La Madeleine (*122 Priory Rd., Lynnwood Ridge, tel 012/361-3667, closed Sun., lunch by appt.*) for the outstanding French and local food and French-rustic decor. Daniel and Karine Leusch, chefs and owners of this Pretoria institution, have won numerous awards for their cuisine over the past two decades or so. The small menu changes frequently, but you might be offered the likes of deboned quail with port sauce and truffle jus, or medallions of springbox sirloin with cranberry sauce and pears poached in honey and red wine. Don't miss it.

and other stately buildings.

The imposing **South African State Theatre** complex on Pretorius Street has six performance venues and a huge public square. On offer at the complex are high-quality drama, ballet, opera, cabaret, and symphony concerts. At the Momentum you can view the work of promising new producers, directors, and performers. The Opera House has a capacity of 1,300, while the smaller-scale Intimate and Rendezvous are designed for cabaret and revues. The Drama Theatre seats 640, all on a single level. Third largest of

INSIDER TIP:

For a fun and vibrant place to hang out, head to Hatfield near the University of Pretoria where there are lots of places to eat, drink, and dance the night away.

—KATE PARR
National Geographic field researcher

the venues is the Arena.

Nearby **Burgers Park** (*Jacob Maré St., bet. van der Walt & Andires Sts.*) is a fine Victorian-style botanical garden, with rows of roses and a Victorian house that now serves as a restaurant.

Built in 1884, the modest Victorian **Paul Kruger Museum,** on the other side of Church Square, appears almost as it did when it was the home of Paul Kruger, president of the Transvaal

South African State Theatre

✉ 320 Pretorius St.

☎ 012/392-4027

www.statetheatre.co.za

Paul Kruger Museum

✉ 60 Church St.

☎ 012/326-9172

💲 $

energy, especially in areas such as Hatfield, where funky bars, discos, and quirky eateries reign.

Visiting Pretoria

Because of their close proximity, the outer suburbs of Pretoria and Johannesburg seem to blend together. But once inside the city center, there are distinct neighborhoods. In the middle is **Pretoria Central,** the heart of the city, with some of its most historic buildings. A statue of President Paul Kruger dominates pretty **Church Square** (*bordered by Paul Kruger & Church Sts.*), Pretoria's hub, surrounded by the **Old Raadsaal** (Council Chamber), **Palace of Justice,**

A bust of Kruger, the great Boer resistance leader, at the Paul Kruger Museum

Transvaal Museum of Natural History

✉ Paul Kruger St.

☎ 012/322-7632

🕐 Closed Sun.

💲 $

Republic between 1883 and 1902 and leader of the Boer resistance to British imperialism.

British interest in the Transvaal Republic intensified after the discovery of gold on the Witwatersrand in 1886, leading directly to the outbreak of the South African War (1899–1902). In concentration camps set up by the British, many thousands of Boer men, women, and children died, along with their African workers.

The house museum contains period furnishings, photographs, and personal items. Note the two stone lions on the veranda, presented to President Kruger as a birthday gift in 1896 by mining magnate Barney Barnato. Exhibits in the adjacent museum trace Kruger's life.

Many of South Africa's statesmen and celebrities are buried at nearby **Heroes' Acre** *(Church St. & D. F. Malan Dr.)*, at Church Street Cemetery. Trees planted in

the 19th century shade the pleasant walkways.

While it's relatively safe and easy to walk around the neighborhoods, a car or taxi is necessary to traverse larger distances.

Transvaal Museum of Natural History

The Transvaal Museum, founded in 1892, is located in the center of Pretoria. Mounted outside its impressive entrance are huge whale and dinosaur skeletons. The traditional sandstone interior is designed around airy and spacious exhibition rooms.

Exhibits include information on important hominid fossils from the Cradle of Humankind World Heritage site (see pp. 226–231) with their associated fossil fauna. Among the museum's other collections are fossils of amphibians, fish, reptiles, and plants from the Karoo; late Permian transitional mammal-like reptiles (also found in the Karoo); and large collections of mounted mammals, birds, reptiles, and invertebrates, especially beetles and butterflies.

But the most famous object in the museum is a cast replica of the **skull of "Mrs. Ples"** (from *Plesianthropus*, meaning "almost human"), the nickname given "her" by journalists. The skull was unearthed at nearby Sterkfontein Caves in 1947 by the Transvaal Museum's Robert Broom (see sidebar p. 23).

It is now thought that small-brained Mrs. Ples walked upright, and she is classed as *Australopithecus africanus,* one of the remote ancestors of humankind. Remains of other members of this species have come from Taung in the North West Province and Makapansgat in the Northern Cape Province. The significance of these fossil finds is immense, as are those by Maeve Leakey, who discovered the fossil bones and teeth of *Kenyanthropos platyops,* dating back some 3.5 million years, possibly an entirely new genus of ancestors; and the discovery at Sterkfontein Caves of a complete fossil skeleton of one of the oldest apelike ancestors of humans by Dr. Ron Clarke, Stephen Motsumi, and Nkwane Molefe of the University of the Witwatersrand, dating back at least 3.5 million years, quite possibly 4.

Visiting the Museum: The attractive and engaging displays have clearly been designed to bring the past to life in an exciting and dramatic way. The museum offers a wide range of programs and guided tours for students (of all ages) and visitors, domestic and international alike. At the **Discovery Centre** (*$, by appt. only),* younger visitors can have a hands-on experience of natural history that engages their five senses. A particularly popular exhibit at the Discovery Centre is a reconstruction

Cheese

Although there's been an established cheese industry in South Africa for some time, artisan cheesemaking has been on the rise over the past few years. About half of the country's cheese is produced around the Western Cape (because of its European influence and mild climate), but you can find cheesemakers all over, including Pretoria. Mild cheeses are the traditional fare, but lately there has been an influx of strong, original blends coming from the smaller fromageries. Try Bokmakiri, a soft goat's milk cheese coated with pepper and garlic.

of a *Deinonychus* dinosaur, one of the "stars" of the movie *Jurassic Park.*

The Transvaal Museum of Natural History is driven by a kind of holy awe at the complexity and wonder of creation. Nowhere is this more apparent than in the permanent displays, such as **Genesis I: Hall of Life,** which is situated, appropriately enough, on the first floor. The exhibit tells the remarkable story of how life originated and developed on our planet, tracing the process from the first blue-green algae 3.5 billion years ago to the amazing biodiversity of the present day.

The **Mammal Hall** focuses on the evolution of mammals, Africa's best known bird book (first published in 1940 and still in print today), who was a former director of the Transvaal Museum. The numbering of Roberts's *Birds of Southern Africa* is used to identify the hundreds of birds displayed on the mezzanine floor.

The Transvaal Museum houses impressive natural history collections.

although it also has displays that deal with dinosaurs and the striking mammal-like reptiles of the Karoo. Reproductions of the skulls of hominids, including *Australopithecus africanus* (Mrs. Ples), are on display. The exhibit strongly makes the point that, based on the present complex evidence of hominid fossils, it is hard to draw up a clear-cut map of the relationships between contemporary humans and their hominid ancestors.

The **Austin Roberts Bird Hall,** showcasing nearly 870 of southern Africa's birds, was named for the author of South

Geoscience Museum: Your inner rock hound will rejoice as the Geoscience Museum, housed in the Transvaal Museum, welcomes you to the fascinating world of precious and semiprecious stones. The museum gathers its collection from geological sites around the country, of which there is no shortage. Alongside the mesmerizing displays are easy-to-understand explanations of the science behind diamonds, geodes, fossils, and meteorites. There is also information on the Tswaing

Meteorite crater, which is only 25 miles (40 km) away.

Pretoria Art Museum

A constantly changing collection of South African art is found in this gallery, located in Arcadia Park, in the eastern part of town. The emphasis is on the so-called Old Masters, namely Pieter Wenning, J. H. Pierneef, Frans Oerder, Anton van Wouw, Hugo Naudé, Irma Stern, and Maggie Loubser. International art here focuses on graphic printmaking from Europe and the United States. Guided tours are available.

Union Buildings

Anyone who watched Nelson Mandela's inaugural speech as the president of South Africa will have caught a glimpse of the Union Buildings, which rose behind him. (A statue of Mandela was to have been erected on the spot where he made his inauguration speech, but instead was placed in Sandton's Mandela Square.)

The Union Buildings, measuring 900 feet (285 m) long, are the masterpiece of British architect Sir Herbert Baker (1862–1946), who designed many public buildings in South Africa. Located on a hill above Pretoria called Meintjies Kop, in the Arcadia neighborhood, the structure is built from a pleasing golden sandstone. The colonnaded central building curves around an amphitheater (which is where Mandela stood). Two impressive wings represent the two languages that were given official status at the time of union in 1910, English and Afrikaans—a symbolism no longer relevant in the new South Africa, with its eleven official languages.

With twin cupola towers at each end of the central colonnade, and ornamental pools, fountains, sculptures, and balustrades within and surrounding the amphitheater, the Union Buildings exude an understated and serene confidence.

The complex was commissioned around the time of union and finished three years later. Since then the Union Buildings have housed the executive branch of government, as they still do today. The president of the republic has his offices here.

There is no public admittance, but you can have a picnic lunch in the gorgeous formal gardens.

INSIDER TIP:

At Pretoria Zoo, see African game and some endangered species up close; a good way to familiarize yourself with the wildlife before you go on safari.

—CAGAN H. SEKERCIOGLU
National Geographic field researcher

National Zoological Gardens of South Africa

Also known as Pretoria Zoo, this is the largest zoo in South Africa and the only one with national status. The zoo's animal collection started modestly in 1899 with just 46 animals, including a

Pretoria Art Museum

✉ Schoeman & Wessels Sts., Arcadia

☎ 012/344-1807

$ $

www.pretoria artmuseum.co.za

National Zoological Gardens of South Africa

✉ 232 Boom St.

☎ 012/328-3265

$ $$ (includes aquarium & reptile park)

www.nzg.ac.za

serval, two suricate, a puff adder, and two gray dormice. Small beginnings indeed for a complex that now spreads across a 210-acre (85 ha) site and boasts international acclaim.

The national zoo has grown to the point where it today houses 202 species of birds, 93 reptile species, 209 mammal species, 4 invertebrate species, and 7 species of amphibian—for a grand total of more than 9,000 individual animals from almost every continent. An interesting aside: The world's first zoo-born white rhino was born at the National Zoological Gardens.

On the expansive grounds you'll come across the Big Five, as well as Sichuan takins, Kodiak bears, singing gibbons, antelope, and Bengal tigers, to name just a few of the zoo's international cast of animals. About 8 miles (13 km) of walkways lace the zoo; the less energetic or physically challenged can rent a golf cart and trundle smoothly past the animals. Alternatively, jump

Satellite Zoos

The zoological gardens manages three satellite facilities: iLichtenburg in the North West Province, Mokopane in Limpopo, and the Emerald Animal World Facility in Vander-bijlpark. These facilities total an additional 779 acres (7,600 ha) and serve as breeding centers for numerous animals, both indigenous and exotic.

on the cable car and get a bird's-eye view of the zoo.

Join a night tour *($$$$)* to explore the behavior of nocturnal animals; a guide will share insights into owls, elephants, lions, and red pandas. Camping tours *($$$)* are also available, allowing you to wake to the roar of Africa's king of the jungle, the lion.

The zoo also boasts the country's largest inland **aquarium,** where you can see ragged-tooth

Flamingos at Pretoria's zoological gardens

sharks, electric eels, piranhas, and jellyfish up close. Tropical fish darting about colorful coral reefs are an ever popular draw. Aquarium evening tours are offered.

The zoo includes a **reptile park** (check out the king crocodiles), a **farmyard** (a favorite among children), and South Africa's third best collection of exotic plants.

There is a restaurant, as well as a picnic area with barbecue facilities alongside the Apies River.

Klapperkop Fort & Military Museum

As a reponse to civil disturbances a decade before the outreak of the South African War (the Jameson Raid and riots in Johannesburg), Fort Klapperkop was constructed to prevent their repetition. It stands high above Pretoria, the city it was designed to protect (though it is said that a shot was never fired in anger from the fort). Building began in December 1896 and took a year to complete. The climb up the hill to Fort Klapperkop is well worth the effort. Its museum has unusual and rare objects on display, and you'll get a spectacular view of the city and the surrounding countryside.

Voortrekker Monument & Museum

Atop a small hill outside Pretoria rises the Voortrekker Monument, inaugurated in 1949 and a national icon for South African Afrikaaners. It honors the thousands of Voortrekkers (pioneers) who left the Cape Colony

between 1834 and 1854 to find independence from the British, called the Great Trek (see p. 26).

Around the building's perimeter, a chain of 64 wagons is carved into the granite wall, representing the Battle of Blood River, in which trekkers and Zulus clashed.

In the massive **Hall of Heroes,** 27 bas-relief panels creating an

INSIDER TIP:

Cenotaph Hall at Voortrekker Monument is designed so that once a year on December 16, the sun shines through the dome roof onto the cenotaph to illuminate the words "Ons vir jou, Suid-Afrika," literally translated "We for thee, South Africa."

—SAMANTHA REINDERS
National Geographic photographer

immense 100-yard (91 m) frieze illustrate the Great Trek, as well as the day-to-day life of Voortrekkers and Zulus. The depiction of indigenous South Africans is obviously biased and inaccurate, but the frieze is impressive nonetheless.

In **Cenograph Hall,** you'll find the museum's central focus, a cenograph that memorializes Piet Retief and all the other Voortrekkers who died during the Great Trek. Flags from the different Voortrekker republics decorate the hall, and several display cases

Klapperkop Fort & Military Museum

✉ Johann Rissik Dr.

☎ 012/460-3235

🕐 Closed Sat.–Sun.

Voortrekker Monument & Museum

✉ Voortrekker Monument Heritage Site, Eeufees Rd., Groenkloof

☎ 012/326-6770, 012/325-7885, or 012/325-0477

$ $$$

www.voortrekker mon.org.za

Smuts Museum

✉ Jan Smuts Ave., Irene

☎ 012/667-1176

$ $

Cullinan Diamond Mine

✉ 95 Oak Ave., Cullinan

☎ 012/305-2649

$ $

contain many period relics, including weapons and household items.

Despite the monument's ideological baggage, it remains historically important. In an attempt to show this, Nelson Mandela visited the monument in 2002, amid threats from the right-wing AWB. There is talk of building a heritage center that ignores political implications of the Voortrekker movement and focus solely on its history.

INSIDER TIP:

For a really special trip, book a scenic hot-air balloon ride through Life Ballooning (www.lifeballooning. co.za) in Cullinan, which can be paired with a tour of the Cullinan Diamond Mine.

—ROBERTA COCI
National Geographic contributor

Near Pretoria: Smuts Museum

In the idyllic village of Irene, southeast of Pretoria, you'll find the farmhouse at Doornkloof, where former Prime Minister Jan Smuts (1870–1950) lived out his retirement. With its spacious and tranquil grounds, the museum's a pleasant retreat from the hurry of a traveler's itinerary. Inside you'll find objects ranging from the historical to the sentimental, plus some dealing with botany, one of Smut's greatest passions.

Cullinan Diamond Mine

The third richest diamond producing mine in South Africa, four times larger than the Big Hole at Kimberley, this fully operational mine in the quaint mining town of Cullinan offers surface and underground tours. You'll also view copies of famous diamonds discovered here (including the Taylor-Burton diamond). The former mining director's Victorian home, the **Oak House** *(103 Oak Ave., tel 012/305-2364),* has been converted into a guesthouse and tea garden. ∎

The Cullinan Diamond

Renowned as the source of the world's only blue diamonds, the Premier Diamond Mine, 25 miles (40 km) east of Pretoria, was opened in 1902. Within three years of operation, it yielded up the Cullinan Diamond, at 3,106.75 carats (621.35 g) the largest gem diamond ever found. A hundred years later the Premier finally changed its name to the **Cullinan Diamond Mine** in honor of its world-famous find. In addition to some 96 smaller brilliants, nine large gems have been cut from the original Cullinan Diamond—the biggest of which is known as the "Star of Africa." All are now in the possession of the British royal family, some of them part of the crown jewels.

EXPERIENCE: Volunteer with Wildlife

South Africa may be renowned for its prolific and varied wildlife, but as elsewhere in the world, its modern lifestyle has taken a heavy toll on nature. Despite many nature and game reserves in the country, there remains a constant battle to fight for the survival of the indigenous species—a battle in which volunteers are most welcome.

Baboons in the Kruger National Park

If conservation appeals to you, there are many options for volunteering in the wildlife sector in South Africa. From tracking elephants to tagging great white sharks, from cleaning penguins to monitoring lions, there is no shortage of adventure with a purpose.

Generally, volunteer programs are self-funded in that you pay a certain amount for accommodation and food, and follow an organized series of shifts. Official programs tend to last anywhere between 1 and 12 weeks, although many organizations, especially those in cities, will accept a few hours of volunteering. Most involve a fair degree of training, which makes it a worthwhile experience for any traveler—a wonderful way to develop your knowledge of nature firsthand while making an ecological contribution.

One such program is **Enkosini's Kariega Game Reserve Project.** On this two-, three-, or four-week program, volunteers are trained in conservation and bush survival through means of bush walks, sleep outs, and day and night game-drives. This is very much a hands-on program in which volunteers (or "conservation managers" as they are known) have the opportunity to work right among the Big Five. You may find yourself monitoring lion kills, tracking hyenas, or conducting research studies on any of the farm's many species. The program is also community based, and volunteers spend one day a week teaching at a local underfunded farm school. Type of work determines type of accommodation. If you decide to track elephants in the desert, be prepared to camp; if you're working with penguins in Cape Town, you can return to your own hotel at night. Most programs provide standard shared accommodation, with decent shower facilities and food.

There is an exceptionally wide choice when it comes to the type of work involved—from cleaning animal pens and building enclosures to tracking and monitoring animals, conducting research surveys, or even cage diving with great white sharks.

International travelers will find it easiest to work through an organization that will book your accommodation and travel, and advise you on the program that will fit your requirements. Contact one of the following: **Enkosini Eco Experience** (tel 082/442-6773, www.enkosiniecoexperience.com) or **Aviva Wildlife Conservation and Community Projects** (tel 021/557-4312, www.aviva-sa.com). Prices vary considerably depending on the type and length of the program.

Cradle of Humankind

Under the burnt earth of western Gautang, a complex of dolomitic limestone caves contains the fossilized remains of our hominid ancestors. This area is interesting geologically, but from a genealogical perspective, it's breathtaking

Displays at the Cradle of Humankind, site of some of the world's most important paleoanthropological finds

Cradle of Humankind

 25 miles (40 km) W of Johannesburg, on R400 just off R563 Hekpoort Rd.

☎ 011/355-1400

$ $$–$$$

www.cradleof humankind.co.za

Understanding where we come from is key to understanding who we are. Getting a clear picture of the environments that were our earliest homes and grasping the evolutionary pressures that formed and forced us to become homo sapiens—and not bonobo chimps—will help us to define what it is to be "human." That definition is to be based on empirical fact: fossil evidence, cranial capac-

ity, dentition, and physiology. And this is why the Cradle of Humankind—also known as Maropeng, which is Setswana for "the place where we once lived"—is so important. It is central to our understanding of who and what we are.

Twenty-five miles (40 km) west of Johannesburg lies a 117,000-acre (47,000 ha) valley. The landscape is undistinguished: thorntrees, scrappy bushes, stone outcrops, low kopjes. The sun burns down, winter and summer. A windswept, almost barren place, you might think, and nothing like the Garden of Eden. Yet this area —Sterkfontein and the Cradle of Humankind—is one of the richest sources of hominid (human-tending) fossils in Africa. The valley contains at least 40 different fossil sites, of which only 13 have been excavated.

Fossil discoveries made at Sterkfontein tell us that our earliest ancestors lived in and around this valley for some three million years. An ancestral Prometheus flourished here: At adjacent Swartkrans there is evidence of the earliest recorded use of fire, as far back as 1.3 million years ago. More than 40 percent of all the existing fossil hominid finds from Africa have been made in and around Sterkfontein—more than 500 hominid fossils in all, along with thousands of stone tools.

The area includes **Bolt's Farm,** where fossil evidence of *Dinofelis*-like (sabre-toothed) cats has been found; **Haasgat,** where there is 1.3-million-year-old fossil evidence of ancestral arboreal monkeys; and **Gondolin,** where 9,000 fossil specimens of a multitude of species have been discovered. Little wonder that this incredibly fossil-rich area was declared a World Heritage site in 1999. Six years later, permission was granted at the 29th session of the Unesco World Heritage Committee to incorporate the geographically distinct but paleontologically associated area of Taung, in North West Province.

However, it's not just the volume or diversity of the fossils that make Sterkfontein stand out. It is the fact that *three* of the most significant fossil hominid finds ever made come from the Cradle of Humankind. The first of these is the **"Taung Child,"** a fossilized skull unearthed at Taung in 1924 by quarrymen working for the Northern Lime Company and whose importance was first recognized by Professor

INSIDER TIP:

Picnics are a great way of experiencing the Cradle. Pack your own and pick a scenic spot, or have the Cradle restaurant organize a picnic basket for you, complete with waiter service.

—ROBERTA COCI
National Geographic contributor

Raymond Dart (he considered it a new species). The second is **"Mrs. Ples"** (possibly *Mr.* Ples, according to new research carried out by Dr. Francis Thackeray of the Transvaal Museum), which dates back 2.5 million years and was found by Robert Broom in 1947 at Sterkfontein. And the third is **"Little Foot,"** discovered by Dr. Ron Clarke and Phillip Tobias in 1995, also at Sterkfontein. Understanding the nature and importance of each of these finds will help you understand the significance of the Cradle and why any visit to South Africa must include a trip there.

Taung Child

Until Professor Dart's breakthrough with the Taung Child, which he named *Australopithecus africanus* (southern African ape), it was thought that humankind had evolved in Asia, not Africa. Prevail-

nothing short of revolutionary. His claim that bipedalism and precision tool use *preceded* the development of the large brain turned upside down all accepted theories of human evolution.

Mrs. Ples

The degree of preservation of Mrs. Ples is extraordinary, and it's easy to understand why the

The ancient cave system at Sterkfontein, a UNESCO World Heritage site

ing opinion was based in part on the existence of a skull found in England, "Piltdown Man," with a large braincase but primitive ape-like features. The idea that humankind had an African origin was paleontological sacrilege. Dart's startling hypothesis—and the fact that Piltdown Man proved to be a competently assembled fake—changed all that.

Dart's understanding that the Taung Child was representative of a species of small erect-walking ancestral hominids who lived 2.6 to 2.5 million years ago was

discovery of this skull caused such a furor when it was first announced. There have been certain problems associated with dating at Sterkfontein; unlike the East African hominid finds, for example, hominids in South Africa are dated using stratigraphic evidence and associated well-dated faunal remains, because the area is not volcanic. That notwithstanding, it appears that Mrs. Ples lived about 2.5 million years ago at a time when the area consisted of woodland, forest, and encroaching grassland.

Although the skull's discoverer, Dr. Broom, initially coined a new genus, *Plesianthropus,* for his find, the skull is now thought to be the most complete cranium of the species *Australopithecus africanus* (the same as the Taung Child), which may be our common ancestor. The decision was later taken to reclassify all the Sterkfontein fossils as *Australopithecus africanus transvaalensis* (still the same genus and species as the Taung fossil but a separate subspecies). The find is important because it provided more fossil evidence and validated Dart's earlier claim that *Australopithecus* predated all other hominid fossils *(Homo erectus, Homo neanderthalensis)* and was in all likelihood a direct "missing link" between ancestral Miocene hominids, *Homo habilis* (handy man), and ourselves.

Little Foot

So many palaeontological finds seem a combination of sheer chance and directed accident— what Carl Jung called "synchronicity." Such was the case with fossil number three. Ron Clarke, the discoverer of Little Foot, was examining fossils excavated years before at Sterkfontein, back in the 1970s, when he came across some foot bones. The clean break in the fossils suggested to him that the rest of the foot bones might still be found at Sterkfontein, and in 1998 he was proved correct. Subsequently, a hominid skeleton has emerged from the calcareous breccia: a complete skull and fragments of arm, foot, and leg bones have been uncovered; the rest of the skeletal remains are presently being excavated with great care. Little Foot is the most complete

---

EXPERIENCE: Observe an Archaeological Dig

Given the abundance of South Africa's fossil life, a visit to one of the country's active archaeological sites is an absolute priority. While viewing publicly displayed treasures such as the famed Mrs. Ples is an incredible experience, it can't beat the excitement of actually watching history being unearthed.

There are several options for observing and participating in archaeological excavations. Previously closed to the public, **Maropeng,** in the Cradle of Humankind, now offers private walking tours to the famous hominid fossil site of Swartkrans. Scientists currently excavating at the site lead the tours and present the public with a rare opportunity to observe an active archaeological dig. Swartkrans has

yielded the largest sample of the *Australopithecus robustus,* a species that went extinct almost one million years ago. It is also internationally renowned for the discovery of the earliest evidence of the use of controlled fire.

After a brief introduction, walking tours depart from Sterkfontein to Swartkrans. There, scientists take guests through the site, presenting an overview of the history of Swartkrans and explaining the current excavations. The tour concludes at a grass amphitheater and with an elegant picnic before returning to Sterkfontein.

Contact **Maropeng** *(tel 014/577-9000, www.maropeng.co.za).* **Tours** *($$$$$),* which are run twice a month, are limited to 12 people.

**Maropeng
Visitor Centre**

✉ On D400 off
R563, just N
of N14 & R563
intersection

☎ 014/577-9000

💲 $$$

**www.maropeng
.co.za**

australopithecine find to date.
Initially dated at between 3.5 and 3
million years old, Little Foot could
be more than 4 million years old,
a more recent study suggests—one
of the oldest known *Australopith-
ecus* fossils, and the oldest from
South Africa.

It's widely held that the
discovery of Little Foot is on a par
with Dart's Taung find, Donald Jo-
hannson's "Lucy" *(Australopithecus
afarensis),* Mary Leakey's Laetoli
footprints, and the discovery of
the "Turkana Boy" *(Homo erectus)*
skeleton made at Nariokotome in
Kenya in 1984.

Visiting the Cradle

The **Maropeng Visitor Centre** at
the Cradle—a brilliant architec-
tural concept in its own right and
winner of the British Guild of
Travel Writers award for the best
new tourism project worldwide—
includes interactive displays,
restaurants, a marketplace, and
an outdoor amphitheater with
cultural presentations.

The center is approached via a

natural bush walkway, and appears
to be a low mound rising above
the surrounding land. This is the
so-called Tumulus, designed to
look like an ancient burial mound.

On entering the Tumulus, you
begin a journey back in time—not
just human time but to an age
before life existed on Earth. The
journey into the past includes a
boat trip on an underground lake
that takes you back four billion
years to the time when the planet
was formed.

The journey continues through
displays brought to life by power-
ful audiovisual shows, sound ef-
fects, state-of-the-art theme-park
technology, and theatrical displays.
They show how the Sterkfontein
Caves were formed, and explore
human evolution, using five
hominid models to illustrate the
process of evolution. At the exit to
the Tumulus, there's an enchant-
ing "Children's Dig" that simulates
a fossil bed.

Down the road from the inter-
pretation center are **Sterkfontein
Caves,** the best known of the

UNESCO Sites

South Africa is home to eight UNESCO
World Heritage sites, the most of any
country in Africa. UNESCO, which stands
for United Nations Educational,
Scientific, and Cultural Organization,
seeks to acknowledge and protect
different sites that benefit humanity.
Globally, there are 878 sites, most of
which are in Europe.

In South Africa, the Cradle of Human-
kind, Robben Island, Mapungubwe, and
the Richtersveld are all deemed to be

sites of cultural importance. The iSiman-
galiso Wetland Park, Cape Floral Regions,
and the Vredefort Dome are important
naturally. The uKhahlamba-Drakensberg
National Park is considered important
both culturally and naturally.

The first site to be recognized was
the iSimangaliso Wetland Park, in 1999.
Most recently (in 2007) the Richtersveld
was recognized. These varied locales pres-
ent a country that is blessed with intense
beauty and cultural significance.

Telling the story of the origins of humankind, Maropeng Visitor Centre

Cradle's sites, where Mrs. Ples, the Taung Child, and Little Foot were found. Guided tours, which begin above ground and take you deep into the bowels of the Earth, last about an hour. An **exhibition center** displays a reconstruction of a mined cave, detailing the stories of cave formation, geology, mammal and hominid fossils, and more.

The only other cave at the Cradle open to the public is **Wonder Cave.** Its enormous cave chamber features beautiful dripstone formations—some stalagmites and stalactites reach 50 feet tall (15 m)—believed to be 2.2 million years old. You can take the elevator down, or, for the adventurous, rappel down. Evening tours are also available, the perfect time to meet the resident bat population.

Beyond the Caves

The Cradle of Humankind offers much more than caves—including numerous game farms, craft shops, restaurants, and guesthouses. The privately owned **Rhino and Lion Nature Reserve** has 600 heads of game, including white rhino, lion, cheetah, and cape wild dog.

You can also visit the **Old Kromdraai Gold Mine,** one of the first mines in the Johannesburg area, where gold was discovered in 1881. On the one-hour tour, you enter a large hole in the side of a hill and walk through rough-hewn tunnels into the heart of the mountain. With a helmet on your head, you get a true sense of what the life of a miner must have been like at the turn of the 20th century.

For the arts and crafts lovers, take the **Crocodile Ramble** *(tel 014/577-9323, www.theramble .co.za)* along the nearby Crocodile River, including the Cradle of Humankind and the Hartbeespoort Dam. The driving route consists of studios, galleries, craft stalls, as well as lodgings and small animal farms. ∎

Wonder Cave
- Map p. 197
- Cradle of Humankind, off Kromdraai/ Broederstroom Rd., Kromdraai Conservancy
- 011/957-0106
- $$

Old Kromdraai Gold Mine
- Map p. 197
- Cradle of Humankind; turn right off N14 between M47 & R563 turnoffs
- 011/957-0211
- $$

www.oldkromdraai goldmine.co.za

Farther Afield in the Interior

Traveling away from the cities takes you into a place entrenched with the past and with nothingness. The interior of South Africa is an elemental land, one lodged in the past. Feel free to muse on the terse poetry of humankind's conception, but remember to wear sunscreen.

A dancer at the Lesedi Cultural Village

Lesedi Cultural Village

⚲ Map p. 197

✉ On R512 en route to Sun City, 6 miles (10 km) N of Lanseria Airport

☎ 012/205-1394

💲 $$$$$

www.lesedi.com

Lesedi Cultural Village

For tourists with limited time, the village of Lesedi (seSotho for "light") provides a quick but effective experience of some of South Africa's indigenous cultures. This multicultural "living village" is home to five traditional homesteads: Zulu, Ndebele, Xhosa, Pedi, and Basotho. Families from each of these ethnic groups live permanently in their own part of Lesedi.

Visitors to the village can come for the day or stay over-

night. Day tours begin either at 11:30 a.m. or at 4:30 p.m. While the morning tour lasts about three hours, the afternoon one tends to be longer—and more dramatic; as dusk falls at Lesedi, the drums start to pound, the night comes alive with traditional singing, and dancing figures throw firelit shadows on the surrounding bushveld.

Both of the day tours include an audiovisual show, a guided tour of the Zulu, Basotho, Xhosa, and Pedi homesteads, and a

INSIDER TIP:

If you are hunting for bargain curios to take home, the vast majority of stalls at Hartbeespoort Dam, near Pretoria, provide the perfect opportunity!

—KATE PARR

National Geographic field researcher

pan African meal served in the 200-seat **Nyama Choma** ("The Greatest African Feast") restaurant. The restaurant, with its genuine African décor, comprises three zones: South Africa, East Africa, and North Africa. The all-African theme has recently been extended by the opening of a new part of the restaurant at Lesedi, the Nile Room, which serves the cuisine of that corner of the continent—couscous and mint-spiced dishes with the aromatic hint of cumin and coriander. After your meal, if you feel so inclined, relax with a hookah pipe, a "hubbly-bubbly" that cools smoke by passing it through a reservoir of water.

Staying Overnight: If you opt to stay the night at Lesedi, you'll find that African hospitality is warm and embracing, and traditional manners impeccable. On your arrival, you'll be greeted and welcomed by the family that owns the homestead where you'll be staying. Guest rooms have been constructed

that offer a unique opportunity—you get to stay with a traditional rural African family and to do so in rooms equipped with all modern home comforts, including en suite bathrooms. The head of the house will be your personal escort, mentor, and guide during your time at the village, and will answer any questions you may have.

Sun City

Map p. 197

118 miles (190 km) NW of Johannesburg

014/557-1000

EXPERIENCE:
From the Air

Don't spend your entire time in this area wading through the artifice of Sun City; instead, go hot-air ballooning. Thanks to the hot, dry climate, the South Africa interior is one of the best places to go ballooning. Try **Bill Harrop's Original Ballon Safaris** (www.balloon.co.za).

Paragliding is popular as well, with one of the best launch sites being Hartbeespoort Dam; contact the **South African Hang Gliding and Paragliding Association** (tel 012/668-1219, www.sahpa.co.za).

For something more demure, take the **Hartbeespoort Cableway** (tel 012/253-1706, $) for mountaintop views of the Hartbeespoort Dam; bring picnic supplies.

Sun City

A two-hour drive northwest of Johannesburg, deep in the wild Pilanesberg mountains, awaits the glitzy, Las Vegas–style entertainment and resort complex of Sun City. It was developed by South African hotel magnate Sol Kerzner, who wanted to create a casino in what was then Bantustan of Bophuthatswane, one of several areas set aside for

Luxury Trains

The world of luxury trains, like that of luxury sea travel, is dominated by nostalgia for the golden age of travel—sparkling crystal, creaking mahogany paneling, fine cuisine, and a decent cocktail in a heavy tumbler to celebrate sunset.

A steam engine wends its way through the eastern Transvaal.

In South Africa you can still experience that glamour and luxury on the Blue Train and on Rovos Rail.

Blue Train

Steeped in mystique, the Blue Train has, over the course of half a century, conveyed government leaders, presidents, kings, princesses, and members of the nobility, all in quiet, unostentatious luxury, grace,

elegance, and romance. The chef-prepared cuisine aboard the Blue Train is faultless, and the meals complemented by the finest wines that the vineyards of South Africa have to offer.

During the daylight hours, you can sit at a writing desk or relax in a comfortable lounge chair in the privacy of your own suite, all the while gazing out the window at the magnificent scenery of Africa. At night, a butler will come by to convert your sitting room into a spacious bedroom, with a custom-designed bed dressed with pure cotton sheets and down duvets. Many of the suites feature double beds. To add to the feeling of sumptuous luxury, there are marble tiles and gold fittings in the bathrooms.

In years gone by, the Blue Train ran on one route only, between Pretoria and Cape Town, but today it goes elsewhere, too: Pretoria to Durban, and Pretoria to the Bakubung Game Lodge. The train is also available for charter to other rail destinations in South Africa.

Contact the Blue Train *(tel 012/334-8459 or 021/449-2672, e-mail: info@bluetrain.co.za, www.bluetrain.co.za).*

Rovos Rail

Three outstanding trains are operated by Rovos Rail. The trains have modern rolling stock, but in addition they also have classic coaches that date from the 1920s and 1930s, each of them meticulously restored to the highest of standards, with wood paneling, period Edwardian features, and every modern convenience and comfort. Of the two dining cars, both of which have been beautifully refurbished, the more formal first saw service in 1911 and is rich with post-Edwardian excess, boasting fluted teak pillars and arches. Overall the traditional décor and period furnishings create a grand, elegant ambience. The Tiffany engines that draw the trains were built in 1893.

Accommodation on Rovos Rail is, in a word, luxurious. Each of the suites are for double occupancy and are furnished either with double bed or twin beds; they also have a roomy lounge. The 118-square-foot (11 sq m) deluxe suites, tastefully restored, also offer double bed or twin bed accommodation for two, a lounge, and en suite bathroom. At about 172 square feet (16 sq m), the aptly named Royal Suites

The observation car of one of the luxury trains operated by Rovos Rail

occupy no less than half a carriage, and include a bathroom with Victorian fittings and bathtub.

Two first-class chefs ensure that meals aboard Rovos Rail are impeccable, with outstanding South African wines to complement the cuisine. Menus can be devised to suit special requirements by prior arrangement. Full bar facilities and room service are available whenever required.

Rovos Rail routes include some of the most romantic and dramatic scenery in southern Africa. You can choose between Cape Town–Pretoria (stopping at Matjiesfontein and Kimberley); the six-day Cape Town–Victoria Falls, which goes via Zimbabwe and includes breathtaking scenery along the way; or trips on the *Shongololo Express,* which offers a range of "Adventure" options, including the Southern Cross Adventure (travels to nine countries on the southern end of the continent: Namibia, South Africa, Lesotho, Swaziland, Mozambique, Zimbabwe, Botswana, Zambia, and Tanzania). Detailed itineraries are available on request.

Contact **Rovos Rail** *(tel 012/553-8000 or 021/421-4020, e-mail: marielle@rovos.co.za or sandy@rovos.co.za, www.rovos.co.za).*

Sun City Hotel
✉ Sun City Resort
☎ 014/554-5110
www.suninter
national.com

The Cabanas
✉ Sun City Resort
☎ 014/557-1580
www.suninter
national.com

The Cascades
✉ Sun City Resort
☎ 014/557-5840
www.suninter
national.com

Palace of the Lost City
✉ Sun City Resort
☎ 014/557-4301
www.suninter
national.com

blacks during apartheid era (making it exempt from the country's strict gambling laws). Officially opening in 1979, Sun City became an international symbol of anti-apartheid sentiment as American and British musicians broke the cultural boycott to play here.

Today, Sun City features slot machines, rock concerts, topless revues, two 18-hole golf courses designed by Gary Player, and every other extravaganza that you can think of.

Four hotels offer different styles and attractions (also see pp. 304–305): glitzy **Sun City Hotel;** the smart, sophisticated **Cascades,** with luxuriant gardens and lots of splashing water; the **Cabanas,** ideal for laid-back family vacations; and the extraordinary, fairy-tale **Palace of the Lost City,** which re-creates the fantasies of Rider Haggard and is adorned with frescoes and hand-painted ceilings depicting the animals and cultures of South Africa.

INSIDER TIP:

Pilanesberg Game Reserve, two hours west of Jo'burg, is full of big game, less crowded than Kruger, and particularly peaceful during the week.

—CAGAN SEKERCIOGLU
National Geographic field researcher

Other facilities at Sun City include the **Valley of the Waves** artificial wave park, archery or clay target shooting under the supervision of trained coaches, quad biking along a wildlife trail, and rides on elephant-back in nearby Pilanesberg National Park.

Pilanesberg National Park

Located within the caldera of an extinct volcano, the 137,000-

At the opulent Palace of the Lost City

False Prophecy

In 1856 a 14-year-old Xhosa girl named Nongqawuse claimed to have seen spirits while she was bathing. They told her that if the Xhosa people slaughtered all of their cattle and destroyed all of their crops, the ancient Xhosa warriors would rise from the dead on February 18, 1857, and drive the British settlers from the Xhosa lands. And after they were done, they would replenish the crops and cattle, and then eliminate illness and old age, just for good measure. The Xhosa had suffered heavily at the hands of the British. At the urging of their chiefs, the Xhosa took to Nongqawuse's millennialist prophecy and destroyed all of their food, including as many as 400,000 head of cattle. The day of reckoning was supposed to be ushered in by a blood-red sun, but February 18 brought with it no unusual astral colors. Without any food, or ghost warriors for that matter, somewhere between 25,000 and 75,000 Xhosas starved, many turning to cannibalism. Nongqawuse narrowly escaped by fleeing to the British, who put her on Robben Island.

acre (55,000 ha) Pilanesberg National Park comprises thickly forested ravines, typical bushveld, and rolling grasslands, as well as **Mankwe Lake,** which is situated on the volcano's central flue. The park occupies an area that is transitional between the higher rainfall lowveld to the east and the arid Kalahari to the west, resulting in a highly unusual overlap of plant, mammal, and birdlife. Species from wetter zones such as cape chestnuts and black-eyed bulbuls occur together with arid-zone species such as red-eyed bulbuls, brown hyenas, and camelthorns. It is also extremely rare for impala and springbok to be found together, as they are here, because the former prefer wetter zones and the latter dry regions.

The Pilanesberg Game Reserve, as it is also called, opened its gates in 1979 after one of the country's biggest ever game-relocation exercises involving animals from across southern Africa. Today the wooded river valleys and thick bush are home to some 10,000 predators, scavengers, and browsing and grazing animals. Lions are doing well here, as are leopards, black and white rhinos, elephants, and buffalo—Africa's Big Five. Other species include the shy, nocturnal brown hyena, cheetah, sable, giraffe, zebra, hippo, and crocodile.

There are nearly 125 miles (200 km) of excellent roads for either self-drives or tours with professional guides, with plenty of blinds and scenic spots to get out and stretch your legs or have a picnic in the wilderness. You'll also see that there are numerous Stone Age and Iron Age sites scattered throughout the park, some of which may be visited by arrangement.

Due to the transitional character of the environment, Pilanesberg is an excellent place for bird-watching, and more than

Pilanesberg National Park

🅰 Map p. 197

✉ Across from Sun City

☎ 014/555-1600

💲 $–$$

www.pilanesberg-game-reserve.co.za

Pilanesberg National Park is a haven for game animals.

can participate in night drives or early morning and early evening game drives.

The park is served by three luxury lodges and two resorts. **Tshukudu Bush Lodge** (tel 014/552-6255, www .legacyhotels.co.za) offers good accommodation in the heart of the Pilanesberg, striking a sensible balance between rustic simplicity and essential luxury. **Bakubung Lodge** (tel 014/552-6000, www.legacyhotels.co.za) with its very own hippo pool, offers hotel-style comfort and tranquillity close to Sun City. At the opulent **Kwa Maritane Lodge** (tel 014/552-5100, www .legacyhotels.co.za) you can gaze out over Pilanesberg's spreading plains. The family-style **Manyane Resort** (tel 014/555-1000, www .goldenleopard.co.za) lies just inside the gates to the Pilanesberg, and features thatched African-style chalets. And, finally, **Bakgatla Resort** (tel 014/555-1000, www .goldenleopard.co.za) offers executive safari tents situated on immaculate lawns, colonial-style chalets, and conference facilities that can accommodate up to 250 guests.

300 species have been observed here. At **Manyane,** in the east, you can enter a huge walk-in aviary for a close-up look at some 80 different kinds of indigenous birds. In the **Manyane Complex's Walking Area** you can learn a lot about the environment on a self-guided trail.

There are many other different ways to enjoy Pilanesberg's natural surroundings. On the Elephant Back Safari, as the name implies, you ride on elephant back through the park for an hour. Or you can get an eagle's-eye view of the game during a hot-air balloon safari. Visitors staying at Bakgatla Resort or Manyane

Swartruggens & Around

This charming Old World town was founded in 1875 on the Scheepersrus and Brakfontein farms. It is part of the **Marico District** and lies about 25 miles (40 km) east of Groot Marico (see opposite).

The name Swartruggens (almost impossible to pronounce convincingly if you don't speak

Afrikaans) means "black ridges" and derives from the appearance of the hills above the town. Today Swartruggens is a typical bushveld settlement, with cattle ranching, wheat, tobacco, and game parks composing the main economic activities of the area. Those with sufficient courage can ride the big birds at the **African Game and Art ostrich farm;** the more prudent can browse in the curio shop.

There are several **diamond mines** still operating in the area, long after the first discovery of diamonds here in 1932.

INSIDER TIP:

Make sure you pay a visit to the delightful Groot Marico—home of the famous writer Herman Charles Bosman who penned some legendary tales.

—KATE PARR
National Geographic field researcher

Ask at the visitor bureau for information on visiting one.

Or visit the **Elands River Battlefield and Graves,** where a fierce battle was fought during the South African War, between August 4 and 16, 1900.

Another unspoiled spot well worth a visit, especially for keen hikers, is the **Kgaswane Mountain Reserve,** situated along the northern slopes of the Magaliesberg to the west of Rustenburg.

A spacious valley, snuggled between two mountain ridges, forms the heart of the park, which boasts a large variety of wildlife best viewed on one of the many excellent hiking trails. There are two overnight trails and two shorter trails to choose from. Birders will enjoy the reserve's 250 recorded species, and conservationists will be pleased to see the breeding colony of cape vultures.

Groot Marico

Like the American West, Groot Marico, on the N4 between Swartruggens and Zeerust, is an example of life imitating art. The area is now in many ways an incarnation of the work of the great South African writer Herman Charles Bosman, once a teacher here in an Afrikaans language school. In *Marico Revisited* he declared of the town, "There is no other place I know that is so heavy with atmosphere, so strangely and darkly impregnated with that stuff of life that bears the authentic stamp of South Africa."

Bosman's best writing is a must-read for anyone interested in South Africa in general and the Marico area in particular. The books are quirky, ironical, strangely moving, hilariously funny, and often quite dark.

Groot Marico in Afrikaans means "big Marico," a real misnomer because it's actually a tiny little town that has remained almost unchanged since the end of the 19th century. Groot Marico

Swartruggens
🅐 Map p. 197

Kgaswane Mountain Reserve
🅐 Map p. 197
✉ W of Rustenburg
☎ 014/533-2050
💲 $–$$$$$
www.tourismnorth-west.co.za

Groot Marico
🅐 Map p. 197
Visitor Information
✉ Main St.
☎ 014/503-0085
www.marico.co.za

may be small, but it is a place that looms large in the history and culture of this part of the country.

The town was founded by the Boer Voortrekkers in the 1850s, and there are rock paintings in the area that were made by early San. Here you can also find the ruins of **David Livingstone's first mission church** at Mabotsa. But this isn't what Groot Marico

units. Another good choice is **Angela's Groot Marico Guest House** (Fakkel & Houkoers Sts., tel 014/503-0082), which offers a pair of double bedrooms and a pair of family bedrooms, all with en suite bathrooms. And for those who want to experience the authentic Marico, try the **Riverstill Guestfarm**, 5 miles (8 km) from town and

EXPERIENCE: Take a Canopy Tour

The Magaliesberg mountain range is an inconceivable 2.4 billion years old, making it one of the most ancient ranges in the world. It is a historian's dream, what with the earliest species of human having been found in the area and several 19th-century battle sites to be explored. But what is often overshadowed by the historical value of the area is the mountain range's unusual beauty. Being a barrier between the lower bushveld areas to the north and the cooler highveld areas, it is a natural meeting point of vastly different species. What better way to explore this than from a bird's-eye view? In the midst of the Ysterhout Kloof, one of the mountain range's most scenic ravines, you'll find the Magaliesberg Canopy Tour. Based on an idea originating

from biologists in the Costa Rican rain forests, the canopy tour is a means of accessing views of otherwise inaccessible flora and fauna by "sliding" via a system of cables through the canopy layer of the trees. For 2.5 hours you will be harnessed, suspended from a cable, and transported through the ravine with expert guides who will delve into the history and ecology of the area for an unforgettable eco-experience. Contact **Magaliesberg Canopy Tours** (tel 014/535-0150, www.magaliescanopy tour.co.za, $$$$$).

Canopy tours are also run in the **Tsitsikamma Forest** (tel 042/281-1836, www.canopytours.co.za) on the Garden Route and at **Karkloof** in KwaZulu-Natal (tel 033/330-3415, $$$$$).

is about. Groot Marico is about experiencing the rural life of the Afrikaner—the food, the drink, the conversation, and the hospitality.

Doing this requires a short stay at one of the simple guesthouses in the area. Perhaps the best is the **Botshabelo Guesthouse** (on Marico River, 1.5 miles/2.5 km from Groot Marico, tel 014/503-0085), which has five lovely en suite

on the banks of the river; it has self-catering cottages, but the owner cooks for guests by prior arrangement.

Other attractions at Groot Marico include a sunset cruise on the **Marico Bosveld Dam** (tel 014/252-1303) and a sampling of potjiekos. Although the dish sounds unpromising (potjiekos translates literally as "pot food"), it is a wonder-

Along the Marico River near Groot Marico

ful stew cooked over open thornwood fires in traditional three-legged pots.

The town's visitor information center can organize a guided tour of the **H. C. Bosman Living Museum** *(Paul Kruger St., tel 083/272-2958)*, housed in a reproduction of the local school where the storyteller taught in 1926. Here bread is baked in an outside oven along with potjiekos, stories are told over the open fire, and performances, readings, and musicals take place.

The **Herman Charles Bosman Festival** takes place every October, while mini-Bosman weekends occur throughout the year.

Zeerust & Around

Situated in the Marico Valley, on the N4 (the chief South Africa–Botswana road) about 150 miles (240 km) northwest of Johannesburg, Zeerust is a commercial hub for the area. The town is named for Casper Coetzee, who in the mid-1860s was engaged to construct a fort and a church here. After his premature death, the little town that sprang up on the site of a former farm acquired the name Coetzee se Rust (Coetzee's Rest), since that time shortened to Zeerust.

Zeerust is a dusty, slightly run-down town these days, but

Kortkloof Village

The indigenous language spoken in the Groot Marico area is Tswana, and the Kortkloof Cultural Village *(tel 018/642-1312)*, in the Groot Marico district, is hosted by the Tswana tribe. Members working here practice traditional Tswana crafts, including wooden furniture and wood carvings from beautiful indigenous trees. Other arts-and-crafts forms include needlework, pottery, and beadwork. You can also enjoy typical traditional food here.

Zeerust
🗺 Map p. 197
Visitor Information
✉ Public Library
☎ 018/642-3713

Botsalano Game Reserve
🗺 Map p. 197
✉ 31 miles (50 km) N of Mafikeng along Botswana border
☎ 018/386-8900
$ $–$$$$

it was a throbbing metropolis at the time when Herman Charles Bosman was teaching in Groot Marico. Bosman's stories often mention *mampoer,* the potent liquor distilled locally from peaches. The alcoholic content of mampoer can be around 64 percent. A true test of its authenticity is to light it with a match: If it doesn't burn with a blue flame, it's not the real thing. **Mampoer tours** can be arranged locally by calling Groot Marico Tourist Information (see p. 239). The tours are an excellent way of getting a taste of the local life as well as a sample of the superb local beverage.

Historical attractions in Zeerust include the **Church of St. John the Baptist,** a national monument built in 1873, and the **Lutheran Dinokana Mission Lehurutshe,** which boasts a painting of Christ dating back to 1889, the foundation year of the church.

Travel back farther in time with a short jaunt out to **Marula Kop,** an Iron Age settlement about 30 miles (50 km) north of Zeerust. There you'll find a rare stone wall and evidence of iron smelting and terracing.

Before you leave Zeerust, make sure you pay a visit to **Ouma se Kombuis** (Grandma's Kitchen) for a real taste of Afrikaans homecooking and a full helping of nostalgic charm. The milk tarts and homemade ginger beer are out of this world. There's also an antique kitchen and farm equipment on display. Contact Groot Marico Tourist

Information *(tel 014/503-0085, e-mail: info@marico.co.za, www .marico.co.za).*

More than 400 species of birds (more than Pilanesberg) are found in the Mafikeng area, immediately to the south of Zeerust. It is a bird-watcher's paradise. Many of these species can be seen at **Botsalano Game Reserve,** 31 miles (50 km) north of Mafikeng along the

Bosman's stories often mention *mampoer,* the potent liquor distilled locally from peaches. Its alcoholic content can be around 64 percent. To test its authenticity, light it with a match: If it doesn't burn with a blue flame, it's not the real thing.

Botswana border. At Botsalano a breeding program for both white and black rhinos has been in operation for some years and is a real success story. This small and intimate reserve is very unpretentious, very untouristy, and offers a rare taste of unspoiled Africa. There's a sizable population of large herbivores: buffalo, giraffe, hartebeest, eland, and kudu, to name a few, which can be viewed in comfort from the very good network of roads.

Other wildlife options near Zeerust include the simple and

Marico Eye Fountain

This is a 56-foot-deep (17 m) fountain that bubbles out crystal-clear water from the Marico River, one of the few perennial rivers in this dryland area. The water is so pure that visibility is around 60 feet (18 m), making the Marico Eye one of the hot favorites with inland scuba fanatics. Night dives are popular, and divers surface with stories of incredible underwater beauty. Enthusiasts camp at the Marico Eye out in the bushveld.

cheetahs first, then wild dogs followed by hyenas and, finally, lions, which came from the Etosha and Pilanesberg National Parks. In the same year, 180 elephants were brought from Gonarezhou in Zimbabwe. The breeding behavior of the Zimbabwean jumbos has not been impaired: The elephant population currently stands at 250.

Around 12,000 animals are at home in Madikwe. All predator species are present as well as black and white rhino, buffalo, giraffe, zebra, and a healthy population of antelope. More than 350 bird species have been recorded. The terrain is open grassland and bushveld plains, interspersed with rocky outcrops and inselbergs. Expect the usual game-viewing options in open safari vehicles guided by a skilled professional.

Accommodation in Madikwe is superior, fully equal to the lodges of the Tanzanian Northern Circuit. Among the choices are **Jaci's Safari Lodge** (tel 014/778-9900, www.madikwe.com), which overlooks a water hole on the banks of the Marico River; the five-star **Buffalo Ridge Safari Lodge** (tel 011/805-9995, www.buffaloridgesafari.com), perched on a ridge with expansive views over the northern plains; and **Jaci's Tree Lodge** (tel 014/778-9900, www.madikwe.com), which consists of eight so-called tree-houses, each standing about 13 feet (4 m) above the ground and constructed around huge leadwood and tambotie trees. ∎

Madikwe Game Reserve

✉ On R49, 62 miles (100 km) from Zeerust

☎ 018/350-9931 or 018/350-9932

💲 $–$$

www.madikwe-game-reserve.co.za

Marico Eye Fountain

✉ Source of Marico River

☎ Marico Ramble Tours, 014/503-0100

rustic **Moretele Tented Camp** (off R511, tel 012/252-0131) on the banks of the Moretele River, which offers guests superb fly-fishing for yellowfish. More than 350 bird species have been recorded in the area (which is malaria free). Accommodation at the Moretele camp is in ten safari tents. There's no electricity at the campground, ensuring that you get all the authenticity you could hope for.

Madikwe Game Reserve

The Madikwe Game Reserve owes its existence to a wildlife initiative called Operation Phoenix. In 1993, the Operation Phoenix translocation project brought more than 8,000 head of game to the park. Three years later, predators were introduced—

A realm of natural wonders: white-sand dunes, crystal-clear springs, ancestral caves, and euphoric fields of wildflowers

Northern Cape

The Goegap Nature Reserve in full bloom

Northern Cape

South Africa's largest but least populated province, the Northern Cape stretches southward from the Gariep (Orange) River. Bordered to the west by the cold waters of the Atlantic, most of the Northern Cape is dry, barren, scrubby semidesert and desert—including the Kalahari, Namaqualand, and Richtersveld—dotted with low, rocky hills. It is an area of vivid contrasts: scorching hot in summer, bitterly cold in winter.

Camels in the Kalahari, the original 4WD for desert safaris

Your memories will be of vast skies and endless landscapes, towering camelthorns (*Acacia erioloba*), huge untidy sociable weaver nests, the roar of lean Kalahari lions, national parks that bequeath a unique wilderness experience, and the incredible annual wild-flower display.

The first people of the Northern Cape, the San were gradually squeezed out of the area by European settlers and migrating African tribes. The few remaining *true* San people still live here. The whole area, especially along the Gariep and Vaal Rivers, is blessed with a bounty of San rock engravings. The province is also rich in fossils.

Mining has always been important, and when diamonds were discovered during the 19th century at Kimberley (the provincial capital), economic and population growth was rapid. Attractions of the Northern Cape include the areas around Alexander Bay and Kimberley,

where diamonds are mined; the Kgalagadi Transfrontier Park, an enormous game reserve straddling the South Africa–Botswana border; and the town of Kuruman, with its remarkable, abundant, crystal-clear spring water and its mission station where David Livingstone and his future wife, Mary Moffatt, first met. Most spectacular of all, though, is Namaqualand in spring (late Aug.–Sept.) when, if the winter rains have been good, the countryside explodes with the yellow, white, purple, and red of millions of daisies and flowering succulents.

Little agriculture is possible in the dry Northern Cape, except for a narrow strip irrigated by the Gariep River in the north, especially around Kakamas and Upington. The major product is grapes for drying, to make

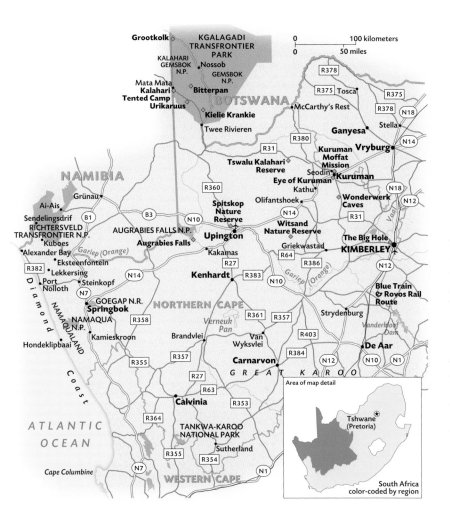

sultanas and raisins, but also for the table; the region is now producing increasing volumes of good table wine as well.

The north is primarily Kalahari Desert, home to huge Kalahari springbok and rapier-horned gemsbok, and is typified by waves of red sand dunes and dry acacia-tree savanna.

Few areas in the province enjoy more than 16 inches (40 cm) of rain per annum. In the west most rain falls in winter, while the east receives the majority of its water from dramatic late summer thunderstorms. Many areas are

extremely hot. (One of the smaller towns is called Hotazel.) The highest temperatures in South Africa are recorded along the Namibian border. Summer maximums sometimes reach the 110°s F (40°s C). Sutherland, on the other hand, is the coldest place in South Africa, regularly recording temperatures below 14°F (-10°C). The cold, clear conditions have made Sutherland an impor-tant center for astronomy, with several major observatories located here. Northern Cape winters are usually frosty and clear, with southern areas becoming bitterly cold. ■

Kimberley

Situated in a dry, dusty area of the Northern Cape, and a shadow of its former self, Kimberley nevertheless retains a mystique dating back to the time when it was the diamond capital of the world.

In 1866 a teenage boy playing alongside the Gariep (Orange) River, near Hopetown, found a shiny pebble that turned out to be a diamond. More finds nearby in 1871 led to a diamond

The Big Hole and, on its edge, Kimberley, the city to which it gave birth

rush, with thousands of miners and laborers pouring into the area. Two years later, their collection of shacks and huts was declared a town and named after the British Secretary of State for the Colonies, John Wodehouse, the Earl of Kimberley. The town rapidly grew into a city, the largest in the interior. Over the years, Kimberley has had a number of "firsts": first city in the Southern Hemisphere to have electric street-lighting (1882); home to the country's first school of mines (1896); and home to the country's first flying school (1913).

The charming period **Railway Station** adjacent to the city center, on Florence Street, is a stopping point for the luxury trains operated by **Rovos Rail** and for the **Blue Train** (see pp. 234–235).

The Big Hole & Kimberley Mine Museum

The largest mine in Kimberley, the so-called **"Big Hole,"** is an astonishing sight. Although now filled with water to within 571 feet (174 m) of the top, the Big Hole is actually 2,624 feet (800 m) deep—the second largest excavation on Earth dug by hand. During the 43 years from 1871 until 1914, when mining here ceased, an astounding 5,996 pounds (2,720 kg) of diamonds

INSIDER TIP:

**Kimberley is famous in birding circles for the recently discovered Kimberley pipit.
It takes special study to distinguish it from other pipits.
A birder's bird.**

—CAGAN H. SEKERCIOGLU
National Geographic field researcher

were removed from the Big Hole. Its surface area is 32 acres (13 ha).

Situated around the edge of the Big Hole are a number of linked attractions forming a museum cum visitor center, including viewing platforms, historic displays, and well-preserved corrugated-metal buildings from old Kimberley. A visit to this little diamond diggers' town is like stepping back in time to the days when Barney Barnato (1852–1897) and Cecil John Rhodes were kings—and diamonds were there for the taking.

In the reconstructed old streets you can visit buildings such as Barney Barnato's Boxing Academy, a tobacconist's shop, a bank, a church, and functioning bars and restaurants. De Beers Consolidated Mines, which has financed much of the construction and renovation here, has on display the old De Beers directors' private railway coach and a reconstruction of a typical farmer's house of the time. If you wish, you can sieve diamond-bearing gravel and perhaps even find your own priceless stone.

A highlight is the suspended aerial platform (the exact size of a 19th-century miner's claim) from which visitors can gaze directly down into the depths of the Big Hole.

On display at the **Diamond Vault** are several thousand genuine diamonds, among them the "616" and the "Eureka." The former (rather unimaginatively named) stone weighs 616 carats and is the world's biggest uncut octahedron diamond, while the Eureka (Greek for "I've found it") was the diamond found by the teenager back in 1866.

Visitors can ride between the city hall and the Big Hole in style aboard a restored century-old tram. Trams run daily from 9:00 a.m. to 4:15 p.m.

Beyond the Mine

The **Ernest Oppenheimer Memorial Gardens** (*Jan Smuts Blvd.*), opposite the Civic Centre, commemorate Sir Ernest Oppenheimer (1880–1957), well-known diamond tycoon and patriarch of the enormous Oppenheimer mining and business empire. He was also the first person to be elected mayor of Kimberley. A bust of Oppenheimer overlooks the **Miners Memorial** or Diggers Fountain, which is sculpted in the form of five miners with upraised arms supporting a giant sieve of the kind used to separate out diamonds from gravel.

The nearby **Duggan-Cronin Photo Gallery** displays the work of Irish photographer and De Beers employee Alfred Duggan-Cronin (1874–1954). In the years between 1919 and 1939, he took

Kimberley

Map p. 247

Visitor Information

Diamantveld Visitor Centre, 121 Bulfontein Rd.

053/832-7298

Closed Sun.

The Big Hole/ Kimberley Mine Museum

Tucker St.

053/830-4417

www.thebighole.co.za

Duggan-Cronin Photo Gallery

Egerton Rd.

053/839-2743

Open Mon.–Fri., weekends by appt.

Donation

McGregor Museum

✉ Atlas St.

☎ 053/839-2722

🕐 Closed Sun. a.m.

💲 $

Pioneers of Aviation Museum

✉ Gen. Kan ver der Spuy Dr.

☎ 053/839-2700

🕐 Closed public holidays

💲 Donation

Kimberley Africana Library

✉ 63–65 Du Toitspan Rd.

☎ 053/830-6247

🕐 Closed Sat.–Sun.

Wildebeest Kuil Rock Art Centre

✉ R31 bet. Kimberley & Barkley West

☎ 053/839-7069 or 082/222-4777

💲 $

www.museumsnc.co.za

It's Still Big

Kimberley's Big Hole has long been touted as the largest hand-dug excavation on Earth, but that came to an end in 2005, when local historian Steve Lunderstedt discovered that the mine in Jagersfontein, hand-dug to 660 feet (200 m), is deeper. He claims that Kimberley never bothered to factcheck its tourism brochures, and, until recently, no one had thought to question the claim.

many photographs of laborers who came from all over southern Africa to work in the Kimberley diamond mines. Duggan-Cronin also made trips to the home territories where his photographic subjects came from. His unique collection of more than 6,000 images documents in detail variations in clothing, facial markings and hairstyles of the region's indigenous peoples. Because many of these cultural markers have now changed or disappeared, the Duggan-Cronin photographs have acquired considerable historical importance.

A sanatorium set up in 1897 by Cecil Rhodes now houses the nearby **McGregor Museum.** After serving as a hotel then a school, this striking building—still retaining the same décor in many rooms that it had in 1900—was officially opened as a museum in 1976. The emphasis of the McGregor Museum and its local satellite museums is on local and natural history. Displays cover prehistory, the diamond rush, the siege of Kimberley during the South African War (1899–1902), and the flora and fauna of the area.

Part of the McGregor Museum, the **Pioneers of Aviation Museum** stands on the site of the town's old flying school. Displays include historic photographs of the beginnings of aviation in the country and a reproduction of the type of Compton-Patterson biplane in which the first pilots were trained.

The stately home **Dunluce** (earlier known as Lillianville) is a fine example of late Victorian domestic architecture. Donated to the McGregor Museum in 1975, Dunluce may be visited only on guided tours organized by the museum.

For bibliophiles, the **Kimberley Africana Library** houses a fine collection of books and documentation on southern Africa. A treasure of the collection is the translation by the missionary Robert Moffatt (father-in-law to David Livingstone) of the King James Bible into the Tswana language.

Some 9 miles (14 km) northwest of Kimberley, **Wildebeest Kuil Rock Art Centre** showcases the rock engravings of the Bushmen, the aboriginal inhabitants of southern Africa (formerly known as San). A 25-minute film provides a useful introduction. Then a half-mile (0.8 km) walk takes you over a sacred hill dotted with more than 400 rock engravings. Information boards and audio commentary instruct you as you walk. Guided tour available. ■

The Kalahari

An unforgiving place of vast distances, silhouetted baobab trees, and a few nomadic San tribes, the Kalahari stretches along the border of Namibia. The name comes from the Tswana word *kgala*–great thirst. When you see the endless red dunes, sparsely punctuated with shrubs, the name makes perfect sense.

At the Tswalu Kalahari Reserve

Kuruman

Kuruman (pop. 216,000), on the N14 between Johannesburg and Upington, is the Kalahari's chief town. It owes its existence to an astonishing spring, known as Gasegonyane (meaning "little water calabash") or The Eye, from which issue 5.2 million gallons (20 million l) of pure, crystal-clear water a day. Agriculture—made possible by The Eye—and mining of manganese, iron, and minerals are the basis of the local economy.

At **Maruping,** close to Kuruman, a mission was begun in 1816 by the London Missionary Society. Soon after 1820, Mothibi, chief of the approximately 10,000 Batswana people living in the area, gave permission to the Scottish missionary Robert Moffatt and his wife, Mary, to move the mission to its present-day site at Seodin, also near Kuruman.

At Seodin, Moffatt learned Setswana and, with helpers, undertook the huge task of translating the King James Bible into

Kuruman

🔺 Map p. 247

Visitor Information

✉ Main St.

☎ 053/712-1001

**www.kuruman
kalahari.co.za**

Kuruman Moffat Mission

✉ Moffat Ln., follow signs from Hotazel Rd.

☎ 053/712-2645

Wonderwerk Cave

✉ 27 miles (43 km) S of Kuruman, on R31 Daniëlskuil-Kimberley Rd., at Wonderwerk farm

☎ 082/832-7226

www.museumsnc .co.za

that language. First, though, he had to develop a spelling system for the purpose. The finished work was set and printed in 1857 on a hand press that still functions today. Moffatt's version was the first complete Bible printed on the African continent.

At the **Kuruman Moffat Mission,** Robert Moffat, assisted by Robert Hamilton and many local people, built an enormous stone church that was for many years the biggest structure on the highveld. One of the most famous visitors to the mission and church was missionary-turned-explorer David Livingstone. Here he met and later married the daughter of Robert and Mary Moffatt, who was also named Mary. On seeing

tion are not just monuments frozen in time. Today the complex functions as an ecumenical center for use by communitiy groups and by the United Congregational Church of South Africa in the wider Kuruman region.

Wonderwerk Cave

This site features a deep cave running far back into the hillside, where excavation and research have been going on for a number of years. It has revealed an archaeological record of virtually continuous human habitation over tens of thousands of years, almost up to the present day. Visitors can learn about the cave and its environment from displays in a small museum close to the site. The cave may be visited by the public, and guided tours are available.

If you wish to stay, three self-catering chalets may be rented at the site, and a central cooking and barbecuing area is also available.

Witsand Nature Reserve

Amid a seemingly endless sea of typical red Kalahari sand stands out this visually extraordinary, 1,000-acre (2,500 ha) island of brilliant white sand.

Geologists believe this extraordinary oasis of whiteness is caused by a quartzite basin forming a natural reservoir of water beneath the dunes. Red Kalahari sand is blown into the basin by the prevailing winds. The oxides that give the Kalahari sand its typical russet color are,

---

EXPERIENCE:
Camel Rides

For camel ride adventures just 25 miles (40 km) from the Namibian border, contact Thinus or Landa Conradie at Koppieskraal Guest Farm (tel 084/564-4613 or 082/336-9110, e-mail: koppieskraal@gmail.com). **Landa's grandfather originally bought camels from the police at Upington, and today Landa and her husband conduct 30-minute and two-hour camelback safaris on animals that are descended from the original stock. An overnight camping safari is also offered.**

---

the new church, Livingstone is said to have commented that it was solid enough "to withstand a cannonading."

Restored by the Kuruman Moffat Mission Trust, the church and the original old mission sta-

Trying out the "roaring sands" at the Witsand Nature Reserve

in time, leached from the sand by rainfall and the prevalent high water table in the quartzite basin, leaving behind the finest silica grains, resulting in this pristine eye-catching whiteness.

The dune system is about 6 miles (10 km) long and almost 3 miles (5 km) wide, and is home to the famous "roaring sands of the Kalihari." Reliable witnesses confirm that the dunes emit eerie roaring sounds when disturbed by man or wind—especially in hot dry weather. Folklore has it that the dunes only roar in the months containing an R (Sept.–April). However, the sand needs to be warm and dry to roar, and has been known to roar through the winter months, too. This bizarre natural phenomenon is certainly worth a listen.

Quite apart from its unusual whiteness and its sound effects, the Witsand (White Sand) Nature Reserve is a naturally scenic park,

teeming with birdlife. More than 170 species of birds are spotted here, including the Namaqua sandgrouse, sociable weaver, and Africa's smallest raptor—the pygmy falcon. The park boasts a sunken bird blind at a secluded water hole where birders and photographers can get an eye-level view of the birds (and game) coming to quench their thirst. Gemsbok, red hartebeest, springbok, duiker, and steenbok are all abundant, and a small herd of kudu has also established itself on the reserve.

Don't miss the self-guided **Botanical Meander.** This 2.8-mile (3.3 km) trail guides you through characteristic Kalahari veld, with information about more than 40 plant species, each of which is numbered. The trail also includes a small outdoor museum and a shaded spot to picnic.

At the **information center** you will find displays on local

Witsand Nature Reserve

🗺 Map p. 247

✉ 170 miles (275 km) NW of Kimberley via R64, Groblershoop (gravel) road, & Witsand (gravel) access road

☎ 053/313-1061 or 083/234-7573

💲 $–$$$$$

wwwwitsandkala hari.co.za

Kenhardt

▲ Map p. 247

Visitor Information

✉ Municipality,
Park St.

☎ 054/651-6500

Upington

▲ Map p. 247

Visitor Information

✉ Kalahari Oranje
Museum
Complex, 4
Schröder St.

☎ 054/332-6064

archaeology and natural history, as well as books, videos, and magazines providing further information. A small shop sells very basic food supplies. Activities such as dune surfing and cycling are offered, and a nearby 4WD route (managed by Witsand but not on the reserve itself) will test your off-road skills in desert sand.

Facilities include ten self-catering thatched chalets (with a four-star rating), carvan and camping areas, a backpacker camp, and picnic areas for day visitors. There is no restaurant, but catering can be arranged upon prior request.

To reach the reserve from Kimberley, drive through Griqua-town toward Upington on the R64, turning off at Griquatown toward Groblershoop. Continue 50 miles (80 km) toward Grob-lershoop, then turn right onto the gravel road at the Witsand sign. Follow the signs for 28 miles (45 km) to Witsand.

Verneuk Pan

The Kalahari desert was for centuries the heartland of South Africa's earliest inhabitants, the Bushmen (the San). They managed to live in this harsh environment by gathering edible plant foods and by hunting. Small groups of Bushmen still live close to the Kgalagadi Transfrontier Park, and you can visit the remains of permanent settlements near the town of **Kenhardt** in the Verneuk Pan, at the Bit-terputs farm.

In 1929 Sir Malcolm Campbell traveled to Vernuek Pan

to try to break the world land-speed record. History records that his attempt was unsuccessful.

Upington

Located on the banks of the Gariep (Orange) River, the town of Upington was founded in 1884 and named for cape attorney-general Sir Thomas

INSIDER TIP:

In Verneuk Pan, look for *karretiemense*, cart people who move from farm to farm using donkeys as their transport. Stop and chat with them for a real insight into the area.

—SAMANTHA REINDERS
National Geographic photographer

Upington. It is the unofficial capital of the Northern Cape.

A mission station was established here in 1875 and in time grew into a town. On the former mission's site stands the **Kalahari Oranje Museum Complex** *(4 Schröder St., tel 054/331-1373, closed Sat.–Sun., donation)*, which provides information about the original inhabitants and about the history of the area.

Two **animal statues** com-memorate Uppington's past—a donkey *(end of Schröder St., at museum complex)* pays tribute to the role of this lowly beast in the town's early development;

and a camel and rider *(entrance of Schröder St., in front of police station)* recalling pre-4WD days when patrols into the forbidding Kalahari were conducted on camelback.

On the outskirts of town, the **South African Dried Fruit Co-operative** *(32 Industrial Rd., tel 054/337-8800)* is the second largest of its kind in the world and famed for its sultanas. Warm in winter, Upington makes a good stopping point for travelers en route to Augrabies Falls, the Northern Cape game reserves, the Kalahari, Namibia, and the Fish River Canyon, and has excellent accommodations, restaurants, and shops.

Before leaving, be sure to stop by the **Orange River Wine Cellars** *(32 Industrial Rd., tel 054/337-8800, www .orangeriverwines.com, closed Mon.)* to sample the various wines produced in irrigated vineyards along the banks of the Gariep. This is the largest cooperative in the country and exports many of its wines to the United States and Europe.

Spitskop Nature Reserve

North of Upington, this reserve—14,000 acres (5,641 ha) in extent, 7,500 acres (3,000 ha) of which are open to visitors—is named for an imposing *kopje* (flat-topped hill) of granite situated within its borders.

You can experience the reserve in a variety of ways. Drive in comfort along 23 miles (37 km) of well-made gravel roads and stop to view game through a telescope at the sheltered viewpoint on top of **Spitskop Hill.** Or, if you feel energetic, walk one or more of the three hiking trails, each a different length; on the longer trail, hikers spend the night at a hut fitted out for the purpose.

Visitors come to experience the fauna that inhabit this semi-arid landscape of rocky outcrops and sandy plains, and for the colorful profusion of wildflowers

Spitskop Nature Reserve

▲ Map p. 247

✉ 8 miles/13 km N of Upington en route to Kgalagadi Transfrontier Park

☎ 054/332-1336

The eponymous rocky hill at the Spitskop Nature Reserve

Khoisan Bushmen

Bushmen (the San or Khoisan) have lived for millennia in the northwestern part of what is now South Africa. Physiological and skeletal evidence indicates that their descendants today bear marked similarities to the ancient Sangoan people who pursued a hunter-gatherer way of life in the southern part of the continent from the early Upper Paleolithic period onward.

Contemporary rock art, at the small town of Andriesvale

It has been said that Bushmen are a kind of genetic "Adam" because their DNA carries the oldest genetic markers so far discovered among humankind. Of all the world's human groupings, the Bushmen seem genetically to have changed least.

Now that their original hunting and gathering grounds have been severely reduced, many Bushmen today live in settlements. But a few bands in the Kalahari still pursue the same way of life that they have followed for 20 millennia— searching for edible plants, roots, berries, and insects, and hunting wild animals with bow and arrow. They use ostrich eggshells for storage. Desert melons and the roots and corms of certain plants are a vital source of water. Bushmen speak a language that is unique for its range of clicking sounds (a number of which have passed into some local African languages).

Traditionally, the Bushmen have been a no-madic people, though archaeological evidence shows that they did settle for extended periods in places where food was abundant. Their dwellings range from simple shelters against the spring rains to more substantial settlements around a permanent water source during the dry months of the year. During this dry season, when game animals stayed close to permanent water holes, the men developed their hunting prowess. In the wet season, the gathering of edible plant foodstuffs by the women became the easier option. Because they moved so often, Bushmen had few possessions. Individuals might carry sticks for digging, a few pieces of firewood, ostrich shells, or perhaps a sling for the baby; they might also have weapons such a hide sling and bow and arrows, and a blanket that additionally served as a bag to carry food.

Arts of the Bushmen

The Bushmen are renowned above all for their remarkable artwork. Ancient San paintings and rock engravings can be found in caves and rock overhangs all across the southern half of Africa. Once seen, you will never forget them. Their renderings of animals, hunters, and creatures that appear to be half human and half beast (believed to be depictions of medicine men, shamans, or healers) are extraordinarily vivid. Fiercely beautiful, the paintings have been executed with a consummate artistic skill that testifies to the almost mystical kinship that the San had with the animals on which they so depended for food and survival.

The San stopped painting long ago, but some groups in the Kalahari still practice rituals that evoke the imagery of the precious rock paintings. In night-long ceremonies, women clap and sing as the menfolk circle around the campfire in increasingly frenzied traditional dances. As they do, an entranced shaman, seemingly bent double in pain, will seek to enter the spirit world. At other times, he may endeavor to transform himself into an animal, drawing on its mystical power to cure the sick, make rain, or bring prey animals to the bow. Some of the figures in San paintings—surreal depictions of figures with irregular nonhuman heads—suggest this altered state of being.

There is an extensive literature on San rock art. The most interesting recent addition to the collection is *The Mind in the Cave,* a book by David Lewis-Williams, senior mentor at the Rock Art Research Institute of the University of the Witwatersrand. It is a profound and scholarly work and well worth a read.

Traditional crafts of the San community

White-water rafting on the Gariep River

that blossom after summer rain has fallen. This is true Kalahari country: dry, with vast pale blue skies and endless sand flats.

On a clear day the towering peak of Spitskop can be seen from 25 miles (40 km) away. In the days of the ox wagon, Spitskop is said to have been a meeting place and rest stop for many a traveler.

Several varieties of antelope can be seen at Spitskop: gemsbok, eland, red hartebeest, steenbok, and sizable troops of Kalahari springbok. Other mammals include zebra and smaller species such as mongoose, suricate, and ground squirrel, as well as reptiles such as puff adders, cape cobras, and tortoises. The substantial birdlife features Namaqua sandgrouse, fiscal shrike, goshawk, kori bustard, and ostrich.

Kalahari Monate Lodge
(*Theuns & Truia Botha, managers of Spitskop Nature Reserve, tel 054/332-1336, e-mail: teuns@ intekom.co.za.*), which is situated

opposite the entrance, has modern facilities.

Gariep River

Longest of South Africa's rivers, the Gariep (Orange) has its beginnings in Lesotho's Drakensberg mountains. From there the river flows northwest through South Africa for 1,367 miles (2,187 km). After joining its chief tributary, the Vaal, near Kimberley, the Gariep continues through the barren semidesert of the Kalahari and Namaqua in the Northern Cape. It pours over the **Augrabies Falls** (see opposite) before eventually flowing into the Atlantic at Alexander Bay.

Naturally, rafting and canoeing are highly popular on the Gariep, especially after the rains of March and April make the waters fast and exciting. Among the favorite activities: Take a several-day rafting safari on the river as it winds through the **Richtersveld Transfrontier National Park** (see pp. 268–269), with its spectacular mountain-desert views.

INSIDER TIP:

At Augrabies Falls National Park look for the endemic Augrabies flat lizard. The males have bright red tails, blue heads and bodies, and yellow front legs.

—RES ALTWEGG
National Geographic field researcher

The rapids above Augrabies Falls provide the opposite experience: a heart-beating, hair-raising ride (see sidebar below).

Augrabies Falls National Park

With its dramatic canyon and huge granite formations, Augrabies Falls National Park is spectacular at any time of the year. But when the Gariep River is in flood and thunders 183 feet (56 m) over the main falls, it is truly awe-inspiring. *Aukoerebis* in the local Khoi language means "place of the great noise," an apt name for the falls at full volume.

While there is much to do in the park, witnessing the falls should be first on your list. Try to go during sunset; it's cooler, and the fading light brings out subtle colors in the surrounding rocks. There are several viewpoints that highlight different aspects of the falls and gorge. For a great panorama of the park, climb to the top of **Moon Rock.**

Augrabies is a place of extreme temperatures. Shade is at a premium in the heat of the day, when small creatures hide out under rock overhangs and trees or in burrows.

**Augrabies Falls
National Park**

▲ Map p. 247

✉ 25 miles (40 km) NW of Kakamas

☎ 054/452-9200

$ $$

www.sanparks.org/parks/augrabies.co.za

EXPERIENCE: Rafting the Gariep

The 1,367-mile-long (2,187 km) Gariep River offers an adventure experience second to none. The river runs all the way from the Drakensberg mountains to the Atlantic Ocean, at Alexander Bay, with particularly striking scenery as it passes through the Richtersveld desert. The banks of the river are filled with semiprecious stones and striking rock formations, and along them roam an abundance of small animals and primates; the birdlife here is extraordinary, too. Because there are no hippos or crocodiles in the river, it is perfect for recreational canoeing and white-water rafting.

Commercial tours are available, and the most popular are four- to seven-day packages, with food and camping equipment provided. On such a tour you will travel anywhere between 25 and 100 miles (40–160 km), depending on the water levels and conditions, and the number of days you choose. Most operators use two-person inflatable canoes. The tours provide a unique and adventure-packed opportunity for swimming, hiking, bathing, bird-watching, game viewing, and, of course, making your way through rapids.

For bookings, contact **Umkulu Safari & Canoe Trails** (*tel* 021/853-7952, www.umkulu.co.za) or **Felix Unite** (*tel* 021/404-1830, www.felixunite.com).

A seven-day trip should cost you about R2,500.

Beyond the Falls: While relatively small (36,000 acres/55,000 ha), the Augrabies Falls National Park is home to a considerable variety of flora and fauna. You can see springbok, eland, klipspringer, kudu, steenbok, and gemsbok. Predators and scavengers include caracal,

EXPERIENCE:
Enjoying Augrabies Falls

You don't need a guide at the park, but it adds to the experience. Highly recommended is the **Gariep 3-in-1** adventure in which trekkers raft down 2 serpentine miles (3 km) of the river, walk 2.5 miles (4 km) through the canyons, and mountain bike 7 miles (12 km) back to camp.

More intense is the **Klipspringer Hiking Trail.** Over three days (two nights in huts), a guide leads you on a 24.5-mile (39.5 km) circuit of the park.

Make reservations for both tours at 012/428-9111, *www.sanparks.org/tour ism/reservations.*

African wildcat, bat-eared fox, black-backed jackal, and leopard. The highly endangered black rhino also resides here; the giraffe at Augrabies have developed a paler coat than elsewhere because of the excessive heat. Dassies and two types of mongoose—the yellow and the slender mongoose—are among the smaller mammals found here.

The river and the surrounding wilderness are a paradise for bird-watchers. Among the local species are rosy-faced lovebirds, African reed jacanas, bee-eaters, masked and sociable weavers, and cormorants; also be on the lookout for goliath, gray, and black-headed herons, fish eagles, and black eagles, as well as pied, giant, and malachite kingfishers, rock kestrels, Egyptian geese, African black ducks, and African shell ducks.

Fishermen can expect largemouth and smallmouth yellowfish, catfish, mudfish, and bream.

On your canoeing or whitewater trip, you're fairly likely to see yellow baboons, vervet monkeys, African scrub hares, ground squirrels, leopards, caracals, African wildcats, bat-eared foxes, cape foxes, jackals, and cape clawless otters.

The Nama are the original inhabitants of the area, and some still pursue a traditional way of life. Watch for their distinctive igloo-shaped *matjieshuise* (mat houses), made from reed mats placed over a framework, and well suited to the Nama's earlier nomadic lifestyle and to the local environment. The reeds in the mats expand in winter to shut out the rain and wind, and shrink in summer to let cooling breezes through.

There are several campgrounds, chalets, and family cabins scattered around the park. Reservations should be made through the park's official website (*www.sanparks.org/ parks/augrabies.co.za*). As with all bookings, procrastination is never a virtue, especially during peak travel months.

Zebras in the Tswalu Kalahari Reserve

Tswalu Kalahari Reserve

Owned by the Oppenheimer family, the luxury Tswalu Kalahari Reserve is located on the largest private concession in southern Africa and caters for the discerning traveler. Tswalu's stated objective is "to restore the Kalahari to itself," and for reintroducing the cheetah and wild dog to the reserve it won the World Wildlife Fund award for "Best Conservation of an Endangered Species."

Tswalu is genuinely exclusive. Guests numbers are restricted to 30, and all are pampered by an attentive staff. Naturally, Tswalu also boasts the ultimate in luxury accommodation. The *motse* (Tswana for "village") is designed to blend inconspicuously into its surroundings and consists of just eight spacious and opulently appointed *legaes* (Tswana for "homes"). The deluxe facilities include an exceptional wine cellar and a private chef who produces superb cuisine.

When to Go
The best time to visit Tswalu is in winter *(April–Aug.)*, when the days are mild and sunny.

Amid the red Kalahari dunes of Tswalu many species of animals may be viewed—waterbuck, tsessebe, kudu, eland, buffalo, nyala, zebra, wildebeest, impala, cheetah, leopard, lion, hyena and black and white rhino. A variety of options is available for game viewing—on horseback, from

Tswalu Kalahari Reserve

🅰 Map p. 247

✉ 185 miles (300 km) NW of Kimberley

☎ 011/274-2299

💲 $$$$

www.tswalu.com

safari vehicles, or on a guided bush walk.

Some of the conservation highlights at Tswalu include the reintroduction of true Kalahari lions, the cheetah, and the endangered wild dog, as well as the critically endangered desert black rhino (the reserve is now home to one-third of the world's desert black rhino population).

The more than 70 species of mammal living here also include sable, Roan antelope, and Kalahari

and though lack of trees means fewer big birds are present, sightings of eagles and the white-backed and lappet-faced vultures do occur. You're likely to see the pale chanting goshawk, pygmy falcon, kori bustard, Namaqua sandgrouse, spotted eagle owl, and crimson-breasted shrike.

Kgalagadi Transfrontier Park

The Kgalagadi occupies 8.9 million acres (3.6 million ha) on

Gemsbok, a local resident of Kgalagadi Transfrontier Park

species like oryx, springbok, and the always entertaining meerkat. Tswalu offers spectacular nighttime game viewing for sightings of aardvarks, aardwolves, porcupines, brown hyenas, and many of the other creatures of the night.

The Tswalu Kalahari Reserve is also known for its superb bird-watching. More than 200 species have been recorded,

either side of the Botswana–South Africa border. In 1999 the two countries agreed to create this gigantic conservation area, the first of southern Africa's transfrontier parks, by merging the Gemsbok National Park in Botswana with South Africa's Kalahari Gemsbok National Park. Common rules govern the whole area, and visitors can move freely

INSIDER TIP:

The Kgalagadi Transfrontier Park is a photographer's dream. Be the first at the gate in the morning to catch the sun's rays sparkling through the dust kicked up by herds of springbok.

—SAMANTHA REINDERS
National Geographic photographer

across borders within the park, although a 4WD will be necessary.

Despite the harsh environment (Kgalagadi is the origin of the word Kalahari, or Thirsty Land), a great variety of animals are at home here, some uniquely adapted to the desert, such as the gemsbok and the black-maned Kalahari lion. The immense size of the park allows for the seasonal migration of herds of eland, red hartebeest, springbok, and blue wildebeest. Secretary birds, buzzards, eagles, and vultures are just some of more than 200 species of bird that occur here. Besides the lion, other predators inlcude the leopard, cheetah, and hyena.

The camps of **Mata Mata, Twee Rivieren,** and **Nossob,** on the South African side of the park, provide accommodation in huts and chalets. All sell fuel and food (Twee Rivieren has its own restaurant) and offer night game-viewing drives. More private, upscale bush camps are now available as well. **Bitterpan Bush Camp** lies on the 4WD route, and **Kalahari Tented Camp** is near Mata Mata. ∎

Kgalagadi Transfrontier Park

🗺 Map p. 247
✉ 160 miles (260 km) N of Upington via R360
☎ 054/561-2000
💲 $$$–$$$$$
www.sanparks.org/parks/kgalagadi

The Curious Lives of Meerkats

The first striking thing about meerkats is their bizarre name, which is Afrikaans for "lake cats." For the record, these small mammals, members of the mongoose family, aren't particularly fond of lakes, nor are there many lakes in their arid Kalahari habitat. But the nominal non sequitur is fitting for such peculiar little mammals.

Meerkats are extremely social creatures. They live in clans with about 20 members, and their daily existence revolves around foraging. Although mainly insectivorous, they'll eat just about anything. They live in colonies that resemble ant hills, spend a lot of time in tunnels, and when they're not looking cute, they're cheating on their mates and eating their young. This infanticide occurs when the alpha female tries to eliminate the litters of other, competing females. These nasty bits aside, they are a cooperative species, designating wet nurses and babysitters to watch groups of infants. Later, the adults teach their young many survival skills, including how to eat scorpions (first you remove the stinger).

Much of what we know about meerkats is due to the Kalahari Meerkat Project. Based in the Kuruman River Reserve since 1993, the project is dedicated to studying the long-term social implications of the meerkat's curious way of life. As meerkats have a lifespan of 12 to 14 years, continuous, long-term study is necessary. Visit *www.kalahari-meerkats.com* for more information.

Namaqualand

Barren and remote, Namaqualand still draws scores of tourists during its brief flower season. On a clear day the blooming countryside exists only in terms of space and color. The severe landscape is also known for less fleeting attractions, like its copper-veined hills, meditative expanses, and curious mining towns.

The Goegap Nature Reserve in flower season

Springbok
 Map p. 247
Visitor Information
✉ Voortrekker St.
☎ 027/712-8035

Springbok

While it might not seem like it at first, Springbok, Namaqualand's main town, might just be as nimble as its four-legged namesake. The settlement was originally built in 1850 during the mining craze, and it has since become the area's impromptu capital. Through a combination of tenacity and luck, Springbok has transitioned to the tourist industry and flourished over the years while the other boomtowns have died as the mines closed down.

The town is huddled in a valley between the granite humps of the Klein Koperberge (meaning "small copper mountains"). Off the N7, Springbok is about 75 miles (120 km) south of the Namibia border, and 375 miles (600 km) north of Cape Town. The town has a variety of stores, restaurants, and accommodations—reservations are recommended during the height of flower season (Aug.–Sept.) when the town is thronged with visitors.

If you need a break from the floral onslaught, there are

other attractions, too. The **Blue Mine** *(Voortreekker Rd., across from Agenbag gas station, tel 027/744-1000, tours on request from Okiep Country Hotel)* was opened in 1852. Long since closed, it attracts many visitors with its azure shafts. Also in town is the **Namaqualand Museum** *(Monument St., tel 027/718-8100, closed Sat.–Sun. Oct. –June, donation)*. Housed in an old synagogue, the museum displays local artifacts of both natural and historical originals.

Five miles (8 km) east of town via the R64 is the **Simon van der Stel Mine** *(request tour at Namaqua Regional Tourism Office, across from Agenbag gas station, Voortrekker Rd., tel 027/712-8035)*, where the former governor mined copper back in 1685. On close inspection, you can still see the graffiti from his party.

Goegap Nature Reserve

The Goegap Nature Reserve, some 10 miles (16 km) out of Springbok, covers 37,000 acres (15,000 ha) of sandy plains interspersed with imposing granite outcrops. The farm, Goegap, was integrated into the reserve in 1990, considerably increasing its size. As in the whole of Namaqua, the chief attraction here is the multicolored annual wildflowers that carpet the area in spring, comprising the majority of the 581 plant species recorded here. You'll also see a range of wild creatures, from lizards and tortoises to insects and small mammals. The 94 bird species that have been recorded include the ostrich, cape eagle-owl, acacia pied barbet, Verreaux's eagle, and spotted dikkop.

Visitors should note that the flowers can be temperamental. They open only when the weather is warm and sunny. The best viewing times are the hours either side of midday, 11 a.m. till 3 p.m. The flowers turn toward the light, so make sure that you get between them and the sun or you may overlook them.

An **information center** provides further data about the plant

Goegap Nature Reserve

✉ 10 miles (16 km) E of Springbok
☎ 027/718-9906
$ $–$$$$$

EXPERIENCE: Wildflower Viewing

If you are lucky enough to be in South Africa during the Namaqualand flower season, a visit to the Northern Cape is not to be missed. But be warned—the flowers can be elusive. Their season is short to begin with, but is entirely dependent on the winter rains and can fall anytime between July and October. It is best to phone the park or one of the hotels in the area beforehand to get a local prediction (loose as it may be) of when and if the flowers will be out.

The easiest way to visit the flowers is by flying either to Upington or Cape Town, from where you can do a scenic drive around the various flower hubs. For more info, call the Namaqua National Park (see p. 264).

Or why not view the wildflowers from horseback? **Namaqualand Horse Trails** *(S of Springbok on N7, contact David or Anne Barnes, tel 027/718-3583)* conducts rides led by expert guides on trails that are particularly beautiful in the wildflower season.

Namaqua National Park

⬛ Map p. 247

✉ 42 miles (67 km) S of Springbok via N7

☎ 027/672-1948

💲 $–$$

www.sanparks.org/parks/namaqua

Hondeklipbaai

⬛ Map p. 247

life of Namaqua, while at the reserve's **Hester Malan Wildflower Garden** a comprehensive range of succulent plants may be viewed. You can move about the reserve in a number of different ways—along a 4WD route, by ordinary sedan round the 10.5-mile (17 km) tourist loop, on foot via two short nature walks, or on two wheels along the reserve's mountain-bike trails. Among the animals you may see are steenbok, springbok, klipspringer, gemsbok, Hartmann's mountain zebra, and bat-eared fox.

Namaqua National Park

Situated some 42 miles (67 km) south of Springbok, this recently opened national park was designed to conserve the plants and animals of Namaqua that were under threat from encroaching farmland. You can hike, drive, and picnic in the reserve. Like the rest of the region it is best visited during August and September when the landscape comes alive with a stunning array of wildflowers.

The park is open only during the wildflower season, every day between 8 a.m. and 5 p.m. **Skilpad Rest Camp** in the park offers four chalets, each sleeping three to four people. The park itself does not provide accommodation. A kiosk at the entrance sells snacks and light meals.

Hondeklipbaai

Hondeklipbaai started life in 1846 as a harbor town. From here, copper ore mined at Okiep near Springbok was shipped to Europe. Initially (and with great difficulty) ox wagons hauled the ore the 65 miles (105 km) from the mines to the coast. However, when a number of copper-ore ships were lost in the heavy mists and rough seas common on

INSIDER TIP:

Book the guesthouse in Goegap Nature Reserve in summer or autumn, when fewer tourists are there, and hike the reserve's trail early in the morning to enjoy fantastic scenery.

—CARSTEN SCHRADIN
National Geographic field researcher

What's in a Name?

No one knows just how Hondeklipbaai (Dog Rock Bay) got its peculiar name. One tale has it that angry townsfolk destroyed a pack of threatening wild dogs near a rock that thus received this odd nickname. A second account says that alongside the police station there used to be rock— later blasted by a lightning bolt—that looked like a sitting dog. Both stories seem little more than urban legends.

this part of the coast, a railway link was constructed from the mines to Port Nolloth in the 1870s. Hondeklipbaai lost its original raison d'être.

Today, the small settlement is a base from which fishing boats and the dredgers that search for diamonds off the coast depart. It also serves as a holiday resort for farmers from the hinterland who come here for their summer vacation.

Diamond Coast

Until recently the entire diamond-rich, northwestern coast of South Africa was part of the Sperrgebiet, or Restricted Zone, forbidden to all but the employees and management of the diamond mines. Now, although movement is still controlled and permits are needed, some parts of the Diamond Coast (see sidebar p. 266) are open to tourists.

Port Nolloth
Map p. 247
Visitor Information
✉ Next to the town hall
☎ 027/851-1111
www.portnolloth .co.za

Springtime at Namaqua National Park

Fish, in particular crayfish, form an important part of the town's economy. Diving for crayfish is strictly controlled, but if you would like to try your luck you may obtain a permit in Springbok.

During August and September, when the wildflowers bloom, it is well worth driving one of the scenic routes in the vicinity of the town; the circular routes that stem off the N7 are the best. The 1945 shipwreck *Aristea* lies off the beach just south of town, a beautiful spot to watch sunsets.

Port Nolloth

Port Nolloth originated in 1854 as a destination for the carts (and later the railways) that transported copper ore to the coast and as a harbor for small craft. Today the town is the only real vacation spot along the Diamond Coast.

At Port Nolloth you can sunbathe or stroll along the spotless beaches, or try your hand with a rod and reel from the shore. Fishing permits are available from the Port Nolloth tourism office, which is located next to the town hall. If you fail to

EXPERIENCE: Tour the Diamond Coast

The Diamond Coast remains to some extent a restricted area. However, some stretches of the coast are now accessible to tourists. The following three tours are available.

Shipwreck Route *(leaves 9 a.m. from Koingnaas Caravan Park or Noup)* This trail within the restricted diamond-mining area takes you along sparkling white beaches to visit several old shipwrecks—among them a Cypriot freighter and a Brazilian steamer—on this dangerous stretch of coast. You will see a number of Late Stone Age middens along the way, and may even catch sight of an endangered species of bird, the African Black oystercatcher. Like all three of the tours featured here, the Shipwreck Route lasts for four hours.

Strandveld Route *(leaves 9 a.m. from Koingnaas Caravan Park or Noup)* Also located within the restricted area, the Strandveld Route takes participants on a spectacular ride over barren yellow sand dunes. You will get to view duikers, springbok, gemsbok, steenbok, small mammals such as suricates and bat-eared foxes, and ostriches in a 74,000-acre (30,000 ha) private reserve. A wide variety of plant types—bulbs, succulents, and low leaf succulents—including several endemic species grow here.

World of Diamonds Mine Tour *(leaves 8 a.m. from the Kleinzee Information Office)* This tour shows visitors the intriguing process of diamond mining. Production schedules permitting, you will be allowed to board the enormous dragline, a piece of machinery that shifts as much as 70 tons of soil 650 feet (200 m) in 60 seconds. The tour also includes a visit to an enormous colony of some 350,000 cape fur seals.

Contact **De Beers** *(tel 027/807-2999 or www .coastofdiamonds.co.za)* for information on all tours.

Richtersveld Transfrontier National Park

 Map. p. 247

 From N7, turn off at Steinkopf and approach via Port Nolloth & Alexander Bay; the last 49 miles (80 km) are dirt

☎ 027/831-1506

💲 $–$$$$$

www.sanparks.org/ parks/richtersveld

land your own yellowtail or snoek, these fish can be bought (subject to availability) from the local fishermen. In addition to tourism, the main economic activities of the town are the processing of crayfish and diamond dredging from the sea.

Cultural tours are offered by the people of the local informal settlement, Sizamile, in which you can visit their shacks and homes. Your guide will bring you up to date on recent developments at the settlement, on its culture and history, and on the challenges it still faces. You will also be shown small-scale economic activities such as day-care centers, vegetable gardening, and chicken farming,

and given the chance to swig Namaqualand whisky at a local shebeen. Contact the Port Nolloth tourism office for tour information.

At **Lekkersing,** northeast of Port Nolloth on the R382, a community group demonstrates examples of local Nama crafts—how to make *velskoene* (rawhide footwear), *riempie* (leather-thong) chairs, and local bonnets and mat houses.

Richtersveld Transfrontier National Park

South African National Parks and the local Nama people (after a landmark court judgement) manage the Richtersveld

Transfrontier National Park in partnership. This is an extremely dry, harsh environment, deriving a major part of its moisture from the dense fog that creeps in from the Atlantic Ocean's freezing waters almost every morning. Some species of plant unique to this area have adapted to these very particular conditions—in spite of which an astonishing variety of small mammals, reptiles, birds, and plants occur in the Richtersveld.

For travel in the park, you're best advised to use a 4WD vehicle, although vans and other high-clearance vehicles are permitted. The only place where you can buy supplies and fuel is at a general dealer (*closed Sat.–Sun.*) in Sendelingsdrift.

The main option for accommodation in the Richtersveld is camping at one of five well-appointed sites: Richtersburg, Kokerboomk-loof, De Hoop, Potjiespram, and Tatasberg & Ganakouriep Wilderness Camps. There is, however, also luxury accommodation available at **Arieb guest cottage,** which offers ten beds, five bedrooms, and two bathrooms. ■

INSIDER TIP:

Richtersveld national park offers an unrivaled 472-mile (760 km) 4WD trail ideal for kicking up a desert storm. Guided trails are an option from April to September, but the trail is well signposted enough to navigate on your own.

—ROBERTA COCI
National Geographic contributor

A 4WD navigating the dunes along the Diamond Coast

TRAVELWISE

Hot-air ballooning at Pilanesberg Game Reserve

PLANNING YOUR TRIP

When to Go

When to visit South Africa depends on where you want to go, and what you wish to do. Most destinations are crowded during the school vacation periods of late June to July, and early December to mid-January. The Kruger National Park and the game reserves of Mpumalanga and KwaZulu-Natal become hot and humid in summer (Dec.–March) and are best visited in spring (Sept.–Oct.), when you will see newborn animals, or in winter (June–Aug.), when the vegetation is thinner and visibility better. The Western Cape and Garden Route are at their best from March to April, though if

you want beaches and heat, go from January to February. Winter is the time to enjoy the dry Northern Cape; summer there is searingly hot. Visitors to the west and northwest coastal regions usually go in late August and September, when the wildflowers bloom. The beaches and coastal resorts of KwaZulu-Natal, hot and crowded in summer, are mild and pleasant during autumn (April–May) and spring (Sept.–Oct.).

Climate

Most of South Africa receives summer rainfall. The exception is the southwestern cape, which has a Mediterranean climate, with wet winters and hot, dry summers. On the highveld, summers are hot with afternoon

thunderstorms, whereas winters are dry and sunny with sometimes frosty nights. Hot, humid, subtropical conditions reign over the lowveld and along the northeastern coast, with heavy summer rainfall; winters are warm and dry. Over the Karoo and northern interior, winter is extremely dry, sunny, and crisp during the day, freezing at night.

Average daily maximum and minimum temperatures, and average monthly rainfall for cities in the different climatic regions, are (from the South African Weather Service):
Cape Town (Mediterranean)
January: 79°F/26°C–61°F/16°C, 0.6 inch/15 mm
July: 64°F/18°C – 45°F/7°C, 3.2 inches/82 mm
Durban (subtropical)
January: 82°F/28°C–70°F/21°C,

5.2 inches/134 mm
July: 73°F/23°C–52°F/11°C,
1.5 inches/39 mm
Johannesburg (highveld)
January: 79°F/26°C–59°F/15°C,
5 inches/125 mm
July: 63°F/17°C–39°F/4°C,
0.15 inches/4 mm
Kimberley (Karoo,
interior plateau)
January: 91°F/33°C–64°F/18°C,
2.2 inches/57 mm
July: 66°F/19°C–37°F/3°C,
0.27 inches/7 mm
Nelspruit (lowveld)
January: 84°F/29°C–66°F/19°C,
5 inches/127 mm
July: 73°F/23°C–43°F/6°C,
0.4 inches/10 mm

For detailed weather information and city and regional forecasts: *www.weathersa.co.za*

What to Take

Visitors will be able to buy or rent everything they need—clothing, medication, camping and hiking equipment, cameras and accessories, and vehicles—in South Africa's cities. It is a good idea to bring a money belt, preferably one that can be worn under clothing, to safeguard your cash and valuables, and a light daypack for touring. Very few establishments in South Africa insist on formal clothing, so you should not need high heels, long dress, suit, or tie. If you're heading off on safari to the country's remoter areas, make sure you take appropriate brown, olive green, or khaki clothing for bush walking, binoculars, hiking boots, backpack, water bottle, sun hat, sunblock, and any prescription medication you need (including malaria medication for the lowveld and far northeast coast).

Insurance

Insure yourself in your home country against travel delays or cancellations, loss or theft of money and belongings, illness or injury. If, however, you have forgotten, you can easily obtain insurance from one of South Africa's large insurance companies. In case of any loss, theft, or crime report the event immediately to the local police station. Your statement will be taken down, and you will be given a case number, which you will need when making an insurance claim. Keep receipts for any items for which you may need to make a claim.

Entry Formalities

You need a passport—valid until at least six months after your arrival date—to enter South Africa. Holders of passports from Australia, Canada, the European Union, and the United States may visit South Africa for up to 90 days without a visa. Travelers from other countries should consult the nearest South African consulate well before their departure date.

You are not required to have any vaccinations before entering South Africa, unless you are entering from a country where yellow fever is found, in which case you need a certificate to prove you have been inoculated against the disease. Although not required, vaccination against hepatitis A and typhoid is recommended if you intend to travel to remote areas.

Persons 18 years of age or more may bring the following into South Africa duty-free:

Flasks of 1.6 fluid ounces (50 ml) of perfume and 8.4 fluid ounces (250 ml) eau de toilette; 0.26 gallon (1 l) of liquor or spirits and 0.52 gallon (2 l) of wine; 200 cigarettes, 50 cigars, and 0.55 pound (250 g) of tobacco; other goods up to the value of R3,000—additional goods up to a value of R12,000 incur 20 percent duty. No narcotics may be imported into South Africa.

You may not bring into or take out of South Africa more than R5,000 in cash.

Festivals

More and more South African cities and towns are creating arts or food festivals to attract tourists. You should check the local news for details. Some of the major established events are the following: For lovers of dance, **Dance Umbrella** (Johannesburg, mid-Feb.–mid-March, *www.at .artslink.co.za/~arts/umbrella*) provides a monthlong celebration, spread over several venues, of South African choreography and performance. Each Easter the huge **Rand Show** (*Nasrec, just S of Johannesburg, www.randshow .co.za*) features trade exhibitions, funfairs, animal events, and pop concerts. The **National Arts Festival** (*Grahamstown, last week June–1st week July, www.na fest. co.za*) is the country's largest annual music, drama, dance, and fine arts event. The **Stellenbosch Wine Festival** (*1st week Aug., www.wineroute.co.za/festival.asp*) allows visitors to sample a huge range of local vintages. When the whales return to breed off the southwestern cape, the **Hermanus Whale Festival** (*late Sept./early Oct., www.whalefesti val.co.za*) celebrates with music, craft markets, and eco-events.

A comprehensive, month-by-month listing of South African festivals can be found at: *www.southafrica.info/travel/cul tural/festivals.htm*.

Further Reading

There are many books you can read before or during your visit to South Africa to get a flavor of the country, its history, peoples, and culture. *South Africa: A Modern History*, by R. Davenport and C. Saunders, will give you the essentials. *Commando*, by Deneys

Reitz, is a classic account of the South African War from the Boer side. Steve Biko's *I Write What I Like* and Nelson Mandela's autobiography, *Long Walk to Freedom*, provide an insight into the thoughts of two great South African leaders. A wonderful account on fossils and Karoo farm life is Eve Palmer's *Plains of Camdeboo*. The short stories of Herman Charles Bosman, published in many different editions, are a must-read if you want to understand South African humor. Other excellent selections from the long roll call of fine South African writing include the following: M. Chapman (editor), *The Paperbook of South African English Poetry*; J. M. Coetzee, *Waiting for the Barbarians* and *Disgrace*; Athol Fugard, *Selected Plays*; Antjie Krog, *Country of My Skull*; Es'kia Mphahlele, *Down Second Avenue*; Alan Paton, *Cry, the Beloved Country*; Richard Rive, *Buckingham Palace: District Six*; Olive Schreiner, *Story of an African Farm*; and Ivan Vladislavi, *The Restless Supermarket*.

HOW TO GET TO SOUTH AFRICA

Almost all foreign tourists enter South Africa by airplane, although a few may cross the border from a neighboring territory by car. Virtually no tourists arrive by sea, except for those on round-the-world cruises.

By Airplane

The country's major hub for air travel is Johannesburg's O. R. Tambo International Airport, but international carriers fly also to Cape Town International Airport and Durban International Airport. Many of the large airlines—among them South African Airways, British Airways, Qantas, Air France, KLM, and Lufthansa—offer direct flights

to South Africa. Flying times to Johannesburg are approximately 17 hours from the U.S., 11 hours from the U.K. and Europe, and 13 to 16 hours from Australia.

All South Africa's international airports are run by ACSA (Airports Company of South Africa), which provides information kiosks at international and domestic arrivals. Visitors are advised only to use porters, shuttle services, and taxis displaying the ACSA logo or bearing an ACSA permit. Johannesburg, Cape Town, and Durban airports are currently undergoing major rebuilding in preparation for the Soccer World Cup of 2010. By that date, Durban's airport is scheduled to change its name to King Shaka International Airport and to move from the south to the north of Durban.

Several ACSA-approved taxi and shuttle services operate at all the large airports; inquire at the information kiosk. **Magic Bus** *(tel 011/548-0822, www.magicbus.co .za)* is a reputable operator offering transport between the three international airports and their respective city centers.

Baggage storage facilities are available at Johannesburg and Cape Town airports.

Useful Websites:
Airports Company of South Africa: *www.acsa.co.za*
Air France: *www.airfrance.com*
British Airways: *www.ba.com*
Cathay Pacific: *www.cathaypacific .com*
KLM–Royal Dutch Airlines: *www.klm.com*
Lufthansa: *www.lufthansa.com*
antas: *www. antas.com.au*
South African Airways: *www.flysaa.com*

By Car

Some tourists may enter South Africa by car from neighboring countries: Namibia, Botswana, Mozambique, Swaziland, or

Zimbabwe. A comprehensive list of border posts, with phone numbers and opening and closing times, is at *www.home-affairs.gov .za/land_border_posts.asp*.

GETTING AROUND
By Air

South Africa is a large country, so travel by air is a good choice for tourists with a limited amount of time. The national carrier, South African Airways (SAA), flies between all the cities and larger towns in the country, while its Airlink and South African Express services fly in smaller aircraft to many regional destinations, including towns close to the Kruger National Park, such as Nelspruit, Phalaborwa, and Hoedspruit; George, at the heart of the Garden Route; Margate, on the KwaZulu-Natal south coast; and Upington, starting point for the Kgalagadi Transfrontier Park or the Gariep (Orange) River adventures.

In recent years South Africa has seen the rise (and, in some cases, demise) of small independent carriers that compete with SAA on the major air routes between Cape Town, Johannesburg, and Durban. Like their international counterparts, they cut costs by charging passengers for in-flight drinks and refreshments. Some of these operators also fly to Port Elizabeth, George, East London, and Nelspruit. The best established air carriers among these smaller operators are Kulula, 1Time, and British Airways (operated in South Africa by Comair).

Good deals are available if you book well in advance online and are prepared to fly at off-peak times, such as on a Sunday, early in the morning or late in the evening.

For domestic flights, passengers are required to be at the airport one hour before the scheduled time of takeoff.

The air-carrier industry in South Africa is very well regulated, with stringent maintenance schedules for all aircraft and an excellent safety record.

Useful Websites:
1Time: *www.1time.aero*
British Airways/Comair:
www.ba.co.za
Kulula: *www.kulula.com*
South African Airways:
www.flysaa.com

By Car
Most South African cities are not well served by safe, efficient public transport suitable for tourists. Thus many visitors use rental cars to travel between and within the country's cities. Driving in South Africa is on the left side of the road. Any valid driver's license will be accepted provided that it is printed in English and bears the signature and photograph of the bearer. Holders of a license not in English should obtain an International Driving Permit before arriving in South Africa.

The country has a good, in many parts excellent, network of asphalt and gravel roads. The major routes are called national roads, designated on signs and maps N1, N2, N3, and so on, whereas regional routes, designated R43, R62, or R306, lead to the national roads or link cities within a region. While "N" roads are generally wider and "R" roads narrower, this is not always the case. The South African Automobile Association website, in its "Travel & Routes" section, carries a comprehensive weekly report on road works and road conditions in the country.

One of the great pleasures of driving in South Africa is to wander off the beaten path and explore the many side routes and secondary roads that crisscross the country, often through areas of startling natural beauty. It is also perfectly feasible for visitors to drive their own or a rental vehicle on safari, through the country's national and private game reserves. Most of these are accessible by ordinary sedan car, though a few require a 4WD vehicle.

Many international car rental companies, such as Avis, Budget, and Hertz, operate in South Africa, with offices at international airports and in the large cities. Motorists can also get good deals from local car rental companies like Tempest and Imperial.

Since South Africa is a big country, with large distances between towns, it's advisable to get an unlimited mileage deal when renting. Before accepting a rental car, make sure to inspect it carefully for any dents or scratches. If found, these should be noted on the rental form, so that you are not charged for them. If you intend to drive extensively on rough, unpaved roads (as, for example, in game reserves), find out in advance whether your car rental contract has any limits in this regard.

Drive carefully. Some South African drivers have little regard for the rules of the road, and vehicle road-worthiness requirements are much laxer than in many Western countries. In many areas, and especially on minor routes through the countryside, roads are not well fenced, and wild or domestic animals may suddenly run out. For this reason, and for reasons of general safety, it is better not to drive long distance at night. Never pick up hitchhikers. Do not stop, even for apparent emergencies; criminals sometimes stage them to rob travelers.

Useful Websites:
South African Automobile Association: *www.aa.co.za*
Avis: *www.avis.co.za*
Budget: *www.budget.co.za*

Hertz: *www.hertz.co.za*
Imperial: *www.imperialcarrental.co.za*
Tempest: *www.tempestcarhire.co.za*

By Public Transportation
The closest South African cities come to having a subway or underground system that would be usable by tourists are the suburban railway in Cape Town and the Gautrain Rapid Rail Link currently being built in Gauteng. Of these two, only the Gautrain will run underground for any appreciable distance.

Cape Town's rail system, operated by Metrorail, links the suburbs in and towns around Cape Town. Their website (*www.capemetrorail.co.za*) provides maps, timetables, station information, news of any delays, and contact details. One-way and round-trip tickets can be bought at most stations. The line that tourists are most likely to use is the one that runs the length of the Cape Peninsula, from the city center to Simon's Town, with stops at each suburb in between. This a convenient way to travel to the rugby and cricket grounds at Newlands; to the False Bay beaches and tidal pools at Muizenberg, St. James, Kalk Bay, Fish Hoek, Clovelly, and Simon's Town. The line is also handy for going to see the penguins at Boulders, just beyond Simon's Town. The stretch from Muizenberg to Simon's Town is particularly worthwhile, since the tracks here are right on the water's edge, with views on the ocean.

Visitors should buy tickets only for first-class coaches, as these are less crowded and more secure. You should note that there have been security problems on the Metrorail system in the past, and guards now travel on the trains. Although you are unlikely to encounter problems, you should remember that the system is not entirely safe.

The other Metrorail line that visitors may want to use is the one linking Cape Town to Stellenbosch, the center of the Winelands.

The Gautrain project (www .gautrain.co.za) aims to connect the center of Johannesburg, Sandton, O. R. Tambo International Airport, and Pretoria with a rapid rail link. The Johannesburg-Sandton line will run underground.

Construction is well under way, and the Sandton-airport link is scheduled for completion by mid-2010, the rest of the system by mid-2011. The trip from the airport to Sandton should take only 15 minutes, the trip from Johannesburg to Pretoria about 40 minutes.

By Bus

Bus links between the cities and large and small towns are well established and frequent. This is a fairly economical option for visitors, although, because of the often great distances involved, it can be a time-consuming experience. In general the prices for long distance travel are proportionately cheaper than those for bus travel between towns close to one another. If you do not have your own transportation and wish to travel independently, bus transport may be the only way to reach some of South Africa's smaller and more remote destinations.

The major intercity bus companies in South Africa are Greyhound, Intercape, Translux, and SA Roadlink. All of these operators offer buses with reclining seats and air-conditioning. Greyhound and SA Roadlink have online reservation facilities; for Intercape and Translux you can book by telephone or at their offices.

A useful facility for tourists on a budget is the Greyhound Travel Pass, giving riders a choice of 7 or 15 days of unlimited travel within 30 days, or 30 days unlimited travel

within 60 days (see website below for prices and conditions).

At present no South African city except Cape Town has a bus system suitable for use by visitors, though this may change before the Soccer World Cup event in 2010. In Cape Town, a service useful to tourists is the shuttle that runs every 10 to 15 minutes between the Victoria & Alfred Waterfront and the main railway station. There are also buses operated by Golden Arrow (www.gabs.co.za) that serve most of the Cape Town area, but only the services running from the city center via Sea Point and Camps Bay to Hout Bay can be recommended to tourists.

Useful Websites:

Baz Bus: www.bazbus.com
Greyhound: www.greyhound.co.za
Intercape: www.intercape.co.za
Translux: www.translux.co.za
SA Roadlink: www.saroadlink.co.za

By Train

The form of train transport in South Africa that tourists are most likely to use are the expensive luxury trains that run on a few set routes within southern Africa. Rovos Rail offers a range of luxury journeys. Their trains run regularly between Pretoria and Cape Town, and less frequently from Pretoria to Durban or to Victoria Falls in neighboring Zimbabwe, or from Cape Town to George. Rovos also offers annual rail trips from Cape Town to Dar es Salaam in Tanzania, and from Pretoria to Swakopmund in Namibia.

The luxury Blue Train departs weekly from Cape Town to Pretoria and vice versa.

Both Rovos Rail and the Blue Train offer every luxury—the trip is not about speed but about sightseeing in luxury from the comfort of your armchair.

Otherwise, intercity travel by train is not recommended for tourists. The trains operated by the parastatal, Shosholoza Meyl, are slow, not efficient and, on many routes, infrequent. For the record, these trains run from Cape Town to Johannesburg and back to Cape Town four times a week and, less frequently, return, between Cape Town and Durban, Cape Town and East London, Johannesburg and Port Elizabeth, and Johannesburg and Nelspruit. If you take one of these trains, make reservations in tourist class with a compartment that sleeps four persons.

Useful Websites:

Blue Train: www.bluetrain.co.za
Rovos Rail: www.rovos.co.za
Shosholoza Meyl: www.spoornet. co.za/ShosholozaMeyl

By Taxi

The word "taxi" in South Africa has two distinct meanings. On the one hand it refers to one of the thousands of minibuses that provide mass transportation along certain routes within and between the urban areas of the country. Although many people use these minibus-taxis safely every day, they are not recommended for visitors unacquainted with South Africa.

On the other hand, "taxi" means what it does elsewhere in the world: a metered car driving people to their destination. Metered taxis cannot be flagged down, but will be found at stations at all the country's major airports, in the city centers, and at large tourist attractions such as Cape Town's Victoria & Alfred Waterfront. Otherwise, you can reserve a taxi to take you from a hotel, store, or restaurant to your desired destination. There are no countrywide taxi companies. To avoid choosing an unsuitable operator, it is best to ask your restaurant or hotel to call a taxi for you.

PRACTICAL ADVICE
Communications

South Africa has an excellent communications infrastructure and provides good postal, Internet, and other telecommunication services.

Post Offices: Mail and postal services are provided by the South African Post Office. Post offices are recognizable by their red-white-and-blue logo showing an open envelope. Postage stamps can be bought at post offices. Large supermarkets sell stamps in booklets. The post office not only handles ordinary mail, but also provides express mail, parcel, and courier services. Rates and tariffs for their services can be found on the (not very user-friendly) post office website. For example, to the U.S. a postcard would cost $0.54 (R4.20) airmail and $0.32 (R2.5) surface mail, and a small letter $0.62 (R4.90) airmail and $0.52 (R4.15) surface mail. The rates to Europe are the same. General delivery addressed with the .0recipient's name can be sent to all the main post offices of South Africa's cities and larger towns to await pick up. You will need some form of identification, such as a passport, to get your mail.

A number of services, formerly the monopoly of the post office, are now also offered by the international company Postnet, with outlets in all the cities and many of the larger towns. Postnet provides, among other things, parcel and courier services and Internet usage.

Useful Websites:
Postnet: *www.postnet.co.za*
South African Post Office: *www.sapo.co.za*

Mailboxes: Envelopes with the correct postage may be dropped in mailboxes, which are bright red and rectangular in shape (though a few old cylindrical mail boxes may still be found). Below the mail slot they normally have a small silver-colored or brass label stating the times when mail is collected from the box.

Telephones: The provision of landline telephone services in South Africa is currently the monopoly of Telkom *(www.telkom.co.za)* though another service provider is due to enter the market. Virtually the whole country has automatic exchanges and direct dialing. You may, however, request operator assistance for making long-distance calls locally and internationally. For calls within South Africa, each town has its own three-digit prefix, while each local number contains seven digits. Thus, for example, the number for the tourist information in Cape Town is 021/487-6800 and the general inquiries number for Durban is 031/311-1111, in each case the city prefix plus the local number. Note that wherever in the country you are calling from, even within the relevant city, you must dial the whole ten-digit number.

Numbers with the prefix 0800 provide calls free of charge.

To make an international telephone call from South Africa, see sidebar p. 11.

Public phones are available all over the country. Look for the green, blue, and white colors of Telkom. Public phones are operated either by coins or more often by an electronic phone card available in denominations of R20, R50, R100, or R200 from most cafés or corner stores around the country. Instructions on how to make a call are listed in all call boxes. Although other local languages may be used, the instructions will always be in English as well.

Useful Telephone Numbers:
Note: All of these numbers incur a charge.
1023   Directory inquiries
1025   Operator help in making a long-distance or collect call within South Africa
10900 Operator help in placing an international call
10903 All other international call inquiries

Cell Phones: Much of the country is covered by cell phone networks, though you may lose connections in rural areas. The chief service providers are Vodacom, MTN, and Cell C, with many outlets at airports and cities all over the country.

Travelers who want to use their own cell phone while in South Africa should first check with the supplier in their home country, to ask whether the phone will work on the networks here. If not, they have the option to buy a starter pack at the airport on arrival and purchase airtime as needed from most supermarkets and cafés around the country. Or they can rent a cell phone with an airtime contract on arrival.

Useful Websites:
Cell C: *www.cellc.co.za*
MTN: *www.mtn.co.za*
Vodacom: *www.vodacom.co.za*

Internet: South Africa is well provided with Internet services, though speed is sometimes compromised by the limited amount of bandwidth available. Travelers will experience no difficulty in getting access to e-mail, the Internet, and Skype in the cities and near major tourist destinations. Many hotels and guesthouses in the larger urban areas make WiFi and Internet connections available to guests. Even in smaller rural areas you will usually be able to gain Internet access.

Conversions

South Africa uses the metric system for all measurements of weight, distance, area, volume, and temperature.

1 kilo = 2.2 pounds
1 liter = 0.2642 U.S gallon
1 kilometer = 0.62 mile
1 meter = 1.093 yards
1 hectare = 2.471 acres

Women's clothing

U.S.					
8	10	12	14	16	8
South African					
87	92	97	102	107	112

Men's clothing

U.S.					
36	38	40	42	44	46
South African					
92	97	102	107	112	117

Women's shoes

U.S.			
6–6½	7–7½	8–8½	9–9½
South African			
5–5½	6–6½	7–7½	8–8½

Men's shoes

U.S.					
8	8½	9½	10½	11½	12
South African					
7	7½	8½	9	10	11

Electricity

The electricity supply is 220–230 volts AC. Sockets take plugs with two or three round pins. U.S. appliances will likely need a transformer to function properly in South Africa. The power supply is mainly reliable in urban areas, though it may be intermittent in remote rural areas. Eskom, the country's power supplier, has been experiencing difficulty in meeting the country's rapidly growing energy demands. Blackouts may occur at times of peak consumption, and it is always advisable to travel with a battery-operated flashlight.

Etiquette & Local Customs

In general, South Africans are warm and friendly, though city people may be more distant. Particularly in small towns and rural areas it is expected that you should exchange the following courtesies on meeting – Local: "Hallo." Visitor: "Hallo." Local: "How are you?" Visitor: "Fine, thanks. And you?" Local: "I'm fine, too." In the country it is common to wave to pedestrians at the side of the road and to receive a wave back.

Black people in South Africa commonly make use of the three-move handshake: Shake Western style, clasp hands with the thumb on top, then repeat the Western style shake. They often give what a Westerner would regard as a very limp handshake; but this is a sign of respect. You will sometimes also find that traditional rural people, out of respect, may speak very softly and not meet your eyes.

Holidays

South Africa has many public holidays, on which banks, businesses, and government offices are closed. (Note that if a public holiday falls on a Sunday, the next day, Monday, is treated as a holiday.)

January 1 New Year's Day
March 21 Human Rights Day
Good Friday (Friday before Easter Sunday)
Family Day (Monday after Easter Sunday)
April 27 Freedom Day
May 1 Workers Day
June 16 Youth Day
August 9 Women's Day
September 24 Heritage Day
December 16 Day of Reconciliation
December 25 Christmas
December 26 Day of Goodwill

Liquor Laws

South Africa has reasonably relaxed liquor laws. Persons 18 or older are legally permitted to buy alcohol. Beer, wine, and spirits can be bought at liquor stores, known locally as "bottle stores," which are open during normal business hours. Larger supermarkets sell wine, but not spirits or beer.

Media

Freedom of the press is guaranteed by South Africa's constitution, and the country has vigorous independent media operating in a number of the 11 official languages. The state broadcaster, the South African Broadcasting Corporation (SABC), can sometimes be too timid or biased in its political reporting, but this reticence is balanced out by assertive commercial media.

Newspapers: Some of the English-language newspapers have been in existence for more than a century. All the cities have their own English morning and evening paper. These are, respectively, in Cape Town the *Cape Times* and *Cape Argus;* in Johannesburg the *Citizen, Sowetan,* and *Mtar;* and in Durban the *Mercury* and *Daily News.* Recently, sensationalist tabloid newspapers have gained a large number of readers in the cities.

The most intelligent and informative of the weekly newspapers is the *Mail & Guardian,* published every Friday, with in-depth reporting on political, economic, and cultural matters.

The major national Sunday newspapers are the Johannesburg-based *Sunday Times,* a mix of tabloid sensationalism, hard-headed reporting, and political commentary, and the lower circulation but good-quality *Sunday*

Independent, incorporating a lot of syndicated material from U.K. and U.S. papers. The Durban area has its own established weekend paper, the *Sunday Tribune.*

The *Sunday Times'* new national daily, *The Times,* is the first multimedia, local paper, with an extensive, interactive website.

Television: The national broadcaster puts out TV programs on its three channels, SABC 1, 2, and 3, in many of the official languages. But English-language news, feature programs, sports, and movies are broadcast at times on each of the three channels. Visitors looking for English-language programming, though, are best advised to tune in to the free-to-air channel, e.tv, or to the pay-channels, M-NET or DSTV. Through DSTV you will have access to CNN, BBC World, and Sky, and also to the e.tv 24-hour local news channel.

Online: You can get good, up-to-the-minute, local and international news via the Web from Internet providers iafrica, iol, and News24. The iol site is particularly useful, in that it supplies links to Web versions of all of South Africa's main newspapers.

Useful Websites:
iafrica: *www.iafrica.com*
iol: *www.iol.co.za*
News24: *www.news24.com*

Radio: The SABC does a remarkable job in broadcasting in most of South Africa's official languages. It puts out a good news and talk-show program on its radio channel, SAFM. Many commercial broadcasters operate on the airwaves, among them 567 Cape Talk in the Cape Town area, and 702 Talk Radio in the Gauteng area, both of which broadcast news, interviews, and talk shows during the day. There are also many regional stations in the country, broadcasting mainly pop music; 5FM is the most popular national music station.

Money Matters
The official currency of South Africa is the rand, subdivided into 100 cents. Rand notes come in denominations of 200, 100, 50, 20, and 10. The coins are bronze-colored 5, 10, 20, and 50c pieces; nickel-silver 1 and 2 rand coins; and a silver-edged, bronze-centered R5 coin.

South Africa's banking system is sophisticated and well developed. The major banks are Standard, First National, Nedbank, and ABSA, all of which have automatic teller machines (ATMs) throughout the country. ATMs can be found at all airports and shopping malls, on many streets of the cities, and even in small rural towns. You should be able to draw local currency from most ATMs via the bank cards you use at home, but you should talk about your travels to your own bank before departure.

Major credit cards are widely accepted, but you should check ahead of time when purchasing goods or services in smaller places. The most common cards are Mastercard and Visa, followed by American Express, and Diners Club.

You can exchange traveler's checks, U.S. dollars, and other major currencies at banks, some travel agencies, and at bureaus de change, which are at many major tourist destinations. Inquire in advance about what commission they charge. The larger hotels will also change checks and banknotes, but take a hefty commission.

Opening Times
Most stores and businesses in the larger urban areas open Monday to Friday at 8:30 or 9:00 a.m. and close at 4:30, 5:00, or 5:30 p.m. They are also open on Saturday from 9:00 a.m. to 12.30 or 1:00 p.m. In smaller towns and country villages stores may close for an hour for lunch between noon and 2:00 p.m. and may be closed on the weekends.

Larger stores in the big urban shopping malls are open much longer, some weekday evenings (especially on Fridays and during the holiday season) until 9 or 10 p.m., and from 10 or 11 a.m. until about 4 p.m. on Saturdays and Sundays.

Banks are normally open from 9:00 a.m. to 3:30 p.m. on weekdays and 9:00 a.m. to 10:30 or 11:00 a.m. on Saturdays.

Most post offices are open from 8:30 a.m. to 4:30 p.m.

Gas stations on major routes operate 24 hours a day, as do larger ones in urban areas. Smaller gas stations are open from about 7 a.m. to 10 p.m., though this schedule may vary from place to place.

Places of Worship
Most South Africans are Christians, members of one of the many African independent churches, or of an Anglican, Catholic, Dutch Reformed, Methodist, or Presbyterian congregation. Others belong to charismatic evangelical churches. There are also a number of Islamic, Jewish, Hindu, and African traditional religious minorities. All these groups have their places of worship, but few of these are visited by tourists, unless they are worshipers belonging to the religion concerned.

Time Differences
South African Standard Time is two hours ahead of Greenwich Mean Time (GMT + 2). The whole country belongs to the same time zone.

Tipping
See sidebar p. 10. Also keep in mind, if you are driving your own or a rental car, you will find that, as soon as you park in the city, informal "car guards," sometimes wearing an official-looking outfit, will approach you to "look after" your car. On your return, depending on how long you have been away, or whether it is cold and dark, you may tip them anything from R2 to R10.

Travelers with Disabilities
Although South Africa's constitution protects the rights of people with disabilities, so far the country has not done much to make things easier for them. Newer public buildings, however, do often incorporate wheelchair ramps, elevators, and restrooms. Parking for the disabled with appropriate signs is also reasonably well supplied in public parking areas. If you depend on facilities for the disabled, you should e-mail or phone ahead to check whether or not they are available at your destination.

Epic Enabled (www.epic-enabled. com) arranges regular safari trips for the disabled, and will design individual tours to suit special needs.

Visitor Information
Every city and town and even small villages have their own tourism information office. You will also find tourist information kiosks at the country's international airports. On arrival in any South African city or town, it's a good idea to head straight for the local tourism office to get an overview of the local and regional attractions that are offered, as well as detailed maps.

The telephone number for general tourism information and safety anywhere in South Africa is 083/123-2345.

Among websites useful for information and planning your trip, www.southafricaholiday.org.uk is noteworthy for its detailed and accurate information. Also helpful are:
> www.sa-venues.com
> www.southafrica.net
> www.southafrica.info

Major Tourism Offices
Cape Town: The Pinnacle, corner of Burg & Castle Sts. (tel 021/426-4260, www.tourismcape town.co.za). This website links to details of tourism information offices in all the towns of the Western Cape.
Durban: Tourist Junction, 160 Pine St. (tel 031/304-4934, www .durban.kzn.org.za)
Johannesburg: 1 Central Place, corner Henry Nxumalo & Jeppe Sts., Newtown (tel 011/639-1600, www.joburg.org.za, www.joburgtour ism.com)
Pretoria: Tourist Information Center, Church S . (tel 012/358-1430). The official tourism site (www.tshwanetourism.com) is very poor. Try www.4pretoria.co.za or www.sa-venues.com.

Regional Tourism Offices
Eastern Cape:
www.ectourism.co.za
Gauteng: www.gauteng.net
KwaZulu-Natal: www.zulu.org.za
Mpumalanga:
www.mpumalanga.com
Northern Cape:
www.northerncape.org.za
Northwest Province:
www.tourismnorthwest.co.za
Western Cape:
www.capetourism.org

EMERGENCIES
Emergency phone numbers for the whole of South Africa are:
Police 10111
Ambulance and fire 10177

National emergency number 107
Emergency number to call from a cell phone 112
Tourism information and safety number 083/123-2345

Crime & Police
In the unfortunate event that you are the victim of a crime, dial 10111, and you will be put in contact with the police station nearest you. Response times vary greatly depending on what area you are in.

You may be asked to come to the police station to make a statement, which will then be written out for you to sign. Make sure to ask for a case number. You will need it for insurance purposes and to follow up on the progress of the case.

Police in South Africa wear dark blue uniforms and a blue cap. Their levels of training are not always high, and you may sometimes have difficulty communicating in English.

Embassies & Consulates
CANADA
Pretoria
Canadian High Commission
1103 Arcadia St. (corner Arcadia & Hilda Sts.)
Hatfield Pretoria 0083
Tel 012/422-3000

UNITED KINGDOM
Cape Town
British Consulate General
15th Fl., Southern Life Centre
8 Riebeeck St.
Cape Town 8001
Tel 021/405-2400
Pretoria
U.K. High Commission
Consular Section
Liberty Life Place
Block B, 1st Floor
256 Glyn St.
Hatfield 0083 Pretoria
Tel 012/421-7500

UNITED STATES
Cape Town
Consulate General
2 Reddam Ave., Westlake
Cape Town 8001
Tel 021/702-7300
Johannesburg
Consulate General
1 River St. Killarney
Johannesburg 2001
Tel 011/646-6900
Pretoria
U.S. Embassy
877 Pretorius St.
Arcadia 0083
Tel 012/431-4000

Lost Property

It's always a good idea to make photocopies or scans of all your important documents, such as passport, tickets, and traveler's checks, and keep them separately from the originals, in case of loss. Immediately report loss of travel documents to the police and to your embassy.

If you lose valuables and intend to make an insurance claim, you should make a statement at the nearest police station and be sure to get a case number (see opposite, Crime & Police).

For further assistance contact the tourism information and safety number 083/123-2345.

What to Do in a Car Accident

If you are involved in a vehicle accident and people are injured, the first thing you should do is call the ambulance number, 10177, or the emergency number from a cell phone, 112. Then call the police on 10111. You may be asked to come to the police station and make a statement. Make sure that you get a case number, for insurance purposes.

If no one is injured and there is no damage other than to the vehicle(s), you are not required

by law to call the police. If there are witnesses, make sure to get their contact information. As usual, get all the details of the other driver, including information on his/her insurance company.

Make sure that the vehicles are not moved before the police arrive. Note that there are many predatory towing companies in South Africa whose vehicles will arrive on an accident scene very quickly. Some of them will try aggressively to get you to use their services. If at all possible, phone your rental car or insurance company to ask them before making a decision on towing.

Be sure to contact your insurance company as soon as possible, whether or not the accident was your fault.

HEALTH
Hospitals & Medical Practitioners

In South Africa's larger urban areas, general medical and hospital services are of a high standard. To find a doctor or dentist, look under "Medical Practitioners" in the local phone book; all doctors and dentists for a particular area are listed there. If it is after hours, an answering machine will normally give you an emergency contact number. Hospitals provide a 24-hour emergency service.

Large State Hospitals

Cape Town: Groote Schuur Hospital, Main Rd., Observatory *(tel 021/404-9111)*
Durban: Addington Hospital, Erskine Terrace, South Beach *(tel 031/327-2000)*
Johannesburg: Johannesburg General, Jubilee Rd., Parktown *(tel 011/488-4911)*
For those who want emergency private hospital services, the two largest providers, with facilities throughout South Africa, are:

Netcare *(tel 011/301-0000, www .netcare.co.za)* and Medi-Clinic *(tel 021/809-6500, www.mediclinic .co.za,).*

Drugs

Pharmacies and dispensing pharmacists will be found in all urban areas, with some 24-hour facilities in the cities. Local pharmacists are well trained and will be able to advise you on medication.

Health Hazards

HIV/AIDS is a serious problem in South Africa, especially among the heterosexual population. If you are sexually active, you are urged to take precautions and to practice safe sex.

If you are traveling to the lowveld areas of Mpumalanga and northern KwaZulu-Natal, you need to take precautions against malaria. Remember that you need to start taking antimalarial medication a week in advance, and for four to five weeks afterward. If you are allergic, or do not wish to take malaria medication, you should cover up well and apply mosquito repellent to exposed skin, especially from dusk to dawn, and sleep under a mosquito net.

Water

It is generally safe to drink tap water in South Africa. In bush camps you should inquire first whether the water is drinkable. If you are hiking and need to drink lake or river water, you should first boil it or add water-purification tablets.

Do not paddle or swim in rivers or lakes without first checking whether bilharzia is present, or whether hippos or crocodiles pose a danger.

Hotels & Restaurants

South Africa's hospitality industry has experienced a massive expansion since the early 1990s. Today visitors will find a wide range of accommodations and dining available in all the major cities and large towns. Even in the tiniest village there will be a reasonable B&B or self-catering establishment and somewhere to get a meal. The overall standards of cleanliness and professionalism in the industry may vary from place to place, but they are generally quite high. Prices by European and U.S. standards are mostly reasonable and good value for the money.

Hotels

The terms used in South Africa to refer to accommodations are generally similar to those used elsewhere in the English-speaking world. On occasion, though, they can be somewhat fluid. Visitors may find that establishments termed "hotel," "lodge," "guesthouse," or "country house" (or a combination of these names) provide facilities that are pretty much the same or quite widely different. In 2000 an official Tourism Grading Council was established, allowing each category of accommodation to be graded on a scale from one to five stars. At present, grading is voluntary and not required by law. The following are the definitions that the council gives for the various types of accommodations relevant to this guidebook (www .tourismgrading.co.za).

Besides accommodations, a hotel should have a reception area and a communal eating area or at least a breakfast room. Though a hotel normally makes food and drink available to its guests, this service may be outsourced to a third party.

Lodges: A lodge is an establishment providing accommodations in natural surroundings. Generally a game lodge's tariffs include meals and some beverages, and may also include activities such as game drives, nature walks, or visits to historical sites. (Gradings apply only to the hospitality side of what a lodge offers.)

Guesthouses: This is usually a mansion or house converted to provide accommodations, though it may be custom-built. Guesthouses are generally managed by the owner, who lives on the premises, but they should have public areas for exclusive use of the guests.

Country Houses: A country house is a larger-scale guesthouse, normally located in quiet, natural surroundings, such as near a lake, nature reserve, or forest. A country house usually offers the same services as a hotel, including dinner.

Hotel Chains: In the listings below, large hotels belonging to major international or local chains, such as Hilton, Sheraton, Sun International, City Lodge, and Protea, are not generally included. Their details are easily available online respectively at:

www.hilton.com
www.starwoodhotels.com/sheraton
www.suninternational.com
www.citylodge.co.za
www.proteahotels.com

Visitors to South Africa wishing to search for their own accommodations will find excellent websites. Several have maps of the country and list places to stay by category, by province, city, and price. Try the following:

www.roomsforafrica.com
www.wheretostay.co.za/
accommodation
www.sa-venues.com/
accommodation
www.south-african-hotels.com
Note that in South Africa

smoking is banned by law from all enclosed spaces open to the public. Since most accommodations are nonsmoking, in the listings this has not been noted for each establishment. But where smoking is allowed, permission is indicated.

Restaurants

Whereas 15 to 20 years ago in South Africa the range of restaurants was limited and the standard of cuisine mediocre, now visitors are spoiled with choices. Cape Town, the Winelands, and the towns of the Western Cape have become gastronomic destinations, offering several outstanding restaurants and dozens of good to excellent ones. In peak vacation season, especially mid-December to mid-January, it is important to make reservations well in advance.

Many hotels have converted their former dining rooms into restaurants—often very good ones—open to both hotel guests and the general public. These restaurants are sometimes run as a separate outsourced operation.

The days of only French cuisine at top restaurants, or of overcooked food at others, are long gone. The current fashion is for fusion cuisine, using South African ingredients but with an international twist. Sushi and Asian fusion styles—influenced by Japan, Thailand, and Vietnam—have also taken a strong hold in the cities. However, visitors will also find the cuisine of most Western European and many Eastern European countries represented here, in addition to traditional South African cooking.

🏨 Hotel   🍴 Restaurant   ⓘ No. of guest rooms   🪑 No. of Seats   🅿 Parking   🕐 Closed

For some reason, though, desserts still tend to be rather unimaginative. Diners will find crème brûlée, ice cream, and chocolate sauce, cheesecake, apple pie, and malva pudding again and again.

Sad to say, in South Africa as in many parts of the world fish stocks are badly depleted. The result is that even specialized seafood restaurants cannot always offer the quality and variety of fish that they had on the menu in the past.

Most restaurants operate with an à la carte menu, though many have "specials of the day." Some offer a fixed-price, set menu exclusively or alongside à la carte. Many restaurants, particularly in the cities, have their own website, and often the current menu is posted there. Most restaurants here offer good value for the money.

A number of estates in the Winelands of the Western Cape offer visitors the choice to buy a prepared picnic basket to enjoy on the estate on fine spring or summer days.

Nowadays you will rarely find a restaurant in South Africa that is not licensed to sell at least wine and beer. It is common practice for diners to bring their own wine to a restaurant—even an expensive one—though a few places do not allow this. BYO (bring your own) is an also excellent option for travelers on a budget, since restaurant markups of 100 percent or more on wine are not uncommon. Even if you pay a cork fee of $2–$7 you will still save money.

Little in the way of a dress code applies at South African restaurants. "Smart casual"—long trousers and an open-neck shirt—is the norm for dinner. At lunchtime shorts are acceptable at most places, particularly if you are eating outdoors. Don't be alarmed if you encounter the word "waitron" when eating out. Many restaurants have adopted this gender-neutral term to refer to both waiters and waitresses.

The listings below make no reference to whether or not a restaurant is nonsmoking, because by law smoking is not allowed in restaurants, cafés, or bars. Smokers have to smoke in a separate area, sealed off from the rest of the establishment.

Two websites give wide and detailed coverage on restaurants. Eat Out (www.eatout.co.za) covers most cities and towns, and has reviews (not always reliable) posted by diners. Dining Out (www.dining-out.co.za) is not as extensive, but offers fuller descriptions, detailed menus, and pictures.

Credit Cards

The vast majority of hotels and restaurants in South Africa accept major credit cards, especially Mastercard and Visa. Diners Club and American Express are also widely accepted.

Listings

Hotels and restaurants are organized by chapter, then listed by price, then in alphabetical order.

For disabled access, it is best to inquire in advance at the hotel or restaurant concerned what facilities they offer.

L = Lunch   D = Dinner

■ CAPE TOWN & THE PENINSULA

CAPE TOWN

CAPE GRACE
$$$$$ ★★★★★
WEST QUAY RD., VICTORIA & ALFRED WATERFRONT
TEL 021/410-7100
www.capegrace.com
The attraction of this hotel—besides its luxury accommodation—is the location, with views of Table Mountain, the harbor, and the waterfront. The restaurant presents seasonal cuisine reflecting the Malay tradition at the Cape.
ⓘ 120 🛏 70 Ｐ ⭯ 🆂 🏊 🆅

🏨 MOUNT NELSON
🍴 **$$$$$** ★★★★★
76 ORANGE ST., GARDENS
TEL 021/483-1000
www.mountnelson.co.za
For over a century the "Nellie" (the locals' nickname for this hotel), with its towering palm trees and lush gardens, has provided fine accommodations close to the city center. Decorated in cool elegant tones, the accommodations range from luxury rooms to deluxe suites and a penthouse. The hotel has a range of bars and restaurants (see pp. 282–283 under **The Cape Colony, Oasis,** and **Planet Champagne Bar**).
ⓘ 201 Ｐ ⭯ 🆂 🏊 🆅

🏨 VINEYARD HOTEL & 🍴 SPA
$$$$$ ★★★★
60 COLINTON RD. (OFF PROTEA RD.), NEWLANDS
TEL 021/657-4500
www.vineyard.co.za
Set within 6 acres (2.4 ha) of beautiful gardens, with a centuries-old homestead at its heart and stunning views of Table Mountain, this is a truly special venue. Rooms are decorated in a clean modern style. The hotel has its own gym and health spa and a range of places to eat and drink, including the award-winning **Myoga** (see pp. 282–283).
ⓘ 175 🛏 210 Ｐ 🏊 🆅 🆂

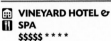

🏨 CAPE HERITAGE HOTEL
$$$$–$$$$$ ★★★★
HERITAGE S ., 90 BREE ST.
TEL 021/424-4646
www.capeheritage.co.za
Delightful boutique hotel located in an old building (1771) right in the historic heart of Cape Town. The rooms have sash windows and period furnishings, with 200-year-old yellowwood and polished hardwood floors. Several good restaurants in the vicinity.
ⓘ 17 🆂

⭯ Elevator 🆂 Air-conditioning 🏊 Indoor Pool 🏊 Outdoor Pool 🆅 Health Club

METROPOLE
$$$–$$$$$ ★ ★ ★ ★
38 LONG ST.
TEL 021/424-7247
www.metropolehotel.co.za
Stylish and modern hotel located in a renovated Georgian building on the city's trendy Long Street. The beige-, black-, and white-colored rooms have travertine marble bathrooms, and French linen on the beds. The hotel's **M-Café** is open for breakfast, lunch, and dinner.
🛏 25 30 🔲 🔾

 THE CULLINAN
$$$–$$$$
1 CULLINAN ST., WATERFRONT
TEL 021/418-6920
www.southernsun.com
Part of the international Southern Sun chain, the Cullinan is a striking multistory building located where the city center meets the Waterfront. Very convenient to the major Cape Town tourist attractions.
🛏 410 ⬛ 15 🅿 🔾 ⛵ ▦

 17 ON LOADER STREET
$$–$$$ ★ ★ ★
17 LOADER ST., DE WATERKANT
TEL 021/418-3417
www.17loader.za.net
Ten minutes from the city center and the waterfront, this B&B is located in the fashionable De Waterkant area, with its cobbled streets and many cafés and coffee bars. Climb to the roof deck for stunning 360 degree views of the city and Table Mountain.
🛏 9 🅿

LEEUWENVOET HOUSE
$$–$$$ ★ ★ ★ ★
8 KLOOF NEK RD., TAMBOERSKLOOF
TEL 021/424-1133
www.leeuwenvoet.co.za
Situated in a renovated Victorian house, Leeuwenvoet offers rooms decorated in cool shades of beige and white. Conveniently located on the edge of the city, with the trendy Kloof Street restaurant area at the doorstep.
🛏 15 🅿 🔾 ⛵

MORNINGSIDE COTTAGE
$$ ★ ★ ★ ★
3 THATCH CLOSE, TOKAI
TEL 021/712-0441
www.morningside-cottage.co.za
Set in the leafy suburbs, close to mountain walks and golf courses, this luxury B&B offers peace and tranquility. All rooms have en suite bathrooms. Guests have access to a sun patio, garden, and pool.
🛏 5 ⛵

SOMETHING SPECIAL

THE CAPE COLONY
$$$–$$$$
MOUNT NELSON HOTEL, 76 ORANGE ST., GARDENS
TEL 021/483-1948
www.mountnelson.co.za
High vaulted ceilings, a large mural of old Cape Town and discreet sounds from the grand piano give this restaurant its distinctive colonial feel. The cuisine, part European, part Asian, is among the best in South Africa. Try the superb lamb or springbok with black Vietnamese sauce.
⬛ 90 🅿 🔾

SAVOY CABBAGE
$$$–$$$$
101 HOUT ST., CITY CENTER
TEL 021/424-2626
www.savoycabbage.co.za
Among the attractions of this eclectic restaurant and champagne bar are the century-old exposed walls and glass stairwell. Specialities include sweetbreads and ceviche of red Roman (a local fish) with pineapple, coconut, and coriander.
⬛ 90 🅿 🕐 Closed D Sun., L Sat.–Sun.

AUBERGINE
$$$
39 BARNET ST., GARDENS
TEL 021/465-4909
www.aubergine.co.za
Stylish decor and classic cooking with a hint of Asia is offered here. Sample the lavender-flavored lamb saddle or salmon tartare with spicy guacamole. The restaurant and its chef,

Harald Bresselschmidt, have won many awards.
⬛ 80 🕐 Closed D Sun., L Sat.–Tues.; 2 weeks June & July

SOMETHING SPECIAL

JARDINE
$$$
185 BREE ST., CITY CENTER
TEL 021/424-5640
This restaurant, named after its award-winning chef, George Jardine, is one of Cape Town's finest. Amid an elegant ambience, Jardine offers such specialities as crayfish risotto, oysters vinaigrette, and oxtail flavored with rosemary.
⬛ 80 🕐 Closed D Mon., L Sat.–Thurs.

SOMETHING SPECIAL

MYOGA
$$$
VINEYARD HOTEL, COLINTON RD. (OFF PROTEA RD.), NEWLANDS
TEL 021/657-4545
www.myoga.co.za
Put award-winning chef Mike Basset together with a stunning, stylish venue, and you have a top combination. The cuisine fuses the best of local

---

and international dishes. Try the prawns with three different sauces for a starter, springbok pepper coriander for a main course, and the "elements of chocolate" dessert. Whatever your choice, though, you will enjoy a feast.

🛏 100 🅿 ⚙

🍴 ANATOLI
$$–$$$
24 NAPIER ST., GREEN POINT
TEL 021/419-2501
www.anatoli.co.za
Located in a converted warehouse with high ceilings, this restaurant is notable for its striking Middle Eastern furnishings and décor. It offers a wide range of Turkish dishes, from kebabs of all kinds to lamb shanks flavored with coriander and orange.

🛏 120 🕐 Closed D Sun., L,
🅿

🍴 BUKHARA
$$–$$$
33 CHURCH ST., CITY CENTER
TEL 021/424-0000
www.bukhara.com
Though the venue is rather hangar-like, Bukhara provides some of the best Indian food in Cape Town. The whole gamut is available here—delicious garlic naan bread, spicy tandooris, lamb and chicken rogan josh, butter chicken, and vegetarian lentil dishes.

🛏 250 🕐 Closed L Sun.

🍴 OASIS
$$–$$$
MOUNT NELSON HOTEL,
76 ORANGE ST., GARDENS
TEL 021/483-1948
www.mountnelson.co.za
Sit on the terrace next to the pool and enjoy a leisurely meal. The outdoor theme is carried indoors into the dining room with its mural of large green leaves. Sunday brunch comes with a complimentary glass of orange juice or sparkling wine and a newspaper.

🛏 100 🕐 D Nov.–March only
🅿 ⚙

🍴 YUM
$$
2 DEER PARK DR.,
VREDEHOEK
TEL 021/461-7607
Yum is a pleasant, reasonably priced restaurant on the lower slopes of Table Mountain. Try the Cajun chicken with guacamole, chili, and coriander, the Italian or Asian style pastas, or the mussels in red Thai curry.

🛏 85 🕐 Closed L Mon.–Thurs., breakfast Mon.–Fri.

🍴 AFRO CAFÉ
$–$$
48 CHURCH ST.,
CITY CENTER
TEL 021/426-1857
Featuring food from all over the continent, this venue carries the African theme through to its fabrics and decor. Patrons come for the stews, spicy curries, and outstanding coffee, and the live music on Thursday and Friday evenings.

🛏 86 🕐 Closed D winter

🍴 PLANET CHAMPAGNE & COCKTAIL BAR
$–$$
MOUNT NELSON HOTEL,
76 ORANGE ST., GARDENS
TEL 021/483-1948
www.mountnelson.co.za
With its décor of twinkling, starry ceiling lights, this is a pleasant place to relax and down a beer or a sparkling wine tinged with cassis. Light meals and canapés are also served. In fine weather, the terrace offers beautiful views over the hotel gardens.

🛏 40 🅿 ⚙

🍴 ROYALE KITCHEN
$–$$
273 LONG ST., CITY CENTER
TEL 021/422-4536
Go upstairs to this unusual gourmet hamburger restaurant, with its quirky interior and sheet music wallpaper. The superb burgers are served with a variety of mouthwatering cheese, mushroom, and chili sauces. There are also vegetarian options.

🛏 50 🕐 Closed D Sun.

🍴 OBZ CAFÉ
$
115 LOWER MAIN RD.,
OBSERVATORY
TEL 021/448-5555
www.obzcafe.co.za
An atmospheric deli restaurant with wooden floors and high ceiling, the Obz Café is a great place for breakfast or a light lunch. The chicken, fried with honey, served on chili mash is a speciality. Evenings often feature intimate theater or stand-up comedy.

🛏 250

🍴 OLIVE STATION
$
165 MAIN RD.,
MUIZENBERG
TEL 021/788-3264
This unusual venue combines a cellar deli where you can buy olive products, and a restaurant housed in an old railway carriage with sea views. The menu is Levantine, offering meze, dolmades, moussaka, and roast lamb, but you can also breakfast here, or just enjoy a coffee and pastry.

🛏 80 🕐 D only Thurs. 🅿

🍴 TONI'S ON KLOOF
$
88 KLOOF ST., GARDENS
TEL 021/423-7617
Offering excellent value for money, Toni's is popular with Capetonians. Sit on the veranda and watch the crowds go by while dining on Portuguese and Mozambican food, such as the excellent prawn rissole or traditional pork, chicken, chorizo, and bean stew.

🛏 48

THE PENINSULA

🏨 THE CELLARS-HOHENORT
$$$$$ ★★★★★
93 BROMMERSVLEI RD.,
CONSTANTIA
TEL 021/794-2137
www.cellars-hohenort.com
This is the place to stay if you want to escape the bustle of the city center. Set in an old manor house surrounded by gardens and vineyards, with fine mountain views, this venue oozes Old World elegance. Enjoy international and Cape Malay

cuisine on the shaded veranda or indoors at the hotel's two restaurants.
🛈 55 🍴 45 🅿 🄂 🏊

🏨 QUAYSIDE HOTEL
$$$–$$$$ ★★★★
JUBILEE SQUARE,
SIMON'S TOWN
TEL 021/786-3838
www.quayside.co.za
Located right in the heart of historic Simon's Town, this hotel looks directly over the waterfront and harbor. The rooms, sea or mountain facing, are decorated in nautical blue and white.
🛈 26 🅿 🄂

🏨 ROCKLANDS
$$
25 ROCKLANDS RD., MURDOCH VALLEY SOUTH, SIMON'S TOWN
TEL 021/786-3158
www.rocklandsbnb.com
Perched on the hillside next to a nature reserve, this B&B offers reasonably priced rooms, some with en suite bathroom. Guests have magnificent views of the ocean from the patio.
🛈 6

🍴 BLACK MARLIN
$$–$$$
MAIN RD., MILLER'S POINT, SIMON'S TOWN
TEL 021/786-1621
www.blackmarlin.co.za
This seafood restaurant, overlooking the ocean, is an ideal place to stop for lunch if you are driving around the Cape Peninsula. Try the crayfish, kingklip, prawns, fish of the day, or lobster bisque. Advance reservations are required.
🍴 180 🅿 🕒 Closed D Sun.

🍴 BLUES
$$–$$$
THE PROMENADE, VICTORIA RD., CAMPS BAY
TEL 021/438-2040
www.blues.co.za
For years a favorite, Blues commands a fine view of the Camps Bay beach and ocean. Specialities here are fresh seafood, steaks, and Italian dishes.
🍴 240 🅿

🍴 CHAPMAN'S PEAK HOTEL RESTAURANT
$$–$$$
CHAPMAN'S PEAK DR., HOUT BAY
TEL 021/790-1036
www.chapmanspeakhotel .co.za
Capetonians love to while away a Sunday afternoon on the terrace here, sipping wine, eating seafood, and enjoying views of sea and mountains. A favorite is the fish, prawns, and calamari combo.
🍴 90 🅿

🍴 BRASS BELL
$–$$$
KALK BAY STATION, MAIN RD., KALK BAY
TEL 021/788-5455
www.brassbell.co.za
Set right on the water's edge between a railway station and the sea, this famous venue consists of several bars and dining areas. Fresh fish from the nearby harbor is the Brass Bell's specialty, served grilled, battered, or in a curry.
🍴 200

🍴 SIMON'S AT GROOT CONSTANTIA
$–$$
GROOT CONSTANTIA ESTATE, GROOT CONSTANTIA RD., CONSTANTIA
TEL 021/794-1143
www.simons.co.za
On the terrace of the oldest wine estate in South Africa you can enjoy a bottle of the local vintage while dining on Cape Malay food, venison, a range of fish dishes, or simply a salad and a burger.
🍴 180 🅿 🕒 Closed D Mon. June–Aug.

🍴 WINESENSE
$–$$
KALK BAY MAIN RD., KALK BAY
TEL 021/788-1869
The attraction of this wine bar and restaurant is that it allows you to sample many local wines without having to buy a whole bottle. You can snack on tapas dishes, or enjoy more substantial grilled steaks or excellent seared tuna.
🍴 60 🕒 Closed D Sun.

■ WEST COAST

CITRUSDAL
───────────────

🏨 HEBRON HIGHWAY HOSPITALITY
$$
ON N7, JUST BELOW TOP OF PIEKENIERSKLOOF PASS (ON CITRUSDAL SIDE)
TEL 022/921-2595
www.hebron.co.za
quaint guesthouse with en suite rooms, each colorfully decorated in an individual style. Breakfast is available, and a coffee shop on the property provides light meals.
🛈 6 🅿 🏊

🍴 PATRICK'S
$–$$$
CITRUSDAL CENTRAL SPORTS GROUNDS
TEL 022/921-3062
The fish on the menu of this Irish-theme pub and restaurant is often caught by the owner himself. Try the kingklip done in a tasty cheese and prawn sauce. Also on the menu are pizzas, schnitzels, burgers, and rich desserts.
🍴 60 🅿 🕒 Closed L & D Sun.–Mon.

DARLING
───────────────

🏨🍴 TRINITY GUEST LODGE
$$$ ★★★★
19 LONG ST.
TEL 022/492-3430
www.trinitylodge.co.za
Tasteful cream-and-green Victorian lodge graced by lavender bushes, offering en suite bedrooms with goose-down duvets and hand-embroidered linen. The restaurant serves trout with potato cake and lamb shanks, and wines of the Darling region.
🛈 8 🍴 30 🅿 🕒 Closed July 🏊

🍴 BISTRO SEVEN
$–$$
7 MAIN RD.
TEL 022/492-3626
Dine out in the garden of this cottage restaurant. A small bar offers pre- or post-meal drinks, while on the menu meat dishes including steaks and hearty casseroles predominate.

───────────────

🛏 36 🅿 🕐 Closed L Mon.–Fri., D Tues.

🍴 EVITA SE PERRON
$
DARLING RAILWAY STATION
TEL 022/492-2831
www.evita.co.za
This restaurant and performance venue was created by South African icon Pieter-Dirk Uys (in his drag persona of Evita Bezuidenhout). Décor and cuisine are thoroughly South African. In fixed-priced buffet, enjoy hearty roast lamb, salad, and vegetables, with cold meats in summer. Lunch most days, but dinner offered only on performance weekends (see p. 87).
🛏 100 🅿 🕐 Closed L Mon.

LANGEBAAN

🏨 FARMHOUSE HOTEL & 🍴 RESTAURANT
$$–$$$
5 EGRET ST.
TEL 022/772-2062
www.thefarmhouselangebaan.co.za
Beautifully located on a rise overlooking the Langebaan Lagoon, this hotel offers a variety of rooms, from budget to luxury. Specialties at their highly rated restaurant include sole, calamari, oxtail in casserole, and rich desserts; dining in summer on the terrace, in winter by the fire inside.
ⓘ 15 🛏 100 🅿 🌊 🎾

🏨 GECKO BEACH HOUSE
$$–$$$ ★ ★ ★ ★
17 BEACH RD.
TEL 022/772-1586
www.geckobeachhouse.com
Private tranquil guesthouse situated right on the beach. The rooms are all en suite and most have a lagoon view. An enormous lounge with fireplace is available to guests.
ⓘ 5 🅿

🍴 DIE STRANDLOPER
$$
ON BEACH OFF ROAD TO CLUB MYKONOS
TEL 022/772-2490
www.strandloper.com
Very popular with locals and visitors, Strandloper is an informal place to gorge yourself on seafood cooked on the beach over open fires. If it all gets too much, stroll down the beach between courses. Advance reservations are recommended. Fixed-price set menu. No credit cards accepted.
🕐 Closed winter

🍴 BOESMANLAND PLAASKOMBUIS
$
AT CLUB MYKONOS
TEL 022/772-1564
www.boesmanlandfarmkitchen.com
The name is Afrikaans for "Bushmanland Farm Kitchen" and the menu lives up to the name. Expect seafood and local dishes such as delicious bread cooked over the fire, and traditional African pap with onion and tomato sauce. Fixed-price buffet.
🛏 450 🕐 L & D Tues.–Sun. 🅿

PATERNOSTER

🏨 BLUE DOLPHIN
$$ ★ ★ ★ ★
2 WARRELKLIP ST.
TEL 022/752-2001
www.bluedolphin.co.za
Comfortable B&B overlooking the dunes and beach. All rooms are en suite with heated towel rails and have sea views. Guests can laze away the afternoons on the daybed out on the wooden deck.
ⓘ 4 🅿

🍴 NOISY OYSTER
$
ST. AUGUSTINE RD.
TEL 022/752-2196
The West Coast is famous for its seafood, and this is an excellent place to enjoy it. Dine indoors or in the cool garden during summer. Try the superb, freshly caught fish cooked Greek style, with tomato, garlic, and onions.
🛏 60 🅿 🕐 Closed L Mon.–Tues., D Sun.–Tues.; closed June–July

🍴 VOORSTRANDT RESTAURANT
$$
ON THE BEACH, STRANDLOPER ST.
TEL 022/752-2038
Situated right on the beach, this small restaurant offers a bar and fine sea views. As at most such venues in the region, seafood—particularly whatever fish has come in with the boats that day—is the chief item on the menu.
🛏 150 🅿

RIEBEEK-KASTEEL

🏨 ROYAL HOTEL
🍴 $$–$$$
33 MAIN ST.
TEL 022/448-1378
www.royalinriebeek.com
Located in a graceful 19th-century building, the Royal offers rooms decorated in beige, black, and white, with en suite bathrooms, a luxuriant garden, a bar, and a dining room for evening meals.
ⓘ 10 🛏 40 🅚 🌊

🏨 OLD OAK MANOR 🍴 GUEST HOUSE
$$
7 CHURCH ST.
TEL 022/448-1170
A Cape Dutch-style homestead turned into a guesthouse, surrounded by old oak trees, with décor using natural wood and antiques. The restaurant here, Café Felix, serves South African cuisine, using fresh, seasonal ingredients. Sit indoors or in the shady garden.
ⓘ 5 🛏 60 🅿 🕐 Restaurant closed L & D Mon. & Thurs. 🌊

🍴 THE BARN
$–$$
34 CHURCH ST.
TEL 022/448-1377
Lovely setting, with oak tree shaded patio in summer, roaring fire in winter, and fine views. The menu offers Mediterranean fare such as meze, pastas, duck with orange, lightly grilled fish, and risotto with porcini mushrooms and butternut squash.
🛏 50 🅿 🕐 Closed L Mon.–Tues., D Sun.–Tues.

WESTERN CAPE

CALITZDORP

 ROSE OF THE KAROO
$–$$
VOORTREKKER RD.
TEL 044/213-3133
www.roseofthekaroo.co.za
The B&B accommodation here
is simple and good value for the
money, and the attached deli,
store, and restaurant provide
hearty country fare. Have the
chicken pie with local salad and
vegetables as main course, and
try a cheese blintz for dessert.
[i]5 [seats]25 [P] [S] [+] Restaurant closed Sun. [pool]

FRANSCHHOEK

SOMETHING SPECIAL

 LE QUARTIER FRANÇAIS
$$$$$ ★ ★ ★ ★ ★
16 HUGUENOT RD.
TEL 021/876-2151
www.lequartier.co.za
A luxurious boutique hotel in
the heart of Franschhoek. The
exquisitely furnished rooms
and suites surround courtyard
gardens planted with shade
trees and lilacs. Expect special
touches, like underfloor heating
in the bathrooms and a hot-
water bottle popped into your
bed in a winter. (For the adjoining **Tasting Room** restaurant,
see at right.)
[i]21 [P] [S] [pool] [TV]

LE FRANSCHHOEK
HOTEL & SPA
$$$$–$$$$$ ★ ★ ★ ★ ★
16 MINOR RD.
TEL 021/876-8900
www.lefranschhoek.co.za
This thatched, Cape Dutch-style
establishment, decorated in
cool whites and restrained colors, offers luxury accommodations, a spa, and fabulous views
of the surrounding mountains.
For dining, guests can choose
from two restaurants and a deli.
[i]79 [seats]200 [P] [S] [pool] [TV]

LAVANDE DE
FRANSCHHOEK
$$–$$$ ★ ★ ★ ★
VERDUN RD.
TEL 021/876-2671

www.ldf.co.za
Stay in air-conditioned luxury,
surrounded by acres of lavender
fields. This upscale B&B offers
rooms decorated in tasteful
pastel shades and a pool terrace
where guests can relax and
enjoy a drink.
[i]4 [P] [S] [pool]

SUNNY LANE
$ ★ ★ ★
30 AKADEMIE ST.
TEL 021/876-4071
http://sunnylane.za.net
Budget accommodations are
hard to come by in Franschhoek, but this venue provides
simply furnished units, supplied
with linen, underfloor heating,
and kitchen facilities. Guests
have the use of mountain
bikes to explore the vicinity.
Credit card deposit; balance
cash only.
[i]2 [P] [pool]

TASTING ROOM
$$$$–$$$$$
16 HUGUENOT RD.
TEL 021/876-2151
www.lequartier.co.za
Consistently rated among the
50 best restaurants in the world,
the Tasting Room offers avant-
garde taste combinations such as
seared tuna with pomegranate
vinaigrette, or foie gras and ham
terrine with yogurt panna cotta.
Choose a four-, six-, or eight-
course menu (the last including
specially selected wines).
[seats]48 [P] [S]

BREAD & WINE
$$–$$$
MÔRESON WINE FARM, LA
MOTTE, HAPPY VALLEY RD.
TEL 021/876-3692
www.moreson.co.za
Lunch on gourmet country fare
at this wonderful venue with a
shady courtyard, surrounded
by lemon trees and vineyards.
Try venison dusted with porcini
mushrooms, or tuna *boerewors*
with chili jelly. Here you can also
buy wine, cheese, salami, and bacon, all produced on the estate.
[seats]70 [P] [closed] Closed D

HAUTE CABRIÈRE
$$–$$$
CABRIÈRE ESTATE, PASS RD.
TEL 021/876-3688

www.hautecabriere.com
Cool in summer, warmed by
heaters in winter, this cave-like
restaurant is built into the
mountainside on the Cabrière
wine estate (whose products
can be tasted at the adjoining
cellar). Excellent contemporary
and fusion food is served here.
[seats]120 [closed] Closed D winter
Sun.–Thurs. [P]

REUBEN'S
$$
OUDE STALLEN CENTER,
19 HUGUENOT ST.
TEL 021/876-3772
Restaurant and bar with views
into the kitchen and exposed
roofing beams. The same
menu serves for both lunch
and dinner, and changes daily.
Food ranges from game such
as springbok or guinea fowl to
Asian-influenced seafood and
noodle dishes.
[seats]150 [P]

TOPSI & CO
$$
7 RESERVOIR ST. W.
TEL 021/876-2952
Amid the expensive gourmet
restaurants of Franschhoek,
Topsi's offers excellent South
African fare at reasonable

prices. You can dine on seasonal food such as a *bredie,* mussel *bobotie,* or pickled fish in comfortable surroundings.
🍴 45 🕐 Closed L & D Tues. 🅿

SOMETHING SPECIAL

🍴 BOSCHENDAL WINE ESTATE
$–$$$
PNIEL RD. (R310), GROOT DRAKENSTEIN
TEL 021/870-4272
www.boschendal.com
The attraction of Boschendal is its tremendous scenic beauty. The estate provides several lunch venues: an elegant fixed-price luncheon in their **restaurant**; a light lunch on the terrace at **Le Café**; or at **Le Pique Nique,** a basket with pâtés, cold meats, and cheese to be enjoyed on the lawns.
🍴 120/180 🅿 🕐 No picnic June–Aug.

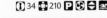

GEORGE

🏨🍴 THE MANOR HOUSE AT FANCOURT
$$$$$ ★ ★ ★ ★ ★
OFF R404, JUST W OF GEORGE
TEL 044/804-0000
www.fancourt.co.za
Whether or not you are a golfer, you can reside in luxury at this hotel on the lush Fancourt golf estate. The hotel, in a 19th-century house that is a national monument, offers six restaurants, a health spa with sauna, steam rooms, and gym.
🛏 34 🍴 210 🅿 🚹 🛗 🏊

🏨🍴 OAKHURST MANOR HOUSE HOTEL
$$–$$$ ★ ★ ★
MEADE & CATHEDRAL STS.
TEL 044/874-7130
www.oakhursthotel.co.za
The thatched country-style hotel in the center of George has comfortable, brightly decorated rooms, all en suite. The restaurant serves breakfast and dinner.
🛏 25 🍴 50 🅿 🏊

🍴 OLD TOWNHOUSE RESTAURANT
$$
CORNER MARKET & YORK STS.
TEL 044/874-3663
In an 1848 meeting hall, this venue concentrates on wholesome food and fresh ingredients. A favorite dish is pork chops done spicy Moroccan style, with a blue cheese filling. Desserts include delicious homemade ice cream.
🍴 60 🅿 🕐 Closed L Sat.–Sun., D Sun.

🍴 MARGOT'S BISTRO
$–$$
63 ALBERT ST.
TEL 044/874-2950
A colorfully decorated house is the venue for this bistro restaurant. By day the menu offers light pasta dishes and salads; by night you can dine on Mexican bean stew or roasted neck of lamb in red wine sauce, with a chocolate cheese blintz for dessert.
🍴 70 🅿 🕐 Closed L Sun.–Mon., D Sun.–Tues.; 2 weeks July

GREYTON

🏨🍴 GREYTON LODGE
$$–$$$
52 MAIN ST.
TEL 028/254-9800
www.greytonlodge.co.za
A tranquil country retreat, offering tasteful, colorfully decorated en suite rooms. From the garden, with its shady trees, you have excellent views of the nearby mountains. The restaurant serves meals prepared with fresh local ingredients.
🛏 15 🍴 80 🅿 🏊

SOMETHING SPECIAL

🍴 254
$$
8 DOMINES BOTHA ST.
TEL 028/254-9373
Spread through the spacious rooms of an old house with period furniture, 254 provides the best food in the area. All dishes, such as light curries, fish, and steaks are prepared from the freshest ingredients. No liquor license, so bring your own wine. Reservations are required; no

credit cards accepted.
🍴 50 🕐 Closed Sun.–Tues. 🅿

🍴 OAK & VIGNE
$–$$
DOMINES BOTHA ST.
TEL 028/254-9037
Popular in summer for its shady courtyard and in winter for its cozy fire, this is the perfect breakfast, brunch, or lunch venue. Continental or full English breakfast is offered, and for lunch a range of soups, light quiches, salads, and panini.
🍴 140

HERMANUS

🏨🍴 THE MARINE HERMANUS HOTEL
$$$–$$$$$ ★ ★ ★ ★ ★
MARINE DR.
TEL 028/313-1000
www.marine-hermanus.co.za
This clifftop luxury hotel has the best location in Hermanus. You can see whales sporting in the ocean from the windows of the lounge and dining areas and from the garden. Accommodations range from standard double rooms to luxury suites. Three restaurants here serve seafood or modern South African cuisine such as flambéed springbok fillet.
🛏 42 🍴 100 🅿 🚹 🏊 🎾

🏨 AUBERGE BURGUNDY
$$$ ★ ★ ★ ★
16 HARBOUR RD.
TEL 028/313-1201
www.auberge.co.za
Admire the view from your bedroom balcony at this Provençal-style guesthouse, near the town center, cliff walks, and old harbor. The rooms are beautifully furnished in quiet colors. Sun worshipers will enjoy the courtyard swimming pool.
🛏 18 🅿 🏊

🏨 MISTY WAVES HOTEL
$$–$$$ ★ ★ ★ ★
40 FERNKLOOF DR.
TEL 028/313-8460
www.hermanusmistybeach.co.za
The hotel is close to the markets and shops of the Village Center and commands

a magnificent view of the sea and frolicking whales in season. Rooms all have a balcony, and some a four-poster bed. Breakfast and à la carte dinner on the premises.

📶 24 🅿 🏊

🏨 BROWN JUG
$–$$ ★ ★ ★
18 MUSSON ST.
TEL 028/312-2220
www.brownjug.co.za
It would be hard to find better value for money than at this B&B with garden and swimming pool, just three blocks away from the town center and whale viewing. All units have en suite bathroom and two rooms are self-catering.

📶 3 🅿 🏊

🍴 HARBOUR ROCK
$$–$$$
FOLLOW WESTCLIFF RD. TO NEW HARBOR
TEL 028/312-2920
www.harbourrock.co.za
From this bar and restaurant high above the new harbor, diners can watch whales in season spouting or leaping from the sea. The menu covers most forms of seafood—shellfish, baked or grilled fish, and sushi—as well as meat dishes.

🪑 130 🅿

SOMETHING SPECIAL

🍴 BIENTANG'S CAVE
$$
BELOW MARINE DR., BET. OLD HARBOR AND MARINE HOTEL
TEL 028/312-3454
www.bientangscave.com
The seafood Bientang's offers—a range of fish and shellfish—is good and tasty. But what is truly exceptional about this restaurant is its magnificent setting, half in a cave, on the rocks, at the ocean's edge. Reservations recommended in season.

🪑 200 🅿 🕐 Closed D Sun.–Thurs.

SOMETHING SPECIAL

🍴 HEAVEN
$$
NEWTON JOHNSON WINERY, ON R360, HEMEL-EN-AARDE VALLEY
TEL 072/905-3947
www.newtonjohnson.com
Just inland from Hermanus, this venue lives up to its name. Perched on a hilltop amid vineyards, Heaven offers stunning views of farmland, mountains, and sea. The food is superb, featuring specialities such as chicken breasts stuffed with cheese and black cherries and poached pear salad. Reservations are required.

🪑 50 🅿 🕐 Closed L Mon.

🍴 FUSION CAFÉ
$–$$
5 VILLAGE S.
TEL 028/312-4277
The patio commands a magnificent view of the bay. The food lives up to the venue's name, including such items as pizza with brie, mozzarella, blue cheese and fig, Cajun burgers, fillet of beef with wild mushroom risotto, and chicken tagliatelle pasta.

🪑 160 🅿 🕐 Closed D Mon.

KNYSNA

SOMETHING SPECIAL

🏨 PEZULA RESORT HOTEL 🍴
$$$–$$$$
LAGOONVIEW DR., EASTERN HEAD
TEL 044/302-3333
www.pezularesorthotel.com
Pezula lies on the easternmost of the two Knysna Heads, with stunning views over the Indian Ocean and Knysna Lagoon. The spacious luxury suites are decorated in contemporary African style with earthy, warm colors. Sports and leisure activities are available, as well as several restaurants, including **Zachary's** (see below).

📶 78 🅿 🎱 🏊 🍷

🏨 THE RUSSEL HOTEL
$$–$$$ ★ ★ ★
UNITY, GRAHAM & LONG STS.
TEL 044/382-1052
www.russelhotel.co.za
Centrally located within walking distance of the main attractions, this hotel offers rooms decorated in white and russet tones, with bathrooms finished in marble. Breakfast is available on request.

📶 18 🅿 🔄 🛎

🏨 SLEEPERWOOD LODGE
$–$$
15 HILL ST.
TEL 044/382-7855
www.sleeperwoodlodge.co.za
Located on a hilltop, the lodge has wonderful views over Knysna and its lagoon with B&B rooms and two self-catering units. Credit card deposit; balance cash only. The lodge requires a small deposit on arrival against loss of keys and breakage.

📶 8 (2 apartments, 4 rooms) 🅿 🏊

🍴 ZACHARY'S
$$$–$$$$
PEZULA RESORT HOTEL, LAGOONVIEW DR., EASTERN HEAD
TEL 044/302-3333
www.zacharys.co.za
This hilltop venue has breathtaking views of the Knysna Lagoon. The menu offers contemporary cuisine, such as prawns flavored with chili, anise, and tomato, pork belly with lentils, or duck breast with shitake mushrooms.

🪑 80 🅿 🕐 Closed L Sun. 🎱

🍴 DANIELA'S
$$
LEISURE ISLE LODGE, 87 BAYSWATER DR.
TEL 044/384-0462
www.leisureislelodge.co.za
Lovely views across the Knysna Lagoon to the surrounding hills distinguish this waterside venue. The decor is crisp and elegant, the daily menu brief but excellent, offering fine fish, meat, and vegetarian choices.

🪑 30 🅿 🕐 Closed Sun.

🍴 ILE DE PAIN
$–$$
10 THE BOATSHED, THESEN HARBOR TOWN
TEL 044/302-5707
Eat surrounded by many

different kinds of bread in this cozy bakery-café. It's the perfect place for breakfast, brunch, or lunch.
🛏 85 🅿 🕐 Closed Mon. & Aug.

🍴 OYSTERCATCHER
$–$$
SMALL CRAFT HARBOR, KNYSNA QUAYS
TEL 044/382-9995
Built on wooden piles in the shallows of the lagoon, this is a good place to feast on Knysna's famous cultivated oysters. Besides shellfish, the menu also offers salads, seafood, and chicken dishes.
🛏 64 🅿 🕐 Closed in bad winter weather

MONTAGU

🏨 MIMOSA LODGE
🍴 **$$–$$$** ★★★★
CHURCH ST.
TEL 023/614-2351
www.mimosa.co.za
Charming Edwardian guesthouse with double rooms or suites opening onto the lovely garden. The restaurant has a high reputation for such dishes as combo of Karoo lamb and beef, clear duck soup, and porcini mushroom ravioli.
🛏 16 🛏 36 🅿 🏊

🍴 ROUTE 62 KLOOF FARMSTALL & RESTAURANT
$
1 LONG ST.
TEL 023/614-2209
The cottage restaurant, with garden attached to its farmstall makes an ideal light meal stop. Try their *uitsmijter* (fried egg on ham and toast), filled pancakes, or fresh cakes.
🛏 110 🅿

MOSSEL BAY

🏨 POINT HOTEL
🍴 **$$–$$$** ★★★★
POINT RD.
TEL 044/691-3512
www.pointhotel.co.za
Located on a rocky promontory jutting out to the sea, this hotel offers en suite rooms with private sea-facing balconies. The accommodations are modern

in style, with touches of bright color.
🛏 52 🛏 90 🅿 🍽 🏊

🍴 CAFÉ GANNET
$$–$$$
BARTHOLOMEW DIAZ MUSEUM COMPLEX, MARKET ST.
TEL 044/691-1885
www.oldposttree.co.za
The restaurant forms part of the Diaz museum complex, housed in one of the town's oldest buildings. The menu focuses on seafood—oysters, fresh fish, calamari, and unusual fare such as shark steaks.
🛏 150 🅿

🍴 BAHIA DOS VA UEIROS
$$
DIAZ STRAND HOTEL, BEACH BLVD.
TEL 044/692-8400
www.diazbeach.co.za
This hotel restaurant commands fine views of the ocean and the Outeniqua Mountains. The decor is subdued and elegant; the food is international in style, with dishes such as five-spice marinated lobster, or ostrich done with garlic and ginger chutney.
🛏 70 🅿 🍽 🚹

OUDTSHOORN

🏨 MOOIPLAAS GUEST HOUSE
$$–$$$
MOOIPLAAS FARM, OFF R328, 6 MILES (10 KM) S OF OUDTSHOORN
TEL 044/279-4019
www.mooiplaasguesthouse.co.za
This guesthouse in the heart of ostrich country offers clean, tastefully furnished rooms, all with en suite bathroom, and some with air-conditioning. The farm runs tours of its own ostrich-farming operation. Credit card deposit; balance cash only.
🛏 8 🅿 🚹 🏊

🏨 QUEENS HOTEL
$$–$$$ ★★★★
5 BARON VAN RHEEDE ST.
TEL 044/272-2101
www.queenshotel.co.za
This is a comfortable old-

fashioned hotel in a delightful Victorian building, decorated with oriental rugs and period furniture. The cool white rooms are all air-conditioned. (For the hotel's **The Colony** restaurant, see below.)
🛏 40 🅿 🚹

🏨 THE CELTIC BUSHMAN
$
29 VAN DER RIET ST.
TEL 044/272-7937
www.celticbushman.com
Reasonably priced, friendly and welcoming B&B in a central location. The rooms are done in ethnic Bushman style. Guests have the use of a secluded garden and pool. Credit card deposit; balance cash only.
🛏 5 🅿 🏊

🍴 KALINKA
$$–$$$
93 BARON VAN REEDE ST.
TEL 044/279-2596
www.kalinka.co.za
The menu at Kalinka offers a range of contemporary dishes with a South African twist. Try crocodile done as sashimi or carpaccio, or a trio of springbok, kudu, and ostrich. Unlike many South African restaurants, this one does imaginative, delicious desserts.
🛏 80 🕐 Closed 7 weeks June–July 🅿

🍴 THE COLONY
$$
QUEENS HOTEL, 5 BARON VAN RHEEDE ST.
TEL 044 272 2101
www. queenshotel.co.za
The Colony evokes an atmosphere of Old World elegance, with period furniture and crisp white napkins. The menu offers good honest food, such as prawn appetizers and lamb main entrées, well cooked and well presented.
🛏 64 🕐 Closed 7 weeks July–Aug. 🅿 🚹

🍴 CANGO CAVES RESTAURANT
$–$$
CANGO CAVES CENTER, SCHOEMANS HOEK
TEL 044/272-7313
The restaurant serving breakfast and lunch

commands superb views over the Cango Valley. This being ostrich country, the menu focuses on ostrich meat prepared in various ways—steaks, burgers, and stews. Other meat, such as lamb, is also available.
150 P

PAARL

GRANDE ROCHE
$$$$$ ★★★★★
PLANTASIE ST.
TEL 021/863-5100
www.granderoche.co.za
At the heart of Grande Roche is a beautifully restored 18th-century Cape Dutch homestead. The luxury rooms and suites, some with private terrace, are dotted about the estate. The **Bosmans** restaurant serves gourmet food based on local ostrich, Karoo lamb, and springbok.
34 80 P

PONTAC MANOR
$$-$$$ ★★★★
16 ZION ST.
TEL 021/872-0445
www.pontac.com
Luxury hotel housed in a historic building, surrounded by mature oaks and fine gardens. Guests have a choice of more traditional or colorfully decorated African-themed accommodations. The restaurant offers classic cuisine with a South African twist. Dining is either indoors or out on the whitewashed patio with superb views of Paarl Rock.
22 45 P Closed D Sun.

LABORIE
 $$
LABORIE WINE ESTATE,
TAILLEFERT ST.
TEL 021/807-3095
www.laborie.co.za
The spot to lunch here in summer is the oak-shaded terrace with superb views over the vineyards. The à la carte menu includes fish, chicken, pasta, and traditional South African food, with daily specials.
120 P Closed 3 weeks July

MARC'S MEDITER-RANEAN CUISINE & GARDEN
$-$$
129 MAIN RD., PAARL
TEL 021/863-3980
An excellent wine list and use of only the freshest local ingredients distinguish Marc's restaurant. The menu constantly changes, but certain items such as fine steaks, paella, and meze platters remain relatively constant.
60 P Closed D Sun.; 3 weeks July

PLETTENBERG BAY

SOMETHING SPECIAL

KURLAND HOTEL
$$$$$ ★★★★★
THE CRAGS, ON N2, 12 MILES (19 KM) E. OF PLETTENBERG BAY
TEL 044/534-8082
www.kurland.co.za
This small luxury hotel in a homestead dating to 1885, surrounded by green meadows and mature oaks, is furnished with antiques and sumptuous imported fabrics. On the surrounding estate are a polo field and fully equipped spa. Gourmet cuisine is served in the hotel dining room.
12 30 P

PLETTENBERG HOTEL
$$$$-$$$$$ ★★★★★
40 CHURCH ST., LOOK OUT ROCKS
TEL 044/533-2030
www.plettenberg.com
Located on a headland with breathtaking views of sea, mountains, and beaches, this hotel offers luxury accommodations. The air-conditioned rooms and suites, are decorated in white and restrained pastel colors. Dining choices include the **Sand Restaurant** (see below).
37 80 P

HALCYON HOUSE
$$-$$$ ★★★★
30 RATTRAY HEAD AVE.
TEL 044/533-2986
www.halcyonhouse.co.za
Guesthouse offering pleasant, elegant rooms on a bed-and-continental-breakfast basis. The

en suite rooms provide either fine sea views or access onto a pretty courtyard.
4 P

THANDA VISTA
$-$$ ★★★★
8 SUSAN ST.
TEL 044/533-1796
www.thandavista.co.za
This B&B, close to the Keurboom Lagoon, consists of five luxurious en suite bedrooms, decorated in warm tones. Guests have access to the lounge, library, WiFi Internet connection, and whale viewing from the rooftop terrace.
5 P

SAND AT THE PLETTENBERG
$$$
PLETTENBERG HOTEL,
40 CHURCH ST.,
LOOK OUT ROCKS
TEL 044/533-2030
www.plettenberg.com
The marine-theme hotel restaurant affords stunning views of the bay. On the menu are duck liver tortellini, salmon ceviche with apricot, duck glazed with maple syrup, and springbok fillet with quince.
80 P

🍴 FRANCO'S KITCHEN
$$
NOEL CENTER, MAIN ST.
TEL 044/533-3693
This restaurant concentrates on Mediterranean and Italian food prepared simply, using local, seasonal materials. Sample the calamari on crunchy spinach with roasted tomato, lightly grilled fish, gourmet pizza, or lamb teriyaki.
🔲 80 🕐 Closed L Mon.–Sat., D Sun.–Mon. 🅿

🍴 FU.SHI/BOMA TERRACE/CHEF'S BAR
$–$$
SHOP 9, THE UPPER DECK, 3 STRAND ST.
TEL 044/533-6497
www.fushi.co.za
The theme of this elegant venue is international and Asian fusion cuisine. At BoMa Terrace you can dine on the airy terrace, at the Chef's Bar, enjoy a drink or late night snack, at the flagship restaurant, Fu.Shi, savor dishes such as prawns sautéed with wasabi and cashew nuts, or teriyaki beef with sweet potato.
🔲 55 🅿

🍴 RISTORANTE ENRICO
$–$$
MAIN BEACH, KEURBOOMSTRAND
TEL 044/535-9818
www.enricorestaurant.co.za
You can't get much closer to the sea than in this large, cheerful Italian and seafood restaurant perched right above the beach. Unusual antipasti include kudu with avocado; for main dishes there are the traditional pizzas, veal Marsala, and osso bucco.
🔲 400 🅿

PRINCE ALBERT

🏨 SAXE-COBURG LODGE
$–$$
60 CHURCH ST.
TEL 023/541-1267
www.saxecoburg.co.za
Relax at the poolside or enjoy mountain views from the garden of this lodge in an 1865 Victorian home. Two rooms have four-poster beds, and all are en suite. Guests can use the lounge and the library.
🛗 7 🅿 ❄ 🏊

🍴 KOGGELMANDER
$$
61 CHURCH ST.
TEL 023 541 1900
www.koggelmander.co.za
Shady outdoor eating under the trees, or indoors in this converted Karoo house. On the menu are both South African items, such as ostrich fillet or lamb burgers, and international dishes such as couscous cakes or pasta putanesca.
🔲 35 🅿 🕐 Closed L Mon.

🍴 KAROO KOMBUIS
$–$$
18 DEURDRIFT ST.
TEL 023/541-1110
The name means "Karoo kitchen." This venue has a good reputation for traditional cape cooking. All the standards feature on the menu: chicken pie, *bredies*, and *bobotie*. Beautifully cooked and flavored lamb shanks are a speciality. No liquor license, so bring your own wine.
🕐 Closed D Sun. 🔲 18 🅿

ROBERTSON VALLEY

🏨🍴 FRAAI UITZICHT 1798
$$–$$$
KLAAS VOODS EAST, OFF R62, BET. ROBERTSON & MONTAGU
TEL 023/626-6156
www.fraaiuitzicht.com
Beautifully decorated guest cottages and suites shaded by old oaks are set amid the vineyards on this estate. The restaurant offers fine dining, including Moroccan chicken tagine, Karoo lamb in red wine, and seared salmon with honey, ginger, and soy.
🛗 8 🔲 35 🅿 🕐 Closed June–Aug. 🏊

🍴 CAFÉ MAUDE
$–$$
BON COURAGE WINE ESTATE, R317, JUST E OF ROBERTSON
TEL 023/626-6806
www.boncourage.co.za
A striking feature of this indoor and garden restaurant is the enormous old pepper tree that shades the terrace. The deli-style lunches encompass salads and gourmet sandwiches filled with ingredients such as bacon, sunflower seeds, and avocado.
🔲 160 🅿 🕐 Closed Sun.

SEDGEFIELD

SOMETHING SPECIAL

🏨 TENIQUA TREETOPS
$$–$$$ ★ ★ ★
TAKE KARATARA/RUIGETVLEI TURNOFF FROM N2 BET. SEDGEFIELD & KNYSNA, CONTINUE 9 MILES (15 KM)
TEL 044/356-2868
www.teniquatreetops.co.za
Tented, self-catering units perched in the treetops amid indigenous forest provide a unique eco-experience. Each unit has its own cooking facility and bathroom, and a deck offering magnificent views. (Teniqua's excellent website describes exactly how to get there, and gives a wealth of information about the resort.)
🛗 8 🅿 🏊

🍴 TRATTORIA DA VINCI
$$
WOODPECKER MALL, MAIN RD.
TEL 044/343-1867
A local favorite, this restaurant has the family members do all the cooking. Favorites include pizza, lamb shank, pork schnitzel with Marsala and mushroom sauce, paella, and excellent desserts.
🔲 65 🅿 🕐 Closed D Sun.

SOMERSET WEST

🏨 SOMERTON MANOR GUEST HOUSE
$$–$$$
13 SOMERSET ST., BRIDGEWATER
TEL 021/851-4682
www.somerton.co.za
This guesthouse is located in a thatched, gabled building boasting period furniture and original artworks. Relax in the *lapa* (open eating area) with its wine cellar, or in the garden. A Jacuzzi, sauna, and billiard room are also available.
🛗 12 🅿 ❄ 🏊 🏋

 Elevator   Air-conditioning   Indoor Pool   Outdoor Pool  Health Club

🍴 96 WINERY ROAD
$$–$$$
ZANDBERG FARM, WINERY RD.
(OFF R44)
TEL 021/842-2020
www.zandberg.co.za
Using only fresh and, where
possible local, organic ingredients, this restaurant offers
dishes such as tagliatelle with
mushrooms, butternut squash,
goat cheese and toasted nuts,
or duck, and cherry pie.
⊞ 100 🅿 🕘 Closed D Sun.

🍴 LADY PHILLIPS
$$–$$$
VERGELEGEN WINE ESTATE,
LOURENSFORD RD.
TEL 021/847-1346
www.vergelegen.co.za
Lunch on the terrace with a
view over the gardens of this
historic wine estate, or sit indoors by the fire. On the menu
is lamb with rosemary sauce
and potatoes au gratin, pasta
with salmon or mustard, cream,
and white wine sauce.
⊞ 100 🅿 🕘 Closed D

STELLENBOSCH

🏨 LANZERAC HOTEL &
🍴 SPA
$$$$–$$$$$ ★★★★★
LANZERAC RD.
TEL 021/887-1132
www.lanzerac.co.za
A 300-year-old wine estate is
home to this luxury hotel and
health spa just outside Stellenbosch. Rooms are individually
decorated in elegant style. Visitors and guests have the choice
of several indoor and outdoor
venues for lunch and dinner.
🛏 48 ⊞ 200 🅿 🕘 ⛱ 🍷

🏨 D'OUDE WERF
🍴 $$$–$$$$ ★★★★
30 CHURCH ST.
TEL 021/887-4608
www.ouwewerf.com
Established in 1802, this
historic hotel in the middle of
town offers luxurious suites
with bathroom, furnished
with antiques. The restaurant,
1802, serves traditional South
African cuisine, such as oxtail
and *bobotie.*
🛏 32 ⊞ 130 🅿 🕘 ⛱

🏨 DE OUDE RYNEVELD
$$ ★★★
71 RYNEVELD ST.
TEL 021/887-7221
www.deouderyneveld.com
The 19th- century slave
quarters have been converted
into this smart B&B, within
walking distance of shops and
restaurants. Rooms, all en suite,
are decorated in white and
pastel shades with touches
of bright color.
🛏 8 🅿 🕘 Some rooms

🍴 LE POMMIER
$$
ZORGVLIET WINE ESTATE,
BANGHOEK VALLEY,
HELSHOOGTE PASS
TEL 021/885-1269
www.lepommier.co.za
The veranda offers vistas over
the vineyards in summer; rooms
with their own fireplace provide
warmth in winter. On the menu
are standards such as *bobotie*
and malva pudding, as well as
international dishes.
⊞ 100 🅿 🕘 Closed D Mon.

🍴 VOLKSKOMBUIS
$$
AAN-DE-WAGEN RD.
TEL 021/887-2121
www.volkskombuis.co.za
This is the place in Stellenbosch
to enjoy traditional fare such
as Karoo lamb, *waterblom-
metjie, bredie, bobotie,* oxtail
stew, or kudu fillet. A garden
restaurant, **De Oewer,** offers
alfresco lunches by the side of
the Eerste River.
⊞ 85 🅿

🍴 DELHEIM GARDEN
RESTAURANT
$–$$
DELHEIM WINE FARM, KNOR-
HOEK RD. (OFF R44)
TEL 021/888-4607
www.delheim.com
Enjoy breakfast, lunch, or
tea surrounded by this wine
estate's gardens. The menu
includes light meals such as
panini with ham, or salmon and
salad, or substantial bratwurst
with homemade mustard, Cape
Malay chicken curry, or lamb
shank with wine and rosemary
sauce.
⊞ 100 🅿

🍴 L'OLIVE
$–$$
OUDE HOEK CENTER,
ANDRINGA ST.
TEL 021/887-8985
Amid tourist shops and galleries, L'Olive offers dining
indoors or on the sidewalk. The
menu uses seasonal ingredients
and changes monthly. Expect
fresh fish, pastas, and meat
dishes prepared with pesto,
garlic, and vegetables.
⊞ 64 🅿 🕘 Closed D Mon.

SWELLENDAM

🏨 HERBERG ROOSJE
🍴 VAN DE KAAP
$$–$$$ ★★★
5 DROSTDY ST.
TEL 028/514-3001
www.roosjevandekaap.com
This Georgian home, with a
garden, offers elegant rooms
and fine dining. The cuisine
includes Cape Malay favorites,
pizzas, beef, and chicken with
French reduction sauces.
🛏 9 ⊞ 46 🅿 🕘 Restaurant
closed mid-Dec.–mid-Jan. ⛱

TULBAGH

🏨 THE OLD TULBAGH
HOTEL
🍴 $$–$$$$ ★★★★
22 VAN DER STEL ST.
TEL 023/230-0071
www.tulbaghhotel.co.za
A historic building houses this
traditional family-run hotel.
Rooms are comfortable, and
guests can enjoy dinner in the
British-style pub and dining
room with open fireplace.
🛏 5 ⊞ 25 🅿 🕘

🍴 READERS RESTAURANT
$$
12 CHURCH ST.
TEL 023/230-0087
A thatched Cape Dutch house,
the oldest (1754) in Tulbagh,
plays host here. The seasonal
menu offers such dishes as pork
chops with grapes and lamb
with ginger.
⊞ 60 🅿 🕘 Closed L & D
Tues.; 3 weeks late July

WELLINGTON

🏨 DIEMERSFONTEIN
🍴 $$–$$$

🏨 Hotel 🍴 Restaurant 🛏 No. of guest rooms ⊞ No. of Seats 🅿 Parking 🕘 Closed

DIEMERSFONTEIN WINE ESTATE, JAN VAN RIEBEECK DR., R301 BET. PAARL & WELLINGTON
TEL 021/864-5060
www.diemersfontein.co.za
This wine estate with beautiful, old trees and garden provides fine accommodations and dining. At the restaurant, **Seasons,** try their pasta of the day or lamb knuckles, washed down with the estate's renowned pinotage.
 21 105 P Some rooms

WILDERNESS

PALMS WILDERNESS GUEST HOUSE
$$$ ★ ★ ★ ★
1 OWEN GRAND ST.
TEL 044/877-1420
www.palms-wilderness.com
Palms is located close to the beauties of the Wilderness area. All rooms have a private entrance, opening onto the luxuriant tropical garden and swimming pool. On site is their own restaurant with open wine cellar.
11 35 P

SERENDIPITY
$$–$$$ ★ ★ ★ ★ ★
FREESIA AVE.
TEL 044/877-0433
www.serendipitywilderness .com
Located in the Wilderness National Park, on the banks of the Touw River, this guesthouse overlooks the lagoon. It also boasts a highly rated restaurant offering a five-course menu that changes often. Regular items include snoek, ostrich, kudu and springbok, and luscious desserts.
4 30 Restaurant closed D Sun.; 2 weeks July P

EASTERN CAPE

ADDO ELEPHANT NP

For additional options, see p. 125

MATYHOLWENI REST CAMP
$$
DIRECTLY ACCESSIBLE FROM N2, 1.8 MILES (3 KM) FROM COLCHESTER
TEL 042/468-0916
www.sanparks.org/parks/ addo/camps/matyholweni/
Accommodations at Matyholweni are in self-catering chalets with showers and toilets, fully equipped kitchens, and barbecue facilities.
12 P

ADDO REST CAMP
$–$$
CLOSE TO MAIN ADDO GATE
TEL 042/233-8600
www.sanparks.org/parks/ addo/camps/addo/
A range of accommodations are available: Self-catering chalets, guesthouses, cottages, and forest cabins, with fully equipped kitchens. A cheaper option is a rondavel with shared cooking facilities and utensils. An à la carte restaurant is available on site.
46 80 P Some units

EAST LONDON

QUARRY LAKE INN
$$ ★ ★ ★ ★
QUARTZITE DR., OFF PEARCE ST., THE QUARRY
TEL 043/707-5400
www.quarrylakeinn.co.za
Bright modern guesthouse, located in the suburbs overlooking a small lake. Rooms all opening onto a balcony or the garden, are decorated in contemporary style in quiet beige, white, and green. Breakfast is served in the dining room or on the wooden deck.
16 P

SMOKEY SWALLOWS
$$–$$$
SHOP 11, CHESS GALLERIA, 20 DEVEREAUX AVE., VINCENT
TEL 043/727-1349
This highly rated restaurant offers items such as prawn salad, fresh fish, and beef fillet, as well as a range of Indian curries and vegetarian dishes. Try the prawn and scallop tempura with avocado ice cream or the delicious butter chicken.
50 P Closed Sun.

AL MARE
$$
AQUARIUM COMPLEX, ESPLANADE RD.
TEL 043/722-0287
Set on the ocean's edge with fine sea views, Al Mare offers a choice of food, ranging from salad, pasta, pizzas, steaks, and seafood and shellfish combinations, to Turkish delight ice cream or citrus cheesecake.
80 P Closed L Sat.– Sun., D Sun.

GRAHAMSTOWN

THE COCK HOUSE
$$ ★ ★ ★ ★
10 MARKET ST.
TEL 046/636-1287
www.cockhouse.co.za
Guesthouse situated within a 19th-century building that is a national monument, offering simply decorated double rooms in the main house and in the converted stables. The in-house restaurant, **Norden's,** provides good South African and international cuisine such as ostrich carpaccio and char-grilled beef fillet on spinach.
9 60 Restaurant closed L Mon. P

MAXWELL'S
$$
38 SOMERSET ST.
TEL 046/622-5119
With a reputation for excellent local meat, Maxwell's offers fine steaks, poultry, and fish. Its garden makes a pleasant lunch venue. Try the delicious mildly spiced Moroccan pie.
66 Closed L Sat.–Mon.; D Sun.–Tues.; closed Dec.

GRAAFF-REINET

DROSTDY HOTEL
$$$–$$$$ ★ ★ ★
30 CHURCH ST.
TEL 049/892-2161
www.drostdy.co.za
The magnificent main hotel building was constructed in 1806 as the *drostdy,* or courthouse. Accommodations are in spacious period rooms and in the nearby cobble-stone Stretch's Court. Candlelit dinner is served in the original courtroom.
39 60 P

🏨🍴 ANDRIES STOCKEN STRÖM GUEST HOUSE
$$$ ★★★★
100 CRADOCK ST.
TEL 049/892-4575
www.stockenstrom.co.za
Located in a beautiful Victorian house, with rooms and suites decorated in bright colors. The menu at the restaurant here emphasizes fresh regional foods and includes such dishes as ostrich liver pâté, smoked kudu salad with sesame wafer, and loin of Karoo lamb with rösti.
ⓘ 6 🛏 12 🅿 🚫 🕐 Restaurant closed D Sun. ⛱

JEFFREY'S BAY

🏨 SEA WHISPER
$$
62 PETUNIA ST.
TEL 082/489-9114
www.seawhisper.co.za
Situated on a hilltop with wide sea views, this B&B provides white-painted rooms with bold touches of maroon and red. For guests who wish to self-cater, a fully equipped kitchen is available.
ⓘ 6 🅿 🚫 Some rooms ⛱

🍴 DE VISWIJF
$$–$$$
55 DIAZ RD.
TEL 042/293-3921
Situated in the building of an old fish factory, this restaurant overlooks the sea. Chicken and *kassler* chops appear on the menu, but the main emphasis is on a wide range of shellfish and seafood dishes.
🛏 120 🅿 🕐 Closed D Sun.

KENTON-ON-SEA

🍴 HOMEWOODS
$$$
1 EASTBOURNE RD.
TEL 046/648-2700
Homewoods has a wonderful setting, with its deck overlooking a beach and river mouth. The food is good standard fare: burgers, steaks, and ribs, calamari in batter with savory rice or fries. *Bobotie* and mild lamb curry are also offered.
🛏 120 🅿 🕐 Closed L Mon., D Sun.–Mon.

LALIBELA

🏨 LALIBELA GAME RESERVE
$$$$
ON N2 BET. PORT ELIZABETH & GRAHAMSTOWN
TEL 041/581-8170
www.lalibela.net
This game reserve offers three luxury lodges, **Mark's Camp, Lentaba Lodge,** and **Tree Tops.** Accommodations are in en suite, secluded, thatched or tented chalets, opening onto gardens that blend into the bush. Each chalet has its own deck from which to observe wildlife. Meals are included.
ⓘ 21 🅿 🚫 ⛱

MOUNTAIN ZEBRA NP

🏨🍴 MOUNTAIN ZEBRA NATIONAL PARK
$$
7.5 MILES (12 KM) FROM CRADOCK, OFF R61
TEL 048/881-2427
www.sanparks.org/parks /mountain/zebra
Accommodations are available in the middle of the park, in the form of four-bed cottages with bathroom and partially equipped kitchen; and a three-room, six-bed, en suite guesthouse with fully equipped kitchen. A licensed à la carte restaurant and a store selling basic supplies are available.
ⓘ 20 🛏 46 🅿 ⛱

NIEU-BETHESDA

🏨 MURRAYFIELD GUEST HOUSE
$
GRAVE & CHURCH STS.
TEL 049/841-1693
You can get information about the town's famous Owl House from the owner, Anne, also author of a book on the subject. Tea and coffee are available in the rooms; breakfast and dinner on request. Credit card deposit; balance cash only.
ⓘ 3 🅿

🍴 VILLAGE INN
$
NEXT TO OWL HOUSE
TEL 049/841-1635
An old building—close to the

PRICES

HOTELS

The cost of a double room in the high season is indicated by **$** signs.

$$$$$	Over $300
$$$$	$200–$300
$$$	$120–$200
$$	$60–$120
$	Under $60

RESTAURANTS

The cost of a three-course meal without drinks is indicated by **$** signs.

$$$$$	Over $50
$$$$	$35–$50
$$$	$25–$35
$$	$15–$25
$	Under $15

---

town's major attraction, the Owl House—is home to this restaurant, open morning through evening. For dinner expect good hearty fare such as roast mutton, curry and rice, and lamb chops. Vegetarian selections are also available.
🛏 30 🅿

PORT ALFRED

🏨 PORTOFINO HOTEL
$$$ ★★★
PARK RD.
TEL 046/624-2223
www.portofinohotel.co.za
The deck at this hotel overlooking the town's marina and small craft harbor provides stunning ocean views. Rooms are en suite and decorated in restrained pastel shades. Breakfast available on request.
ⓘ 11 🅿 🚫 ⛱ ⛱

🍴 GUIDO'S
$–$$
WEST BEACH DR.
TEL 046/624-5264
With its fine setting on the beach at the mouth of the Kowie River, Guido's becomes fairly crowded in summer, despite its vast size. Wood-fired pizzas, seafood, and juicy ribs

---

 Hotel   Restaurant   No. of guest rooms    No. of Seats   Parking   Closed

and steaks form the backbone of the menu.
🛏 450 🅿

PORT ELIZABETH

🏨 THE KELWAY HOTEL
🍴 $$–$$$ ★ ★ ★ ★
BROOKES HILL DR., HUMEWOOD
TEL 041/584-0638
www.thekelway.co.za
This newly opened hotel offers rooms decorated in cool tones. Its hilltop location means wonderful sea views from many rooms and the terrace of the hotel restaurant, **Farriagers.**
ⓘ 62 🛏 120 🅿 ⊟ 🛗 Some rooms 🌊

🏨 MILLBROOK HOUSE
$$ ★ ★ ★
2 HAVELOCK S., CENTRAL HILL
TEL 041/582-3774
www.millbrookhouse.co.za
Located on a quiet square in the historic heart of Port Elizabeth, this long-established B&B offers tastefully decorated rooms, most en suite, with 24-hour Internet connection.
ⓘ 4 🅿 🌊

🍴 34° SOUTH
$$
BOARDWALK COMPLEX, MARINE DR., SUMMERSTRAND
TEL 041/583-1085
www.34-south.com
Enjoy views over the water from the balcony of this Mediterranean and sushi restaurant. The extensive menu ranges from soups, meze, and fresh fish to dishes made with chicken and ham.
🛏 250 🅿

🍴 WICKER WOODS
$$
MOUNT CROIX, 99 CAPE RD., MILLPARK
TEL 041/374-8170
Situated in a quaint old house that retains its beautiful Oregon pine floors and original fittings. The food ranges from salmon and spring roll starters, through Cajun and stir-fry main courses, to deserts such as deep-fried Lindt balls.
🛏 50 🕐 Closed D Sun.–Mon.

SIBUYA GAME RESERVE

🏨 SIBUYA GAME RESERVE
$$$$
UP KARIEGA RIVER FROM KENTON-ON-SEA
TEL 046/648-1040
www.sibuya.co.za
Sibuya is approached in unique fashion—by boat up the Kariega River from Kenton-On-Sea. Accommodations are in luxury tents at the **River Camp** or the **Forest Camp.** All tents are on raised wooden platforms with mosquito netting and en suite bathrooms. Sit-down dinners are cooked over open fires.
ⓘ 9

■ DURBAN & KWAZULU-NATAL

BALLITO

🏨 HOTEL IZULU
$$$–$$$$
REY'S PL.
TEL 032/946-3444
www.hotelizulu.com
Accommodations at this hotel are in luxurious suites. Stroll across the palm-shaded lawns, or let yourself be pampered in the spa. Guests can dine at several venues.
ⓘ 18 🛏 84 🅿 🛗 🌊 🎽

🍴 MOZAMBIK
$$
BOULEVARD CENTER, JACK POWELL ST.
TEL 032/946-0979
Informal venue in the style of a beach hut, with ocher walls and reed screens. The Portuguese-Mozambican food includes chicken livers *peri-peri*, salad of chickpeas and roasted vegetables, chicken or grilled prawns with garlic or peri-peri flavoring.
🛏 105 🅿 🕐 Closed L Mon., D Sun.

CLARENS

SOMETHING SPECIAL

🏨 SEDIBA LODGES
$$–$$$
6 MILES (10 KM) FROM CLARENS, ON R711 TO FOURIESBURG
TEL 058/256-1028
www.sedibalodge.co.za

Sediba consists of three luxury, self-catering lodges sleeping four to six persons. Two lodges are on a trout dam, the third is on a hill—all with magnificent views. Each furnished lodge has its own dining room and lounge.
ⓘ 7 🅿

🍴 CLEMENTINES
$$–$$$
315 CHURCH ST.
TEL 058/256-1616
The bright red-and-green exterior is matched by the colorful interior. The patio provides wonderful views of the surrounding mountains. Sample the prawns with coriander and Pernod, or duck velouté soup.
🛏 50 🕐 Closed L & D Mon.

🍴 CAFÉ MOULIN
$–$$
410 MAIN ST.
TEL 082/690-1382
Offering superb mountain views, this restaurant serves country food. You are charged by weight for what you eat, with choices of red beets with pears, seafood pasta and roasted butternut squash with sundried tomatoes.
🛏 80 🕐 Closed L Tues.–Wed., D Sun.–Wed. & during winter

DURBAN

SOMETHING SPECIAL

🏨 THE ROYAL
🍴 $$$$$
267 SMITH ST.
TEL 031/333-6000
www.theroyal.co.za
This city-center hotel with its liveried doorman is a Durban institution. Rooms are decorated in royal blue with yellowwood finishings, and the hotel houses a range of restaurants and bars. Best known are the **Ulundi Restaurant,** serving fine Indian cuisine, and the **Royal Grill,** offering classic and contemporary food.
ⓘ 251 🅿 ⊟ 🛗 🌊 🎽

🏨 BEVERLY HILLS
🍴 $$$$
71 LIGHTHOUSE RD.,

UMHLANGA ROCKS
TEL 031/561-2211
www.southernsun.com
Almost on the beach, with views over the Indian Ocean, this is the place for a seaside stay. The hotel's restaurant, **Sugar Club**, affords a panoramic sea view and serves good light meals and substantial dishes such as prawns in coconut milk and rib roast.
🛏 89 🅿 ⬒ ⬓ ⛵ 📺

🏨🍴 SOUTHERN SUN ELAN GENI
$$$–$$$$ ★ ★ ★ ★
63 SNELL PARADE
TEL 031/362-1300
www.southernsun.com
This large beachfront hotel provides a choice of rooms with dramatic ocean views from the upper story sea-facing rooms. The hotel's **Daruma** restaurant, with its clean Zen-like decor, offers authentic Japanese cuisine, including a wide range of tempura and sushi dishes. There is also an Indian restaurant, and a restaurant serving breakfast and dinner buffets.
🛏 449 🍴 380 🅿 ⬒ ⬓ ⛵ 📺

🏨 BLUE WATERS HOTEL
$$–$$$ ★ ★ ★
175 SNELL PARADE
TEL 031/327-7000
www.bluewatershotel.co.za
This establishment provides good, reasonably priced accommodations right on the beachfront. Every bedroom has its own balcony with fine ocean view. Both à la carte and buffet dining are available.
🛏 278 🍴 250 🅿 ⬒ ⬓ ⛵

🏨 JOAN'S BED & BREAKFAST
$$ ★ ★ ★ ★
3 MATHIAS PL., DURBAN NORTH
TEL 031/563-3220
www.joansbxb.co.za
This upscale B&B is situated close to tourist attractions, between the city center and the beach resort of Umhlanga. All the cool, tastefully furnished rooms are air-conditioned and have a private entrance.
🛏 7 🅿 ⬓ ⛵

🏨 RIDGEVIEW LODGE
$$ ★ ★ ★ ★ ★
17 LOUDOUN ST., BEREA
TEL 031/202-9777
www.ridgeview.co.za
Decorated in traditional style with warm colors, this lodge offers good value and quiet, luxurious accommodations, close to the city center. Enjoy a cool tropical garden and fine city views. Breakfast is served.
🛏 7 🅿 ⬓ ⛵

SOMETHING SPECIAL

🍴 9TH AVENUE BISTRO
$$–$$$
SHOP 2, AVONMORE CENTER, 9TH AVE., MORNINGSIDE
TEL 031/312-9134
This award-winning, elegantly decorated restaurant offers a small, frequently changing menu, concentrating on Continental fusion cuisine. Sample grilled springbok loin on gingered carrots, veal belly with prunes and mushrooms, and the fresh berry soup.
🍴 65 🅿 🕐 Closed L Sat.–Mon., D Sun.

🍴 HEMINGWAY'S
$$
131 DAVENPORT RD., GLENWOOD
TEL 031/202-4906
Decorated in an unusual Afro-Latino style, Hemingway's is located in the rooms and on the veranda of a converted house. The food is international, ranging from escargot, eggplant with parmesan, and nachos, to Portuguese and Italian meat and seafood dishes.
🍴 75

🍴 OYSTER BAR/ZENBI SUSHI
$$
WILSON'S WHARF, VICTORIA EMBANKMENT
TEL 031/307-7883
Overhanging the water at Durban's small-craft harbor, the deck at this venue provides magnificent views. Fresh oysters from Knysna and the West Coast are offered, as are prawns and a selection of sashimi and sushi.
🍴 60 🅿

🍴 SOCIETY
$$
HOLLIS HOUSE, 178 FLORIDA RD., MORNINGSIDE
TEL 031/313-3213
Located in a handsome old house decorated in colorful Pacific style, Society focuses on Asian and fusion cuisine with sushi and Vietnamese rice pancakes, springbok loin with mango, and Szechuan duck. A bar and lounge upstairs hosts live entertainment.
🍴 70 🅿 🕐 Closed L Sun.–Mon., D Sun.

🍴 SPIGA D'ORO
$$
200 FLORIDA RD., MORNINGSIDE
TEL 031/303-9511
Enjoy breakfast, lunch, or dinner out on the bustling sidewalk, or in the cool, airy black-and-white interior of this Italian restaurant. The menu covers the range of international Italian cuisine, with all sorts of pizzas and pastas plus chicken and beef dishes.
🍴 120

🍴 BEAN BAG BOHEMIA
$–$$$
18 WINDERMERE RD., MORNINGSIDE
TEL 031/309-6019
Light, airy, arty venue set in an old house that is a national monument, with a bar and a courtyard for eating alfresco. The menu covers both light meals (burgers and pizzas) and more serious dining on Mediterranean and fusion cuisine.
🍴 200 🕐

🍴 INDIAN CONNECTION
$–$$
485 WINDERMERE RD., MORNINGSIDE
TEL 031/312-1440
www.indian-connection.co.za
In a city with many Indian restaurants, this is one of the best. Spread throughout the rooms of an old house, it serves mainly northern Indian food, including several *breyanis*, and lamb, chicken, and seafood curries, with the traditional accompaniments.
🍴 80 🅿

🏨 Hotel   🍴 Restaurant   🛏 No. of guest rooms   🍴 No. of Seats   🅿 Parking   🕐 Closed

LITTLE INDIA
$–$$
155 MUSGRAVE RD., MUSGRAVE
TEL 031/201-1121
A restaurant that aims to cover the full spectrum of Indian cuisine, from north to south. Northern dishes include *breyanis*, chicken *tikka*, and tandoori choices; southern dishes range from a variety of vegetarian meals to spicy fish curry.
175 **P**

SNAP WINE BAR
$–$$
41 MARRIOTT RD., BEREA
TEL 031/309-4160
This trendy venue with its modern décor offers over 70 South African wines, 9 of them by the glass, and live entertainment. The menu features Mediterranean starters and gourmet burgers, Cajun chicken, and fish dishes.
70 **P** Closed L Sat.–Mon., D Sun.; 2 weeks late Dec.

MANNA
$
40 MARRIOTT RD., MORNINGSIDE
TEL 031/309-8581
Busy breakfast and lunch venue with shady patio. Although it may take a while to reach your table, the food is wholesome. Try the chicken wrap with sweet chili and roast peppers, sesame lentil burger with mayonnaise and red beets, or tasty fishcakes.
100 Closed Sun.

FREE STATE

HALEVY HERITAGE HOTEL
$$$–$$$$ ★★★★
MARKGRAAFF & CHARLES STS.
TEL 051/403-0600
www.halevyheritage.com
This hotel in the heart of the city began life as a humble boardinghouse in 1893. Now it provides a range of luxurious accommodations. Breakfast, lunch, and dinner are serves in the hotel's two restaurants.
21 62 **P**

DE OUDE KRAAL COUNTRY HOUSE
$$–$$$ ★★★★
21 MILES (35 KM) S OF BLOEMFONTEIN ON N1
TEL 051/564-0733
www.oudekraal.co.za.
Located on a working sheep farm, Oude Kraal offers guest rooms each with its own open fireplace, en suite bathroom, and private patio, some with underfloor heating. The restaurant has a fixed-price five-course menu, concentrating on South African specialities.
10 30 **P**

PROTEA HOTEL
$$–$$$ ★★★★
202 NELSON MANDELA DR., BRANDWAG
TEL 051/444-4321
www.proteahotels.com
Member of a countrywide hotel group, this establishment lies in the center of the business area. It offers light, modern rooms, all en suite and air-conditioned. The hotel has a restaurant, the **Amoretta**.
94 65 **P**

OOLONG LOUNGE
$$
16A SECOND AVE., WESTDENE
TEL 051/448-7244
The cool glass and black-and-white interior creates a metropolitan feel at this venue, open for lunch, dinner, and late night cocktails. The menu is Eastern fusion, offering Thai skewers of mildly curried meat, stir-fries, Indian curries, and sushi.
60 **P** Closed Sun.

HOWICK

FERN HILL HOTEL
$$–$$$ ★★★
ON R103, MIDMAR/TWEEDIE/HOWICK
TEL 033/330-5071
www.fernhillhotel.co.za
Set amid gardens with mature tree ferns and ponds, this hotel offers country tranquility. The historic main building began as a trading post. Rooms are decorated in deep warm colors. Breakfast, lunch, and dinner are served.
35 65 **P**

YELLOWWOOD CAFÉ
$–$$
1 SHAFTON RD.
TEL 033/330-2461
Located in a delightful historic farmhouse, set in a garden, the Yellowwood serves food from breakfast through dinner. The small seasonal menu offers dishes such as Camembert parcels, oxtail, and lamb shanks.
120 **P** Closed Mon.

PIETERMARITZBURG

PROTEA HOTEL IMPERIAL
$$–$$$ ★★★
224 JABU NDLOVU ST.
TEL 033/342-6551
www.proteahotels.com
Housed in a charming century-old building, this hotel offers the spaciousness and solidity of a past era. The decor of the rooms, though, is modern. The hotel has its own restaurant.
70 120 **P**

THE BUTCHERY PUB & GRILL
$$
101 ROBERTS RD.
TEL 033/342-5239
Rustic steak house specializing in top-grade aged steaks. Meat is the focus here, with such cuts as oxtail, lamb shanks, chops, steaks, and *eisbein* on the menu. For lunch you can have less substantial fare, such as sausages and mash.
200 **P** Closed 1 week late Dec.

EATON'S ON EIGHTY
$$
80 ROBERTS RD.
TEL 033/342-3280
You'll find simple elegance here—exposed brick, black chandeliers, white walls. The small menu offers daily specials, including chicken breast filled with shitake mushrooms and ham, or beef Wellington served with macadamia nuts.
40 **P** Closed L Sat.–Tues., D Sun.–Mon.

ST. LUCIA

🏨 MAKAKATANA BAY LODGE

$$$$$ ★ ★ ★ ★

LOT 1 MAKAKATANA, WESTERN SHORES, GREATER ST. LUCIA WETLANDS PARK

TEL 035/550-4189

www.makakatana.co.za

The only private lodge within the St. Lucia park, Makakatana offers luxury en suite accommodations with lake, forest, or wetland views. The lodge has viewing decks, a central lounge, bar, dining room, and *boma* (open-air cooking and eating area).

🛈 6 🅿 ⚅ ⚅

🏨 UMLILO LODGE

$$ ★ ★ ★ ★

9 DOLPHIN AVE.

TEL 035/590-1717

www.umilodge.co.za

This friendly, welcoming establishment offers safari-style accommodations within walking distance of St. Lucia's amenities. Guests can laze on the wooden deck next to the pool and, by request, enjoy dinner in the *boma* (open-air cooking and eating area).

🛈 11 ⚅ ⚅

SOUTHBROOM

🏨 FIGTREE LODGE

$$–$$$ ★ ★ ★

30 NORTH RIDGE RD.

TEL 039/316-6547

www.figtreelodge.co.za

Set amid lush subtropical vegetation, the lodge offers four en suite bedrooms. Beautiful views from the lodge's covered and open wooden decks. Breakfast is served. Credit card deposit; balance cash only.

🛈 4 🅿 ⚅

🍴 TRATTORIA LA TERRAZZA

$$

UMKOBI LAGOON, 17 OUTLOOK RD.

TEL 039/316-6162

The restaurant enjoys a good location, overlooking the Umkobi Lagoon, with indoor dining during inclement weather. On the menu are standard Italian dishes such as pizzas and pastas, but T-bone steaks, seafood, and chicken dishes are also featured.

🌣 120 🅿 🕐 Closed L Mon.–Tues., D Sun.–Mon.; & 2 weeks April

UKHAHLAMBA-DRAKENSBERG NP

A variety of accommodations are available in the resorts and camps run by the Ezemvelo KwaZulu-Natal Wildlife organization. Only a selection of camps is given here. Most camps accommodate guests in self-catering chalets and rustic huts with kitchen and barbecue facilities. For a full list and further details consult the website (*www.kznwildlife.com*). Note that all reservations have to be fully paid in advance.

🏨 GIANT'S CASTLE CAMP
🍴

$$–$$$

OFF N3, 40 MILES (65 KM) FROM ESTCOURT, 40 MILES (64 KM) FROM MOOI RIVER

TEL 036/353-3718

Most of the accommodations are in two-bed, en suite chalets, each with its own fully equipped kitchen and lounge/dining area. There are also a few four- and six-bed chalets with the same facilities. The camp has a store, as well as a restaurant and bar.

🛈 43 🌣 56 🅿

🏨 LOTHENI

$$

31 MILES (50 KM) FROM UNDERBERG, 38.5 MILES (62 KM) FROM NOTTINGHAM RD.

TEL 033/702-0540

The accommodations here are entirely self-catering, all with bathroom and fully equipped kitchen. Visitors can choose between chalets sleeping two, three, or six persons. Lotheni has a store selling basics.

🛈 14 🅿

🏨 THENDELE CAMP

$$

ROYAL NATAL NATIONAL PARK, 4 MILES (6 KM) FROM GATE

TEL 036/438-6411

Visitors to Thendele have the choice of chalets, sleeping from two to four persons, or six-bed cottages. All the accommodations are en suite.

Chalets are self-catering, while at the cottages a cook will prepare the food you bring. A store is also available.

🛈 29 🅿

🏨 INJISUTHI

$–$$

NORTHERN SECTION OF GIANT'S CASTLE AREA, 3 MILES (5 KM) FROM INJISUTHI GATE

TEL 036/431-7848

Injisuthi has 15 self-catering chalets, each accommodating four persons. Each chalet has a bathroom, fully equipped kitchen, and a shared lounge with fireplace. There is a shop selling basic supplies on-site.

🛈 15 🅿

■ KRUGER & MPUMALANGA

BARBERTON

🏨 BARBERTON MANOR GUEST HOUSE

$$ ★ ★ ★ ★

81 SHEBA RD.

013/712-4826

www.barbertonmanor.com

This mansion, built in 1927 from a design by architect, Sir Herbert Baker, retains its period

atmosphere, with ceilings of pressed steel and large fireplaces. The accommodations have been modernized, all with en suite bathrooms.

🛏 3 🅿 🌊

🍴 BYE APART ATE
$–$$
27 DE VILLIERS ST.
TEL 013/712-2846
Located in an old Barberton house, this restaurant serves good old-fashioned country fare with a Portuguese twist. Try the seasoned strips of steak, or their speciality, a seafood platter loaded with fresh fish and shellfish.

🪑 100 🅿 🕐 Closed D Tues.

DULLSTROOM

🏨 PEEBLES COUNTRY RETREAT
$$$$–$$$$$ ★ ★ ★ ★ ★
LYON CACHET & BOSMAN STS.
TEL 013/254-8000
www.peebles.co.za
This family-owned hotel has luxury suites, each with open fireplace, bathroom with extra large bath, private dining area and patio. Peebles has its own bar and restaurant. Guests have exclusive use of one of the large fly-fishing facilities in Dullstroom.

🛏 10 🪑 35 🅿 🌊

🍴 MRS. SIMPSON'S RESTAURANT
$–$$
194 TEDING VAN BERKHOULD ST.
TEL 013/254-0088
www.mrssimpsons.co.za
Amid kitsch decor celebrating the Duke and Duchess of Windsor, this venue serves excellent food. Sample the springbok carpaccio, the Moroccan-style prawns and mussels, or the grilled pork chops with apricot and honey.

🪑 60 🅿 🕐 Closed Tues.–Wed. & D Sun.

HAENERTSBURG

🍴 RED PLATE
$–$$
161 RISSIK ST.,
HAENERTSBURG VILLAGE
TEL 083/305-2851
Colorfully decorated restaurant

with outside deck. The menu changes often but features stir fries, seafood platters, and soups. Signature dishes are the lamb burger with avocado, and pork neck with apple, honey, and mustard.

🪑 70 🕐 Closed L & D Tues., Wed. D Sun.

HAZYVIEW

🏨 BLUE MOUNTAIN 🍴 LODGE
$$$$$ ★ ★ ★ ★ ★
ON R514 TO KIEPERSOL
TEL 013/737-8446
www.bluemountainlodge.co.za
This luxury country lodge has a range of suites each furnished in an individual style—Provençal, African, or Camelot—some with private plunge pool. The restaurant has a five-course set menu, including fresh fish, pastas, and venison dishes.

🛏 15 🪑 34 🅿 🕙 🌊

🏨 RISSINGTON INN 🍴
$$–$$$ ★ ★ ★ ★
ON R40 OUTSIDE HAZYVIEW
TEL 013/737-7700
www.rissington.co.za
Relaxed thatched inn with rooms and suites, set in 10 acres (4 ha) of gardens. Rooms are furnished in rustic style with shower and bath. The restaurant has an à la carte menu featuring venison stew, seafood and chicken dishes, and, as a vegetarian option, vegetable vermouth pasta.

🛏 16 🪑 40 🅿 🌊

KRUGER NATIONAL PARK

The park is the size of a small country, and the range of accommodations available is large. Most accommodations are in the $$ range, with some lower and a few higher priced units. Below is only a representative sample covering the main areas of the park. For more details consult the Kruger pages of the South African National Parks website (www.sanparks.org), as well as the Kruger park entry on pp. 176–184. Reservations should be made in advance with a major credit card.

Southern Kruger

🏨 BERG-EN-DAL 🍴
$$–$$$$
7.5 MILES (12 KM) FROM MALELANE GATE
TEL 013/735-6106
Accommodations range from three-bed bungalows and six-bed family units, to luxury guesthouses in the best position in the camp for up to eight people. All units are self-catering and air-conditioned. The camp has a shop, restaurant, and cafeteria.

🛏 95 🅿 🕙 🌊

🏨 SKUKUZA 🍴
$–$$$$
24 MILES (39 KM) FROM PHABENI GATE
TEL 013/735-4152
Largest of the Kruger camps, Skukuza is the size of a small village; facilities include two restaurants, a deli, bank, and car rental. Stay in furnished tents on stilts, with communal facilities; thatched en suite huts, some self-catering; fully equipped guest cottages; or luxury, multiroom guest cottages and houses.

🛏 230 🪑 270 🅿 🕙 Some units 🌊

Central Kruger

🏨 OLIFANTS
$$–$$$$
51.5 MILES (83 KM) FROM PHALABORWA GATE
TEL 013/735-6606
Available are en suite two- to four-bed bungalows, some with kitchenettes, others with communal cooking facilities, and large luxury guesthouses, sleeping up to eight persons. Some units have kitchens and superb views, so state your preference when booking. Restaurant, shop, and cafeteria are on site.

🛏 109 🪑 56 🅿 🕙

🏨 SATARA 🍴
$$–$$$$
30 MILES (48 KM) FROM ORPEN GATE
TEL 013/735-6306
Choose between two- or three-bed en suite, self-catering bungalows; five- or six-bed

guest cottages with the same facilities; or three luxury guest-houses in prime position. Store, restaurant, and deli are available in the camp.

 151 75 P S ⛱

 LETABA
$–$$$$
31.5 MILES (51 KM) FROM PHALABORWA GATE
TEL 013/735-6636
Permanently furnished safari tents on stilts and rustic huts with communal bathroom and kitchen facilities; en suite self-catering bungalows, with two or three beds; and larg er guest cottages and guesthouses make up the range of accommoda-tions. Restaurant, store, and cafeteria on-site.

113 44 P S Some units ⛱

Northern Kruger

BATALEUR
$$$
87 MILES (140 KM) FROM PHALABORWA GATE
TEL 013/735-6843
One of the smaller bushveld camps, Bataleur offers six- and four-bed en suite cottages, with fully equipped kitchen.
It is important to note that there is no restaurant here, and the small shop does not sell food. Guests must bring their own supplies.

7 P S Some units

PUNDA MARIA
$$–$$$
6 MILES (10 KM) FROM PUNDA MARIA GATE
TEL 013/735-6873
Accommodations here range from permanently furnished safari tents on stilts, en suite, with cooking facilities; to en suite two- or three-bed bungalows, some with, some without kitchen; and larger, fully equipped bungalows, sleeping up to six. Restaurant, cafeteria, and store are available.

31 20 P S Some units ⛱

SHINGWEDZI
$–$$$$
44 MILES (71 KM) FROM PUNDA MARIA GATE

TEL 013/735-6806
This camp offers rustic three-bed huts with communal kitchen and bathroom facilities; two- to five-bed en suite, self-catering bungalows, with open air or enclosed kitchen; a four-bed cottage; and a luxury three-bedroom guesthouse, both with full facilities. The camp has a store, restaurant, and cafeteria.

66 24 P S Some units ⛱

PRIVATE GAME LODGES IN & AROUND KRUGER

For additional options, see pp. 182–184.

LUKIMBI SAFARI LODGE
$$$$$
16 MILES (26 KM) FROM MALELANE GATE
TEL 011/431-1120
www.lukimbi.com
The lodge in the southern part of Kruger offers 16 luxury air-conditioned suites decorated in contemporary African style, each with bathroom and private deck with river views, and most with private pool. All meals are included in the price.

16 P S ⛱

SINGITA BOULDERS & SINGITA EBONY
$$$$$
IN SABI SAND RESERVE, 40 MILES (64 KM) FROM HAZYVIEW ON R536
TEL 021/683-3424
www.singita.com
In the Sabi Sand conservation area, these two lodges provide luxury accommodations and game viewing, overlooking the Sand River. All suites are air-conditioned and have their own swimming pool, lounge with open fireplace, bathroom and outside shower. All meals are included.

24 P S ⛱

JOCK SAFARI LODGE
$$$$
WITHIN KRUGER, 22 MILES (35 KM) FROM MALELANE GATE
TEL 041/407-1000
www.jocksafarilodge.com
Close to the southern end of Kruger, this lodge has two sites,

Main Jock and Little Jock, less than a mile (1.6 km) apart. The thatched, air-conditioned luxury suites each have a game-view-ing deck overlooking the river, bathroom and outdoor shower, and most an individual plunge pool. Meals are included.

15 P S ⛱

SINGITA LEBOMBO & SINGITA SWENI
$$$$
WITHIN KRUGER, 40 MILES (64 KM) FROM ORPEN GATE
TEL 021/683-3424
www.singita.com
These luxury private lodges are in the southeastern part of Kruger, on the Mozam-bique border. The beautifully appointed suites, built on raised platforms provide superb game viewing. Each suite is air-conditioned, and has its own fridge, bathroom, and outside shower. Meals are included.

21 P S ⛱

PILGRIM'S REST

MOUNT SHEBA COUNTRY LODGE HOTEL
$$$–$$$$ **
GROOTFONTEINBERG, 561 KT LYDENBURG RD.
TEL 013/768-1241
www.mountsheba.co.za
Located in the mountains above the town, this hotel offers thatched suites, each with their own bathroom, fireplace, and patio overlooking a nature reserve. Breakfast and lunch are available, and dinner is served in the hotel's **Chandelier** restaurant.

24 86 P ⛱

SABIE

THE WOODSMAN
$$ **
94 MAIN ST.
TEL 013/764-2204
www.thewoodsman.co.za
Enjoy lovely views of the Sabie Valley at this B&B. Accommo-dations are in spacious suites, decorated with period furniture and dark wood. All rooms are en suite, some with balcony with fine valley view. Meals are

available in the **Woodsman** restaurant.
(i) 12 **🛏** 180 **P**

🍴 COUNTRY KITCHEN
$–$$
73 MAIN ST.
TEL 013/764-1901
This pleasant, casual venue serves up good South African food with a contemporary accent, including a range of vegetarian dishes. Sample the trout with mustard and tarragon-flavored mash, or the *waterblommetjie* casserole, with juniper and brandy sauce.
🛏 40 **P** ⏱ Closed Sun.–Tues.

TIMBAVATI

🏨 KINGS CAMP
$$$$$
6 MILES (10 KM) FROM TIMBAVATI GATE, OUTSIDE HOEDSPRUIT
TEL 015/793-1123
Roomy air-conditioned suites, each set well apart from the others, feature a well stocked minibar, secluded veranda, showers inside and out, and a Victorian-style bath.
(i) 11 **P** 🅢 🏊 🐚

TZANEEN

🏨 COACH HOUSE
🍴 $$$$–$$$$$ ★ ★ ★ ★ ★
OLD COACH RD., AT AGATHA, 9 MILES (15 KMS) FROM TZANEEN
TEL 015/306-8000
www.coachhouse.co.za
On a hilltop, with gardens and views, the Coach House offers country luxury. All the rooms have a private veranda and en suite bathroom with heated towel rail. Dine in the candlelit dining room on oysters, local trout, lamb, or their famous chicken pie.
(i) 39 **🛏** 130 **P** 🅢 🐚 🏊

WHITE RIVER

🏨 WINKLER HOTEL
$$ ★ ★ ★
4 MILES (6 KM) NORTH OF WHITE RIVER, ON NUMBI GATE RD. (R538)
TEL 013/751-5068
www.proteahotels.com
One in the national chain of Protea hotels, the Winkler is set in lush, green gardens close

to the Kruger National Park. All rooms are air-conditioned, en suite and have a balcony with view over the grounds. Breakfast, lunch, and dinner are served.
(i) 87 **P** 🅢 🏊 🏊

🍴 FEZ
$–$$
BAGDAD CENTER, ON R40 OPPOSITE CASTERBRIDGE FARM
TEL 013/750-1253
Dine on the veranda, with its olive and orange trees, and blue-checked tablecloths. The food is North African-Moroccan in style, but there is also sushi on the menu.
🛏 80 **P** ⏱ Closed Mon. & D Sun.

▋ JOHANNESBURG & THE INTERIOR

JOHANNESBURG

🏨 GRACE HOTEL
🍴 $$$$$ ★ ★ ★ ★ ★
54 BATH AVE., ROSEBANK
TEL 011/280-7200
www.thegrace.co.za
Luxury hotel, with rooms decorated in subdued classically elegant fashion, offering an English-style garden on the rooftop terrace. The **Dining Room** serves dishes such as duck cooked with port and blueberries, and springbok shank with chestnut, and does a popular lunch on the terrace.
(i) 60 **🛏** 105 🐚 🏊 🏊 **P** 🅢

🏨 MELROSE ARCH
🍴 HOTEL
$$$$$ ★ ★ ★ ★ ★
1 MELROSE S., MELROSE ARCH
TEL 011/214-6666
www.africanpridehotels.com
Contemporary African-theme hotel, with rooms in bright colors, and a pool bar where your table sits in the shallow water. **Restaurant March** serves international and African fusion cuisine, such as roasted beet and butternut curry, or salmon sashimi.
(i) 180 **🛏** 110 **P** 🅢 🏊 🏊

🏨 THE MICHAELANGELO
$$$$$ ★ ★ ★ ★ ★
SANDTON S., SANDTON
TEL 011/282-7035
www.legacyhotels.co.za
This modern, Italian Renaissance–style hotel in the heart of Sandton is the last word in comfort with luxury rooms and suites, a pillared portico, indoor swimming pool, grassy sun deck, gym, health spa, and several bars and restaurants.
(i) 240 **🛏** 305 **P** 🅢 🏊 🏊 🐚

🏨 THE SAXON BOUTIQUE HOTEL & SPA
$$$$$ ★ ★ ★ ★ ★
36 SAXON RD., SANDHURST
TEL 011/292-6000
www.saxon.co.za
High fortress-like walls surround the luxurious Saxon. This boutique hotel in the northern suburbs offers African-theme suites, acres of landscaped gardens, gracious dining, and a health spa, steam room, and heated lap pool.
(i) 26 **P** 🏊 🅢 🏊 🐚

🏨 PEECH HOTEL
🍴 $$$$ ★ ★ ★ ★
61 NORTH ST., MELROSE NORTH
TEL 011/537-9797
http://thepeech.co.za
Small hotel with rooms in contemporary African style, with feather duvets and unlimited WiFi access. The **Bistro** restaurant serves fish, ostrich, and lamb, prepared with Cape Malay flavors.
(i) 10 **🛏** 45 **P** ⏱ Restaurant closed Sun. 🅢 🏊

🏨 QUATERMAIN INN
🍴 $$$–$$$$$ ★ ★ ★ ★
137 WEST RD. S., MORNINGSIDE, SANDTON
TEL 011/290-0900
www.falstaff.co.za
Located near the center of Sandton, with a golf course nearby, this hotel provides rooms and suites with restrained décor. The **Sel et Poivre** restaurant serves French cooking with Belgian leanings. Try the smoked salmon or *rösti*, or slow-roasted duck with goose-berry sauce.
(i) 104 **🛏** 110 **P** 🅢 🏊 🐚

🔃 Elevator 🅢 Air-conditioning 🏊 Indoor Pool 🏊 Outdoor Pool 🐚 Health Club

🏨 VILLA VITTORIA
$$$
21 MELVILLE RD., HYDE PARK
TEL 011/788-0708
This guesthouse is located in the city's northern suburbs, between Rosebank and Sandton, in the former British consulate. The en suite double rooms, with dark wood and light fabrics, have king-size beds and WiFi connection. Breakfast is served, and dinner on request.
🛏 10 🅿 🏊

🏨 COTSWOLD GARDENS
$$–$$$
46 COTSWOLD DR., SAXONWOLD
TEL 011/442-7553
www.cotswoldgardens.co.za
This guesthouse is in the leafy suburb of Saxonwold, near the zoo and the amenities of Rosebank. It has a garden and offers B&B and self-catering rooms. An Internet-enabled PC is available to guests.
🛏 4 🅿 🏊

🏨 PREMIERE CLASSE SUITE HOTEL
$$–$$$ ★ ★ ★
62 CORLETT DR., MELROSE
TEL 011/788-1967
www.premiereclasse.co.za
This hotel offers reasonably priced rooms, close to Rosebank and Sandton. The suites are self-catering, each with their own kitchen. Breakfast and dinner available on request.
🛏 30 🅿 ⬆ 🅢 Some rooms

🏨 HIGHGROVE GUEST HOUSE
$$ ★ ★ ★ ★
1 SIDE RD., MORNINGSIDE, SANDTON
TEL 011/884-3680
www.high-grove.co.za
Georgian in style, this gracious guesthouse provides tasteful en suite rooms, all with Internet-ready connection. Each room looks onto the garden and pool from a balcony or patio. Breakfast is served.
🛏 8 🅿 🏊

🏨 MELVILLA GUEST HOUSE
$$
75 AUCKLAND AVE., AUCKLAND PARK (BORDERING MELVILLE)
TEL 011/726-1325
www.melvilla.co.za
Located in a quiet neighborhood, but close to the trendy restaurants and bars of Melville's Seventh Street, this guesthouse offers rooms decorated in modern African style. Breakfast is served.
🛏 10 🅿

🏨 MELVILLE TURRET GUEST HOUSE
$$ ★ ★ ★
118 SECOND AVE., MELVILLE
TEL 011/482-7197
www.melvilleturret.co.za
This guesthouse is in a historic building more than a century old, with self-catering or B&B accommodations. Some rooms open onto the garden, others have city views.
🛏 9 🅿 🅢 Some rooms

🍴 AUBERGE MICHEL
$$$$–$$$$$
122 PRETORIA AVE., SANDTON
TEL 011/883-7013
A cool black-and-white interior characterizes one of the city's leading restaurants (which requires fairly formal dress). The menu offers fine French cuisine, such as crab soup with mushroom and coriander tortellini, or springbok with prawns and gingerbread sauce.
🪑 60 🕐 Closed L Sat.–Mon., D Sun.; 3 weeks Dec. 🅿

SOMETHING SPECIAL

🍴 LINGER LONGER
$$$–$$$$
58 WIERDA RD. W., WIERDA VALLEY, SANDTON
TEL 011/884-0465
Dine in the colorful interior or in the garden summerhouse. The award-winning menu includes crocodile and prawn in mango curry, a trio of beef, lamb, and venison with polenta and roasted garlic, or Atlantic salmon with Moroccan crust.
🪑 70 🕐 Closed L Sat.–Sun, D Sun.; 2 weeks late Dec. 🅿

PRICES

HOTELS
The cost of a double room in the high season is indicated by **$** signs.

$$$$$	Over $300
$$$$	$200–$300
$$$	$120–$200
$$	$60–$120
$	Under $60

RESTAURANTS
The cost of a three-course meal without drinks is indicated by **$** signs.

$$$$$	Over $50
$$$$	$35–$50
$$$	$25–$35
$$	$15–$25
$	Under $15

🍴 BUTCHER SHOP & GRILL
$$$
SHOP 30, NELSON MANDELA S., SANDTON
TEL 011/784-8676
Restaurant with a high reputation for its well aged meats: T-bone, fillet, sirloin, and rump steaks, as well as beef ribs, pork chops, and kebabs, all with a choice of sauces.
🪑 300 🅿

🍴 ASSAGGI
$$–$$$
POST OFFICE CENTER, 30 RUDD RD., ILLOVO
TEL 011/268-1370
Expect a warm welcome, starched white linen, and Italian food. Assaggi specializes in risottos with scampi, mushrooms, or asparagus. Or, try their brie lasagne, or fried veal with parmesan.
🪑 90 🕐 Closed L Sun.–Mon., D Sun; 2 weeks late Dec. 🅿

🍴 MELVILLE GRILL & ABYSSINICA
$$–$$$
THIRD AVE. & SEVENTH ST., MELVILLE
TEL 011/726-2890

 Hotel   Restaurant   🛏 No. of guest rooms   🪑 No. of Seats   🅿 Parking   🕐 Closed

Two formerly independent restaurants blended into one, with an East African décor. The menu offers grilled steaks, and Ethiopian and East African specialties.
🛏 110 🅿 ⊕ Closed Sun. winter

🍴 MOYO
$$–$$$
SHOP 5, HIGH ST., MELROSE ARCH
TEL 011/684-1477
One in the chain of Moyo African-food restaurants, this venue extends up five levels, linked by a series of copper-and-steel staircases. The menu covers Moroccan lamb, East African curries, and South African seafood and ostrich.
🛏 500 🅿

🍴 YAMATO
$$–$$$
196 OXFORD ROAD, ILLOVO
TEL 011/268-0511
This is as authentic Japanese as you will find in South Africa. In addition to sashimi and sushi, the chef also offers *nabe mono*, a hot pot in which diners cook at their own table.
🛏 120 🅿 ⊕ Closed L Sat

🍴 ZAFFERANO
$$-$$$
PARK HYATT HOTEL, 191 OXFORD RD., ROSEBANK
TEL 011/280-1234
Chic restaurant serving international cuisine. Artichoke frittata and duck prosciutto with grilled melon and mushrooms feature here and osso bucco and stuffed chicken breast.
🛏 80 🅿 ⊕ Closed 2 weeks late Dec.

🍴 GOURMET GARAGE
$$
ATHOLL S . CENTRE, WIERDA RD. E. & KATHERINE ST., SANDTON
TEL 011/883-2226
A 1950s retro-style venue serving gourmet hamburgers of all sorts: beef, ostrich, lamb, bacon, and vegetarian. Steaks, chicken, and pork chops are also available.
🛏 280 🅿

🍴 LEKGOTLA
$$
5 NELSON MANDELA S .,

SANDTON
TEL 011/884-9555
African décor and modern African cuisine characterize this venue, which means "meeting place." Sample fish cakes with Madagascan green peppercorn sauce and Zanzibar chicken with tomato and chili on couscous.
🛏 370 🅿

🍴 SOULSA
$$
16 SEVENTH ST., MELVILLE
TEL 011/482-5572
Trendy restaurant with arty split-level interior and tables on sidewalk. Try their "day-long brunch," or Asian-spiced tofu pockets, followed by springbok shanks with black currant jus, or seared tempura tuna with pickled ginger.
🛏 80 ⊕ Closed Mon.

🍴 RED CHAMBER
$-$$
68 HYDE PARK CENTER, JAN SMUTS AVE., HYDE PARK
TEL 011/325-6048
A well-established Chinese restaurant serving authentic Mandarin cuisine. Try the Monk's dish with glass noodles, Peking duck, or vegetarian.
🛏 130 🅿

🍴 SOPHIA'S MEDITERRANEAN RESTAURANT
$-$$
SHOP 311, ROSEBANK MALL, CRADOCK AVE., ROSEBANK
TEL 011/880-7356
Named for Sophia Loren, whose image appears on the walls, this venue concentrates on seafood, Mediterranean cuisine, and pizzas.
🛏 150 🅿 ⊕ Closed D Sun.

PILANESBURG NP

For options see p. 238.

PRETORIA

🏨 SHERATON
$$$$–$$$$$ ★★★★★
CHURCH & WESSELS STS.
TEL 012/429-9999
www.starwoodhotels.com/sheraton
This hotel, part of the international chain, is centrally located

in the quiet embassy quarter, overlooking the Union Buildings with views of the city.
🛏 175 🛏 260 🅿 ⬛
⬛ 🌊 Some rooms 🏆

🏨 COURTYARD HOTEL
$$$–$$$$$ ★★★★
PARK & HILL STS., ARCADIA
TEL 012/342-4940
www.citylodge.co.za
Despite being close to the city center, this hotel lies in an estate with gardens. A century-old manor house forms its core. The self-catering rooms are decorated in colorful fabrics. Breakfast is served; dinner can be in your room.
🛏 69 🅿 ⬛ 🌊
⬛ Some rooms

🏨 PREMIER HOTEL
🍴 PRETORIA
$$$–$$$$$ ★★★★
573 CHURCH ST., ARCADIA
TEL 012/441-1400
www.premierhotels.co.za
This hotel, opened in 2007, in the Premier chain, provides guests with rooms in the heart of the city. Decorated in white, and dark shades of brown. The hotel has its own restaurant, the **Ambassador,** serving breakfast, lunch, and dinner.
🛏 118 🛏 96 🅿 ⬛ ⬛ 🌊

🏨 LERIBA LODGE
🍴 $$$ ★★★★
245 END AVE., CLUBVIEW, CENTURION
TEL 012/660-3300
www.leriba.co.za
This lodge, located on 20 acres (8 ha) along the banks of the Hennops River, provides a unique bush experience five minutes' drive from Pretoria. The en suite rooms are decorated in East African style and have fine views onto the garden. South African cuisine is served at the lodge's **Pinotage** restaurant.
🛏 58 🛏 120 🅿 ⬛ Some rooms 🌊 🏆

🏨 40 ON ILKEY
$$ ★★★
40 ILKEY RD., LYNNWOOD GLEN
TEL 012/348-3766
www.40onilkey.co.za
This new B&B lies a couple of minutes from the city's

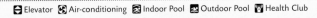

shopping mall of Menlyn Park, with a 27-acre (10 ha) bird sanctuary close by. En suite rooms are decorated in honey tones and beds made with percale linen.

[1] 7 P

MOLOPO VIEW GUEST HOUSE
$–$$
264 MOLOPO AVE., SINOVILLE
TEL 083/459-7209
www.molopoview.co.za
Enjoy views over northern Pretoria from the veranda of this venue. The rooms are simply furnished; some have shared bathrooms, but most are en suite. Breakfast is served.

[1] 6 P [S] Most rooms ⌘

OXNEAD GUEST HOUSE
$ * * *
802 JOHANITA ST., MORELETA PARK
TEL 012/993-4515
www.oxnead.co.za
Offering excellent value, this guesthouse in a quiet suburb, is just the place for a stopover when traveling north-south on the N1. The tastefully decorated rooms are self-catering, but a full breakfast is served.

[1] 10 P

BRASSERIE DE PARIS
$$$–$$$$
381 ARIES ST., WATERKLOOF RIDGE
TEL 012/460-3583
Situated in an architect-designed 1960s house, this venue with separate rooms and balconies has a high reputation for French food. The brief menu changes constantly.

40 P [C] Closed L Sat.–Sun., D Sun.; 2 weeks late Dec.

FAIRHILL BISTRO
$$–$$$
849 ARCADIA ST., ARCADIA
TEL 012/344-0140
www.fairhillbistro.co.za
Eat inside or out at this relaxed venue in an old house. The cuisine is Portuguese, with strong Mozambican and Mediterranean influences. Dine on seafood *peri-peri*, or on cuts of venison, beef, or pork.

40 P [C] Closed L Sat.–Sun., D Sun.; 4 weeks Dec.–Jan.

IMAGINE RESTAURANT & DELI
$$–$$$
310 EASTWOOD ST., ARCADIA
TEL 012/342-9281
At this cheerful restaurant and deli, lunch guests help themselves and are charged by the weight. Dinners are less casual, offering fine dining on Mediterranean-style dishes such as lamb with rich port reduction, or ostrich fillet.

82 P [C] Closed Sun.

WING HIN CHINESE RESTAURANT
$$
BUSINESS SUITE 13B, MAROELANA CENTER, MAROELANA ST., MENLO PARK
TEL 012/460-6180
Patronized by local Chinese, Wing Hin serves wonderful pork morsels with plum sugar sauce, chopped chicken with cashew nuts, *peri-peri* prawns, and beef with mushroom and oyster sauce. There's even Tsingtao Chinese beer.

150 P

DIE WERF
$–$$
66 OLYMPUS AVE., FAERIE GLEN
TEL 012/991-1809
Rustic farm-style venue 9 miles (15 km) from the city center, offering South African cuisine. Expect hearty chicken pie, *bobotie*, stews in enamel dishes, and tripe done in three-legged pots, rump steak in red wine, or mushrooms in port.

300 P [C] Closed L Mon., D Sun.–Mon.

ZEMARA
$–$$
ARCADIA PARK GALLERIES, PARK & WESSEL ST., ARCADIA
TEL 012/344-1526
One of the very few African-cuisine restaurants in the area. The Congolese chef here offers dishes like grilled tilapia with lemon, grilled chicken with palm nut, and plantain fries.

60 P

SOWETO

B'S PLACE
$
5541 SHUENANE ST., ORLANDO EAST
TEL 011/935-1766
B's is located in an extension to a Soweto house of the 1930s, its walls decorated with historical newspaper clips. Dine on African specialities, such as *pap*, meat, and spicy sauce, and sip sorghum beer from a calabash. Fixed-price menu.

35

WANDIE'S PLACE
$
618 MAKHALEMELE ST., DUBE, CRAIGHALL
TEL 011/982-2796
Wandie's, by now an institution, offers indoor and outdoor dining and is a favorite for Soweto tours. The buffet includes local fare: fish, beef, oxtail, and mutton stews, *mogodu* (tripe), and grilled chicken, or vegetarian. Fixed-price menu.

160 P [S]

SUN CITY

Located 18 miles (190 km) northwest of Johannesburg in the Northwest Province, Sun City consists of a complex of entertainment venues, restaurants, and four hotels (listed below) that offer a wide variety of accommodation and facilities.

THE CABANAS
$$$–$$$$ * * * *
SUN CITY RESORT
TEL 014/557-1000
www.suninternational.com
Located in verdant gardens that stretch all the way to the Sun City Lake, ideal for laid-back family vacations. You have the choice of either larger family cabanas, which accommodate four, or smaller standard cabanas. Both provide all necessary comforts. There are two restaurants, the **Palm Terrace** and **Butchers Grill Steakhouse**, and a pool bar.

[1] 380 P [S] [S] ⌘ [W]

THE CASCADES
$$–$$$$ * * * *
SUN CITY RESORT
TEL 014/557-1000
www.suninternational.com
Smart, sophisticated, and

tranquil, with luxuriant gardens and lots of plashing water. Luxury rooms and suites have spa baths. The **Peninsula Restaurant** offers international cuisine and a resident pianist. Lighter meals can be enjoyed at the **Fishmonger**.
ℹ️ 243 P ⬆️ ❄️ 🌊 🍸

🏨🍴 PALACE OF THE LOST CITY
$$–$$$$$ ★ ★ ★ ★
SUN CITY RESORT
TEL 014/557-1000
www.suninternational.com
Re-creating the fantasies of Rider Haggard, the Palace of the Lost City is adorned with frescoes, mosaics, and hand-painted ceilings devoted to the animals and cultures of South Africa. Here you can enjoy luxury accommodations, with each sumptuous suite containing a Jacuzzi and sauna.
ℹ️ 338 P ❄️ 🌊 🍸

🏨🍴 SUN CITY HOTEL
$$–$$$$$ ★ ★ ★ ★
SUN CITY RESORT
TEL 014/557-1000
www.suninternational.com
Pulsing with excitement, Sun City has world-class casinos, a variety of bars (the **Lobby Lounge, Sun Terrace, Harlequins**), restaurants (the **Orchard** is Eastern, the **Calabash** serves traditional South African food), and other eateries that will suit every pocket and palate
ℹ️ 340 P ⬆️ ❄️ 🌊 🍸

SWARTRUGGENS

🏨🍴 WOODRIDGE PALMS BOUTIQUE HOTEL
$$$$$
BET. KOSTER & SWARTRUGGENS ON R509
TEL 014/544-6911
www.woodridgepalms.co.za
This hotel and wellness center attempts a fusion of Africa and the East. Set on a vast rolling estate, it provides on-site access to nature walks and bird-watching. A restaurant is on the premises.
ℹ️ 7 🛏️ 32 P ❄️ 🌊 🍸

ZEERUST

🏨 ZEERUST SELF-CATERING
$$
10A RUST ST.
TEL 083/777-6670
www.zeerust.za.org
This self-catering establishment provides luxurious rooms, handsomely decorated in bright, bold colors. Guests have access to a fully equipped kitchen, barbecue area, lounge, and garden. Note that smoking is permitted. Credit card deposit; balance cash only.
ℹ️ 6 P

◼ NORTHERN CAPE

AUGRABIES FALLS NATIONAL PARK

🏨 AUGRABIES REST CAMP
$–$$
30 MILES (49 KM) FROM KAKAMAS ON R359, THEN FROM PARK GATES
TEL 054/452-9200
www.sanparks.org/parks/augrabies
Accommodations are in air-conditioned, en suite chalets, each with two or three single beds, and family cottages, sleeping four. All units have their own fully equipped kitchen. A restaurant and shop are available on site.
ℹ️ 59 🛏️ 96 P ❄️ 🌊

DIAMOND COAST

🏨 NARIES NAMAKWA RETREAT
$$–$$$$$
STEENVLEI, KLEINZEE
TEL 027/712-2462
www.naries.co.za
In the heart of Namakwa this retreat has en suite accommodations: A family self-catering unit sleeping up to four; three thatched units, built like Namakwa huts; and a manor house with five bedrooms. Breakfast and dinner are included in the price.
ℹ️ 12 P

🏨🍴 DIE HOUTHOOP
$–$$
STEENVLEI, KLEINZEE

TEL 027/821-1669
www.houthoop.co.za
This remote establishment provides accommodations either in rustic wooden huts, which are simply sleeping units, or in a few en suite self-catering chalets. The on-site guesthouse has a lounge available to guests, and there is a restaurant on-site.
ℹ️ 9 🛏️ 20 P

KAKAMAS

🏨🍴 VERGELEGEN GUEST HOUSE & RESTAURANT
$$–$$$ ★ ★ ★ ★
ON N14 BET. KAKAMAS & KEIMOES
TEL 054/431-0976
The rooms, with en suite bathroom, range from standard to luxury. Views take in the barren semidesert surroundings, as well as lush irrigated vineyards. On the menu are South African specialities made from fresh local produce.
ℹ️ 22 🛏️ 85 P ❄️ 🌊

KGALAGADI TRANSFRONTIER PARK

Kgalagadi is an enormous park. Listed here are only those camps that provide reasonable amenities, and do not require visitors to bring their own water and firewood. For full details, consult the Kgalagadi pages of the South African National Parks website (www.sanparks.org). Reservations should be made in advance with a major credit card. Note that, below, times rather than distances are given to camps, because of the often poor state of the roads.

🏨 TWEE RIVIEREN
$$
165 MILES (265 KM) FROM UPINGTON TO GATE, THEN ANOTHER 9 MILES (15 KM)
TEL 054/561-2000
This largest camp in the park, provides accommodations in en suite family cottages or chalets sleeping two to six people. Units are air-conditioned and self-catering, with their own small kitchen. Electricity is

available 24 hours a day. A restaurant and well-stocked store is on site. Note: This is the only camp with cell phone reception.

ⓘ 31 🏕 72 🅿 🅢 🏊

🏨 MATA-MATA REST CAMP
$–$$
2.5 HOURS FROM TWEE RIVIEREN
TEL 054/561-2000
Accommodations here are in en suite units, some with kitchens, some with basic self-catering facilities, sleeping from two to six persons. There is a well-stocked store on site, but no restaurant. Electricity is available 18 hours a day.

ⓘ 6 🅿 🏊

🏨 NOSSOB REST CAMP
$–$$
3.5 HOURS FROM TWEE RIVIEREN
TEL 054/561-2000
Nossob offers visitors the choice of chalets, family cottages, or a guesthouse, sleeping from two to six persons. All units are en suite, some have a kitchen, and some basic self-catering facilities. There is a well-stocked store on site, but no restaurant. Electricity is available 18 hours a day.

ⓘ 16 🅿 🏊

KURUMAN

🏨 TUSCANY GUEST HOUSE
$$
83 MAIN ST.
TEL 082/423-6311
Located right in town, this guesthouse offers cool, tastefully decorated rooms. Continental breakfast is served. Note that smoking is permitted here.

ⓘ 6 🅿

PORT NOLLOTH

🏨 PORT INDIGO
$–$$ ★★★
125 KAMP ST.,
MCDOUGALL'S BAY
TEL 027/851-8012
Port Indigo offers self-catering units, sleeping from two to eight. Almost all are on the beach with fine Atlantic Ocean views. At most units breakfast is available on request, and all

have barbecue facilities.

ⓘ 26 🅿 None

🍽 VESPETTI
$
BEACHFRONT RD.
TEL 079/866-9960
Colorful Italian restaurant offering both indoor and outdoor dining, with good sea views. Starters include grilled calamari Napolitana and sautéed chicken livers; entrées range from pizzas to pastas.

🏕 60 🅿 🕐 Closed Mon.

SPITSKOP

🏨 KALAHARI MONATE LODGE
$$
13 KM N. OF UPINGTON ON R360
TEL 054/332-1336
www.spitskopmonate.com
This lodge, set in nearly 22 square miles (57 sq. km) of nature reserve, offers self-catering, thatched chalets. Each unit has its own fully equipped kitchen and a patio with built-in barbecue.

ⓘ 6 🅿 🅢 🏊

SPRINGBOK

🏨 MOUNTAIN VIEW GUEST HOUSE
$$–$$$ ★★★★
2 OVERBERG AVE.
TEL 027/712-1438
www.mountview.co.za
Granite boulders, valley, and mountain views are offered at this guesthouse. Each room is individually decorated and has its own fridge and tea- and coffee-making facilities. Breakfast is served. Lunch and dinner on request.

ⓘ 13 🅿 🅢 🏊

🏨 SPRINGBOK HOTEL
🍽 $$ ★★
VAN RIEBEECK ST.
TEL 027/712-1161
Pleasant, traditional hotel right in the middle of town. The hotel provides air-conditioned suites, each with either bath or shower. Décor is colorful, with floral fabrics. The dining room provides a substantial buffet dinner, and there is also a shady

beer garden.

ⓘ 28 🏕 56 🅿 🅢

UPINGTON

🏨 LE MUST RIVER MANOR
$$ ★★★
12 MURRAY AVE.
TEL 054/332-3971
www.lemustupington.com
This delightful guesthouse has gardens ranging down to the Gariep (Orange) River. The rooms have percale linen, are en suite, some with a balcony and garden or river view. Guests have access to the lounge. Breakfast is served. Credit card deposit; balance cash only.

ⓘ 6 🅿 🅢 🏊

🍽 LE MUST
$–$$
11 SCHRODER ST.
TEL 054/332-6700
Decorated in a kitsch retro style, this restaurant serves quality South African cuisine. Try something different like the *biltong* and *bobotie* spring rolls, the springbok shank with prune sauce, or the fine sultana crème brûlée for dessert.

🏕 70 🅿
🕐 Closed L Sat.–Sun.

 Hotel   Restaurant   ⓘ No. of guest rooms   No. of Seats   Parking   🕐 Closed

Shopping

Most of the expensive goods you will find in the stores of South Africa are imported brands that you can buy anywhere. The pleasure of shopping here comes rather from discovering locally made works of arts and crafts. There are many original artists working in oils, mixed media, ceramics, glass, wood, and stone. But South Africans are also inventive at creating objects out of galvanized wire, colorful beads, and recycled materials such as plastic bags and soda cans. Even from the vendors at traffic lights you can sometimes buy remarkably creative craft objects.

Markets

Markets can be found all around the country. Some are in proper roofed buildings, others in the open air. Wherever tourists congregate, at the entrances to Cape Point Nature Reserve, at the Kruger National Park, or on the Durban beachfront, you will find African sculpted animals and curios for sale. Much of this material comes from central suppliers, and you will see the same stuff over again.

Stores

All the cities have big U.S.-style shopping malls (a full list is at www.mallguide.co.za). If you are concerned about security, these are safe places to shop. Few cities have districts of small specialty shops, the exception being Cape Town's Long Street, with many antiaue and book shops. Smaller towns may have antiques stores, where you can make discoveries.

■ CAPE TOWN

Malls

The best malls are: **Canal Walk** (N1, Exit 10, Sable Road exit, just outside Cape Town CBD, tel 021/555-4433), **Cavendish S uare** (Vineyard Rd., Claremont, tel 021/657-5620), **Constantia Village** (Constantia Rd., Constantia, tel 021/794-5065), and **Victoria & Alfred Waterfront** (tel 021/408-7600).

Markets

Greenmarket S uare (54 Shortmarket St., tel 021/423-3266) is a long-established open-air market selling clothes, jewelry, candles, and African curios.
Pan African Market (76 Long St., tel 021/426-4478) offers a wealth of African crafts from all over the continent.
The Red Shed Workshop (Victoria &Alfred Waterfront, tel 021/408-7860), a covered venue, sells handmade crafts, including jewelry, woodwork, and pewter.

Specialty Stores

A.R.T. Gallery (3 St. George's Mall, tel 021/419-2679) sells ceramics, glass, and jewelry.
The **Cape Quarter** (72 Waterkant St., tel 021/421-0737) is a modern gallery area with designer and lifestyle stores.
Diamond Works (Lower Long St. & Coen Steytler Ave., Foreshore, tel 021/425-1970) Watch diamonds being made into jewelry.
Everard Read Gallery (3 Portswood Road, Victoria & Alfred Waterfront, tel 021/418-4527) deals in South African fine art.
The Scratch Patch (Victoria & Alfred Waterfront, tel 021/419-9429, Dido Valley Rd., Simon's Town, tel 021/786-2020) sells inexpensive semiprecious stones. (Kids love it.)

■ WESTERN CAPE

FRANSCHHOEK: Many galleries here sell South African arts and crafts. Try **African Art Gallery** (40 Huguenot St., tel 021/876-2960) or **Bordeaux Street Gallery** (42 Huguenot Rd., tel 021/876-2165). **Bread & Wine** (Happy Valley Rd., tel 021/876-3692), a farm store, sells local wine and cheese.

HERMANUS: A large market on Market S uare sells clothing and crafts. **Wine Village** (Sandbaai & Main Rds., tel 028/316-3988) has a wide selection of South African wines.

KNYSNA: Shops are at the **Boatshed** (Thesen Harbour Town) **Knysna Waterfront** (21 Waterfront Dr., tel 044/382-0955) and **Woodmill Lane** (bet. Rawson, Main, & St. George Sts., tel 044/382-3045).

OUDTSHOORN: Buy ostrich leather and eggs at **Bushman Curios** (76 Baron van Rheede St., tel 044/272-4497).

PLETTENBERG BAY: Old **Nick Village** (N2 just E of town, tel 044/533-1395) sells uality antiques and crafts.

STELLENBOSCH: Try **Africa Silks** (36 Church St., tel 021/882-9839) for fine fabrics; **Mirko Jewelry** (Andringa & Church Sts., tel 021/886-8296) for handmade design pieces; or **Oom Samie Se Winkel** ("Uncle Samie's Shop," 84 Dorp St., tel 021/887-0797)for its eccentric mix of local merchandise; **Vineyard Connection** (Muldersvlei Rd. & R44 toward Paarl, tel 021/884-4360) for a selection of wines.

■ EASTERN CAPE

EAST LONDON: Lock Street

Gaol *(Fleet St.),* formerly a prison, now a market and shops.
PORT ELIZABETH: The Board-walk *(Marine Dr., Summerstrand, tel 041/507-7777)* has jewelry, crafts, and designer goods, and **The Bridge Mall** *(Langenhoven Dr., tel 041/363-8914)* has all the resources of a shopping mall.

■ DURBAN & KWAZULU-NATAL

DURBAN

Malls

The Workshop *(99 Aliwal St., tel 031/304-9894)* has curio, jewelry, antiques, and spice shops. Other malls are **Berea Centre** *(249 Berea Rd., tel 031/202-7888);* the **Gateway Theatre of Shopping** *(1 Palm Blvd., Umhlanga Ridge, tel 031/566-2332);* **Musgrave Centre** *(115 Musgrave Rd., tel 031/201-5129);* **The Pavilion** *(Jack Martens Dr., Westville, tel 031/265-0558);* and **The Wheel** *(55 Gillespie St., tel 031/332-4324)*

Markets

Every day, the **Amphimarket** *(Beachfront, Bay of Plenty, tel 031/301-3200)* sells curios, books, clothing, and CDs. **Victoria Street Market** *(Queen & Victoria Sts., tel 031/306-4021)* showcases the spices, foods, fabrics, and brassware of Durban's Indian traders.

Specialties

The **African Art Centre** *(94 Florida Rd., tel 031/312-3804)* has KwaZulu-Natal crafts. The **BAT Centre** *(Small Craft Harbor, Victoria Embankment, tel 031/332-0451)* offers local arts.

MIDLANDS

Shoppers for arts and crafts should not miss the **Midlands**

Meander *(www.mid landsmeander. co.za),* an art route of more than a hundred dealers from Pieter-maritzburg to Mooi River.

■ KRUGER & MPUMALANGA

Much of the interesting merchandise here is at roadside stalls in the **Kruger National Park.** The following venues are also worth visiting:

HOEDSPRUIT: Monsoon Gallery *(R527 W of town, tel 015/795-5114)* offers high quality African artwork and crafts.

NELSPRUIT: Riverside Mall *(White River Rd., tel 013/757-0080)* offers more than 140 shops.

VAALWATER: Black Mamba *(Spar Complex, tel 014/755-3518)* sells original arts and crafts from Africa.

■ JOHANNESBURG & THE INTERIOR

CLARENS

This small Free State town is a hub for fine art galleries. On the main street visit the **Addy Hoyle Gallery** and others.

JOHANNESBURG

The **Rosebank Rooftop Market** *(roof of Rosebank Mall, Cradock Ave., tel 011/442-4488)* takes place each Sunday, with more than 600 stalls. The adjacent **African Craft Market** *(Cradock & Baker Sts., tel 011/880-2906)* is open daily. At the **Melville Market** *(Kingsway & University Rds., Auckland Park, tel. 011/482-2118)* you can browse for bric-a-brac Mon.–Sat.

Malls

Major centers are the **Hyde Park Shopping** *(Jan Smuts Ave., Hyde Park, tel 011/325-4340);* **Mall of Rosebank** *(bet. Bath & Cradock Aves., Rosebank, tel 011/788-5530);* and the most opulent of all, **Sandton City** *(Sandton Drive & Rivonia Rd., Sandton, tel 011/217-6000).*

Specialty Stores

The best of local, African, and international fine art is found at **Goodman Gallery** *(163 Jan Smuts Ave., Parkwood, tel 011/788-1113)* and the **Kim Sacks Gallery** *(153 Jan Smuts Ave., Parkwood, tel 011/447-5804).* **Collectables** *(32 Tyrone Ave., Parkview, tel 011/646-4211)* deals in antique jewelry, silver, glass, and furniture. The **Oriental Plaza** *(corner Bree & Malherbe Sts., Fordsburg, tel 011/838-6753)* is an excellent place to bargain hunt for fabrics, clothing, and spices.

PRETORIA

Hatfield Market *(Hatfield Plaza, Burnett St., tel 012/442-4488)* every Sunday, for collectibles, furniture, jewelry, arts and crafts. **African Diamonds & Jewelry** *(Shop 5.3 Hatfield S ., tel 012/362-6455)* is the place to go for jewelry.

Malls

Some of the bigger malls are **Hatfield Plaza** *(1122 Burnett St., Hatfield, tel 012/362-5842),* catering to a younger crowd; the vast **Menlyn Park** *(Atterbury Rd. & Lois Ave., Menlo Park, tel 012/348-8766);* **Brooklyn Mall** *(Fehrsen & Lange Sts., New Muckleneuk, tel 012/346-1063);* and **Kolonnade Shopping Centre** *(Van der Merwe St. & Zambesi Dr., Montana Park, tel 012/548-1902),* offering a craft market and dozens of shops.

Entertainment

In the last three decades South Africa has made great strides in developing indigenous entertainment. Although most movies are imported, in theater, dance, and music local material predominates. Cultural forms of European origin, such as opera, classical ballet, and symphony concerts receive less funding than before, but are still successfully staged in the larger cities. Arts festivals around the country (see p. 271) showcase the country's performance talent.

COUNTRYWIDE

Cinemas

Two movie-distribution companies Ster Kinekor *(www.sterkinekor.com)* and Nu Metro *(www.numetro.co.za)*, have movie houses—mainly in malls—across South Africa. Both show popular movies, Hollywood blockbusters, and some Bollywood productions. Details of what's on, where and when, can be found on their websites. In Cape Town, Durban, Johannesburg, and Pretoria, Ster Kinekor also has Cinema Nouveau venues that show art movies from Europe and other countries.

Theater

Barnyard Theatre *(www.barnyardtheatres.co.za)* is an innovative type of entertainment. At the Barnyard venues you sit on benches in a rustic ambience and enjoy food, drink, and musical theater (mainly show tunes from musicals).

▓ CAPE TOWN

Cinemas

Many movie theaters are located at **Cavendish Square** and the **Victoria & Alfred Waterfront** (see Cape Town Malls p. 307). An unusual independent venue, the **Labia** *(68 Orange St., City Center, tel 021/424-5927, www.labia.co.za)* shows both commercial and art movies.

Music

The **Buena Vista Social Café** *(81 Main Rd., Greenpoint, tel 021/433-0611)* features Latino music.
The Cape Town Philharmonic Orchestra *(tel 021/410-9809, www.cpo.org.za)* performs regular symphony concerts at Artscape, the City Hall, and other venues.
The Green Dolphin *(Victoria & Alfred Waterfront, tel 021/421-7471, www.greendolphin.co.za)* is a major venue for local jazz.
Long Street is the place to go at night for many clubs and bars featuring live and recorded pop music.

Theaters

Artscape *(D. F. Malan St., Foreshore, tel 021/410-9800, www.artscape.co.za)* puts on performances of opera, ballet, and drama in three performance areas.
Barnyard *(Willowbridge Lifestyle Centre, 39 Carl Cronje Dr., Tygervalley, tel 021/914-8898)*
The **Baxter Theatre** *(Main Rd., Rondebosch, tel 021/685-7880 www.baxter.co.za)* stages music, dance, drama, and theater in three venues.
Theatre on the Bay *(1A Link St., Camps Bay, tel 021/438-3301, www.theatreonthebay.co.za)* is an intimate theater, staging successful local and international drama, music, and cabaret.

▓ DURBAN

Cinemas

For movie theaters visit the many venues in the local malls

Berea Centre, Gateway, Musgrave Centre, The Pavilion and **The Wheel** (see Durban Malls, opposite).

Music

BAT Centre *(Small Craft Harbor, Victoria Embankment, tel 031/332-0451)* hosts regular concerts and other live music events.
KZN Philharmonic *(tel 031/369 9438, www.kznpo.co.za)* performs classical music regularly at venues in Durban and elsewhere in KwaZulu-Natal.
Rainbow Restaurant & Jazz Club *(23 Stanfield Road, Pinetown, tel 031/702-9161)* is one of the best local venues for jazz.
Reform Club *(198A Florida Rd., Morningside, tel 083/786-8027)* Cocktails and the best in dance music.

Theaters

The **Elizabeth Sneddon Theatre** *(University of KwaZulu-Natal, King George V Ave., tel 031/260-2065)* performs student productions and visiting drama, dance, rock concerts, and musicals.
The **Playhouse** *(231 Smith St., tel 031/369-9596, www.playhousecompany.com)* has three performance venues, staging drama, music, opera, and dance.
Barnyard *(Gateway Mall, 1 Palm Blvd., Umhlanga Ridge, tel 031/566-3045)*

▨ JOHANNESBURG

Cinemas
Many movie theaters can be found in the malls at **Hyde Park Shopping**, the **Mall at Rosebank** and **Sandton City** (see Johannesburg Malls on p. 308).

Music
For the best of local jazz visit the **Bassline** *(10 Henry Nxumalo St., Newtown, tel 011/838-9145, www.bassline.co.za)* or **The Blues Room** *(Village Walk, Rivonia & Maude Sts., tel 011/784-5527, www.bluesroom.co.za)*.
Catz Pyjamas *(12 Main Rd., Melville, tel 011/726-8596, www.catzpyjamas.co.za)* is a 24-hour bistro, featuring live music performances.
The **Johannesburg Philharmonic Orchestra** offers concerts at the Linder Auditorium *(27 St. Andrews Rd., Parktown, tel 011/717-3223)*.
    For clubs and dance music, visit the Moroccan-theme nightclub **Shoukara** *(Mutual & Rivonia Blvds., Rivonia, tel 082/855-2584)*, **Sudada** *(12 Friedman Dr., Sandton, tel 011/884-1980)*, or the **Venue** *(Melrose Arch, tel 011/214-4300)*.

Theaters
Barnyard *(Shop L205, Cresta Shopping Centre, Beyers Naude Dr., tel 011/280-4370)*
Civic Theatre *(Loveday St., Braamfontein, tel 011/877-6800, www.showbusiness.co.za)* stages drama, opera, and ballet performances, as well as musical theater in its three performance venues.
Market Theatre *(56 Margaret Mcingana St., tel 011/832-1641, www.markettheatre.co.za)* has three venues staging local and international drama and other performance arts.

Teatro at Montecasino *(William Nicol & Witkoppen Rds., Fourways, tel 011/510-7000, http://montecasino.tsogosun.co.za)* stages musicals and light entertainment.
Theatre on the Square *(Shop 121 Nelson Mandela Sq., Sandton, tel 011/883-8606, www.theatreonthesquare.co.za)* stages drama and musical performances.

PRETORIA

Cinemas
Multiscreen movie theaters will be found at **Brooklyn Mall** and **Menlyn Park** (see Pretoria Malls p. 308).

Music
The **University of Pretoria Symphony Orchestra** *(tel 012/420-2947, www.upso.up.ac.za)* performs orchestral works at various venues in the city.
    Dance music clubs include the huge **Boston Tea Party** *(Louis & Glen Manor Ave., Menlyn, tel 012/365-3625)* and the mainly student venue **Recess** *(Lenchen St. N & South St., Centurion, tel 012/663-7862, www.recess.co.za)*.

Theaters
The **State Theatre** *(320 Pretorius St., tel 012/392-4066, www.statetheatre.co.za)*, the largest theater complex in the country, houses six performance venues where opera, ballet, drama, cabaret, musicals, and film festivals are staged.
Barnyard *(Shop UF57, Menlyn Park, Atterbury Rd. & Lois Ave., Menlo Park, tel 012/368-1555)*

Activities

With its fine weather, wide open spaces, beaches, game parks, rivers, and mountains South Africa is a great destination for outdoor pursuits. In many parts of the country visitors can engage in adventure activities, such as scuba diving, canoeing, kayaking, white-water rafting, mountain biking, climbing, parachuting, and rapelling, known as "abseiling" here. Leisure pursuits such as golf, hiking, horseback riding, bird-watching, and fly-fishing are also available.

COUNTRYWIDE

Getaway is a monthly safari and travel magazine with details on adventure activities *(www.getaway.co.za)*.

South African National Parks offer hiking, canoeing, birding, mountain biking, and stargazing *(www.sanparks.org,* click on *"Activities & Facilities"* link).

Wildthing Adventures *(tel 021/556-1917, www.wildthing.co.za)* offers canoeing, hiking, bridge jumping, and safaris.

Birding
Lawsons *(tel 013/741-2458, www.lawsons.co.za)* organizes birding, butterfly, mammal, and general wildlife tours in KwaZulu-Natal.

Monty Brett *(tel 033/266-6113, www.sappibrett.co.za)* organizes birding tours, courses, and other safaris.

Climbing
The **Mountain Club of South Africa** *(tel 021/465-3412, www.mcsa.org.za)* and **Climb ZA** *(www.climbing.co.za)* provide information on climbs of all grades in the country.

Fly-Fishing
You will find details on the sport in South Africa at *www.flyfishing.co.za*.

Golf
Descriptions of the major golf courses, with pictures and maps, can be found at *www.golf-safari.com*.

Motorcycling
Karoo Biking *(www.karoo-biking.de/en/)* offers tours by BMW motorcycle.

Mountain Biking
Comprehensive information about South African mountain-bike trails, e uipment, and tour operators is found at *www.mtbonline.co.za*.

Sea Kayaking
PaddleYak *(tel 021/790-5611, www.seakayak.co.za)* offers kayak tours in Cape Town, along the West Coast, and the Garden Route.

■ CAPE TOWN

Adventure Activities
Downhill Adventures *(tel 021/422-0388, www.downhilladventures.com)* offers cycling, sand-boarding, paragliding, abseiling, cage diving, and uad biking.

Abseil Africa *(tel 021/424-4760, www.abseilafrica.co.za)* specializes in rapelling off Table Mountain.

Cape Xtreme *(tel 021/788-5814, www.cape-xtreme.com)* organizes shark-cage diving, cycling, surfing, and climbing.

Scuba Diving
Orca Industries *(tel 021/671-9673, www.orca-industries.co.za)* provides scuba training, equipment, and dives.

Sea Kayaking
Sea Kayak *(tel 082/501-8930, www.kayakcapetown.co.za)* leads kayak tours off the city's coast, where you may see whales and penguins.

■ WEST COAST

Adventure Activities
Eden Adventures *(tel 044/877-0179, www.eden.co.za)* in the Wilderness National Park on the Garden Route, organizes canoeing, abseiling, hiking, and cycling.

Bridge & Bungee Jumping Face Adrenalin *(tel 042/281-1458, Bloukrans; 044/697-7001, Gourits)* offers the world's highest bungee jump at the Bloukrans and Gourits River bridges.

Forest Canopy Tours *(tel 042/281-1836, www.tsitsikam ma canopytour.co.za)* offers a safe glide from platform to platform.

Flower Tours
Tours & Trails *(tel 021/762-3530, www.toursandtrails.co.za)* take tours to the Nama ualand flowers and the cape floral kingdom in late August and in September.

Hiking
Oystercatcher Trail *(tel 044/699-1204, www.oystercatchertrail.co.za)* is a three-day coastal hike from Mossel Bay.

Boating
Breede River House Boat Hire *(tel 028/542-1049, www.houseboathire.co.za)* operates on the Breede River near Swellendam.

Lightleys (tel 044/386-0007, www.houseboats.co.za) offers fully equipped houseboats on the Knysna Lagoon.

Mountain Biking
Mountain Biking Africa (tel 044/382-0260, www.mountainbik ingafrica.co.za), based in Knysna, does half- and full-day bike tours.

Shark Diving
Operators in the Western Cape offer viewing of the great white shark from ship deck or from an underwater cage.
Shark Africa (tel 044/691-3796, www.sharkafrica.co.za) operates from Mossel Bay.
White Shark Diving Co. (tel 021/461-6583, www.sharkcagediv ing.co.za) operates out of Kleinbaai (near Hermanus).

Skydiving
Sky Dive Ceres (tel 021/462-5666, www.skydive.co.za), about 1.5 hours from Cape Town, offers same-day training and tandem jumps.

Whale-Watching
On the whales' return to the southern cape from July to December several operators offer whale-watching.
Dyer Island Cruises (tel 028/384-0406, www.whalewatchsa .com) and **Ivanhoe Sea Safaris** (tel 028/384-0556, www.whalewatch ingsa.co.za) operate from Gansbaai near Hermanus.
Ocean Safaris (tel 044/533-4963, www.oceansafaris.co.za) go out from Plettenberg Bay.

■ EASTERN CAPE

Boating
Lightleys (see p. 311) also offers houseboats on the Kowie River from Port Alfred.

Hiking
Wild Coast Holiday Reservations (tel 043/743-6181, www .wildcoastholidays.co.za) organizes seven different coastal hiking trails on the Wild Coast.

Outdoor Activities
The Edge resort (tel 045/962-1159, www.theedge-hogsback.co.za) at Hogsback offers 4WD trails, hiking, mountain biking, and trout fishing.

■ DURBAN & KWAZULU-NATAL

Outdoor Activities
Ezemvelo KZN Wildlife (www .kznwildlife.com, click on "eco-tourism," then "activities"), the KwaZulu-Natal Parks organization, offers birding, boating, climbing, hiking, fishing, horseback riding, and cycling
Sani Pass Hotel (tel 033/702-1320, www.sanipasshotel.co.za) has uad biking, fishing, golf, and 4WD tours.

Canopy Tours
Karkloof Canopy Tour (tel 033/330-3415, www.karkloofcano pytour.co.za) near Howick lets you glide on cables above the forest floor.

Deep-Sea Fishing
Magnum Charters (tel 035/571-0043, www.sodwanabaylodge .com) organize ocean trips for game fishing.

Hang Gliding
Silent Wings (tel 039/832-0268, www.silentwings.co.za) provides training in the Midlands, and hang-gliding tours to the Western Cape and interior.

Hiking
Wonderful hikes are available in the Ukhahlamba-Drakensberg (see Ezemvelo KZN Wildlife).

Scuba Diving
PADI 5 Star Dive Centre (tel 035/571-6015, www.sodwanabay lodge.com) offers scuba courses and dives at Sodwana Bay.

■ KRUGER & MPUMALANGA

Bush Walks
The Kruger National Park and private game lodges offer bush walks with an experienced armed ranger.

Canopy Tours
Skyway Trails (tel 013/737-8374, www.skywaytrails.com) lets you slide on steel cables from platform to platform over a valley near Hazyview.

Fly-Fishing
Mpumalanga and the Dullstroom area are known for fly-fishing: www.flyfishing.co.za.

Horseback Riding
Horizon (tel 014/755-4003, www.ridinginafrica.com) organizes horseback adventures in Limpopo's Waterberg region.

■ JOHANNESBURG & THE INTERIOR

Outdoor Activities
Adventure Addicts (tel 012/711-0264, www.adventure-addicts.com) at Dinokeng near Pretoria offers quad biking, microlight flights, elephant-back rides, and more.
Jacana (tel 012/734-2978, www. jacanacollection.co.za) offer hiking and horseback trails, mountain

bike, quad bike, or 4WD, in Gauteng and the Eastern Free State.

Boating
Harties Houseboat Cruises *(tel 073/825-4409, www.hartieshouse boats.co.za)* offers charters on Hartbeespoort Dam near Johannesburg and Pretoria.

Old Willow Houseboat Charters *(tel 016/973-1729, www .oldwillow.co.za)* rent boats on the Vaal River.

Canopy Tours
Magaliesberg Canopy Tour *(tel 014/535-0150, www.magalies canopytour.co.za)* takes you gliding on steel cables from platform to platform set on a mountain cliff face.

Hot-Air Ballooning
The generally stable conditions on the highveld make this the ideal location for ballooning.

Air Ventures *(tel 011/793-5782, www.air-ventures.co.za)* operates from the Cradle of Humankind and the Magaliesberg.

Bill Harrop's Balloon Safaris *(tel 011/705-3201, www.balloon.co .za)* offers balloon flights near the Magaliesberg mountains.

Mountain Adventures
GoVertical *(tel 082/731-4696, www.gotrekking.co.za)* organizes caving, abseiling, and rock climbing in the Magaliesberg area.

■ NORTHERN CAPE

Outdoor Activities
Gariep 3-in-1 Adventure This challenging half-day adventure offered by the Augrabies National Park *(www.sanparks.org)* involves canoeing down the Gariep (Orange) River, walking a couple of miles, then returning to camp by mountain bike.

Kalahari Adventure Centre *(tel 054/451-0177, www.kalahari .co.za)* based near Augrabies offers river trips, bird-watching, and desert safaris

Canoeing & Rafting
Safaris and canoeing and rafting down the Gariep (Orange) River are major activities here.

Bushwacked *(tel 027/761-8953, www.bushwhacked.co.za)* operatesriver-rafting trips between half-day and six-day durations.

Felix Unite *(tel 021/404-1830, www.felixunite.com)* reliably operates canoe and raft safaris. **River Rafters** *(tel 021/975-9727, www.riverrafters. co.za)* organizes raft trips in this region.

MENU READER

English is used on all menus in South Africa, but there are a few local terms that may puzzle the visitor.

achar condiment of green mangoes, oil, and spices
biltong air-dried meat flavored with salt and coriander
blatjang spicy fruit chutney, often made with apricots
bobotie curried minced meat topped with an egg custard
boerewors sausage made from coarsely chopped meat spiced with coriander
borrie turmeric
braai to grill on an open fire (also short for *braaivleis*)
braaivleis a barbecue
bredie stew made with lamb or tomatoes, including waterblommetjie
bunny chow half a loaf of bread hollowed out and stuffed with curry
crayfish lobster
kabeljou (also called *kob*) a firm, white-fleshed marine fish
kingklip a fine, eel-like, white-fleshed marine fish

koeksuster plaited strips of deep-fried dough soaked in very sweet syrup
malva pudding caramelized sponge cake, made with apricot, spiced with ginger
mampoer white brandy made from peach, plum, or other fruit
marula edible yellow berry of a lowveld tree
mielies corn
mogodu tripe
monkey gland sauce piquant sauce for steak made from onion, tomato, and Worcestershire sauce
mopane worms dried caterpillars of the emperor moth
morogo wild spinach
pap a stiff white porridge made from ground corn
perlemoen abalone
potjie three-legged cast-iron cooking pot
potjiekos food (usually meat and vegetable stew) slow-cooked in a potjie
rooibos a bush indigenous to the Cederberg area, from which rooibos tea is made
samoosa a small, spicy, triangular, deep-fried pie
samp crushed corn kernels
skilpadjie liver wrapped in caul fat and fried
snoek popular Western Cape marine fish, often made into pâté
sosatie kebab
umngqusho Xhosa dish made from samp and beans flavored with spicy ingredients
Van Der Hum popular local liqueur, made from brandy, tangerine peel, herbs and spices
vetkoek a small cake of deep-fried dough
waterblommetjie edible waterlily-type plant (cape pondweed)
witblits "white lightning," another name for mampoer

INDEX

ILLUSTRATIONS CREDITS

National Geographic

TRAVELER

South Africa

Published by the National Geographic Society

John M. Fahey, Jr., *President and Chief Executive Officer*
Gilbert M. Grosvenor, *Chairman of the Board*
Tim T. Kelly, *President, Global Media Group*
John Q. Griffin, *President, Publishing*
Nina D. Hoffman, *Executive Vice President; President, Book Publishing Group*

Prepared by the Book Division

Kevin Mulroy, *Senior Vice President and Publisher*
Leah Bendavid-Val, *Director of Photography Publishing and Illustrations*
Marianne R. Koszorus, *Director of Design*
Barbara Brownell Grogan, *Executive Editor*
Elizabeth Newhouse, *Director of Travel Publishing*
Carl Mehler, *Director of Maps*
Barbara A. Noe, *Series Editor*
Cinda Rose, *Series Art Director*

Staff for This Book

Barbara A. Noe, *Project Editor*
Kay Kobor Hankins, *Art Director*
Kevin Eans, *Photo Editor*
Robin Currie, Karin Kinney, *Text Editors*
Lise Sajewski, *Editorial Consultant*
Roberta Cosi, *Researcher*
Steven D. Gardner, Michael McNey, Nicholas P. Rosenbach, and Mapping Specialists, *Map Research & Production*
Al Morrow, *Design Assistant*
Jan Mucciarone, *Indexer*
Hunter Braithwaite, Bridget A. English, Elliana Spiegel, Jane Sunderland, *Contributors*
Richard Wain, *Production Project Manager*
Sam Corum, Meredith Wilcox, *Illustrations Specialists*

Jennifer A. Thornton, *Managing Editor*
R. Gary Colbert, *Production Director*

Manufacturing and Quality Management

Christopher A. Liedel, *Chief Financial Officer*
Phillip L. Schlosser, *Vice President*
Chris Brown, *Technical Director*
Nicole Elliott, *Manager*
Monika D. Lynde, *Manager*
Rachel Faulise, *Manager*

National Geographic Traveler: South Africa
ISBN: 978-1-4262-0333-6

NATIONAL GEOGRAPHIC

T R A V E L E R